JACKSON SCHOOL PUBLICATIONS
IN INTERNATIONAL STUDIES

JACKSON SCHOOL PUBLICATIONS
IN INTERNATIONAL STUDIES

Senator Henry M. Jackson was convinced that the study of the history, cultures, political systems, and languages of the world's major regions was an essential prerequisite for wise decision-making in international relations. In recognition of his deep commitment to higher education and advanced scholarship, this series of publications has been established through the generous support of the Henry M. Jackson Foundation, in cooperation with the Henry M. Jackson School of International Studies and the University of Washington Press.

The Crisis of Leninism and the Decline of the Left: The Revolutions of 1989, edited by Daniel Chirot

Sino-Soviet Normalization and Its International Implications, 1945–1990, by Lowell Dittmer

Contradictions: Artistic Life, the Socialist State, and the Chinese Painter Li Huasheng, by Jerome Silbergeld with Gong Jisui

The Found Generation: Chinese Communists in Europe during the Twenties, by Marilyn Levine

Rules and Rights in the Middle East: Democracy, Law, and Society, edited by Ellis Goldberg, Resat Kasaba, and Joel S. Migdal

Can Europe Work? Germany and the Reconstruction of Postcommunist Societies, edited by Stephen E. Hanson and Willfried Spohn

Marxist Intellectuals and the Chinese Labor Movement: A Study of Deng Zhongxia (1894–1933), by Daniel Y. K. Kwan

Essential Outsiders: Chinese and Jews in the Modern Transformation of Southeast Asia and Central Europe, edited by Daniel Chirot and Anthony Reid

Essential Outsiders

Chinese and Jews in the Modern Transformation of Southeast Asia and Central Europe

Edited by

Daniel Chirot

and

Anthony Reid

University of Washington Press

Seattle and London

Library of Congress Cataloging-in-Publication Data

Essential outsiders : Chinese and Jews in the modern transformation
  of Southeast Asia and Central Europe / edited by Daniel Chirot and
  Anthony Reid.
      p.   cm. — (Jackson School publications in international
  studies)
    Includes index.
    ISBN 0-295-97613-6 (alk. paper)
      1. Chinese—Asia, Southeastern—History.   2. Asia, Southeastern—
  Ethnic relations.   3. Asia, Southeastern—History.   4. Jews—
  Europe, Central—History.   5. Europe, Central—Ethnic relations.
  6. Europe, Central—History.   I. Chirot, Daniel.   II. Reid,
  Anthony, 1939-   .   III. Series.
  DS523.4.C45I57   1997   96-6516
  959'.004951—dc21   CIP

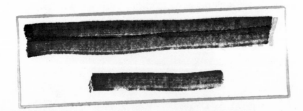

Contents

v

Acknowledgments

We would like to thank the Social Science Research Council for funding the conference in La Jolla, California, that produced these papers, and especially Toby Volkman, who was then the council's staff person responsible for Southeast Asian studies. On the last morning of the conference we were all awakened early in the morning by the January 1994 earthquake that jolted southern California and caused so much damage in Los Angeles. This may have been a sign of how dangerous the ground on which we were treading really is.

Elizabeth Perry and Timothy McDaniel attended this conference as commentators and provided many useful suggestions. Hillel Levine and Tan Liok Ee also participated and added valuable insights and criticisms of the papers. Robert Hefner's invaluable advice from afar made the entire project possible.

Several anonymous reviewers contributed comments that we sometimes took to heart. We are grateful to Eric Larsen for his editorial help.

The Henry M. Jackson Foundation helped fund the publication of this volume, and the Department of Sociology at the University of California at San Diego funded Daniel Chirot while he was working on the final revisions of the manuscript.

Both of us would like to thank the participants at the conference, some of whom came from very far away, and all of whom wrote and rewrote excellent papers. We certainly did not all agree, but we argued cordially and with good results.

Finally, we would like to thank Naomi Pascal, the editor-in-chief at the University of Washington Press, for her careful reading of the manuscript, her understanding of its importance, and her patience.

DANIEL CHIROT AND ANTHONY REID

PART ONE

Similarities and Disparities

An Introduction

to the Comparison

of Entrepreneurial Minorities

1 / Conflicting Identities and the Dangers of Communalism

DANIEL CHIROT

Comparing the two most prominent entrepreneurial minorities in the modern world, European Jews and Southeast Asian Chinese, raises questions about almost every important and controversial aspect of nationalism and ethnic conflict. Because of what appears to be intensified xenophobic nationalism and the spread of bloody ethnic wars in parts of Asia, Europe, and Africa in the late 1980s and the 1990s, the salience of such questions is at its peak in the social sciences as well as in the general public's awareness.

Presenting information about these two successful but often persecuted minorities offers insights about the very formation of ethnic and nationalist identities, and clues about when such a process is more or less likely to lead to either violent social separation and conflict or peaceful accommodation. It also addresses contemporary debates about whether or not ethnonationalism is a recent or an ancient phenomenon. Furthermore, any study of these two groups raises venerable but still relevant controversies about why certain ethnic groups seem able to adapt more successfully to modern capitalist economies than others. Are there cultural traits that determine groups' prospects in modern economies that are so deeply rooted as to be virtually hereditary properties transmitted from generation to generation? Or is the success of any particular ethnic group simply situationally determined and explainable in terms of recent, almost chance political and economic configurations?

In the case of most of Europe's Jews, such questions are of greater historical than contemporary interest. The extermination of some two-thirds of European Jews from 1939 to 1945 has made them less a focus for hatred and jealousy than was the case before. It is possible, though hardly certain, that anti-Semitism could once again play a political role in some parts of the collapsed Soviet Union, but it seems almost inconceivable that there could

3

be any repetition of such virulent anti-Semitism in Central or Western Europe.

But in Southeast Asia, any discussion about the role of the Chinese is of pressing contemporary importance. Even though, as some of the chapters in this volume show, tension between Chinese and non-Chinese throughout Southeast Asia is less problematic today than it was in the 1960s and 1970s, the potential for conflict remains. The alleviation that has occurred in the past quarter-century is due to the phenomenal economic boom that has enriched a growing proportion of the region. What would happen, as Linda Lim and Peter Gosling ask in chapter 11, if economies declined, or even if they stopped growing so quickly? Would this exacerbate economic conflict between ethnic communities and raise the specter of renewed intercommunal warfare? Is the fact that the Chinese have been disproportionately more enriched by the boom than other communities going to make them a more obvious target of resentment? And how has their growing wealth affected the self-image and ethnic confidence of the various Chinese communities in Southeast Asia?

At one time it was thought by many European liberals, both Christian and Jewish, that growing prosperity and modernization, along with the elimination of legal discrimination, would eliminate anti-Semitism. In a sense, despite lingering prejudices against Jews, that is roughly what happened in Britain and North America, although rather more slowly and far less completely than optimists expected. But in France, despite its tradition of liberal emancipation of Jews during the Revolution, the period from the 1880s until World War II saw an intensification of anti-Semitism, which became one of the central ideological positions of the nationalist right. And in Germany and Austria, what had been a tradition of growing legal and official tolerance in the second half of the nineteenth century was sharply reversed, and anti-Semitism became the defining political ideology of the state in the 1930s. For certain countries farther east and south, especially Russia, Poland, and Romania, anti-Semitism became, in the late nineteenth and early twentieth centuries, an essential component of their nationalist identities.[1]

Is there any possibility that ethnic hostility on such a level could be directed toward the Chinese in Southeast Asia by those who consider themselves "natives"? Might the lessening of recent ethnic conflict be the same kind of lull before the storm that Europe experienced in about the middle of the nineteenth century? There have been enough examples of brutal anti-Sinicism in some Southeast Asian countries over the past four decades to remind us that the phenomenon is neither illusory nor just a declining holdover from the colonial past. These examples range from the forced expulsions of large parts of the Chinese community in Vietnam after 1975 and the massacres of Chinese in Cambodia in the 1970s (though the larger Vietnamese minority was more heavily targeted, under both Lon Nol and the subsequent Khmer Rouge regime) to lesser but still significant outbursts of killing and official government discrimination against Chinese in Burma, Indonesia, and Malaysia (although in Burma, too, another community, this time the Indians, was more directly targeted by the government, and there have also been incessant ethnic wars throughout much of the country since 1948). Is the worst over? Is the new prosperity a guarantor that it will never happen again, much less ever reach the level that anti-Semitism reached in Europe in the 1930s?

It is easy to see how quickly a discussion of these matters could become sensitive and controversial, even among supposedly dispassionate scholars. But if that is so, the potential for trouble is far greater if such a project comes to the attention of political ideologues and opportunistic political figures in Southeast Asia. Even the most elevated review of the historical record and of competing social scientific theories that try to elucidate some of the questions raised by the comparison of Jews and Chinese can lend itself to gross misrepresentation and abuse.

This is all the more the case because "Jews" are not a neutral category in Southeast Asia, especially in its Muslim parts. The identification of Malay and Indonesian Muslim nationalists with the rest of the Islamic world, and of Jews with the state of Israel, combined with the anti-Sinicism, however muted, that exists in these countries, has made the very mention of such a comparison inflammatory. This issue is approached rather gingerly by An-thony Reid in the concluding remarks of his chapter. To avoid a distracting focus on emotive rhetorical controversies and to concentrate, instead, on the important questions raised by the essays in this volume, he decided to underplay his analysis of contemporary anti-Semitism in Muslim Southeast Asia.

The analogy with Jews is not welcomed among Chinese intellectuals in Southeast Asia, though in Singapore's early days of independence after its break with Malaysia, the "Israeli" model of self-reliance as an isolated for-tress in a sea of religious and ethnic enemies was popular, at least with the government. But today, even to suggest the validity of the broader Jewish-Chinese comparison raises a terrifying specter and certainly has the potential to antagonize Muslims. It also associates the group being compared to Jews with the persisting negative image that Jews have throughout much of the Christian world, as well as the Muslim. It is one thing to say that in Europe the experience of the 1930s and 1940s will never be repeated, and quite another to claim that anti-Semitism has entirely vanished. Rather, it persists as a set of derogatory cultural stereotypes, and some groups compared to Jews sometimes take offense for that reason.

Nevertheless, despite the dangers of misinterpretation, and despite the sensitivity of the issues raised by such a discussion, it is possible, on the basis of the essays presented in this volume, to offer some conclusions that shed light on three of the many questions our inquiries raised. First, what are the sources of modern anti-Semitism and anti-Sinicism? Second, under what circumstances can these prejudices be reduced and, if not resolved, at least marginalized and made relatively harmless? Conversely, what might cause them to be exacerbated and to evolve toward ethnic warfare? And third, what are the prospects for the future of ethnic relations in Southeast Asia? Even though the answers offered in this volume are tentative, they are at least suggestive and, to a limited extent, generalizable to other, analogous cases of ethnic conflict in the world.

I should add an important disclaimer on behalf of the contributors to this book. The conclusions I offer are those I have drawn from reading their essays. All these authors are highly accomplished, well-known scholars, and it would be silly to pretend that they agree about every point among themselves. In the conference at which the papers that became these chapters were first presented, there were some heated arguments. It should be equally evident that the contributors might not all agree that I am drawing the proper conclusions from their work. Ultimately, any synthesis of such complex issues has to be personalized in order to present a coherent viewpoint. I have done this, drawing not only on these essays but also on my own research about nationalism and ethnic violence in the twentieth century.[2] The responsibility for what I write is mine alone.

THE REASONS FOR MODERN ANTI-SEMITISM AND ANTI-SINICISM

The most widely accepted explanation for the dislike directed against successful entrepreneurial minorities is simply that as successful outsiders they make native populations jealous. Such minorities occupy lucrative economic positions that are coveted by aspiring members of the majority, they are often owed money, and it seems difficult to compete with them. Their superior commercial skills may be attributed to innate traits, to their secretiveness and closed but international social networks, or to their collaboration with political elites (colonial or domestic) who use them to oppress the people. Such widely held and popular explanations cannot be dismissed easily. Not only do they appeal to common sense but they also have been buttressed by a long tradition of scholarship, many examples of which are cited in the chapters that follow, especially in Anthony Reid's.[3] The trouble is that these types of explanations fit the historical descriptions of the phenomenon with respect to the Southeast Asian Chinese and Central or East European Jews in the late nineteenth and early twentieth centuries only partly, and in some ways not at all. This is most evident in the chapters by Hillel Kieval and Takashi Shiraishi, but it can be seen to some extent in the other essays as well.

By showing that anti-Sinicism developed quickly at a specific time, just as new nationalist ideas were taking root in Java and as both the economy and the political-administrative system were being opened, rationalized, and modernized, Shiraishi makes a strong case against any claim that in Java, and by analogy throughout Indonesia, anti-Chinese sentiment was strongly connected simply to old patterns of economic specialization and prejudice. Something more was required.

Hillel Kieval brings a similar point out clearly in his account of how accusations of Jewish ritual murder of Christian children in Central and Eastern Europe produced some notorious, officially sanctioned trials in the late nineteenth century. Though such accusations had a long history, for centuries they had been treated as mere folk superstitions unworthy of being dignified by state authorities. Then, suddenly, a number of such cases resulted in well-publicized trials, and the myth of Jewish blood rituals returned in full force.

By looking specifically at a case in Hungary in the early 1880s, Kieval shows that none of the ordinary theories about anti-Semitism works well to explain what happened. The trial occurred in a village where Jewish-peasant relations were good, and in Hungary, unlike in Poland (then mostly part of Russia), Russia proper, or Romania, the ruling elites were specifically opposed to political anti-Semitism. This fact is also emphasized in Victor Karady's thorough review of the historical relationship between Jews and Hungarians. That a wave of such incidents swept the entire region at the same time suggests that a new, anti-Enlightenment and antiliberal form of anti-Semitism was growing. Although the outward form of these blood ritual cases may appear to hark back to medieval tales of sorcery and magic spells, the trials were modern events with much deeper implications than they would have had if they had been mere survivals of old superstitions.

To be sure, resentment of Jews or Chinese based on the perception that they are closed groups of greedy interlopers who have gained unfair commercial advantages in one way or another over naive but purer and more deserving natives has been common enough. Yet the evidence presented in this volume suggests that starting some time in the last third of the nineteenth century with respect to European Jews, and a couple of decades later with respect to Southeast Asian Chinese, new and more systematic programs of ethnic hatred were directed against them than had existed in the earlier part of the nineteenth century. Because Jews and Chinese had already occupied commercial, artisanal, tax farming, moneylending, and other similar, specialized economic niches for centuries, this intensification of prejudice in new forms needs more explanation.

A clue may be found in the rise of nationalist consciousness at about that time, its spread through the growth of literacy, and the development of markets that upset older, more patrimonial economic relationships. These transformations entailed a large bundle of related changes: the gradual, or sometimes rapid, privatization of what had been large tracts of communal lands, the extension of labor markets and resulting mass migrations, the growth of a substantial literate middle class neither quite in the elite nor, any longer, a part of the peasant masses, the rationalization of previously highly localized legal systems, and other transformations that are easily recognized as being part of the process of modernization. Aside from being unsettling to many, these transformations also created new possibilities for social mobility and expanded the political horizons of large numbers of people. Therefore, they raised new questions about the identities of those most affected by the changes. In that context, the rise of modern nationalism hardened attitudes toward those newly viewed as outsiders. Entrepreneurial minorities, previously seen as just one more among many specialized ethnic and religious groups that existed in most complex, premodern agrarian societies, now became, in the eyes of the new nationalists, something considerably more threatening.

This explains what might otherwise seem paradoxical. What classical nineteenth-century liberal theory had identified as major progressive steps in the modernization of society (and this was an error perpetuated by many of their mid-twentieth-century followers in the social sciences, the so-called "modernization theorists") turned out in many cases to be the prelude to rising xenophobia. Increasing education, growing consciousness among a people of their common cultural bonds, the drive toward independent nationhood among previously subjected people, and increasing political activism among once passive segments of the population are supposed to produce freer and more democratic societies. But they may set in motion forces that instead raise the flag of ethnoreligious war, provoke panic about a people's economic security and sense of identity, and so promote a politically defensive reaction that leads to the opposite—to restrictions on liberty and brutal dictatorship.

A classic case of how this happened is explained in Steven Beller's chapter about late-nineteenth- and early-twentieth-century Vienna. It was not the mercantile, old-fashioned, culturally distinctive Jews who provoked the new anti-Semitism but those who assimilated most thoroughly to the new, cosmopolitan, liberal German culture of Central Europe that was in the vanguard of progress. There were economic forces at work, to be sure, and leading Jewish entrepreneurs and financiers became the target of the anti-Semites. But far more important than this was the revolt of the frustrated urban and small-town German Austrians who did not accept the new liberal ethos, who did not succeed as well as the emancipated Jews in entering the ranks of the new cultural elite, and who, in general, were uneasy about the unsettling effects of the rapid economic progress of the period. Beller speculates that this new anti-Semitism, which was really part of a broader reaction against liberalism, may have been set off by the financial panic of 1873. But it persisted and intensified for decades afterward and was, in fact, never permanently reversed in Vienna. Carl Schorske has shown how strongly it affected fin-de-siècle Vienna and set the stage for the atmosphere the young Adolf Hitler found when he moved there in 1907.[4]

There is a further and deeply disturbing paradox to this development. Although many German and Austrian anti-Semites claimed to be revolted by the culture of Orthodox, small-town, traditional Jewry, it was the most assimilated, the least easily identified, the most cosmopolitan and liberal Jews who were the most resented and who, more than their more backward brethren, provoked outrage in Vienna. Not only were they successful competitors in the economic and cultural marketplace, but they were also interpreted as insidious agents of antinationalism who poisoned the purity of the nation by introducing foreign—that is, liberal and antinationalist—ideas and practices.

More than structural social and economic changes were at work in European society during the late nineteenth century. In 1886, Edouard Drumont's *Jewish France* was published and became an immediate best-seller in France. Its basic thesis was that parasitical Jewish financiers owned half the capital in France and were impoverishing the population by ruining legitimate commerce and industry.[5] This absurd claim would not have resonated so widely had there not been more complicated currents of thought in the air as well. After all, whereas nationalism and modernization were relatively recent phenomena in most of Central and Eastern Europe, they were far older in France, which had experienced little anti-Semitism in the first three quarters of the nineteenth century. So France should have been better prepared to cope with the accelerated rate of change in the later part of the century.

With the popularization of Darwinism and its use (or misuse) to explain human history, the notion that the mainspring of history was a desperate struggle for survival between "races," interpreted as "nations," became common across the European political spectrum. This happened in France, but even more so in Germany.[6] The notion appealed greatly to the Russian intelligentsia, too, and Robert Tucker writes that Stalin dated the beginning of his conversion to atheism, and eventually to Bolshevism, from the time when, at the age of thirteen, he read the forbidden Darwin while in his seminary school.[7]

To Darwinism were added, also in the 1860s, the startling revelations of Europe's other popular scientific superstar, Pasteur. The idea that invisible agents caused disease and proliferated in mysterious ways was seized upon almost immediately by intellectuals to explain much that was poorly understood about the great transformation going on in economic and social life.[8] Synthesizing his understanding of Darwin and Pasteur, the German ideologue Paul de Lagarde could explain that Jews were bacilli that had to be exterminated in order to save the German race from being fatally polluted.[9]

It took about two decades, from the 1860s to the 1880s, for such views to become fully ingrained in Europe's general thinking. When they did, the century of liberalism came to an end as intellectuals and many among the growing body of bourgeois and working-class readers came to view the world in racial-national terms and to fear that their nation was beset by implacably hostile racial enemies, both internal and external. The sense that the struggle for survival was between nations legitimized the race for objectively useless colonies in remote parts of the world, provoked an armaments race, and eventually led to world war.[10]

Thus, in the case of the new anti-Semitism in Europe, a whole constellation of forces contributed to its rise, including economic change, political liberalization, increasing education and literacy, and a new vision of how world history worked, based on poorly understood notions of Darwinian evolution and the fear of contagion through unseen social "bacteria." Jews, particularly the emancipated ones who no longer dressed distinctively or served in traditional Jewish occupations as small merchants and artisans, became the symbol of forces over which, in fact, they themselves had little control. Attacking them became a way of reacting to the fears raised by the coming of a new, less stable, and more dangerous world.

Changes in Southeast Asia at the start of the twentieth century were connected to those in Europe. The colonial powers and the Thai monarchy sought to modernize economies and administrations in line with the rationalization of European state bureaucracies. Education spread, and Darwinian ideas appealed particularly to the small but important class of new Asian nationalists. Kasian Tejapira's essay in this book emphasizes that it was the European-educated Thai King Vajiravudh (who reigned from 1910 to 1925) who first proposed that the Chinese in Thailand were foreign, antinational parasites just like the Jews in Europe. Such a notion would have been unthinkable earlier, not least because the Thai royal family was itself partly Sino-Thai.

Similarly, Edgar Wickberg's chapter suggests that late nineteenth-century changes in the Spanish Philippines, including attempts to rationalize the colonial state, combined with renewed Chinese immigration to create a new type of anti-Sinicism that became part of the Filipino nationalist movement, even though a good portion of the educated nationalist elite itself descended from previous generations of Chinese immigrants.

But there were so many differences between Europe and Southeast Asia in the early twentieth century that it would be unwise to draw too direct a comparison between them. For one thing, Western and Central Europe either were already substantially industrialized or at least had major urban industrial centers like Vienna, Budapest, and Warsaw. Southeast Asia was still overwhelmingly rural and agricultural. On the other hand, better analogies suggest themselves if the comparison is extended to Southeast Asia in the late twentieth century, when the region was rapidly industrializing, urbanizing, and going through an unparalleled burst of economic growth.

CONFLICTING IDENTITIES AND THE DILEMMAS OF ASSIMILATION

It may seem trivially obvious, but it must be said that the biggest objective difference between the Jews in Europe and the Chinese in Southeast Asia is that China, which borders on Southeast Asia, is the world's most populated country. In the early twentieth century there was no Israel, and even if there had been, it could never have been large or powerful. Chinese imperial power in Southeast Asia, however, had been present at least since the thirteenth century (when the Yuan, or Mongol, dynasty launched invasions of Burma, Vietnam, and the East Indies), and even earlier in the case of northern Vietnam. The notion that the Jews were ever a serious threat to the independence of any European state may seem laughable in comparison.

But we are not dealing with a purely objective phenomenon. Anti-Semites in late-nineteenth- and early-twentieth-century Europe believed that Jews could exercise great power by their secret control of vast amounts of capital and systematic political and cultural subversion of great nations. The triumph of Bolshevism and its seizure of the powerful Russian Empire after 1917 were seen as conclusive proof of Jewish power. The disproportionate number of Jews in the high ranks of the Communist party, at least until the purges of the late 1930s, was evidence enough for those who wanted to believe. Hitler and other anti-Semites were obsessed by the dangers of Judeo-Communism.

Their fear has even had a recent echo in the "historians' dispute" in Germany about the origins and nature of Nazism. Some historians, most notoriously Ernst Nolte, have found some exculpation of Nazi crimes by saying that, after all, they were driven chiefly by fear of communism, and Stalin started the mass murders which, in a sense, the Nazis then replicated out of a somewhat justified fear that Germany would undergo the same fate if it lost its struggle.[11] Nolte's reasoning may hold no objective merit at all, since it would be difficult to claim that Germany was threatened by Bolshevism at any time after 1923 (until it brought the Red Army down on its head by invading the USSR in 1941), and even more preposterous to claim that the Jews of Europe were in any sense responsible for Stalinism. (Stalin himself, in his later years, turned into a vicious persecutor of Jews.)[12] But Nolte is right in one sense. The Nazis and many other anti-Semites did perceive the existence of a monstrous Jewish threat, and they interpreted the rise of Soviet totalitarianism as evidence of what this threat could lead to if left unchecked. How far this interpretation was removed from any traditional dislike of little Jewish entrepreneurs in premodern Europe, or how marginally it was connected to the economic role of Jews in Germany at the time (where they were less than 1 percent of the population), should be obvious.

The fear of Jews went much further than communism, however, because somehow Jewish capital and journalism were assumed to be responsible not only for Bolshevism but also for taking over the main liberal powers of the West—France, the United Kingdom, and the United States. Thus, the perceived threat was truly all encompassing. In his political autobiography, *Mein Kampf,* Hitler wrote (while in prison in 1923) that the only major power that could be fully trusted in the long run was Japan, because it alone could never be subverted by secret Jewish influence. Presumably, it was beyond the power even of diabolical Jews to turn themselves into Japanese.[13]

In other words, the perception of a major foreign threat existed as strongly in the minds of European nationalist anti-Semites, especially after the Bolshevik revolution, as it would have if there really had been a huge, threatening, neighboring Jewish great power. All that mattered was the perception that local Jews, whatever their economic class or political leanings, would automatically side with this hostile foreign danger because all Jews were assumed to be part of a solidary community.

Jews throughout Europe indeed once had a unifying bond, religion, as well as a historical myth of common kinship. But Zionism, which was a reaction by emancipated (that is, secularized and modernized) Jewish intellectuals in the late nineteenth century to the discovery that they might never be accepted as equals no matter how much they tried to assimilate, was originally hostile to religious tradition. And for many Jews, neither traditional religion nor Zionism was a satisfactory base for their identity. As Karady explains in his chapter on Hungarian Jews, some sought relief in socialist and communist movements that promised to do away with religion and ethnicity altogether. Others tried to assimilate by changing their names and converting. In the end, no strategy was entirely satisfactory. No one, not even the communists, allowed Jews to become fully assimilated, and those who tried to maintain a distinct identity were increasingly rejected as aliens in Central and Eastern Europe.

But despite this divergence of strategies among Jews, in the view of anti-Semites all Jewish attempts to create new identities or reaffirm old ones were fronts that hid underlying Jewish solidarity. Zionists, communists, and various kinds of socialist Jews were antinationalists and subverters of private property. Liberal Jews were carriers of cosmopolitan corruption and greed. Rich Jewish capitalists were more loyal to international capital than to the nation in which they lived. And those who held onto old religious traditions were considered repulsively barbaric and cruel, capable even of sacrificing Christian children in their strange rituals. Indeed, the whole lot were condemned by those who feared them. That divisions among liberals, socialists, Zionists, and Orthodox religious Jews were as intense and bitter as any within parallel segments of Gentile society meant little to anti-Semites. In the end, this is the key to understanding anti-Semitism. Once the Jews were identified as the antinationalist enemy, each and every Jew was condemned as a member of his or her hereditary community. Political and national allegiances were assumed to be ascriptive. There was no way out.

The Chinese in Southeast Asia at the start of the twentieth century had even less of a common bond than did European Jews. They were divided by their regions and languages of origin, which were themselves different from the Mandarin used by the Chinese state as its bureaucratic language. And over generations, many had intermarried and mixed in with local populations. (Of course, so did Jews, but in general to a lesser extent; in both cases there was a lot of variation.) As Wickberg's chapter shows, at certain times in the past the Southeast Asian Chinese had even been rejected by the Chinese Empire, although the Dutch and Spaniards had on several occasions been fearful that China might use its tenuous links with its overseas communities in the Dutch East Indies or the Philippines to extend its political control. Such fears lay behind some of the early massacres of Chinese in the Dutch and Spanish colonies.

This lack of a common identity among the Chinese began to change with the rise of modern Chinese nationalism at the very end of the nineteenth century and in the first decade of the twentieth. Shiraishi makes it a central theme of his chapter to show that the creation of Chinese nationalism played a decisive role in making the Chinese in the Dutch East Indies begin to feel that they were a unified, historically rooted community. This new identity as Chinese nationals in turn played an important part in convincing Javanese intellectuals that they, too, had to forge their own identity, one entirely different from that of the Chinese or the Dutch.

Later in the twentieth century, Southeast Asian Chinese would try many of the same approaches as earlier European Jews to resolve the problem of what their new identity should be. Some became Chinese nationalists, others became communist internationalists, and some tried to mix the two identities. Kasian's chapter poignantly describes some of the dilemmas this raised. Had this collection included an essay about the Malayan communist movement, which tried to be nationalist and anticolonial while never quite managing to enlist many followers beyond a certain portion of the Malayan Chinese community, the analogy between the Jewish and the Chinese search for identity would have been further reinforced.

Still other Chinese tried to become various kinds of local nationalists, especially if they came from mixed parentage, which was common. Some retreated into apolitical concentration on their business affairs, and many tried to assimilate into their surroundings, with greater or lesser success. Some Chinese became highly Westernized, using English or Dutch as their major language and becoming Christians. Some urged conversion to Islam. But anti-Chinese local nationalists, like European anti-Semites, viewed all these strategies as duplicitous and subversive, serving only to conceal the real danger of Chinese ambitions. The issue, which is far from settled, hinged on the question of whether or not the Chinese were to be viewed as a single "race" with its own interests and goals, or whether, on the contrary, individuals were to be judged according to their political or economic interests and by their very different kinds of ideological stances.

The game of competing identities, which becomes so important as the unsettling effects of modern social change force growing numbers of people to question and redefine their place in society, can quickly turn into a vicious circle. If a nation needs to be solidary in order to survive, and if competing identities within its body are seen either as a form of illness or as the opening wedge for foreign invasion and domination, then part of the national task is to rid itself of such dangers. But then those targeted for elimination, or even for assignment to permanently inferior political status, have no choice but to react with their own newly defensive sense of identity.

In Europe this happened not only between Jews and Gentiles but also between most nations bordering each other and previously mixed together. Romanians and Hungarians discovered entirely imagined hostile histories going back a thousand years; Serbs and Croats turned a religious difference between them into a supposedly racial one; Poles and Germans, as well as Czechs and Germans, who had mixed freely in their border areas, decided that they were mutually exclusive and hostile peoples, as did the French and Germans, and so on. That the process began a short while later in Southeast Asia and produced similar effects also extends well beyond the question of Chinese identity and anti-Sinicism. In that sense, the phenomena of anti-Semitism and anti-Sinicism are only partly related to whatever distinctive economic and cultural traits and common bonds the Jews and Chinese may actually possess. All that was needed to set off some such hostility in the age of nationalism was the existence of distinctive minority communities. In these two cases, their great success and adaptability to economic and social modernization fueled greater resentment, no doubt, as did their increasing search for their own identity. But there was no way to avoid some kind of reaction once modernization and the concept of nationalism were under way.

And yet, nationalism has not set off wars between culturally distinct populations in all instances. In nations with significant numbers of Jews, anti-Semitism was not equally virulent everywhere, nor did it exist at a constant level anywhere. It was worse in Central Europe (if Germany is included in the definition of this region, as it should be) than in Western Europe, although in the late nineteenth century it seemed that it was getting worse in France than in Germany. It was less serious in England, the United States, and Canada than in continental Europe. Even within Central Europe, it was less intense in Hungary than in Romania, Poland, or Austria, all four of which had large Jewish minorities, especially in their cities. But it got worse almost everywhere in Europe in the 1920s and 1930s. These differences should warn us away from simplistic structural explanations and alert us to historically specific differences and changes.

The same applies in Southeast Asia. Anti-Sinicism was stronger in Thailand and the Philippines than in the rest of Southeast Asia from the 1910s into the 1930s, but since the 1940s it has lessened in those countries and has played a less important role there than in the rest of Southeast Asia. On the other hand, since the 1960s anti-Sinicism has flared on and off, with varying degrees of intensity—including, in some places, much violence—as a significant aspect of nationalism in Malaysia, Indonesia, Cambodia, and Vietnam. Even in the 1990s it would be difficult to claim either a uniform level of anti-Sinicism throughout the area or to preclude the possibility that it might increase in some places and decrease in others.

What accounts for such differences, when in fact the negative stereotypes of both Chinese in Southeast Asia and Jews in Europe (and North America) have been pretty similar everywhere? Why have conflicting identities led to such violence in some cases and to relative assimilation and considerably more harmonious relations elsewhere? The tendency of both Jews and Chinese to rise to positions of cultural as well as economic prominence has been high throughout Europe and North America and is in any case not correlated with degrees of anti-Semitism or anti-Sinicism. The Central European country in which Jews were probably the most economically powerful in the first third of the twentieth century was Hungary, not Romania, Poland, Austria, or Germany, even though Jews held a disproportionately high number of important cultural and professional urban positions in all those countries. And in Southeast Asia, although Chinese were a large and powerful minority in Malaysia, they were economically at least as centrally important, if not more so, in Thailand. As the chapter by Gary Hamilton and Tony Waters illustrates, the economic power of the Sino-Thais throughout the twentieth century has been, and continues to be, immense.

What the essays in this collection show is that variations in the degree of anti-Semitism or anti-Sinicism cannot be explained by analyzing purely objective structural factors: the size of the minority community, its degree of economic influence, the general level of economic development in the society, the speed of modernization, or the presence of any measurable threat to nationalist goals presented by the existence of the minority. All of these may contribute to antiminority sentiments, but they are not sufficient explanatory variables. Rather, the prospects of relatively benign assimilation, or its opposite, must ultimately be found elsewhere.

DIFFERING DEFINITIONS OF NATIONS AND COMMUNITIES

The most important difference between the objective analysis of any version of nationalism and the vision of the committed nationalist is that the former begins with the understanding that nationalism is always at least partly, and often largely, based on a historical myth. The committed nationalist's version of history, on the other hand, is uncritical and accepts myth as self-evident truth. For the analyst, it is always a difficult problem to explain why this or that form of nationalism actually came into being, whereas for most nationalists, the question is easily answered by reciting a largely fabricated history that points to the inevitability of "our" nation's existence.

Among professional social scientists, the most-cited recent works on nationalism all emphasize its contingent nature and artificiality. The very title of the most famous of these works, Benedict Anderson's *Imagined Communities,* conveys the sense that the nation is an artificial entity.[14] Even Anthony Smith, the foremost proponent of the thesis that nationalism is an ancient phenomenon originally based on real blood ties, insists that he is not a "primordialist." Whatever tendency there is for people to seek solidarity in some community, there has been nothing inevitable about the rise of certain nations at the expense of others. Modern nations are all more or less artificial groupings far more heterogeneous than the small tribes of the past, which were, according to Smith, the founders of a few, but hardly all, subsequent nations.[15]

But regardless of the historical truth about their foundations, various nations that have established themselves have two quite different types of founding myths. One, by far the commonest, is that the members of the nation are the modern descendants of an ancient tribe, a "folk," whose common kinship and united struggle to achieve sovereignty and security in their territory over many centuries laid the basis for the modern nation. It is of almost no consequence that the overwhelming majority of these stories are recent inventions, most going back no farther than the nineteenth century, because they almost all claim great antiquity. According to this first type of "foundation story," the members of the nation share common characteristics and interests because of their common kinship, and those who are not members cannot possibly be loyal citizens.

The second type of foundation story is that the nation consists of various groups and individuals who have formed a united whole and who deserve citizenship by virtue of their behavior, their demonstrated loyalty and adherence to the values and codes of the nation. It is clearly much more likely that nations made up of recent immigrants, like those in the Americas, will adopt this kind of story to explain their existence. The United States is the most important example. On the other hand, the Francophone people of Quebec have a vision of their "nation" that is far closer to one based on a "tribal blood" foundation story. This may seem odd, because in France itself the national myth of a universalistic "citizenship" that has the power to convert foreigners has prevailed, with some interruptions during periods of rightist ascendancy, since the time of the French Revolution. Explanations about why one kind of nationalism and not the other have become dominant in any particular place are not readily available.[16]

Why do some national myths insist that blood is primordial and that, as the Germans and Russians believed (and to a considerable extent still do), the nation is a large, kin-based kind of *Volksgemeinschaft?* Why do others, most notably the English, the French, and the people of the United States, believe, on the contrary, that the nation should be able to absorb different types of unrelated people by converting them to a national way of behaving and thinking?[17]

Liah Greenfeld claims that the answer has to do with the situation of the small elites (or potential elites) who, in each case, created modern national- ism, and on their image of themselves at the moment of creation. If national- ism was the invention of a self-confident elite that wanted to justify its expanding power and legitimize social mobility, as was the case in England and the United States, a generous, inclusive, "civic" nationalism was more likely to emerge. If, on the other hand, it was the creation of a group under attack, which felt its very existence threatened by powerful outside forces, a more closed, resentful, defensive nationalism was more likely to emerge. There is also the tradition of Enlightenment thinking in Western Europe, particularly evident in the writings of John Locke, that emphasized individ- ual over group rights and obligations.[18]

These are not, in themselves, entirely satisfactory explanations, because both types of founding nationalist myths are just that—creations which simplify historical reality and avoid dealing with the complexity of what really happened. Neither Russia nor Germany has ever been as closed, much less culturally or racially "pure," as its extreme nationalists have pretended, and England, France, and the United States have frequently violated their stated principles of respecting individual over group rights. Also, opinion within any nation varies, and over time there may be changes in the relative weights given to certain aspects of the nationalist myth. For example, the concept of "race" as "nation" was on the ascendant through- out the world in the 1920s and 1930s, but it waned somewhat in the years after World War II.[19]

Nevertheless, even with all these qualifications, the nature of the basic founding national myth counts. In every nation it is possible to find a time when such a myth came into being and became widely accepted. Such stories, once established, are subject to change only slowly, and the basic element of either "blood" or "civic" nationalism (perhaps a more descriptive term would be "assimilation" nationalism, but "civic" has become widely used) as the basis of national identity has so far proved highly durable in nationalisms formed from the eighteenth to the early twentieth centuries. In a crisis, that is what the people in a nation refer to as a guide. In its moment of greatest national crisis, the United States fought a bloody civil war to end slavery, and in its time of greatest modern crisis, Germany fought a far bloodier war to purify itself and its neighbors of polluting races. In its moment of immense national crisis, Russia in the 1990s appears to be reverting to a traditional conception of itself as a communal, "blood"-based nation on the defensive against the corrupting influence of greedy Western individualism and the dangerous incursions of Oriental (in this case Islamic) barbarism. Such ingrained myths may blind a people to the reality of their situation, but that does not make the myths any less potent as a base for political mobilization and action.

Without going into detail, it is evident that where conceptions of blood nationalism prevailed, Jews were unlikely to be accepted as full citizens. Because throughout Central Europe, nationalism grew as an essentially defensive reaction—with the Germans galvanized into nationalism by defeat and occupation at the hands of the French during the Napoleonic War, the Hungarians reacting against Habsburg Germanization policies, the Romanians (in Transylvania, where Romanian nationalism began) and Croats reacting against Hungarian domination, the Poles reacting against Prussian and Russian conquest and subsequent cultural imperialism, and so on— nationalist elites were predisposed toward carrying a bitter sense of having been wronged and toward the necessity of purging baneful foreign influences and potential traitors from their ranks. In those circumstances, Jews, especially as they moved into the urban professions and adapted well to commercial intercourse with the more developed and dangerous great powers, were bound to be viewed with suspicion.

Yet, as Karady emphasizes in chapter 5, official Hungarian nationalism was far more tolerant toward Jews than might have been expected. The reason for this was that late nineteenth-century Hungary was above all a multiethnic, multilingual political entity in which Magyar (Hungarian) speakers were a minority. The willingness of emancipated urban Jews to convert to Magyar speech and to declare their loyalty to the Hungarian nation was decisive. No matter what the anti-Semitic sentiments of the elites, they accepted Jews as converts to the national cause because they needed all the support they could get in a political atmosphere that was moving surely, if hesitantly and slowly, toward the extension of voting and political rights. Furthermore, the sentiment that Jews could be loyal was extended long past 1918, after which Hungary lost almost all of its minorities except Jews and Gypsies.

In other cases in the region, among Hungary's neighbors, the nationalists felt that they represented clear majorities, and if only they could be rid of foreign domination and infiltration, they would easily prevail. So the "blood" nationalism of political elites was less constrained in its anti-Semitism than it was in Hungary.

To be sure, in the end it is not clear how much difference all this made. Anti-Semitism was a fundamental aspect of the drift to the right that occurred throughout the region in the 1930s, and during World War II the Germans found abundant help in all the societies they came to dominate, including, though with some delay, Hungary. (Budapest's large Jewish community was spared early persecution because it was protected by the Hungarian government until 1944.)

In chapter 2, Reid suggests that the distinction between "blood" and "civic" nationalism is useful in Southeast Asia, too. Indonesian nationalists, by virtue of having to deal with significant religious and ethnic minorities throughout the immense and varied territory controlled by the Dutch, were obliged to create a more civic than a blood type of nationalism. It was not just, or even mainly, the Chinese as such who were at issue, but whether or not the inhabitants of the outer islands would accept being part of the same nation as Java, and whether or not Christians and Muslims could be loyal to a common anti-Dutch cause.

Indonesia has so far been an extraordinary example of a nation created consciously, with a new language, a founding myth, and a whole identity that dates from no earlier than the start of the twentieth century. (Bahasa Indonesia, the official language taught in all schools, is derived from a widespread form of market Malay that has existed for a long time but that, in the twentieth century, has been turned into a sophisticated, literary modern language that has its own vitality even though the vast majority of Indonesia's people, including the majority Javanese, still have their own distinct and mutually incomprehensible native languages.)

Under such circumstances, no matter how much anti-Chinese sentiment may flare up from time to time, one may suppose that the possibility of acceptance through cultural conversion is higher than it would be if Indonesian nationalism were based on notions of blood. Thus, the Suharto government has been able to collaborate with Chinese businesses quite comfortably, even as it claims to be genuinely nationalistic. On the other hand, there is no guarantee that "blood" definitions will not come to the fore in the future, as some Indonesians are demanding.

In Malaysia, particularly peninsular Malaysia (the old colony of Malaya), the situation is quite different. The majority Muslim Malays once felt themselves to be an endangered minority. But they managed to establish, with British help, almost complete domination over the political system, and they now have a demographic majority great enough to ensure continuing control through elections. Yet because the political system remains democratic and the government must face periodic elections, the possibility of strong opposition from within Malay ranks (today that would mean Muslims trying to create a fundamentalist religious state), along with the fact that about a third of the population is Chinese, means that it is necessary to forge alliances with the significant Chinese voting block, too.

The founding national myth among Malays is one of an endangered pure Malay people defined by its Muslim culture that must defend itself against foreign, particularly Chinese, power, originally manifested as a powerful Chinese-led communist insurgency in the late 1940s and 1950s. But even though this myth has led to discriminatory laws favoring majority Malay over Chinese businesses, a process described in K. S. Jomo's chapter, as well as in the one by Linda Lim and Peter Gosling, it has never led to the kind of anti-Chinese legislation that threatened to deprive them of their property and basic political rights. So long as Malaysia remains a functioning democracy in which a large portion of the Malay elite is wedded to notions of economic and social modernization, there is a limit beyond which angry Malay nationalism cannot be allowed to go. To allow the polity to become too anti-Chinese would badly disrupt the economy, because, as Jomo shows, the Chinese still control a large portion of it. Allowing anti-Sinicism too much power would also unbalance the political situation in favor of religious extremists.

This situation is somewhat reminiscent of the Hungarian one until the late 1930s and even through the early days of World War II. The Hungarian elite was unwilling to tolerate persecution of its urban Jews because that would have been too destructive of the economy and would have meant giving power to the most extreme nationalists, who wanted to create a Nazi type of state. In both cases, "blood nationalism" was kept under control by political elites for quite practical reasons.

In other words, "blood" and "civic" conceptions of nationalism emerge slowly, and conflicting forces are at work in determining which one finally prevails. Political compromises that may seem to be merely expedient can change behavior toward minorities and decrease the likelihood of future conflict. On the other hand, the fundamental nature of the founding national myth, once a widespread consensus emerges among the political and intellectual elites of a nation, will predispose that nation toward a certain outcome in times of economic or political crisis. Though Malaysia is more democratic than Indonesia, an unbiased observer must wonder what the long-term consequences will be of a founding national myth that so emphasizes hereditary ethnic interests and makes them the basis of nationhood.

In Central Europe, the idea of blood nationalism was so fixed that bitter wars to the finish were fought and are still being fought with the same ultimate goal—ethnonational purification. The Nazis did not begin the process, and it did not go away with their defeat. Most of the multiethnic states that emerged in the region after World War I have become largely monoethnic by some combination of breaking up, having their borders moved, mass killings of minorities, and the forcing of emigration. Poland, Hungary, the Czech Republic, Slovenia, and Austria (which emerged from the ruins of the Habsburg Empire as overwhelmingly German Catholic) are now rid of their old ethnic problems. Romania, which was over one-third non-Romanian after World War I, is now over 90 percent ethnic Romanian, but with a significant potential for ethnic war in Transylvania, which has a large Hungarian minority. Slovakia's relations with its Hungarian minority present a similar potential for trouble. As for the remaining Balkan states with significant minorities—Serbia, Croatia, Bosnia, Albania, and Macedonia—they are either at war or in danger of being subjected to future violence.

Can Southeast Asia escape such a fate, one that has already befallen Vietnam and Cambodia? The question is especially relevant for Malaysia, because of its large Chinese minority, and for Indonesia, where the Chinese are only 2 or 3 percent of the population but where they are economically very important. There, the debate about the meaning of the nation—about competing "blood" versus "civic" definitions—has to be watched closely to see where it is heading and what consensus, if any, is emerging. This point may seem less relevant for Thailand and the Philippines, where anti-Sinicism has not been so pronounced, but the same debates exist in those countries, too, and the outcome is far from being decided.

This brings us to another aspect of Liah Greenfeld's typology, which is not as well explored in her book but which is equally, if not more, significant: the difference between "individualistic" and "communal" definitions of society. England and the United States, the two most strongly "civic" nations, Greenfeld claims, are also individualistic societies, whereas Germany and Russia, the nations that most strongly base membership on notions of "blood," are communal. She takes this to mean that the defense of the individual is important for one set of nations, whereas in the other, not only are the community's rights and needs paramount but the individual is almost assumed to have no possibility of political existence outside of his or her national community.

This may be too Manichean and simplistic a view of vastly complicated societies, but again, as in the ideal types of "blood" and "civic" nationalisms, the theory is useful for understanding important aspects of political behavior. There is a strong hypothesis in Greenfeld's work that only individualistic civic nations can be fully democratic, because in the communal view, the interests of the nation entirely override those of the individual. Especially in times of crisis, this is a strong argument in favor of unanimity. The community, the nation, is the relevant political actor and should speak with one voice, that of its elite. Consequently, individual rights and interests are trampled and dissent becomes a betrayal of the national community.

In agrarian states that made no claims to being modern nations, defining political actors according to their ascribed communal status was common and usually had benign implications. The "millet" system in the Ottoman Empire was like this, as was the position of Jews throughout much of premodern Central and Eastern Europe. It seems that the Chinese in much of Southeast Asia were treated similarly.

Though certainly not democratic in any sense of the word, the Ottoman Empire was relatively tolerant and ran well enough in a prenationalist age to hold together for a long time. It was a polity in which communities were divided on the basis of ethnoreligions, or "millets." Each millet had a considerable degree of legal and even political autonomy so long as it recognized the ultimate sovereignty of, and paid its dues to, the Ottoman state. Most premodern agrarian states, including both independent and colonial ones in Southeast Asia, accommodated their major ethnic or religious communities in this way most of the time. But in an age of rising nationalism, this kind of structure could not hope to survive as the mixed populations asserted their conflicting identities and claims and began a process of homogenization into national boundaries that is still far from completed in the former Ottoman lands. The wars, expulsions, massacres, and general political tensions that "nationalization" of this territory has produced explain why, in the context of the contemporary Middle East or the Balkans, Ottoman rule appears in retrospect to have been far more benign than early-twentieth-century nationalists claimed.[20]

For similar reasons, there has been a good bit of nostalgia about the nineteenth-century Habsburg Empire in Central Europe, because it evolved into an antinationalist political entity ready to accommodate various ethnic communities so long as they did not question the existence of the central state. This is why, for German nationalists in the empire, the Habsburgs were anathema, and why Hitler hated them as racial traitors.[21]

"Millet" systems became unworkable because modern states and economies cannot live with such a high degree of communal separation and specialization, and each community that is unable to take control of a state becomes threatened by the forced homogenization that follows inevitably from the strengthening of the state and the modernization of technology. In Central Europe, and increasingly throughout the world in the twentieth century, multiethnic, multireligious states either have come under enormous pressure to split into separate homogeneous nations or, in moments of crisis, have degenerated into ethnic and religious warfare. What is going on in former Yugoslavia in the 1990s is not the revival of an ancient process but the culmination of one that is barely one hundred years old and that became genocidal only during World War II.

Yugoslavias, Sri Lankas, and Rwandas are not the exceptions that horrified journalists claim to see whenever they occur. Rather, they become inevitable if the definition of political actors remains based on their hereditary, communal affiliation. In a modern society, where control of the state is all-important because of the state's enormous potential power in all aspects of life, from education to the defense of property rights, and where the semi-independence accorded to various communities by a millet-like system is impossible, if communal organizations and solidarities do develop strongly, or remain alive from the past, they quickly become the main political actors competing for control of the state.

If, on the contrary, a society views individuals, each with his or her own rights and capacity to make political choices, as the main actors, then compromise in times of crisis becomes much easier. Modern individuals have many different memberships in occupational, religious, political, and social organizations. They possess what sociologists call crosscutting roles and allegiances. Furthermore, in reality in modern economies, many people move, or may expect to move, into different economic classes, different neighborhoods, and therefore different political categories over time. Under those circumstances, it is difficult to mobilize people on the basis of hereditary characteristics, and no political outcome is as threatening to the losers as the risk of being confined to permanent powerlessness and inferiority by virtue of their birth.

If anti-individualism becomes the ideology of the state, however, then communal categories become fixed groups into which people are placed and from which they cannot escape. Communal membership, rather than indi-vidual traits, determines a person's place in the political system, and whether or not one belongs to a particular community tends to be ascriptively assigned. Lines of conflict become hereditary and lose their fluidity. The power of the state that makes it almost impossible for traditional ascriptive communities to survive as semi-independent entities dooms a modern soci-ety based on the modern reincarnation of similar groups to an eternal war of survival between them. Where the individual is defined primarily by his or her community, rather than as a distinct entity, uneasy truces between competing religions, races, ethnicities, or classes eventually degenerate into wars of extermination or expulsion as the victors eliminate their rivals. The point is that once modern states and economies break down old communal solidarities, re-creating them as the basis for political competition and then recognizing them, rather than individuals, as the main political actors elimi-nates the single chance those societies have to harmonize the many conflict-ing interests, groups, and cultural elements that exist within all modern states.[22]

It may seem possible for a kind of "communal democracy" to exist, as indeed it has in Malaysia. The problem is that the record of long-term stability and peaceful conflict resolution in societies dominated by commu-nal politics in the twentieth century has been extremely poor. Except for the case of India, which is hardly reassuring, it would be difficult to point to another example except, perhaps, Switzerland, which is so anomalous as to be almost useless as a model. Western societies, particularly the United States, that have managed to retain individualistic ideologies curb endemic tendencies toward primarily communal politics by allowing people to mix, change their identities, and vote freely. Individuals, not communities, have legal rights, at least until now. If that were ever to change, then the United States would not survive as a democratic, stable society.

This point brings up important questions about the future of Southeast Asia's Chinese communities and about the fate of the region as a whole.

For whatever combination of reasons, the Chinese in Southeast Asia, like Europe's Jews, have produced an astounding number of success stories in business and what used to be called the "liberal professions." Much of this success is owing to a high degree of adaptability.

In chapter 5, Karady's account of how urban Hungarian Jews "over-invested" in education helps explain how this last significant Jewish community in Central Europe managed to remain disproportionately important in Hungary's life as the country moved through repeated periods of political turmoil and drastic change from the late nineteenth to the late twentieth century. It was certainly not just their capital as such that guaranteed this importance, but also the intellectual capital and flexibility of some Jews. What is particularly striking is how many different paths were followed by skilled individual Jews. Some were entrepreneurs, some were attorneys, some became professional communist activists, some anticommunist dissidents, some leading academics and scientists, and so on. Of those who escaped extermination, then, there were always some who were well placed for whatever change occurred, so that their intelligence, education, and resourcefulness could be put to good use. It was, in fact, this diversity, rather than any cohesive commonality of interests and opinions, as the anti-Semites supposed, that helped so large a proportion of Hungary's surviving Jews to continue playing an important role in society under different sorts of regimes, even though they did so as individuals rather than as a unified community.

All this is truer still for the Chinese in Southeast Asia, who belong to even more diverse communities than did Europe's Jews. So far as business success goes, the essays presented in this volume suggest that, if anything, Chinese accomplishments have been considerably more impressive than those of Jews in Europe. Even in countries where they make up only a small percentage of the population, notably Indonesia, the Chinese have played a vastly disproportionate role in developing the modern economy.[23] In Malaysia, according to the figures presented by Jomo in chapter 9, after two decades of policies systematically favoring bumiputera (majority Malay) entrepreneurs over the Chinese, the latter still own more than twice as large a share of all the capital in the country as the former, even though in the general population Malays now number over 50 percent.

Chinese success in Southeast Asia is not merely a matter of certain types of business, either, but of a wide range of economic activities, from control of some of the world's largest multinational corporations to ownership of small shops throughout the countryside, especially in Indonesia, Thailand, and Malaysia. Moreover, there is a growing number of Chinese or part-Chinese intellectuals, attorneys, doctors, and so on. Kasian, in chapter 3, suggests that this professional segment of the urban Sino-Thai population, particularly its younger members, has been in the forefront of political modernization and the liberalization of Thai society in the 1980s and 1990s. As such, he suggests, it is in the vanguard of the more cosmopolitan, open, and prosperous future that awaits Thailand.

This is certainly one of the paths that may lead toward the future. The three essays in this volume on contemporary Chinese businesses in Southeast Asia (Jomo, Hamilton and Waters, and Lim and Gosling) hold out this possibility. Open and official discrimination against the Chinese has diminished in all of Southeast Asia, particularly in the ASEAN countries. Political and social integration and mixing, as well as general prosperity, seem to be allaying what might have become greater resentment among non-Chinese as Chinese have benefited disproportionately from economic growth. Many non-Chinese have benefited, too, and the long decades of security since the 1960s have calmed ethnic tensions.

And yet, as we have seen, optimists in Europe in the second half of the nineteenth century expected that anti-Semitism would also vanish with time. If Kasian's essay is compared with Beller's, there is a haunting parallel. The new anti-Semitism in Vienna and throughout Europe in the late nineteenth century was directed against the liberalization of society as a whole, and Jews happened to be a visible, somewhat suspect, ostensibly somewhat alien population in the forefront of this change. Old prejudices based on Jews' traditional entrepreneurial roles and on ancient religious differences played their part, but they were not the essential cause of what happened. It was precisely because Jews had moved into successful new roles, both in business and in cultural life, and because they also were increasingly active politically and were visibly in favor of cosmopolitan liberalizing changes, that they came to be so feared and hated by reactionary nationalists.

Could something like this happen in Southeast Asia? The Chinese minorities are playing such a large role in the economic transformation there that they could easily become targets of those frustrated by some of the changes taking place. Many in the majority populations have not done as well as they might have hoped. There may one day be serious economic or political reverses to the recent progress. Are there not forces of resentful nationalism calling for a return to a more traditional, less aggressively capitalist, less consumer oriented, more modest, respectful, and less mobile social order? How do they view the increasingly assertive and self-confident professional and business Chinese who are not loathe to flaunt their success and modern opulence?

For those who seek a guilty party to blame for the negative aspects of economic growth, marketization, and decline of tradition, the Chinese are an excellent target. Their very success—the flexibility and diversity of career paths and life-styles of the Chinese—ensures, as it did for Jews a century ago, that there will be some in every category of those considered responsible for the changes. There are plutocrats and student radicals, nationalists who claim that "Chineseness" does not matter and nationalists who assert their Chinese identities, journalists and shopkeepers, union leaders and politicians, conservatives and socialists, converts to Islam or Christianity and traditionalists who maintain their old religious ways. For those who want to blame a group of supposed outsiders for what they dislike about modernization, it is not difficult to turn a diffuse rage against large and incomprehensible forces into a focused anger toward what appears to be a united and duplicitous community of strangers who take different roles only to fool their enemies.

Many observers, including writers in the *Far Eastern Economic Review* and also, in a subtler and more scholarly way, Kasian Tejapira in this volume, have noted the increasing self-assertiveness of Southeast Asian Chinese.[24] Some younger ones are learning Mandarin and trying to reclaim a Chinese identity that their ancestors, who had regional identities rather than Chinese ones as such, never had. And it is a fact that many Chinese businesses, large and small, are managed in a closed way and use what appears to outsiders, as Jomo suggests, to be their own way of communicating and doing business. It is not difficult to understand why non-Chinese nationalists who view change as threatening and who feel that their own community is endangered would interpret such behavior as confirming their worst suspicions. This happened with Europe's Jews as well.

None of this need be terribly threatening if politics and society are based primarily on well-developed individualism. If, on the other hand, it is automatically assumed that the ethnoreligious, hereditary community is the main political actor, and if individuals are expected to behave according to communal, not personal, interests, then "the Chinese," or "the Christians" in Indonesia, or "the Muslims" in the Philippines, or any other identifiable minority group becomes a potential traitor to the national cause, which is itself identified as the cause of the majority community. Though particularly dangerous for the Chinese, this is a threat to all groups in the multiethnic and multireligious societies of Southeast Asia, as it was elsewhere in the world and as it was for Europe's Jews.

Given the recent tendency in U.S. universities, in the government, and in related cultural institutions to assign positions on the basis of hereditary ethnic characteristics, it is inappropriate for an American academic to lecture others about the dangers of doing this or about the even greater risk of assuming that everyone's primary interests are determined by his or her ascribed ethnic status. Nevertheless, it is important to note that in the modern world there have been no good solutions to the tensions raised by the competition of different culturally defined groups if those groups become fixed hereditary categories and if the basic orientation of societies becomes communal. To assume that hereditary racial, linguistic, or religious categories are paramount in all cases means that distrust of communities other than one's own becomes more or less inevitable. Premodern societies could survive this way, but not those with urban, mobile populations interacting in modern economies under the rule of an officially nationalistic, powerful, bureaucratic state. An expanding economy may accommodate the resulting tensions for a while, but communal thinking and bargaining will so dominate political thinking that in times of retrenchment or exacerbated competition, communal hatreds, jealousies, and fears must come to the fore.

One of the common threads running through the successful East and Southeast Asian societies of today, particularly in Japan, Chinese-dominated Singapore, and Malaysia but increasingly elsewhere as well, is a rather smug dismissal of the West, particularly of the United States. The West, it is claimed, has become too selfish and individualistic to maintain its strength. The more communal approach of the Asians is better. Whatever this means for Japan, communalism in Southeast Asia is ethnic and religious. Add to this the fact that Darwinian thinking about evolutionary competition is popular among Southeast Asian intellectuals as well, and the recipe for something more somber than a group of happy, united national communities cooperating for the national good lies just around the corner.

But this takes us beyond what the essays in this volume demonstrate. They are suggestive and sometimes provocative, but they are also meticulously documented and carefully reasoned. They provide a base from which one may speculate, but none of the authors is foolish enough to venture into punditry, which by its very nature rarely produces carefully marshaled evidence or scholarly subtlety. We know that even though common social forces act in similar ways throughout the globe, no two situations are exactly alike, and history never repeats itself. Whatever our differences, we all hope that the following chapters will make readers think carefully about the different paths that lead to the future in Southeast Asia, and about the issue of minorities and ethnic conflict throughout the world.

NOTES

1. Hans Rogger, *Jewish Policies and Right-Wing Politics in Imperial Russia* (London: McMillan, 1986); Celia S. Heller, *On the Edge of Destruction: Jews of Poland between the World Wars* (New York: Columbia University Press, 1977); William O.

Oldson, *A Providential Anti-Semitism: Nationalism and Polity in Nineteenth Century Romania* (Philadelphia: American Philosophical Society, 1991). A particularly useful account of how anti-Semitism became one of the dominant ideologies of twentieth-century Romanian nationalists, and of how little this had to do with traditional economic roles, is found in the recent work by Irina Livezeanu, *Cultural Politics in Greater Romania: Regionalism, Nation Building, and Ethnic Struggle* (Ithaca, New York: Cornell University Press, 1995).

2. Daniel Chirot, *Modern Tyrants: The Power and Prevalence of Evil in Our Age* (New York: Free Press, 1994).

3. In much of the classical sociological analysis on minority entrepreneurs (though far less in Weber than in Sombart), there is a considerable strain of anti-Semitism that takes the form of an attack on, or at least a dismissal of, the utility of petty commerce and usury, which are seen as inherently parasitical and unclean. This is evident in much of the Marxist literature as well, especially in Marx's own expression of loathing and horror at all money-making activities and the Jews' propensity to succeed at them. His essay "On The Jewish Question" is pure venom. See Karl Marx, *Early Writings,* introduced by Lucio Colletti (Harmondsworth: Penguin, 1975).

To this day, the hatred of markets and capitalist activity easily lapses into blame of minority entrepreneurs for serving the interests of the oppressive elites, be they capitalists, colonial masters, or local landowners. In this fashion, Marxist analysts, like Marx himself, can have it both ways. Minority entrepreneurs are seen to be stealing from the people, but the onus of being racially prejudiced is removed from the critical analyst by putting even more blame on cynical higher powers who use the minorities. This excuses anti-Semitism, or anti-Sinicism, as a misplaced but essentially justified form of revolutionary activity by the oppressed.

A good example of such a position is found in Edna Bonacich's defense of urban looting and violence in Los Angeles's 1992 Rodney King riots. She calls Los Angeles a colonial society oppressed by racist, thieving, capitalist whites. Korean shopkeepers, who bore the brunt of much of the looting, she writes, play the same role as East European Jews and Southeast Asian Chinese. They are cynically used by the powers that be, and so become the targets of those legitimately angered by superexploitation. Because the Koreans are themselves oppressors, scant sympathy is shown them. On the other hand, the white elite is much more guilty, and after the revolution, presumably, Koreans can be brought back into the fold of the deserving majority. See Edna Bonacich, "Thoughts on Urban Unrest," in Fred L. Pincus and Howard J. Erlich, eds., *Race and Ethnic Conflict: Contending Views of Prejudice, Discrimination, and Ethnoviolence* (Boulder, Colorado: Westview Press, 1994), pp. 404–407. Marx, too, held out hope for Jews, whose culture and society he found so repulsive, because after the fall of capitalism they would presumably give up their ways and become normal people.

4. Carl E. Schorske, *Fin-de-Siècle Vienna: Politics and Culture* (New York: Vintage, 1981), chapter 2.

5. Edouard Drumont, in Paul Mendes-Flohr and Jehuda Reinharz, eds., *The Jew in the Modern World: A Documentary History* (New York: Oxford University Press, 1980), pp. 276–77.

6. Alfred Kelly, *The Descent of Darwin: The Popularization of Darwinism in Germany* (Chapel Hill: University of North Carolina Press, 1981), pp. 30, 37, 125.

7. Robert C. Tucker, *Stalin as Revolutionary* (New York: W. W. Norton, 1974), p. 78. See also Tibor Szamuely, *The Russian Tradition* (New York: McGraw-Hill, 1974), pp. 169–70.

8. Eric J. Hobsbawm, *The Age of Capital 1848–1875* (New York: Charles Scribner's, 1975), p. 285.

9. Fritz Stern, *The Politics of Cultural Despair* (Berkeley: University of California Press, 1974), pp. 63–65.

10. I have expanded on this theme in more detail in *Modern Tyrants,* chapter 2.

11. Charles Maier, *The Unmasterable Past: History, Holocaust, and German National Identity* (Cambridge, Massachusetts: Harvard University Press, 1988).

12. Adam B. Ulam, *Stalin: The Man and His Era* (New York: Viking, 1977), pp. 684, 730–31.

13. Adolf Hitler, *Mein Kampf,* translated by Ralph Mannheim (Boston: Houghton Mifflin, 1971), pp. 637–38.

14. Benedict R. Anderson, *Imagined Communities: Reflections on the Origin and Spread of Nationalism* (London: Verso, 1983). See also Eric J. Hobsbawm, *Nations and Nationalism since 1780* (Cambridge: Cambridge University Press, 1990); Ernest Gellner, *Nations and Nationalism* (Ithaca, New York: Cornell University Press, 1983).

15. Anthony D. Smith, *The Ethnic Origins of Nations* (Oxford: Blackwell, 1986), particularly chapters 1 and 2.

16. Liah Greenfeld's willingness to address this question by going directly to the intellectual discourse that established the foundations of the major modern European nations is what has made her book on nationalism so important and controversial. See her *Nationalism: Five Roads to Modernity* (Cambridge, Massachusetts: Harvard University Press, 1992).

17. Rogers Brubaker explores the differences between French and German notions of citizenship in his *Citizenship and Nationhood in France and Germany* (Cambridge, Massachusetts: Harvard University Press, 1992).

18. For an elaboration of this point and its implications for contemporary debates about nationalism and identity, see my "Modernism without Liberalism: The Ideological Roots of Modern Tyranny," *Contention* (Fall 1995), pp. 141–66.

19. It is interesting to ask, although the question is far from the scope of this book, whether or not the concept of "race" as "nation" is on the rise again in today's world.

20. For a remarkable and accurate picture of what Ottoman society was like in an area that has come to be highly contested—Bosnia—see Ivo Andric's *Bridge on the Drina* (Chicago: University of Chicago Press, 1972). Mass expulsions or exterminations did occur in agrarian states, but the object was to break the political power of a threatening community, not to purify the society. Otherwise, the persistence of mixed religious societies for centuries, even millennia, would be inexplicable. Such events were rare, though they began to crop up in late medieval and early modern western Europe as defenseless communities of Jews and, later in Spain, Muslims were forcibly ejected. It was actually in Spain that the idea of the nation of "blood" was first found; even the descendants of converts were suspected because of their hereditary ties to alien communities. See Peggy K. Liss, *Isabel the Queen: Life and Times* (New York: Oxford University Press, 1991). Indeed, the exterminations of Chinese that occurred in Batavia (the chief city of the East Indies, now Jakarta) and in the Philippines were the work of Dutch and Spaniards who were developing modern notions of the nation-state.

21. Schorske, *Fin-de-Siècle Vienna*, chapter 2.

22. I have expanded on these points in "Modernism without Liberalism."

23. Arief Budiman, in a recent editorial essay in *Far Eastern Economic Review* (December 22, 1994, p. 21), suggests that Suharto's government in Indonesia is shifting its favors from the Chinese community toward indigenous groupings. But this repeats the old error of thinking that somehow Chinese success in Indonesia is a function of government favors. It is, if anything, the other way around, as it has been in this century in Thailand, too, and as it was with Jews in Hungary in the late nineteenth and early twentieth centuries. The government of President Suharto became dependent on the Chinese for investment, expertise, and economic drive and so made a useful political bargain with the top Chinese entrepreneurs. Reversing this bargain would certainly threaten the Indonesian economy with capital flight, though it would undoubtedly please many Indonesian nationalists.

24. See George Hicks and J. A. Mackie, "Overseas Chinese: A Question of Identity"; Michael Vatikiotis, "Malaysian First"; Lynn Pan, "Ersatz Chinese?"; and Hicks and Mackie, "Tensions Persist: But Official Discrimination Is on the Decline," all of which appear on pp. 46–51 in *Far Eastern Economic Review*, July 14, 1994.

2 / Entrepreneurial Minorities, Nationalism, and the State

ANTHONY REID

Periods of rapid economic expansion and relatively weak government tend to widen the differences between individuals and social groups. Risk takers and innovators are rewarded more than most, sometimes by their ability to enter the yawning gap between the laws and values of an older era and the economic needs of the new one. Cultural minorities exist wherever international business is done, but their salience, and indeed their importance to the transformation taking place, becomes greater at such times. The European "miracle" known by such terms as the "capitalist transformation" or the "birth of the modern" is impossible to conceive of without the Jews, Hanseatic Germans, Lombards, and other entrepreneurial minorities who moved into innovative roles, first in trade, then in money management, and finally in manufacturing.

This crucial role in the modern transformation comes with high risks. Finding the pace of change unsettling to established values and life-styles, some majority spokesmen fasten on foreigners and minorities the aspects of change they find most distressing. To the everyday resentment of people with wealth is added an element of moral indignation against the increasing commercialism of the age. That this takes place as states become absolutist, populist, and democratic, and as they encourage the sense of national or racial community necessary to give themelves coherence in this process, creates immense dangers for the very minorities who lie at the heart of the modernization process.

The contributors to this book examine these dilemmas in relation to the two most important entrepreneurial minorities of the modern transformation: "Jews" in Central Europe and "Chinese" in Southeast Asia. I will not tiresomely repeat the quotation marks upon future use, but they are necessary here to emphasize what assumptions are already made in bringing together even two minority ethnic labels. After a century of strident nationalism and racism, the labels "Jew" and "Chinese" have come to be widely accepted internally, even though, like most other ethnic terms, they originated with frequently hostile others. But it is difficult to establish any common criterion for members of either category, except that they have been seen as outsiders in the societies to which they migrated. By the nature of the migratory process, they lived and operated in different places and cultures, spoke a great variety of languages, and adhered to different religious traditions. Many made a successful passage into a different ethnic category; those who did not now carry one of the two labels, though always alongside others. Some were entrepreneurs or urban professionals, but most were salaried workers, peddlers, miners, or agriculturalists. Some were rich or educated, but most were poor and ignorant. It is not our assumption in this book that "Jews" as a whole or "Chinese" as a whole can be usefully considered to have common characteristics, and still less that they should be compared with one another. The important comparison is in their creative and vulnerable role as "outsiders at the center" in dynamic processes of change.

That the Jewish role in the transformation of Central Europe ended in the most traumatic way a half-century ago, whereas the Chinese role in Southeast Asia's transformation is currently at its most robust, made it clear, at the conference where these essays were first presented, that the comparison had greater urgency and intensity than it would have if we had generalized the issues to entrepreneurial minorities everywhere. We were prepared for the moral dilemmas that arose from this simple two-way comparison, and we believed scholars had an important responsibility to examine them fully. While attuned to the problems posed to sober analysis by the heritage of anti-Semitism and the guilts of Holocaust remembrance in European discourse, we were disconcerted to find that a derivative anti-Jewish rhetoric in Southeast Asia also presented problems. In some reformist Islamic circles in Malaysia and Indonesia, a demonization of the concepts "Jew" (Yahudi) and "Zionist" has recently taken root that makes this book more important, despite the risk that in some quarters it could be distorted rather than read. I will return to this dilemma at the end of these remarks.

ENTREPRENEURIAL MINORITIES

Specialized minorities have played a crucial role in the development of trade, money management, and capital accumulation in most of the Old World—with some interesting exceptions in eastern Asia. Kings and magnates needed such minorities, found them less threatening than their own subordinate populations, and encouraged them, rather than the upstart majority middle classes, to take on crucial brokering roles. Nevertheless, relations between the two groups could be poisoned by guilt, because the pariah minorities were not only religious or racial outsiders but were also engaged in protocapitalist activities (moneylending, petty trade, tax farming) denounced by the guardians of social morality. Much debate has centered on the two factors that kept the minority separate: its own desire to maintain its religious, racial, or ritual distinctiveness, and the majority's forcing economically distinctive roles upon it by denying access to preferred occupations.

Although numerous writers in both East and West had noticed the phenomenon well before the modern era, comparative theories began to be developed by European (chiefly German) social scientists during the late nineteenth century. The Jews of Europe were, naturally, the central example for these writers, but even as early as Roscher (1875), analogies were made to the Chinese in Southeast Asia.[1] Most influential were the theories of Werner Sombart and Max Weber. Sombart made the case that capitalism flourished where Jews were given the greatest economic freedom, and he attributed Jewish economic success to the more positive attitudes toward wealth expressed in the Torah than in the Christian New Testament.[2] His views have been less quoted than Weber's, probably more because of his later sympathy for Nazism and anti-Semitism than because his argument on this point was any less cogent.

Weber sought to draw a sharp distinction between the "pariah capitalism" of the Jewish minority and the "rational capitalism" that developed from Puritan values into the dominant phenomenon of modern times:

> To the English Puritans, the Jews of their time were representatives of that type of capitalism which was involved in war, Government contracts, State monopolies, speculative promotions, and construction and financial projects of princes, which they themselves condemned. In fact the difference may, in general, with the necessary qualifications, be formulated: that Jewish capitalism was speculative pariah-capitalism, while the Puritan was bourgeois organization of labour.[3]

In Weber's view, the capitalism of pariah minorities was incapable of becoming generalized or of stimulating modern rational capitalism because of the ritual distinctiveness of the pariah groups, who were segregated from the majority by their outcaste status and also by "taboos, hereditary religious obligations in the conduct of life, and the association of salvation hopes with their pariah status."[4] Although Weber's terminology has remained influential among modern theorists, including those dealing with Southeast Asia's Chinese,[5] the accumulating evidence for Chinese leadership in Southeast

Asia's economic transformation makes his distinction untenable today in that case. And recent scholarship on the development of early modern European economies makes it difficult to sustain there as well.[6]

Other terms have therefore been coined to deal with this widespread and persistent phenomenon. Philip Curtin developed the notion, originally proposed by Abner Cohen, of a "trade diaspora" of merchant networks remaining distinct among the larger host population. He saw this as a long-term historical phenomenon, the need for which disappeared with the industrial era and domination by a single world trade culture.[7] In a looser sense, the term "diaspora" has undoubtedly become more popular of late, notably in the first worldwide "International Conference on the Chinese Diaspora" held in Berkeley, California, in November 1992. On that occasion, some Southeast Asian representatives objected to the term because of its origins in the Greek Bible, with its Jewish messianic implications that the diaspora would one day be regathered to the motherland.[8] It should be made clear that most of those using the term, including the contributors to this book, do so with no such implications. Instead, we use it in Cohen's modern sense: "a nation of socially interdependent, but spatially dispersed communities."[9]

Some sociologists have argued for a more specific historical conjunction they label the "status gap" as the key to understanding why entrepreneurial minorities become necessary. Such minorities appear to fill "the discontinuity, the yawning social void which occurs when superior and subordinate portions of a society are not bridged by continuous, intermediate degrees of status."[10] In many societies, including feudal Europe, prerevolutionary Eastern Europe, and colonial Asia and Africa, the ruling group was so determined to maintain its distance from the subordinate majority population that a dysfunctional economic gap appeared that could be filled only by outsiders.

In what could be seen as a variation of the foregoing theme, Stanislav Andreski sought to explain the rise of anti-Semitism and other forms of hostility toward minorities by the emergence of small traders and urban artisans from the previously rural host population.[11] Andreski identifies this new competitiveness with the entrenched Jews as the source of anti-Semitism in Poland, as Wertheim and others have done for anti-Chinese movements in Southeast Asia.[12]

The most recently fashionable term in the North American sociological literature is "middleman minority." The term is rather too broad to be useful in the context of this book; it seeks to embrace not only the "status gap" type of historical society but also, and preeminently, such an advanced economy as that of the United States, where successive waves of immigrants occupy particular niches in small business without thereby presenting political problems.[13]

Perhaps the central issue of this literature is whether the prominence of entrepreneurial minorities results from economic causes likely to occur in any society at some stage in its transition to capitalism, or whether it is rooted in particularly intractable cultural and political configurations. If the former, then the trauma such minorities undergo at the hands of nationalists can be seen as a temporary phenomenon that should ease if rational capitalism becomes generalized. If the latter, then racial hostility is likely to be an enduring feature of such societies, breaking out along particular fault lines whenever economic or political conditions deteriorate. As always, neither economics nor culture can explain everything. Cultural divides usually have origins at least partly economic, and they may in turn prolong and endanger the spread of market forces, locking some elites into a vicious circle in which they punish minorities with one hand while using them with the other.

NATIONALISM

Despite its enormous contribution to the making of the modern world, nationalism has until recently been poorly served in the literature. While self-evidently "natural" to its adherents, nationalism tended to be seen by scholars as a perverse false consciousness. "It claims to protect an old folk society while in fact it is helping to build up an anonymous mass society."[14] The political power of nationalisms, Benedict Anderson points out, contrasts with "their philosophical poverty and even incoherence."[15] Only after the nationalist tide had receded in Western Europe, four decades after the world war it had produced, did the new comparative work of Anderson, Gellner, Anthony Smith, Eric Hobsbawm, and Liah Greenfeld produce a body of theory useful for both Europe and Asia.[16]

Nationalisms share the project of creating a link between a state and an artificial (or "imagined") community brought into being through modern communications. Immediately one must distinguish between "liberation" movements seeking to create a national state and "official nationalisms," in Anderson's term, seeking to build mass support for an existing state or dynasty. Anderson has made a case for distinguishing racism as a separate phenomenon linked with the "official nationalism" sponsored by imperial states.[17] For most writers, however, and particularly for those researching Central and Eastern Europe, popular nationalisms arrange themselves along a kind of continuum between the incorporative, or civic, and the exclusive, or ethnic. Nationalism, says K. R. Minogue, "begins as Sleeping Beauty and ends as Frankenstein's monster."[18] The variety romantically associated with a presumed ethnocultural identity, dubbed "biological nationalism" by Kohn, "ethnic nationalism" by Smith, and "blood nationalism" by Greenfeld,[19] made its appearance in the wake of Darwinian theory in the second half of the nineteenth century and obtained a more strident character after 1880 with the development of germ theories of contagious disease and eugenic theories about improving the gene pool. It thus flourished during a particular period in European intellectual and social history (roughly 1880–1945) and had its greatest popularity east of the Rhine, where earlier civic nationalisms had not taken root.

In Southeast Asia, nationalisms are only now emerging from the enchanted honeymoon phase, during which they could not be subjected to rigorous analysis without seeming to give comfort to colonialism or its successors. They began life as the incorporative "liberation" type, directed primarily against foreign rule, with the Philippine movement against Spanish rule in the 1890s as the prototype. Only in the cases of Siam-Thailand (because it was never colonized) and Malay and Khmer nationalists (because they felt more endangered by Asian "immigrants" than by European rule) did the definition and defense of the race or people (Malay *bangsa,* Thai *chat*) often take precedence over the project of national sovereignty within colonial boundaries.[20] The civic variant of nationalism has been the dominant official ideology, particularly in Indonesia and the Philippines, where no single ethnic group dominates, but ethnic nationalism lives uneasily with it, seldom far from the surface where the Chinese are concerned. "Malaysian" nationalism is a fragile and very recent phenomenon (though proposed by Malaysian Prime Minister Mahathir to have become the norm by the year 2020), whereas Malay nationalism has been a vigorous reality since the 1920s.

COMPARING EUROPE AND SOUTHEAST ASIA

The context in which Southeast Asia is being economically transformed in the late twentieth century is far removed from that of Central Europe in the period 1880–1945. The Central European transformation combined boom and bust economic development, populist electoral politics, the consequences of a terrible war and a vengeful peace in 1918, and the intellectual climate not only of nationalism and Marxism but also of social Darwinism and eugenics. None of these will necessarily be replicated in Southeast Asia in the coming decades, and certainly not in combination. The globalization of economic and cultural life, in which eastern Asia has been a major player, makes any revival of economic nationalism extremely costly.

In cultural and religious terms, moreover, the Chinese experience is about as far from that of European Jewry as is possible within the spectrum of entrepreneurial minorities. The Jews were preeminently a homeless, vulnerable diaspora, maintaining some semblance of common identity only by ritual barriers against commensalism and intermarriage (imperfectly observed, of course), a heroic tradition of learning, and the hostility of their neighbors. Chinese emigrants were the superfluous, omnivorous, and relatively pragmatic errant sons (virtually no women left China until the late nineteenth century) of the greatest of empires, for whom, until the last century, the twin options of returning to China or assimilating into the majority population would have eliminated a common identity altogether were it not for periodic new waves of emigration.

Nevertheless, an explicit comparison of the situations of these largest and economically most important entrepreneurial minorities is overdue. It contributes to our understanding of the multiple paths that can be taken toward an advanced and expansive market economy and of the particular possibilities and limitations of vanguard minorities on those journeys. In this respect, the growing debate over the Chinese role in the flourishing economies of Southeast Asia, taken up by several writers in this volume, can reinvigorate the stalled discussion of the Jewish role in European capitalism. Southeast Asia and Central Europe provide abundant case studies of the effects of different types of relationships between the nation-state and economically powerful but politically disadvantaged minorities. Finally, the disastrous outcome in Hitler's Third Reich needs to be approached in contexts broader than those of the fateful histories of Germany and the Jews. It may be that the moral weight of the Shoah (the "catastrophe," a word now preferred among specialists to the more popular term "Holocaust") lies too heavily on those histories in isolation for fruitful analysis; comparison with less tragic outcomes can suggest some new ways forward.

In Asia, memories of these and other traumas of the 1940s are differently shaped. As Ian Buruma reminds us, "much of what attracted Japanese to Germany before the war—Prussian authoritarianism, romantic nationalism, pseudo-scientific racialism—had lingered in [postwar] Japan while becoming distinctly unfashionable in Germany."[21] Even less than Japanese politicians do Southeast Asian ones have a habit of public apology or self-criticism. Thanks to the colonial heritage, the sense of being historical victims rather than actors is even stronger in Southeast Asia than in Japan. When traumatic bouts of violence have occurred, as they did in Indonesia in

1965–66, Malaysia in 1969, East Timor in 1975–76, or Vietnam in 1978, the instinctive reaction has been not to probe and reeducate but to prescribe narrower limits to public discussion lest popular passions again get out of hand. As Ruth Benedict pointed out a long time ago, those who inhabit Protestant Christian "guilt cultures" should not expect the rest of the world to behave in the same way. Elsewhere (not only in Southeast Asia or Japan), shame is a stronger social sanction than guilt, and "confession appears only a way of courting trouble."[22]

The killing fields of Cambodia, too, have given rise to more public self-criticism in the United States than in Cambodia or its neighbors. Western scholars, increasingly dismayed by the persistence of ethnic nationalism in post-1978 Cambodia, have begun to interpret the killings under Pol Pot as a product, at least in part, of glorification of a certain kind of "Khmerness" at the expense of "alien" Vietnamese, Chinese, and bourgeois elements.[23] In Southeast Asia, however (as perhaps in Eastern Europe), neither these nor other events have yet served to disenchant ethnic nationalism of the romanticism and righteousness it acquired in the anticolonial struggle.

For Southeast Asia's Chinese, the reluctance to draw comparisons from European history have to do with a long experience of hearing the comparison made only in negative terms. Throughout the period from 1600 to 1900, Europeans repeatedly labeled the Chinese "the Jews of the East" in terms that stressed commercial ability, greed, and subservience. Now that Europeans are less likely to continue these stereotypes, some of the Muslim fellow-countrymen of Southeast Asian Chinese have begun to take up the same shopworn anti-Semitic theories.

In the rest of this essay, I raise some comparative questions about three transitions through which the two minorities have passed, particularly in their relations to the economy and the state—the rise of key brokers for the expanding state; emancipation; and nationalism. There do appear to be some instructive parallels in the types of problems that emerged as societies became more complex and commercialized and as new, imagined communities replaced older, experienced ones. Although Europe experienced the transitions discussed here earlier than Southeast Asia (and Germany and France earlier than the Slavic lands), there is nothing linear or necessary about these processes of change.

SOURCES OF THE CHINESE AND JEWISH DIASPORAS

The stable and substantial Jewish community of Central and Eastern Europe originated in the late Middle Ages, from the thirteenth to the fifteenth centuries, when many long-established Jewish communities in Western Europe moved eastward to escape the heightened danger of persecution and pogrom in the aftermath of the Crusades. In 1264 the Polish king Boleslav granted an unusually liberal charter of self-government to Jews, so eager was he to encourage these productive settlers. The expulsion from Spain and Portugal in 1492, persecution, and the wars of religion in England, France, and Germany drove more Jews eastward. Jewish communal life flourished particularly in the enlarged kingdom of Poland-Lithuania in the century before the Cossack destruction of 1648. The Jewish population of Poland grew to about 150,000 in 1576 and 450,000 in 1648, by which time it represented between 5 and 10 percent of the Polish population and almost half the world's Jews.[24]

Southeast Asia has been the principal overseas destination of Chinese traders and migrants throughout the second millennium of the modern era. Until the Southern Song Dynasty (1127–1279), foreigners had carried most trade from the south to China. Thereafter, Chinese knowledge of the southern regions grew steadily. But private trade was banned, with varying effectiveness, before 1567, and as late as 1749 Chinese returning after making a fortune in the south could be imprisoned or executed for the crime of emigrating.[25] Substantial injections of Chinese population into Southeast Asia probably occurred by defection from massive imperial naval expeditions during two periods—under the Mongols in the 1290s, and in the reign of the Yungle (Ming) emperor in 1402–24. These people appear to have assimilated locally, because of the difficulty of maintaining contact with China.[26] After Chinese trade from Fujian and Guangdong to the south was legalized and licensed in 1567, however, stable and distinct Chinese communities became a feature of Southeast Asia. In the mid-seventeenth century there were communities of 3,000 to 5,000 Chinese in the major port cities of Batavia and Banten in Java, Ayutthaya in Siam, and Hoi An in Vietnam. About twice that many lived in Manila, so the total Chinese population in Southeast Asia must have been at least 40,000.

The Chinese were only one commercial minority among many, including Gujaratis, Chettiars, Malays, Portuguese, and Japanese until the middle of the seventeenth century. Dutch and English dominance in the Indian Ocean then severely damaged the trade of all the rival networks. Subsequently, the Chinese remained dominant in East Asian trade, took over roles surrendered by the Japanese in the 1630s, and became indispensable buyers from and sellers to the large European companies. By 1700, Chinese were unrivaled as the preeminent commercial minority everywhere in Southeast Asia. From this date, at least, their position can usefully be compared with that of Jews in Central and Eastern Europe.

In the early centuries of immigration, both minorities were always welcome—the Jews first in Western and then in Eastern Europe, the Chinese in all the Southeast Asian states as well as in the European enclave cities of the region. Both were valued positively for their wealth, skills, and international contacts and negatively for their disinclination to resort to arms. They virtually introduced urban life and manufacture to many areas that had known little of either. They made it possible for struggling dynasties or colonial port cities to aspire to become something more like states through a much broader revenue base and the commercial primacy of one city over others. If they grouped together, it was more for the convenience of trade and social life than because of legal restriction. In the Southeast Asian case, Chinese intermarried with or even created ruling dynasties, notably in Ayutthaya, Brunei, Melaka, and Demak, during this early and relatively open stage.

Commercial skills and disposition, along with international contacts, made it possible for the wealthiest migrants to dominate certain avenues of trade, while various crafts became the virtual preserve of poorer urban settlers. In the seventeenth century a visitor remarked that "almost all trade is in their [Jewish] hands" in Poland;[27] similar comments were made about Chinese in Cambodia, Patani, Jambi, and elsewhere in Southeast Asia.[28] They made their living through retailing, manufacture, or service functions, notably the keeping of inns (by Jews) and of drinking and gambling houses (by Chinese).[29] The ruling class in both cases (including both colonial and native rulers in Southeast Asia) found them indispensable as producers and providers of goods and as brokers with the majority agricultural population.

The gruesome slaughters that occasionally occurred in this situation were as much outbreaks of international or intertribal warfare as they were pogroms against minorities. Some of them could be seen as related to the mid-seventeenth-century economic, political, and demographic crisis that affected Europe and eastern Asia in surprisingly parallel ways. The worst horrors in Central Europe were those the Cossacks visited on the Jews of Poland in the years following 1648. But Polish nobles and priests were equally the targets of these depredations, because it was Polish dominance that was under attack. Island Southeast Asia and China, like Poland, suffered from economic decline and a fragmentation of power (except in areas under Dutch control) in the mid-seventeenth century. After the collapse of the Ming Dynasty in China (1644), the Zheng (Koxinga) resistance to its successor, based on sea power in Fujian, Taiwan, and the South China Sea, caused anxieties about the Chinese "threat" in the Philippines, Vietnam, and Cambodia because it seemed to foreshadow a Chinese naval expansion. But it was Europeans who were most inclined to respond to these anxieties by massacre and expulsion, notably the Spanish attacks on the Chinese in Manila in 1586, 1603 (the bloodiest, with almost 20,000 victims), 1639, 1662, and 1686. The Muslim sultanate of Aceh also banned Chinese in the 1630s, and again around 1700, during periods of religious zealotry.

The character of the interaction between Chinese and Southeast Asians was undoubtedly altered by the Europeans who established demographically insignificant but militarily impregnable footholds in Southeast Asia—in Melaka (Portuguese, 1511; Dutch, 1641), Manila (Spanish, 1571), Batavia or Jakarta (Dutch, 1619), Makassar (Dutch, 1669), and elsewhere. In these enclaves, and by example elsewhere, the Europeans provided an opportunity and even encouragement for the Chinese to remain distinct rather than assimilate into the indigenous majority.

Local-born Chinese willingly assimilated into a high-status ruling category whenever this was advantageous and possible, as it was in Thailand, Cambodia, and pre-Dutch Javanese and Malay societies. But where Europeans occupied the highest status category, they were as hostile as the Polish or Russian aristocracy to outsiders marrying their daughters (they were not so averse to taking local women as concubines themselves). For the Chinese, then, intermarriage with Southeast Asians was no longer a path to elite assimilation but instead created creole communities distinct from the China-born, from indigenous people, and from Europeans. People in these communities typically began speaking dialects based on the local vernacular.[30] These *peranakan* (to use the Indonesian word) Chinese of the European enclaves thereby became distinctive diaspora communities with their own legal and cultural institutions, a position European Jewry had long enjoyed.

BECOMING BROKERS TO THE EXPANDING STATE

The stronger states that emerged in Europe in the seventeenth and eighteenth centuries, and in Southeast Asia in the nineteenth, developed a new revenue base in the cash economy that transformed society during these periods. Minorities such as the Jews and the overseas Chinese were the quickest to exploit the opportunities of the new commercialism because they were uninhibited by feudal tradition or landholding and because they had the necessary international contacts to move capital and goods across boundaries. Having initially little to lose and a world to gain, they tended to be the greatest risk takers, especially in trading across the battle lines and enmities that made life in both regions unstable. Their communities grew in wealth and mobility, but a few key figures flourished out of all proportion to others as tax farmers and purveyors to governments.

The rulers (or colonial regimes) that were growing in power at the expense of local lineages needed arms and supplies for their expanding armies and cash to pay for their public works and palaces. In Central Europe, the court Jews (*hofjuden*) became indispensable financiers and purveyors to German and Austrian rulers, living dangerously by providing what the ruler needed, including cash through revenue monopolies and straight loans. The most spectacular was perhaps Samuel Oppenheimer of Heidelberg, originally contractor of the Palatinate Elector, to whom the Austrian Emperor Leopold I turned to supply the armies he needed to resist the onslaught of Louis XIV of France at the end of the seventeenth century. Oppenheimer was able to raise the money by turning to his fellow Jewish contractors at the courts of Mainz, Bamberg, and Hesse. Both ruler and contractor occupied lonely, vulnerable pinnacles of power, and there sometimes developed between them real affection on this account. Isolated and exceptional as they were, such figures could often provide protection and patronage for their fellow Jews still chiefly living in poverty in the ghettos, which in turn increased their ability to mobilize this useful underclass for their tax collection, commerce, and manufacturing purposes.[31]

The Jewish community as a whole lived an unstable life centered on the market towns of the Austrian Empire and Poland. Although Leopold I, later patron of Oppenheimer, had expelled all Jews from Vienna and Lower Austria in 1669–71, by the middle of the following century there were about 150,000 Jews in the Hapsburg Empire, mostly concentrated in what is today Czech and Hungarian territory. The largest group of Jews at that time was in Poland, however, where they numbered about 800,000, or 10 percent of the population, at the 1764 census, living chiefly around the Baltic ports.[32]

In Southeast Asia, the system of farming the collection of state revenues to prominent Chinese was at its height in the nineteenth century, but it had begun soon after the Dutch East India Company began to govern its enclave in Batavia in 1619. The Dutch appear to have introduced a system of farming taxes on gambling, alcohol, the slaughter of livestock, the weighing of goods, and so forth, because they were familiar with it in Europe, but it proved a particularly efficient means of drawing revenue from the Chinese commercial community without having to understand its inner workings.[33]

In the eighteenth century, the monopoly over opium imports became the main source of Dutch Company revenue, and in the nineteenth, the expanding colonial governments obtained much of their tax needs by farming the sale of opium to prominent Chinese entrepreneurs. The Singapore opium farm alone realized about 40 percent of Singapore's revenue in the 1860s and nearly 50 percent in the 1880s.[34] The Netherlands Indies government made greater use of land taxes and import duties (Singapore being a free port), but Chinese-run tax farms there represented more than a quarter of all revenue in the 1840s and over 20 percent in the 1880s. The opium farm again provided the lion's share. In 1870 there were more Chinese engaged in tax-farming operations—about 7,000, or 6 percent of adult male Chinese—than there were Dutchmen in government service in the Indies.[35] The Chinese tax farmer and his agents were the economic arms of government in rural areas. Buying a farm to operate tollgates and pawnshops, or to tax markets or the slaughter of cattle, enabled Chinese entrepreneurs to evade the many restrictions that the colonial government placed on their movements outside the cities. As a hostile Dutch report noted in 1897:

> The cattle slaughter farm gives the Chinese a means to move about in the villages without being controlled to any great extent. Persons authorized by the farmer are kept in almost all district and subdistrict towns to spy on behalf of their employer. They devote every moment to penetrating into the inner circles of the villages. The pass system is not applied to these people, a reason why the Chinese spend so much money on setting them up as part-employees. Where it would be necessary to engage three people, permission is asked for six.[36]

The system of farming revenues to Chinese appears to have been copied by Javanese rulers in the 1680s directly from Dutch practice, no doubt encouraged by the Chinese entrepreneurs who spread inland from the Dutch-governed coastal towns. By the late eighteenth century the quasi-independent rulers of Java were primarily dependent on revenues from such farms to develop a state apparatus that could compete with the growing power of the Dutch.[37] Thai and Malay rulers also adopted the system in the eighteenth century, probably on Chinese urging, and by the second half of the nineteenth century most of their revenues came from it. Incomplete Thai records show the revenue from Chinese-run revenue farms growing from 3 million to 13 million baht between 1871 and 1888, a period when King Chulalongkorn was desperately in need of resources to create a government capable of withstanding growing European pressures.[38] Through this system of revenue farming, a few Chinese became immensely powerful with both colonial and indigenous governments in the late nineteenth century: Thio Thiau Siat in Sumatra and Penang; Tan Seng Poh in Singapore; Loke Yew in Kuala Lumpur; Khaw Soo Cheang in South Thailand; Oei Tiong Ham in Java. They used their strategic positions in charge of the opium and other farms to become the dominating figures in the Chinese economy of Southeast Asia.

The mid-eighteenth century had been a watershed in relations between

Chinese and Europeans in Southeast Asia, after which a distinction must be drawn between European-ruled and Asian-ruled areas. The alliance between Dutch and Chinese in Java was under increasing strain in the 1730s, as ever larger numbers of Chinese were attracted to Batavia after Beijing's restrictions on foreign trade were lifted. Dutch anxieties increased as regulations first to restrict and then to deport recent arrivals seemed impossible to enforce. When some criminal Chinese gangs began to attack Europeans outside the city in October 1740, a crackdown quickly degenerated into a wholesale massacre in which 10,000 people—most of the Chinese living in Batavia—were thought to have died. Other Chinese fled to join the enemies of the Dutch Company in Java, some becoming Muslims in the process.

It may be that this exceptional bloodbath was related to a structural shift in Dutch interests from trade to agricultural production in Java.[39] Such was more clearly the case in the Philippines, where a growing local-born middle class (Spanish, Chinese mestizo, and *indio*) resented the control of the domestic economy by China-born Chinese.[40] Non-Catholic Chinese were expelled from the Philippines in 1755 under a regulation repeated in 1766. Although the Chinese government's relationship with overseas Chinese is often seen as a major distinction from the Jewish predicament, since the Jews had no great imperial homeland, this was not so under the emperors, who were little interested in disasters befalling Chinese so unfilial as to have left the middle kingdom.

After these traumatic mid-eighteenth-century events, the Chinese population of the Spanish and Dutch colonies was reduced to initially smaller but more stable creole communities, secured against further pogroms at European hands by their essential loyalty to and symbiosis with the European order. The Chinese mestizos of the Philippines formed a flourishing Catholic middle class, representing 4.8 percent (120,000) of the Philippine population by 1810 and 5.2 percent (290,000) in 1890, by which time they were becoming integrated into a new Filipino elite. The Chinese *peranakan* of Java were a smaller creole minority, representing between 1 and 2 percent of Java's population (about 100,000 in 1810 and 250,000 in 1890). Like the *baba* of the British Straits Settlements (Singapore, Penang, and Melaka), the *peranakan* saw no attraction in assimilating into a subordinate indigenous community.[41] *Baba* and *peranakan* therefore remained as stable communities, retaining a form of Chinese religion (a shift from an older pattern in the Malay world of assimilation through Islamization) but speaking a Malay-based creole.[42] If *peranakan* speech (and *baba* Malay) was closer to standard Malay than Yiddish was to German, this was largely because of the important role these Chinese-descended urban Malay speakers played in the way modern Malay itself evolved. (An analogy might be the way Yiddish influenced the Viennese German dialect.)

By keeping a firm grip on the opium farms and other crucial bridges to the European administration, the Chinese tax farmers maintained control over the continuing influx of China-born Chinese into Netherlands India and Malaya throughout the nineteenth century. All three Sino–Southeast Asian communities were kept legally distinct by the colonial order in terms of residence, landowning, education, and dress. They largely governed their own affairs. Although they had lost much of their Chineseness, they were less likely to assimilate or integrate than they had been in the seventeenth century.

In Asian-ruled states, on the other hand, the second half of the eighteenth century witnessed a much-increased influx of Chinese miners, planters, traders, and settlers, who often formed highly productive enclave economies. States such as Siam, Vietnam, Riau-Johor, Brunei, Sambas, and Sulu welcomed the new influx, which included some refugees from the European settlements, and profited greatly from them. In Siam, the Thonburi (1767–82) and Bangkok dynasties that restored Siam's fortunes after the Burmese conquest were themselves half-Chinese and very dependent on other Chinese as traders in Bangkok, commercial cultivators in the southeast, and tin miners in the south. Autonomous Chinese polities were established at Hatien in the Vietnam-Cambodia borderland and in the goldfields of western Borneo. Except in Malaya-Singapore, where they were a far larger proportion of the population, the number of Chinese in the various populations of Southeast Asia in 1800 varied from the 1 to 2 percent of Java to over 10 percent in Siam and Borneo.[43] The earliest global estimate, in the 1830s, was of "nearly a million" Chinese in Southeast Asia—more than 2 percent of the total population.[44]

Relations with these autonomous communities were often tense and conflicts frequent over the proportion of the proceeds paid to the local elite. The Chinese as a group aroused resentment because of the influence they had over rulers and because of their direct authority as tax farmers. Peter Carey mentions the large number of attacks on Chinese tollgate keepers and traders in the Javanese princely states in the 1820s, as their demands on peasants for revenue increased. The rebel followers of Dipanegara put "whole Chinese communities . . . to the sword" in 1825, just as the Tay-son rebels had done in the Saigon area of southern Vietnam in 1782.[45] Further massacres occurred in southeastern Siam in 1848, in Brunei in the early 1800s, and in the gold-mining area of upriver Kelantan (Malaya) in the 1830s.[46] These massacres were all authorized by rulers in response to some

Chinese act of violence, usually provoked, in turn, by increased demands for taxes. Nevertheless, the killing went beyond the normal limits of Southeast Asian warfare. Thousands of Chinese were killed in each of these cases, and often whole communities were wiped out.

In both Southeast Asia and Europe, the entrepreneurial minorities were crucial to the growth of a commercial economy on the one hand, and an absolutist state on the other. In both areas the minority communities re- mained distinct from the majority populations in culture, religion, resi- dence, and law, partly by choice and partly through the policies of govern- ments that found their distinctiveness useful. A few of their number climbed dangerous pinnacles of power and wealth through their closeness to the ruling courts. Assimilation and intermarriage still occurred around the fringes of the minority community, though probably on a reduced scale as the communities became more settled and self-conscious.

EMANCIPATION AND MASS EDUCATION

A major transformation reshaped and modernized European Jewry between 1780 and 1848; the analogous period for Chinese in Southeast Asia was much shorter, between 1890 and 1920. The self-governing autonomy of the minor- ity was lost in both cases, as was the privileged position of its leaders as brokers and financiers to the state. In exchange, more exciting opportunities were held out to members of the minority as citizens of a modern state, entitled to take part in the upward march of Enlightenment ideas— education, progress, science, liberalism, and nationalism. The minority was able to play a disproportionately large role in the urban and educated middle class which the newly complex state required. The miserable poverty and insecurity of its poorer members were alleviated, even as the pinnacles of power of the few court brokers were toppled. Massacres and expulsions appeared to be things of the past. Yet the path out of the ghetto and into modern mass society was a potentially dangerous one as identities were redefined and questioned.

The process by which Jews on a large scale moved out of ghettos and into the mainstream of European cultural and commercial life was part of the broader development of investment capitalism, the rise of an urban, profes- sional middle class, the spread of Enlightenment ideas, the growth of popu- lar education, and the creation of the modern nation-state.

In economic and cultural terms, it was the Jews of the German cities who led the way, though they were relatively few in number. The most promi- nent Jewish success story was that of the Rothschilds, whose fortune began with Meyer Amschel Rothschild (1743–1812) in Frankfurt. Rothschild became immensely wealthy by taking judicious but ingenious care of the fortune of the ruler of Hesse-Cassel when that prince had to flee Napoleon. His Frankfurt bank became the epitome of successful Jewish international banking in the first half of the nineteenth century, and its influence spread throughout Europe. By contrast, Berlin was the center where German-Jewish intellectuals such as Moses Mendelssohn (1729–86) and Heinrich Heine (1797–1856) were able to make their biggest contribution to the German Enlightenment. The Jews of the Hapsburg Empire and the Slav lands—poorer, more numerous, and more autonomous in their shtetls—were nevertheless influenced in due course by this flowering of Enlightenment ideas in the German language.

The emancipation of the Jews of the Austrian Empire, whose numbers doubled in 1772 when the Hapsburgs annexed Polish Galicia, was begun by the reforming Emperor Joseph II (1780–90). He gave Jews near equality before the law and decreed their right to attend schools and enter the professions. This impetus toward transforming Jewry into a religious minority of equal citizens was taken up by the French revolutionaries, who gave Jews full legal equality, and it was carried across Europe by Napoleon. Napoleon called together a "Sanhedrin" in Paris in 1807 which declared, in effect, that the Jews were not a separate people but a religious minority who were equal citizens of Napoleon's First Empire. Ideas of citizenship and equality before the law certainly had their setbacks in the years that followed, but they ultimately triumphed in Central Europe in the period from 1848 to 1871, and they were influential even in Russia, where, however, full legal equality was never achieved under Czarist rule.

Emancipation made possible a massive movement of Jews into the growing cities, the professions, and middle-class life in general. Vienna had counted only about 6,000 Jews before 1848, but the Jewish population rose even faster than that of the city as a whole, to 40,000 in 1869 and 175,000 (8 percent of Vienna's 2 million) in 1910. Budapest counted 45,000 Jews in 1869 and 204,000 (23 percent of the city's population) in 1910.[47] In the rapid modernization of Central European society, Jews seized the new opportunities particularly rapidly. In Vienna, as in the Austrian Empire as a whole, Jews were about three times as likely as non-Jews to attend the *Gymnasien* (elite academic high schools) before the First World War. Over 60 percent of those graduating from such schools in Vienna to become lawyers and doctors in that period were Jews, most of them from commercial family backgrounds.[48] Throughout Central Europe, urban middle-class Jews, largely excluded from positions in the bureaucracy, were playing a disproportionate, dynamic role in the key agencies of the intellectual and economic transformation of Europe—the universities, the press, commerce, the arts, and the new sciences.

In Southeast Asia, the equivalent of emancipation was the abolition of the revenue farms and the lifting of residence and travel restrictions on the Chinese. Beginning with the opium farm in Java in 1894, all the opium and pawnbroking farms of Southeast Asia were dismantled by 1910. The gambling farms under British and Dutch auspices followed in the next decade.[49] As a recent study put it, "revenue farming . . . sowed the seeds of its own destruction. By funding the revenue needs of the weak state, it helped to nurture a strong state, which eventually could establish the local control necessary to raise its own taxes."[50] Colonial states, and also Siam under Chulalongkorn and his European advisers, became more knowledgeable, powerful, and European in composition. They took over the application of these "vice taxes" themselves and raised vastly larger revenues from customs duties and individual and corporate taxes.

The new bureaucracies began to rule the Chinese directly, rather than through Chinese headmen (*Capitan China*), with specialist services such as the Protectorate of Chinese in Singapore (1877) and the Bureau of Chinese Affairs in Netherlands India. The British had begun during the nineteenth century to consider Chinese as citizens of their colonies, entitled to protection, and similar attitudes spread to the other colonies around the turn of the century. As they lost access to the hinterland through their revenue farms, Chinese demanded the right to travel freely in Netherlands India, a right effectively granted to them between 1900 and 1910. Finally, all governments began to take an interest in modern education for their subjects, including local-born Chinese. As the most urban, commercial, and uprooted of Southeast Asia's communities, the Chinese responded vigorously to these opportunities.

Despite their relatively modest numbers, the Sino–Southeast Asian minorities played a role perhaps even more striking than that of European Jewry in the creation of the new national cultures that began to emerge at this time. The Chinese mestizos of the Philippines had been emancipated earlier through adoption of Catholicism, and in the late nineteenth century they seized the opportunity of Spanish education and manners. The national hero José Rizal, whose writings (in Spanish) remain the great classics of Philippine national literature, was but one of a brilliant *ilustrado* generation, descended from Chinese mestizos, who created both a Filipino identity and the political revolution of 1896 in its name. In the cities of Malaya and Netherlands India, the turn of the century marked what Claudine Salmon has called "the Sino-Malay moment," when the *peranakan* Chinese laid the basis for national literatures in Malay and Indonesian through Chinese-owned newspapers and publishing houses.[51] The creole Malay patois began to give way to standard Malay and standard Chinese as well as English and Dutch, variously favored by the new schools and printers. In Bangkok it was Sino-Thais who pioneered the early publishing houses, newspapers, and film corporations.

NATIONALISM, MARXISM, AND RACE

The same forces and ideals that emancipated minorities thrust previously autonomous communities into direct competition with each other and gave rise to intellectual currents and mass movements that were ultimately the greatest dangers to minorities. Education, the printed word, a new rapidity of communication, and a gradual extension of suffrage encouraged peoples from widely different local, ethnic, cultural, and social groups to identify with new imagined communities that conferred pride and status. The romantic movement celebrated rural landscapes and communities and empathized with "the people"—often imagined to embody the harmony and collective values urban intellectuals had lost. Socialism promised an egalitarian future in which workers would discover a new international solidarity in freeing themselves from capitalist exploitation. In the last quarter of the nineteenth century, social Darwinism encouraged the idea of history as a struggle for survival among peoples, whereby every group had to strengthen and mobilize itself internally. These currents all contended in nineteenth-century Europe. In Southeast Asia they came first to the Philippine *ilustrados* in the late nineteenth century but spread everywhere in the first two decades of the twentieth.

Because they were relatively urban, uprooted, educated, and commercial, entrepreneurial minorities tended to feel all these currents earlier and more strongly than the majority communities. They contributed more than their share to the early stages of forging new socialist and nationalist identities in both regions. In their case, however, an additional possibility arose of imagining a new national community *as* minority diaspora, and of creating the common language, memory, school system, reform agenda, and eventually territory to give this possibility substance. It was those who acquired the best educations in the dominant European languages (German, Russian, French, and English in Europe; Spanish, Dutch, French, and English in Southeast Asia) who felt these pressures for new community most strongly.

Whereas overseas Chinese nationalism somewhat preceded majority nationalisms in Indonesia, Malaysia, and Thailand, its Jewish equivalent was held back by the impracticality of having no territory to relate it to. Only in the 1880s and 1890s, after German, Italian, and Slavic nationalisms were well established, did Zionism emerge as a coherent option. The writer Eliezer Perlman (also known as Eliezer Ben Yehuda, one of the main architects of the revival and modernization of the Hebrew language) in 1878 was one of the earliest to react to pan-Slav enthusiasm by asking the nationalist question, "Why should we be any less worthy than any other people? What about our nation, our language, our land?"[52] The rise of extreme and programmatic anti-Semitism in Germany, Austria, and France in the 1870s and 1880s, and the draconian measures taken against Jews in the Russian laws of May 1882, certainly encouraged the trend. When, in 1895, the Vienna columnist Theodore Herzl published his *Der Judenstaat* (The Jewish State), even this most international of diasporas now had its nationalist program, which would compete for half a century with various brands of socialism, liberalism, religious revival, and assimilation for the mind of European Jewry.

The enormous factor of China dominated the analogous phenomenon in Southeast Asia. To the great diversity of ancestral speech groups (Hokkien, Cantonese, Teochiu, and Hakka were the most numerous) was added the deeper division between the local-born and the China-born, whose numbers increased as contract laborers traveled south in unprecedented numbers after 1880. The first explicitly nationalist impetus came from China, in the form of visits by Sun Yat-sen and other nationalists in 1900. Support for their ideas, however, proved to be more widespread among the uprooted Chinese of Southeast Asia than in China itself. Modern schools began to be established using Mandarin, the "standard" speech of north China, rather than the dialects familiar to the migrants. In the first decade of the twentieth century there were strong moves to stress a "Chinese" identity, fostered by the changes in the colonies described earlier. Enthusiasm was by stimulated by the Chinese Nationality Law of 1909, with its *jus sanguinis* claim over all overseas Chinese, and by the Chinese revolution of 1911.

The year 1910 has been identified as a watershed in the relationship between Thais and Chinese in Siam. Not only was there a change of ruler from Sinophile Chulalongkorn to Sinophobe Vajiravudh, but also a severe Chinese strike took place against the imposition of a uniform tax, bringing Bangkok to its knees.[53] The establishment of modern Chinese nationalist organizations in the Netherlands Indies and Malaya occurred at about the same time.[54] These organizations would remain a periodic problem for governments in Southeast Asia for the next three decades. Their attempts to organize boycotts of Japanese goods, most dramatically in 1928 and 1937, served more to underline how powerful a grip the Chinese had on many sectors of the economy than to deter Japanese aggression in China.

Diaspora nationalism gave rise to Chinese schools of modern type and to new collective organizations dedicated to reforms that would increase the status and strength of China as well as its overseas sons and daughters. Except in the Philippines, these organizations were led by prosperous, local-born Sino–Southeast Asians, but their formation was much influenced by the massive influx of Chinese contract laborers between 1880 and 1930. About 200,000 Chinese a year left southern China for Southeast Asia in the last decades of the nineteenth century, and nearer to 300,000 per year emigrated in the first decade of the twentieth. Most returned after some years of harsh labor in tin mines or on estates, but enough remained to shift the demographic balance sharply in favor of the China-born in Malaya and to produce large Chinese-speaking populations everywhere. This shift added to nationalist pressures on the Sino–Southeast Asians to redefine their culture and loyalties in a more Chinese direction, especially in Malaya, where the *baba* gradually declined into insignificance.

The attractions of Marxism for entrepreneurial minorities merits particular attention. Somewhat simplistically taking Jews as a collectivity, Milton Friedman has recently drawn attention to the paradox that they "owe an enormous debt to free enterprise and competitive capitalism" and yet have been "consistently opposed to capitalism and have done much on an ideological level to undermine it."[55] On a practical level, too, Jews were heavily overrepresented even in the Social Democratic party (12 percent of its Reichstag members in 1912) of Germany, where Jews were a tiny and affluent group.[56] In Russia, where Jews formed a real proletariat, socialism was still more attractive, and the Jewish Bund provided mass support for socialism. In Southeast Asia also, the Chinese minority has produced more ideologues of the left than of the free-market right and has given disproportionate support to communist parties.

Undoubtedly, Marxism's theoretical internationalism and its rejection of racial and cultural loyalties as false consciousness were welcome to minority intellectuals weary of attempting to reconcile conflicting and burdensome identities. So long as they were in the opposition, communist parties in Southeast Asia, like those in Europe, were consistent opponents of majority racism. Given the added factor of the strength of communism in China itself, it is not surprising to find that the Malayan Communist party was virtually a Chinese creation (1934), always struggling to find token Malays and Indians to broaden its Chinese image, that the Communist party of

Thailand drew much support from ethnic Chinese, or that leading non-Chinese communists such as Ho Chi Minh and Tan Malaka spent many years in China and leaned heavily on Chinese support. Although the smaller, relatively affluent Chinese minorities in Indonesia and the Philippines found Marxism less attractive, the Indonesian Communist party (PKI) was the only mainstream Indonesian party to give political leadership to *peranakan* Chinese such as Tan Ling Djie and Tjoo Tik Tjoen.[57]

The factor of China and Chinese communism had, of course, only an indirect analogy in Europe. Nevertheless, the perception of the anti-Semitic right in Europe after 1917 that Russia had fallen under the control of a "Judeo-Bolshevik" conspiracy created a fear about the giant, supposedly Jewish-dominated revolutionary power to the east somewhat similar to the worries that China engendered among anticommunists in Southeast Asia after 1949.

Although Comintern policy in the 1930s required that the communists of Malaya organize themselves in a national party that formally espoused independence for Malaya, its links with the Chinese Communist party were so close and its Chinese membership so overwhelming that the problems of identity were all on the side of non-Chinese who joined the party. And once communism triumphed in China, fear of China and suspicion of the overseas Chinese became more important sources of anticommunism than ideological commitment to private enterprise.

Colonial policies encouraged a division of function, a dual economy, between the "native" majority of peasants, under their own, often anticommercial, aristocratic-bureaucratic hierarchy, and the commercial sector of Europeans, Chinese, and other minorities. In consequence, a majority bourgeoisie was slow to develop in Southeast Asia, as in Eastern Europe, and participation by majority groups in the modern economies that took shape in the twentieth century was initially slight. Paradoxically, at first this limited the potential for anti-Chinese nationalism. In the 1920s and 1930s, anti-Chinese political rhetoric was most pronounced in the Philippines, partly because it was the only Southeast Asian country to experience mass-based democracy, but also because a relatively stronger Filipino bourgeoisie, most of it of mestizo Chinese descent, felt able to compete with the Chinese in commerce. The president of the Commonwealth of the Philippines, Manuel Quezon, could boast in 1941 (probably with exaggeration) that as a result of his curbs on Chinese business, Filipino control of retail trade had increased to 37 percent from less than 20 percent at the time the commonwealth was inaugurated in 1935.[58]

Nationalism in Southeast Asia was not necessarily directed against the entrepreneurial minorities. For the Western-educated intelligentsia, foreign, European rule was the enemy, and the Chinese were a problem primarily insofar as they supported that regime. For a time, Chinese and Southeast Asian nationalisms shared common goals of overthrowing Western domination and strengthening the Asian state. At the level of leaders and intellectuals there was much cooperation between Chinese and indigenous nationalists.

On the other hand, the initial financial support for nationalist causes came from indigenous merchants such as the Muslim batik producers of Java and the Vietnamese silk producers of Cochin China, who were fighting unequal battles with stronger Chinese competitors. Hence the popularity, during the period 1910–25, of appeals to anti-Chinese sentiment, and the periodic attempts to boycott Chinese goods.

This undernourished bourgeoisie could not sustain effective national movements, but it did largely define the content of nationalism during that critical period. While many other foreign influences were accepted as part of the new national identities—Indian mythology, Buddhism, Islam, Christianity (in the Philippines), European dress, and "modernity"—Chinese influences were generally excluded from the package. Chinese cultural icons were being assertively mobilized at this time in the service of the competing overseas Chinese identity, and therefore Chineseness became one of the most important "others" against which the new national identities defined themselves.

As the nationalist movements of Vietnam and Indonesia broadened their bases, they found Marxist prophecies of the coming demise of both imperialism and capitalism more effective among the mass of the population than anti-Chinese economic nationalism. In the bigger colonies, therefore— Netherlands India, Burma, and Vietnam (or its three colonial constituents)— foreign rule always took precedence over anti-Chinese polemic as a focus of nationalist campaigns.

In independent Thailand, on the other hand, Chinese distinctiveness, economic success, and, during the nationalist phase, perceived arrogance were easier targets than Europeans for those wanting to mobilize opinion around the national idea. In the 1910s it was the king himself who blazed this trail. The first Thai ruler to receive all his education in England, Rama VI (Vajiravudh) had picked up anti-Semitic stereotypes in Europe and used them to attack the Chinese, following a pattern already well established by the European "Jews-of-the-East" school. In 1914 he pseudonymously published a series of articles in the Thai press that were later published as an influential pamphlet, "The Jews of the East." He explained the factors behind anti-Semitism in Europe and attacked the Chinese of Siam for characteristics he claimed to be the same as those of Jews: "racial loyalty," by which they regarded outsiders as mere barbarians, a double standard of morality toward themselves and others in business dealings, and a pursuit of money above all else.[59] More than anything else, he faulted Chinese entrepreneurs for being entrepreneurs:

> There are many reasons why the Chinese are able to make money more rapidly than other people, most of them no different from those that apply to the Jews.... According to Chinese thought, money is the beginning and end of all good. There is nothing greater. Chinese appear to be willing to do anything and everything for money.... Chinese are willing to endure every sort of privation for money.... No matter how small the wages, they are ready and glad to accept them, since they know how to sustain life on an incredibly small amount of food.... There is no kind of work that they will not do, provided that they are paid for it.... In matters of money the Chinese are entirely devoid of morals and mercy. They will cheat you with a smile of satisfaction at their own perspicacity.[60]

Mass politics in Thailand began, however, only with the 1932 revolution against absolute monarchy, which celebrated the race or nation (*chat*) rather than the monarch and sought greater control of the economy, largely at the expense of Chinese. Local Chinese support for China in the Sino-Japanese War, and the government's for Japan, exacerbated the tensions. Anti-Chinese polemics and discriminatory measures reached their peak under the nationalist government of Pibun Songkhram in 1938–45.[61]

In the Philippines, too, Chinese control of the economy was the major nationalist issue during this period, for some of the same reasons. Because the United States overlords had already committed themselves to independence by 1946, colonialism itself was not the issue it was in Vietnam or Netherlands India. Malay and Khmer ethnic nationalists, by contrast, were in no hurry to remove the protective colonial umbrellas under which the two peoples had come to see themselves as endangered nations. More threatening to their newfound communities than colonialism was the prospect of being marginalized or absorbed by minorities more successful in both commerce and education—Chinese and Indians in Malaya, Chinese and Vietnamese in Cambodia.

The anticolonial nationalisms of Southeast Asia show some similarities to Gellner's "Hapsburg" type, in which powerless and education-deprived groups share related cultures that, "with a good deal of effort and standardized and sustained propaganda, can be turned into a rival new high culture," leading to the establishment of a state that sustains the reborn culture.[62] More careful distinctions, however, are required. Benedict Anderson differentiates Thai nationalism from the anticolonial nationalisms of the rest of Southeast Asia as a staged "official nationalism" like those of Japan, Austria, and Russia,[63] even though it appeared at the same time as similar anti-Chinese populisms in Vietnam and Indonesia. The more important distinction in the long run is between all the nationalisms of the Southeast Asian mainland, on the one hand, and the polyethnic new constructions of Indonesia and the Philippines, on the other.

Burmese, Thais, Khmers, Vietnamese, and Malays were all peoples of historically shifting boundaries, or no boundaries at all, who felt the call of nationalism to try to extend one particular construction of ethnolinguistic and historic identity to fill the larger fixed boundaries created by colonial rivalry. A variety of minorities, not only Chinese, had thereby to be included and given citizenship, but their relationship to the "definitive people," to use Prime Minister Mahathir's phrase,[64] had considerable potential for violence if mismanaged—as it notably has been in Burma, Laos, and Cambodia. Even in Thailand, probably the most successful country in this process, the project "to make this cultural community coterminous with the autonomous and sovereign political unit . . . requires constant tinkering and coercion."[65]

Indonesia and the Philippines, on the other hand, expressed themselves in nationalisms so manifestly new, without any single dominant language, that they had no alternative but to be nationalisms of citizenship. Although both nationalisms have so far been ambivalent or negative about including Chinese cultures among the ethnic diversity in which they rejoice, their inherent pluralism provides a framework within which it could be done. On the other side of the balance is the possibility in the particularly diverse Indonesian polity that the nationalism seen so far, for all its anticolonial vigor and ingenious cultural syncretism, has not yet defused the possibility of more virulent and exclusivist nationalisms built around "definitive" ethnolinguistic groups—Acehnese, Toba-Batak, Javanese, Balinese, Timorese (Tetum), and so forth.

Although the ethnic nationalisms of the former Soviet and Yugoslav states are discouraging on this score, my belief is that the everyday openness and acceptance of diversity in countries such as Indonesia, the Philippines, and India will prove a stronger safeguard against such dangers than the outward conformity of the Soviet or Chinese systems.

WAR AND CRISIS

The catastrophe that descended on Europe in 1933–45 has become the moral allegory par excellence for all who are tempted to blame their misfortune or disadvantage on a particular ethnic group. Hatred of Jews was the most consistent political passion of Adolf Hitler, the Viennese painter who came to power in Germany in 1933. In consequence, six million Jews died from his systematic extermination campaign—most of them from the Central and Eastern European lands conquered by or allied with Germany after 1939. The number of Slavs who died at Hitler's hands was several times greater. The racial theories of Hitler and his followers became a license for killing whoever was deemed inferior.

History offers innumerable examples of violence against entrepreneurial minorities, violence from which not only Jews and Chinese but also Indians, Armenians, Parsees, Germans, Lebanese, Palestinians, Greeks, Vietnamese, and many others have suffered. The Holocaust was different from all others both in scale and in having been carried out systematically over a period of several years by a democratically elected government that had made its racist policies clear from the beginning. In the modern world of mass politics, the dangers of racist political programs could not again be taken lightly.

This catastrophe was not inherent in a particular set of economic factors. The collapse of confidence in the liberal capitalist order caused by the Great Depression of 1929–35, along with the particular problems Germany and Austria faced after a cruel peace was imposed on them in 1918, played its part in the scapegoating of Jews and the consequent rise of Nazism. But as this book shows, Europe offered a diversity of relations between majority nationalists and entrepreneurial minorities even at a time of economic crisis and racial theorizing. Although Berlin's conquest or bullying of various governments gives the last stage of the history of Central European Jewry an appearance of uniform horror, the governments concerned reacted to Nazi demands in a wide variety of ways, from eager collaboration to heroic resistance.

Is a repetition of this European nightmare possible? Even more than lessons consciously drawn from the Holocaust, the structural changes that have taken place during the long postwar boom have rendered any major conflict between a nationalist majority and an entrepreneurial minority unlikely in the democratic advanced economies. In those countries, racial theories remain largely discredited, even if they are sometimes privately expressed or even presented in tendentious pseudo-academic form. The public expression of racial hostility must be carefully camouflaged or it will lose more votes than it wins. In market economies where consumerism has become general and the majority have become educated employees of the service sector, distinctive entrepreneurial minorities are no longer as essential or as salient as they once were.

Moreover, the world economic system has changed profoundly since the 1930s, to the point where arguments stemming from the needs of the nation-state have to be balanced by the multinational needs of large corporations. After considering the arguments for the waning of nationalism, Ernest Gellner, in his book *Nations and Nationalism,* took the view that "the sharpness of nationalist conflict may be expected to diminish" but the congruence of political unit and culture will continue to apply.[66] Yet if one looks at the economic basis for nationalism that he erected in earlier chapters of the book—"a mobile, literate, culturally standardized, interchangeable population"—it is clear that it now points toward internationalism.[67] Tariff barriers have been lowered until no one knows where an "American" or "Japanese" brand name has been produced. Capital, management, and increasingly even labor are becoming mobile internationally, just as a century ago they became mobile nationally. Similarly, the "print capitalism" that Benedict Anderson described as defining potential nations begs for an analysis of the effect the replacement of newspapers by global electronic media networks has had on cultures, consciousnesses, and identities.[68] If explanations for the rise of homogeneous nation-states in the nineteenth century are adapted to contemporary economic conditions, they support hypotheses about still larger units of effective interchangeability.

Within each of the advanced economies, hostility toward the pioneers of capitalist activity weakens as a shared consumerist culture becomes generalized. Entrepreneurs are more likely to be upheld as models than deplored as greedy signs of disorder. In states such as Australia and Canada, multiculturalism is pursued as a national goal not only to civilize eating habits but also because cosmopolitan, multilingual citizens are particularly valuable in an increasingly integrated global economy.

World War II was a trauma of a different sort for Southeast Asia. The period of war and revolution that followed the Great Depression might be seen in hindsight as a mid-century crisis of large proportions, from which the region began to emerge only in the 1970s. Mass migration from China largely ceased with the depression in 1930, and the Chinese minority everywhere gradually became a stable one in which the local-born formed an ever larger majority. A high birth rate nevertheless saw the numbers of those who self-identified as Chinese grow even faster than they had during the previous period of migration, from a total of about 4 million in 1930 to about 10 million in 1960 and perhaps 24 million in 1990—a growth not unlike that of European Jewry fifty years earlier. As a proportion of total population, the Chinese ranged from about 40 percent in Malaysia-Singapore down to merely 1 percent in the Philippines and North Vietnam.[69] The end of colonial privilege created opportunities to replace European firms in the higher peaks of commerce and industry, which more than compensated for the controls that economic nationalism sought to place on Chinese minorities. The turbulence of the 1940s and 1950s ensured that most of those who did flourish in this era, however, were newcomers ready to take big risks rather than the established families of the colonial era.

Although patriotic passions were stirred in the 1930s and 1940s by the Sino-Japanese war and the eventual reconstitution of China under communist leadership, the subsequent Maoist period rendered the ancestral land unusually unattractive as a magnet or focus of loyalty. The idealistic youth who "returned" in the 1940s to build a fatherland they had never known suffered miseries that became known in the diaspora. The minorities who could be manipulated by Beijing or Taipei became ever smaller, so that subsequent decades have seen a process of weaning the Southeast Asian Chinese away from the diaspora-nationalist push for identification with China. The antithesis between this process and Israel's effect on Jewish diasporas in the same period is striking. Whereas the core of the self-perceived Chinese community in each of the Southeast Asian countries in the early twentieth century, except Java, was *totok* (first-generation), the only remaining *totok* are now elderly (though they include the most powerful entrepreneurs). By its considerable demographic growth in the same period and the education of two new generations in the national vernaculars, the Chinese diaspora has become more similar to pre-Holocaust European Jewry.

It would be difficult to say with confidence that the narrowing cultural gap between minority and majority which these changes entailed has reduced the threat of violence beneath the surface. Each major political upheaval has created new dangers for the resented minority. The Japanese occupation in 1941–45 created sharp cleavages between Chinese, who had tended to be anti-Japanese since the Sino-Japanese war and who supported guerrilla resistance in Malaya and Borneo, and majority nationalists, for whom the Japanese brought some opportunities. The months immediately following the Japanese surrender in August 1945 witnessed an outbreak of racial violence almost everywhere as scores were settled by both sides and Chinese nationalists made provocative claims of victory. Revolutionary upheavals followed, particularly in Indonesia, where Chinese shops provided a safer and more profitable target than Dutch colonial institutions. Chinese suffered disproportionately in all such political violence, even when they were not its primary target.

No more than in Europe is it easy to relate outbreaks of violence in

Southeast Asia with particular economic or cultural conditions. In Thailand, where barriers to assimilation were lowest, there has indeed been little explicitly anti-Chinese violence since the 1950s. Yet at the other extreme, Malaysia, where the social and legal barriers between Chinese and Malay are highest, there has been only one major outbreak of violence since 1946, though this was the particularly traumatic riot and killings of May 1969. Indonesia has seen repeated outbreaks, in 1946 (Tanggerang in particular), 1959–60, 1963 (Sukabumi), 1965–67, 1973 (Bandung), 1980 (Ujung Pandang), 1982 (Surakarta), 1994 (Medan), and 1996 (Situbondo and Tasikmalaya).[70]

The most systematic governmental attempt to destroy or expel an entrepreneurial minority occurred in Vietnam in 1978–79, as relations between Beijing and Hanoi broke down. The million or more Hoa (ethnic Chinese) in the south were largely Vietnamese citizens but were pressured into becoming boat people by deprivation of their livelihood and the double prejudice against them as potential fifth columnists and as bourgeois. The smaller number of Hoa in the north previously had been allowed to retain Chinese citizenship, escape the draft, and act as intermediaries with the giant neighbor. Yet despite centuries of accommodation with the majority Vietnamese, this community was put under such pressure that almost all of its members had been forced to leave for China by April 1979. Recent census data show only 5,000 Hoa in northern Vietnam, against 174,000 in the 1960 census.[71]

Though international hostility was the immediate cause of this crackdown, it also points to the paradoxical relationship between ruling communisms and nationalism. Marxist parties took strong theoretical stands against nationalism and racism as false consciousnesses, yet much of their appeal in Asia was, to parody Lenin, as "a higher stage of nationalism." For Western-educated intellectuals, Marxism was attractive because it could provide a rational, modern, nonracial explanation of why the currently poor and weak nations might hope to rise. To the broader population, communists appeared willing not simply to talk about overthrowing foreign control (Japanese in China, Western colonialism in Southeast Asia, "neocolonial" enterprise after the war), but to get on with it.

The weakness of a majority bourgeoisie in Indonesia, Vietnam, and Burma made a corporatist style of economic nationalism virtually irresistible there. The governments of these three countries in the 1950s and 1960s all had to deal with a political public that was passionately anticolonial and believed that private capitalist activity was corrosive and antinational and that the new states should intervene in the economy to deliver a good life for all. As in Eastern Europe, politically correct attitudes toward racial equality imposed from above did nothing to deal with the resentment of unequal (individual and group) success in the marketplace or, in the end, to educate citizens to handle questions of identity in a politically mature manner.

The spectacularly successful opening of the Southeast Asian economies to foreign and domestic investment since 1970 (except for Burma and Indo-China, which started on the same path some twenty years later) has improved living standards throughout the region. The 1970s brought Malaysia and Singapore a burst of phenomenal growth, averaging 7.6 percent a year throughout the decade in real terms, so that national income more than doubled during this period. In these most advanced Southeast Asian economies, the economic gap between Chinese and others may be narrowing, though with the danger in Malaysia of making the Malay business elite more rather than less dependent on government discrimination in its favor.[72]

In Thailand and Indonesia, economic growth in the 1980s, also at rates higher than any ever experienced in Europe, increased the share going to risk-taking Chinese entrepreneurs to an extent well beyond what any minority group could have aspired to in the modern European cases.[73] Yet this danger is more than offset by an acceptance, to a degree unthinkable even in the 1960s, that money-making activity is legitimate and positive for the nation. In chapter 3 of this volume, Kasian Tejapira describes how fully Sino-Thai individuals and values have been incorporated into the newly dominant middle-class ethos of Thailand. Although one cannot be as optimistic about Indonesia, even in the face of the Medan riots one internal commentator declared that "a multi-ethnic capitalist class is ... in active formation, economically and politically. Although this class remains far from anything near hegemony over Indonesian life, its very formation has helped soften old racial antagonisms."[74]

The negative side of this phenomenally rapid economic growth is the dissolution of established ties of kinship and locality, the challenge of competitive consumerism to cherished values, and the anomie of newly urban life. The increasing identification of young Malays and Indonesians with a scriptural and morally prescriptive definition of Islam is understandable in this context, particularly to anyone who has examined evangelical revivals in Europe and America. The new Islamic movements have provided both community and a moral anchor in the changing world. In Malaysia, Malay identity is always a further factor, and Islam has become more salient there as a boundary marker since the Malay language was imposed on the whole Malaysian education system in 1969–70.[75]

For the young activists who drive these movements, scripturalist Islam helps resolve the dilemma of modernity. It provides a coherent morality that marks them off from both the old-world village syncretism of their parents and the godless consumerism and corruption they see around them in the cities. At an earlier stage these negative aspects of modern commercialism could be comfortably associated with Chinese and Europeans. But as Muslims themselves join the new rich in ever-growing numbers, narrower explanations for these negative aspects have been imported from the Middle East and ultimately from the West.

In Malaysia and Indonesia today, the crudest racial formulations of the demonology of modernization are directed against a "Jewish" minority known only as a theoretical construct. The secularism and the separation between church and state that these groups deplore in the modern West have made Christianity a less satisfactory target, particularly because Christian minorities in Malaysia and Indonesia are not easily demonized. There are real personal and political costs in attacking them, whereas Jews seem a disembodied, costless target for group hatreds and ambivalence about the modernization process.

The return of many students from periods of study in Egypt and Arabia, increased contacts with Middle Eastern governments, and the interest of young idealists in the Iranian revolution of 1979 have exposed Southeast Asians to explanations for Muslim weakness deriving from the Middle East, in which Israel and the "international Jewish lobby" play a large part.

In the 1980s in Malaysia and the 1990s in Indonesia, some of the explicitly anti-Semitic publications circulating in the Middle East began to appear in Malaysian and Indonesian editions. They ascribed all the evils of the modern world, particularly colonialism, communism, secular liberalism, and commercialization, to Jewish conspiracies along the lines of those sketched in the notorious Czarist forgery, "The Protocols of the Learned Elders of Zion."[76] The political configuration in Malaysia makes it difficult to condemn such excesses once they become associated with Islam, and Mahathir himself appeared to encourage them during the first six years of his prime ministership.[77]

In Indonesia, home of the world's largest Muslim community, Islamic ideas are much more diverse and more autonomous from the political needs of government, and cultural identities are less embattled and defensive than those of Malaysian Malays. The pleas of leaders such as Abdurrahman Wahid and Nurcholis Madjid to disentangle Islamic revitalization from the failed political struggles of the past have led in the direction of tolerance and openness. Nevertheless, the current of Jewish-conspiracy theories has recently increased in virulence. Its most influential champion since 1991 has been *Media Dakwah,* a Jakarta Muslim monthly whose circulation has been rising along with its extremism and in 1994 stood at about 20,000. In attacking opponents such as Nurcholis Madjid, it regularly labels them agents of the Jews or of Zionism, whose only aim is to destroy Islam.

In August 1993, this campaign was extended to William Liddle, one of the world's leading analysts of Indonesian politics. In an analysis of contemporary Indonesian Islam, Liddle had given *Media Dakwah* a paradigmatic place within the current he called "scripturalist," as opposed to the "substantialist" stream of Nurcholis Madjid and Abdurrahman Wahid, and he had deplored the anti-Semitic stereotypes into which the journal's defensive insularity was leading it.[78] The *Media Dakwah* response was to devote a whole issue to an attempt to discredit Liddle as part of the international Jewish conspiracy, arguing that all the evil and bloodshed that has befallen the world arose from the scheming of Jews.[79]

Anger over Israel's treatment of Palestinians only partially explains why such fantastic ideas have suddenly become popular and believable in Islamic Southeast Asia. Scapegoating and conspiracy theories are more credible as a familiar social system dissolves and the boundaries of the new remain unclear. Periods of rapid economic expansion followed by crisis encourage beliefs that the system is not working in "our" interests—as happened in Europe and the United States after 1873, during World War I, and again, catastrophically, in the 1930s. Malaysia's sudden economic downturn in 1985–87, after a period of dramatic growth, may well be an indication of such dangers. Moreover, the decline of Marxism has increased the desire for some coherent critique of Western hegemony that does not jettison modernity altogether.

One of the most extreme anti-Jewish diatribes (this one fortunately buried in a low-circulation university staff newsletter) emerged from the Malaysian debate in 1994 over whether to ban the film *Schindler's List.* The prominent Malay novelist Shahnon Ahmad argued that it was Hitler, not Schindler, who should be praised. The Jews whom the Nazis had regrettably failed to kill, in Shahnon's apocalyptic vision, were now responsible for leading the world to its destruction. The signs he perceived of this imminent collapse were precisely the ills of rapid economic growth—consumerism, commoditization, the rule of money, and the abandonment of traditional values in the name of a spurious freedom.[80]

Alienation from the onward rush of commercialization is familiar from European history and is inescapable in the much faster pace of Asian development. It is, on balance, remarkable (and a tribute to the smaller number of economic casualties suffered thus far in Southeast Asia's transition than in Europe's) that there has not been more scapegoating and that the Jewish target identified for demonization is such an unreal and abstract one. Nevertheless, the experience of Europe strongly suggests that racist theory never stops with one target group. Whenever a large segment of society begins to find explanations acceptable that proceed from political arguments (whether about the role of Israel, the excessive consumption of the rich, or the extent of foreign influence) to the demonization of whole racial groups, then the outlook for all minorities (and ultimately also majorities) becomes dark.

There are still crises of transition to be negotiated in Southeast Asia before minority status ceases to be a salient and resented feature of economic and political life. If the economies falter, domestic political conflicts again get out of hand, and desperate politicians look for scapegoats and saviors, the dangers of violence remain real. Yet this book is a statement of confidence that the region will learn from the salutary experience of the European transition and avoid its poisonous racial conflicts.

NOTES

This chapter has been through many drafts, and its present form has been influenced by a diversity of views—not all by any means compatible. I wish especially to acknowledge Steve Beller, Dan Chirot, Harold Crouch, K. S. Jomo, Victor Karady, Clive Kessler, Dan Lev, Tan Lay Cheng, and Tan Liok Ee, though none of them is responsible for the outcome.

1. W. Roscher, "Die stellung der Juden in Mittelalter vom Standpunkt fur die allgemeine Handelspolitik," *Zeitschrift fur gesamte Staatswirtschaft* 31 (1875), as cited in Walter P. Zenner, *Minorities in the Middle: A Cross-Cultural Analysis* (Albany: State University of New York Press, 1991), p. 2.

2. Werner Sombart, *The Jews and Modern Capitalism* (Glencoe, Illinois: Free Press, 1951 [1911]).

3. Max Weber, *The Protestant Ethic and the Spirit of Capitalism,* translated by Talcott Parsons (London: Unwin University Books, 1930), p. 271.

4. Max Weber, *The Sociology of Religion,* translated by E. Fischoff (London: Methuen, 1963), p. 109.

5. Joseph P. Jiang, "Towards a Theory of Pariah Entrepreneurship," in G. Wijeyawardene, ed., *Leadership and Authority: A Symposium* (Singapore: University of Malaya Press, 1968); Gary Hamilton, "Pariah Capitalism: A Paradox of Power and Dependence," *Ethnic Groups* 2 (Spring 1978), pp. 1–15; Allen J. Chun, "Pariah Capital-

ism and the Overseas Chinese of Southeast Asia: Problems in the Definition of the Problem," *Ethnic and Racial Studies* 12:2 (April 1989), pp. 233–56.

6. For example, Jonathan Israel, *European Jewry in the Age of Mercantilism, 1550–1750* (Oxford: Oxford University Press, 1985).

7. Philip Curtin, *Cross-Cultural Trade in World History* (Cambridge: Cambridge University Press, 1984).

8. Although primarily a New Testament term (John 7:35; 1 Peter 1:1), the concept of the Diaspora harks back to Deuteronomy 28:25—"The Lord shall cause thee to be smitten before thine enemies; thou shalt . . . be removed into all the kingdoms of the earth."

9. Abner Cohen, "Cultural Strategies in the Organization of Trading Diasporas," in Claude Meillassoux, ed., *The Development of Indigenous Trade and Markets in West Africa* (London, 1971), cited in Curtin, *Cross-Cultural Trade,* p. 2n.

10. Irwin Rinder, "Strangers in the Land: Social Relations in the Status Gap," *Social Problems* 6 (1958–59), pp. 253–60.

11. Stanislav Andreski, "An Economic Interpretation of Anti-Semitism in Eastern Europe," *Jewish Journal of Sociology* 5:2 (1963), pp. 201–13.

12. W. Ph. Wertheim, *East-West Parallels: Sociological Approaches to Modern Asia* (The Hague: van Hoeve, 1964), pp. 76–80.

13. Edna Bonacich, "A Theory of Middlemen Minorities," *American Sociological Review* 38 (1973), pp. 583–94, and "Middleman Minorities and Advanced Capitalism," *Ethnic Groups* 2 (1980), pp. 311–20; Walter Zenner, "Middleman Minority Theories: A Critical Review," in R. S. Bryce-Laporte, D. M. Mortimer, and S. R. Couch, eds., *Sourcebook on the New Immigration* (New Brunswick, New Jersey: Transaction Books, 1980), pp. 413–25; Zenner, *Minorities in the Middle.*

14. Ernest Gellner, *Nations and Nationalism* (Oxford: Blackwell, 1983), p. 124.

15. Benedict Anderson, *Imagined Communities: Reflections on the Origin and Spread of Nationalism* (London: Verso, 1983), p. 14.

16. Anderson, *Imagined Communities;* Gellner, *Nations and Nationalism;* Anthony Smith, *The Ethnic Origins of Nations* (Oxford: Blackwell, 1986); Eric J. Hobsbawm, *Nations and Nationalism since 1780* (Cambridge: Cambridge University Press, 1990); Liah Greenfeld, *Nationalism: Five Roads to Modernity* (Cambridge, Massachusetts: Harvard University Press, 1992).

17. Anderson, *Imagined Communities,* pp. 129–40.

18. K. R. Minogue, *Nationalism* (London: Batsford, 1967), p. 7.

19. Hans Kohn, *Nationalism: Its Meaning and History* (Princeton, New Jersey: Van Nostrand, 1955); Smith, *The Ethnic Origins of Nations;* Greenfeld, *Nationalism.*

20. For Malay nationalism, see Tan Liok Ee, *The Rhetoric of Bangsa and Minzu: Community and Nation in Tension, the Malay Peninsula, 1900–1955* (Clayton, Victoria: Centre of Southeast Asian Studies, Monash University, 1988); and Ariffin Omar,

Bangsa Melayu: Malay Concepts of Democracy and Community 1945–1950 (Singapore: Oxford University Press, 1993). For Thailand, see Craig J. Reynolds, ed., *National Identity and Its Defenders: Thailand 1939–1989* (Clayton, Victoria: Centre of Southeast Asian Studies, Monash University, 1991); and Scot Barmé, *Luang Wichit Wathakan* (Singapore: Institute of Southeast Asian Studies, 1993).

21. Ian Buruma, *The Wages of Guilt: Memories of War in Germany and Japan* (New York: Farrar Straus Giroux, 1994), p. 8.

22. Ruth Benedict, *The Chrysanthemum and the Sword* (Boston: Houghton Mifflin, 1946), as cited in Buruma, *The Wages of Guilt,* p. 116.

23. Penny Edwards, "Cambodia's Melting Pot," *The Woodstock Road Editorial* (Oxford, 1992); Ben Kiernan, *The Pol Pot Regime: Race, Power, and Genocide in Cambodia under the Khmer Rouge, 1975–79* (New Haven, Connecticut: Yale University Press, 1996).

24. Hillel Levine, *Economic Origins of Anti-Semitism: Poland and Its Jews in the Early Modern Period* (New Haven, Connecticut: Yale University Press, 1991), p. 32.

25. Ng Chin-keong, "The Case of Ch'en I-lao: Maritime Trade and Overseas Chinese in Ch'ing Policies, 1717–1754," in R. Ptak and D. Rothermunde, eds., *Emporia, Commodities and Entrepreneurs in Asian Maritime Trade, c. 1400–1750* (Stuttgart: Franz Steiner, 1991), p. 395.

26. Anthony Reid, "Flows and Seepages in the Long-term Chinese Interaction with Southeast Asia," in Anthony Reid, ed., *Sojourners and Settlers* (Sydney: Allen & Unwin, 1996), pp. 17–33.

27. Levine, *Economic Origins of Anti-Semitism,* p. 33.

28. Anthony Reid, *Southeast Asia in the Age of Commerce,* vol. 2 (New Haven, Connecticut: Yale University Press, 1993), pp. 312–13.

29. Levine, *Economic Origins of Anti-Semitism,* p. 9; William Dampier, *Voyages and Discoveries,* edited by C. Wilkinson (London: Argonaut Press, 1931 [1699]), pp. 94–95.

30. An excellent discussion of this phenomenon is that in G. William Skinner, "Creolized Chinese Societies in Southeast Asia," in Reid, *Sojourners and Settlers,* pp. 51–93.

31. Howard M. Sachar, *The Course of Modern Jewish History* (New York: Vintage Books, 1990, rev. ed.), pp. 22–27. Levine, however, in *Economic Origins of Anti-Semitism,* pp. 136–41, rejects a similar constructive role for the Jewish managers of feudal estates in Poland (the *arendar*) compared with that of the *hofjuden* in German-speaking Europe, largely because Poland's economy was in steady decline after 1648 and its religious atmosphere was growing increasingly intolerant.

32. William O. McCagg, *A History of Hapsburg Jews, 1670–1918* (Bloomington: Indiana University Press, 1989), p. 12; Levine, *Economic Origins of Anti-Semitism,* p. 32n.

33. John Butcher and Howard Dick, eds., *The Rise and Fall of Revenue Farming: Business Elites and the Emergence of the Modern State in Southeast Asia* (Basingstoke: Macmillan, 1993), pp. 73–77.

34. Butcher and Dick, *The Rise and Fall of Revenue Farming*, p. 172.

35. Butcher and Dick, *The Rise and Fall of Revenue Farming*, pp. 198–204.

36. F. Fokkens, translated in M. R. Fernando and David Bulbeck, eds., *Chinese Economic Activity in Netherlands India: Selected Translations from the Dutch* (Singapore: ISEAS/ECHOSEA, 1992), pp. 63–64.

37. Peter Carey, "Changing Javanese Perceptions of the Chinese Communities in Central Java, 1755–1825," *Indonesia* 37 (1984), pp. 8–9, 24–25.

38. Butcher and Dick, *The Rise and Fall of Revenue Farming*, pp. 156–57.

39. This argument is forcefully made in A. R. T. Kemasang, "The 1740 Chinese Slaughters in Java: Officially Orchestrated Pogroms," *Kabar Seberang* 16 (December 1982), pp. 65–91. Most other authorities see the massacre as having been more spontaneous.

40. Edgar Wickberg, *The Chinese in Philippine Life, 1850–1898* (New Haven, Connecticut: Yale University Press, 1965), p. 22.

41. Ong-Tae-Hae (Wang Ta-hai), *The Chinaman Abroad: An Account of the Malayan Archipelago, Particularly of Java*, translated by W. H. Medhurst (London: John Snow, 1850 [1791]), pp. 14–18; Claudine Salmon, "Ancestral Halls, Funeral Associations, and Attempts at Resinicization in Nineteenth Century Southeast Asia," in Reid, *Sojourners and Settlers*, pp. 197–202.

42. Skinner, "Creolized Chinese Societies in Southeast Asia," pp. 59–61.

43. The rapidly increasing outflow from southern China in the nineteenth century was balanced by the high number of returnees, of deaths without issue, and of Chinese assimilated into Southeast Asian populations. In Java, for which figures are the least unsatisfactory, Ong-Tae-Hae (1791) and Raffles (1814) estimated that there were 2 percent or more Chinese in the population, compared with only 1.39 percent in the 1930 census (Carey, "Changing Javanese Perceptions," p. 14). In the Philippines, the group classified as "Chinese" has been well below 1 percent in the twentieth century, as compared with 5 percent Chinese mestizo in the nineteenth, the descendants of whom are now considered Filipino.

44. T. J. Newbold, *Political and Statistical Account of the British Settlements in the Straits of Malacca* (London, 1839; reprinted Kuala Lumpur: Oxford University Press, 1971), p. 8.

45. Peter Carey, *Babad Dipanegara* (Kuala Lumpur: MBRAS, 1981), pp. xlii–xliii; Alexander Woodside, *Vietnam and the Chinese Model: A Comparative Study of Nguyen and Ch'ing Civil Government in the First Half of the Nineteenth Century* (Cambridge, Massachusetts: Harvard University Press, 1971), pp. 3–4.

46. G. William Skinner, *Chinese Society in Thailand: An Analytical History* (Ithaca,

New York: Cornell University Press, 1957), p. 144; Spenser St. John, *Life in the Forests of the Far East,* vol. 2 (London: Smith, Elder & Co; reprinted Kuala Lumpur: Oxford University Press, 1974), pp. 312, 320–21; W. A. Graham, *Kelantan: A State of the Malay Peninsula* (Glasgow: Maclehose, 1908), p. 103.

47. McCagg, *A History of Hapsburg Jews,* pp. 145, 191; Steven Beller, *Vienna and the Jews 1867–1938* (Cambridge: Cambridge University Press, 1989), p. 44.

48. Beller, *Vienna and the Jews,* pp. 49–67.

49. Butcher and Dick, *The Rise and Fall of Revenue Farming,* pp. 35–36.

50. Butcher and Dick, *The Rise and Fall of Revenue Farming,* p. 9.

51. Claudine Salmon, ed., *Le moment "Sino-Malais" de la littérature indonésienne* (Paris: Cahiers d'Archipel, 1992).

52. Cited in Sachar, *The Course of Modern Jewish History,* p. 306.

53. Skinner, *Chinese Society in Thailand,* pp. 155–63; Victor Purcell, *The Chinese in Southeast Asia* (London: Oxford University Press, 1965, 2d ed.), pp. 118–19.

54. L. E. Williams, *Overseas Chinese Nationalism: The Genesis of the Pan-Chinese Movement in Indonesia, 1900–16* (Glencoe, Illinois: Free Press, 1960); Wang Gungwu, *Community and Nation: Essays on Southeast Asia and the Chinese* (Singapore: Heinemann, 1981), pp. 128–58.

55. Milton Friedman, "Capitalism and the Jews: Confronting a Paradox," *Encounter* 63:1 (1984), p. 74.

56. Sachar, *The Course of Modern Jewish History,* p. 335.

57. Leo Suryadinata, *Pribumi Indonesians, the Chinese Minority and China* (Singapore: Heinemann, 1992, 3d ed.), pp. 12–14, 36–38.

58. Purcell, *The Chinese in Southeast Asia,* p. 546.

59. The pamphlet is quoted in full in Kenneth P. Landon, *The Chinese in Thailand* (London: Oxford University Press, 1941), pp. 34–43.

60. Landon, *The Chinese in Thailand,* pp. 38–39.

61. A few months before Pibun came to power, his cultural commissar, Luang Wichit Wathakan, himself a *lookjin* (Sino-Thai) like many other leaders of anti-Chinese opinion, made a famous speech at Chulalongkorn University, where, after referring to Hitler's actions against Jews, he declared that "it was high time Siam considered dealing with their own Jews"—i.e., Chinese. See Barmé, *Luang Wichit Wathakan,* pp. 133–36.

62. Gellner, *Nations and Nationalism,* p. 97.

63. Anderson, *Imagined Communities,* pp. 94–95.

64. Mahathir bin Mohammed, *The Malay Dilemma* (Singapore: Asia Pacific Press, 1970), pp. 122–30.

65. Reynolds, *National Identity and Its Defenders,* pp. 24–25.

66. Gellner, *Nations and Nationalism,* pp. 114–22.

67. Gellner, *Nations and Nationalism,* p. 46.

68. Anderson, *Imagined Communities,* pp. 66–97.

69. Mary Somers Heidhues, *Southeast Asia's Chinese Minorities* (Hawthorn: Long-man Australia, 1974), p. 3; Purcell, *The Chinese in Southeast Asia,* pp. 169–75; "The Overseas Chinese," *The Economist,* July 18, 1992, p. 21.

70. For the earlier sequence, see J. A. C. Mackie, "Anti-Chinese Outbreaks in Indonesia," in J. A. C. Mackie, ed., *The Chinese in Indonesia* (London: Nelson, 1976), pp. 77–138. The latest are described in *Far Eastern Economic Review,* January 9, 1997, pp. 14–15.

71. *Vietnam Population Census 1989,* vol. 1 (Hanoi: Central Census Steering Com-mittee, 1991). For the crisis of 1978–79, see Michael Godley, "A Summer Cruise to Nowhere: China and the Vietnamese Chinese in Perspective," *Australian Journal of Chinese Affairs* 4 (1980), pp. 35–59; Charles Benoit, "Vietnam's 'Boat People,' " in David W. P. Elliott, ed., *The Third Indochina Conflict* (Boulder, Colorado: Westview Press, 1981), pp. 139–62.

72. Pang Eng Fong, "Race, Income Distribution and Development in Malaysia and Singapore," in Linda Lim and Peter Gosling, eds., *The Chinese in Southeast Asia* (Singapore: Maruzen, 1983), pp. 316–35; Harold Crouch, "Malaysia: Neither Authori-tarian nor Democratic," in Kevin Hewison, Richard Robison, and Garry Rodan, eds., *Southeast Asia in the 1990s* (Sydney: Allen & Unwin, 1993), pp. 133–58.

73. Some gross estimates are found in *The Economist,* July 18, 1992, p. 21. In 1993 the Indonesian magazine *Info Bisnis* produced a list of the country's 300 richest taxpayers, 247 of whom were Chinese. The proportion is probably similar in Thai-land, though the line between who is and is not "Chinese" is even less clear or meaningful there.

74. Ariel Heryanto, "A Class Act," *Far Eastern Economic Review,* June 16, 1994, p. 30.

75. Chandra Muzaffar, *Islamic Resurgence in Malaysia* (Petaling Jaya: Penerbit Fajar Bakti, 1987), especially pp. 13–29; K. S. Jomo and Shabery Cheek, "Malaysia's Islamic Movements," in Francis Loh and Joel Kahn, eds., *Fragmented Vision: Culture and Politics in Contemporary Malaysia* (Sydney: Allen & Unwin for ASAA, 1992), pp. 79–106.

76. The "Protocols" were first published in Malaysia in 1983, and in Indonesian translation in 1992. Other publications of this genre include two in English published by the "Thinker's Library" at Sungei Tua just outside Kuala Lumpur, both dated 1991: Shakil Ahmed Zia, *A History of Jewish Crimes* (first published in Karachi, 1969), and Misbahul Islam Faruqi, *Jewish Conspiracy and the Muslim World* (first published in Karachi, 1967). In Indonesia, Lukman Saksono translated from English both the "Protocols" and Gerald L. K. Smith's "Jewish-Zionist Capitalists," published in Henry Ford's private anti-Semitic newspaper, *The Dearborn Independent,* in the 1920s (Jakarta: Grafikatama, 1991). More of this type of literature published in 1991–92 and

more typically translated from Arabic intermediaries is reviewed by Margot Cohen in *Sources Age* (Melbourne), March 26, 1994.

77. This phase appeared to end after a couple of public brawls with the international press. The first was over a cancelled visit of the New York Philharmonic to Kuala Lumpur in 1984, which first revealed to the world Malaysia's policy of discouraging "works of Jewish origin." There was then a series of confrontations in 1986, culminating in the visit of the Israeli president to Singapore in November, against which Malaysian protests were vigorous.

78. Liddle's article was published in a rival journal as "Skripturalisme *Media Dakwah:* Satu Bentok Pemikiran dan Aksi Politik Islam Masa Orde Baru," *Ulumul Qur'an,* July 1993. The English version is *"Media Dakwah* Scripturalism: One Form of Islamic Political Thought and Action in New Order Indonesia," in Mark Woodward and James Rush, eds., *Towards a New Paradigm: Recent Developments in Indonesian Islamic Thought* (Tempe: Arizona State University Press, 1996).

79. *Media Dakwah,* Shafar 1414/August 1993.

80. Shahnon Ahmad, "Pola Pemikiran di Sebalik Halal-Haramnya *Schindler's List,"* *Lidah* (Penang), 2 (1994), pp. 9–12.

PART TWO

Identity, Choice, and the Reaction to Prejudice among Chinese and Jews

3 / Imagined Uncommunity

The *Lookjin* Middle Class and

Thai Official Nationalism

KASIAN TEJAPIRA

One night in September 1992, four months after an uprising by the cellular phone–wielding, sedan-driving Thai middle class had
toppled the military government of General Suchinda Kraprayoon, the
top-rated drama "Lod Lai Mangkorn" (Through the Dragon Design) was
broadcast on a state-run television channel. It contained the following
dialogue:

> THAO KAE: Pipow like you gek evely ceng ley hef fom leir palengs. Lazybongs
> lares lung after my logter. Shem ong you. Go away![1]
>
> SA-NGIAM: You have come to settle here in the land of the Thais. How dare
> you insult a Thai like me![2]
>
> THAO KAE: Yek, I hef come to settle here. Buk lik ik Thailaeng, nok your
> laeng. Pipos like me are weilling to kowtow to lik laeng ang to le Thais who are
> hark-working, buk never to pipow like you.[3]

THE LEGACY OF IMAGINED UNCOMMUNITY

The television drama "Lod Lai Mangkorn" was adapted from a Thai novel of
the same name that was serialized in *Sakul Thai* magazine during 1989 and
1990. The book was written by Praphassorn Sewikul, a middle-ranking official in the Ministry of Foreign Affairs and a successful, part-time popular
novelist of ethnic Thai origin. It was reputedly based on the real life stories
of two Chinese immigrant multimillionaire tycoons, Chin Sophonphanich
of the Bangkok Bank and Thiam Chokwatthana of the Sahaphatthanaphi-
boon consumer products manufacturing conglomerate. The novel depicts
the rags-to-riches story of Ah-Liang Seuphanich, a Chinese immigrant who
arrives penniless in Thailand on the eve of the Second World War and then

painstakingly, parsimoniously, and ingeniously builds up a family business empire despite war, bankruptcy, coups, military dictatorship, political exile, family conflicts, and tragedies.[4]

Drawing on and portraying the widely held image of inherent Chinese immigrant entrepreneurial virtues (diligence, patience, self-reliance, discipline, determination, parsimony, self-denial, business acumen, friendship, family ties, honesty, shrewdness, modesty), the novel's tragic, heroic, and triumphant plot has a profound appeal among the Chinese immigrant and *lookjin* (Sino-Thai) community that belies its rather dry and terse narrative style.[5] Defying the convention in Thai literary and entertainment circles of portraying Chinese characters as mafia villains, stingy, bloodsucking shopkeepers, and uncultured buffoons, all of whom "phood thai mai chad" (literally, "to speak unclear Thai," but more accurately, "to speak Thai with a thick Teochiu-accent"), the novel's protagonist is a "phood thai mai chad" Chinese immigrant merchant rather than the usual Thai foreign-educated nobleman or military officer. Moreover, this unschooled Chinese merchant manages to win the heart of the story's beauty (Thao Kae's daughter) in fierce and persistent competition with her ethnic Thai, university-educated boyfriend, Sa-ngiam.[6]

As of February 1993, the novel had gone through its eleventh printing. The phenomenal impact of *Lod Lai Mangkorn*'s dramatized version on viewers can be gauged from the following incident. Shortly after the series premiered on television, a popular-music radio program, "Smile Radio," asked its listeners of Chinese descent to call in and disclose their clan names. They flooded the radio station with calls, indicating that the Thai-speaking *lookjin* middle class, after many years of public reticence about their Chineseness, were now finally "coming out of the closet."

The revolutionary nature of *Lod Lai Mangkorn* and its television adaptation lies in its implicit and explicit challenges to the hegemonic imagination of the Thai nation. This "official nationalism" was conceived by King Vajiravudh (1910–25), the chief ideologue of Thai royalist absolutism, and was later consolidated, expanded, and intensified by Prime Minister Field Marshal Plaek Phigunsongkhram (1938–44; 1948–57), the führer and pioneer of Thai militaristic statism.[7] It is narrowly based on the Thai race and is politically centered on and arbitrarily defined by the state. Some basic canons of its doctrine are as follows.[8]

During the initial phase of official nationalism under King Vajiravudh, which may be called the phase of "negative politicization of Thai ethnicity," the majority Thai ethnic group was politically "interpellé" as the mainstay of the multiethnic Siamese nation.[9] This is evident in the King's oft-quoted poem "Sayamanusati" (Maxim for Siam), which maintains the distinction between "la patrie siamoise" and "le peuple thai" as follows:

> If only Siam still stands,
> then all of us can survive.
> But if Siamese land is lost, alas,
> it's as if Thai lives and race were gone.

King Vajiravudh's willful politicization of the Thais was achieved negatively, however, by singling out the Chinese as their archenemy.[10] Dubbed "the Jews of the Orient" by the king, the Chinese in Siam were showered with epithets, among them the following: "[Siamese] are no more like the Chinese than any of the European races are like the Jews," "exclusive and unneighborly," "neither knows nor understands nationality or patriotism," "loyal to the power that owns his fickle allegiance only so long as his own interests happen to coincide with those of his master's," "regard their residence as temporary and . . . refuse to be assimilated," "share the benefits of citizenship . . . but . . . evade . . . duties," "never dreams of dealing honestly or fairly with any of us," "every bit as unscrupulous and as unconscionable as the Jews," "his courtesy is merely assumed and his fair speech mostly lying flattery," "acute . . . money-making instinct," "utterly without morals, without conscience, without mercy, without pity . . . where money is concerned," "Honour and Good Name, Honesty and Truth, Love and Mercy, the Milk of Human Kindness, all are offered on the altar of the Money God," "no more Buddhists than are the Jews Christians," "aliens by birth, by nature, by sympathy, by language, and finally by choice," "born intriguers and conspirators," "bound one day to come into bloody conflict with the inhabitants."[11]

In independent Siam, a colonial "plural society"–like situation (à la J. S. Furnivall),[12] in which people of different ethnicities "mix but do not combine" and "live side-by-side but separately," the king simply denied any possible co-identity, union, combination, or even mediation and middle ground between the two races and communities. Hence:

> One is either a Chinaman or a Siamese; no one could be both at the same time, and people who pretend that they are so are apt to be found to be neither. Such people, like the Chameleon, change their colour to suit their surrounding; when they come among us they are Siamese, but when they go among the Chinese they become Chinese, while many of them also owe their allegiance to some European Power. These latter are usually the "politicians" among the Chino-Siamese community, the self-constituted leaders of "Modern Thought," the demagogues and journalists of Bangkok. . . .

We can only count as Siamese those who have *definitely* decided to adopt the Siamese nationality, cutting themselves quite completely from all Chinese association. They must throw their lots in with us *absolutely* before we accept them as one of us. We cannot accept those who call themselves "Chino-Siamese" as Genuine Siamese.[13]

What this amounts to is the imagining of an "uncommunity" between the Thais and the Chinese in Siam in which a Chino-Siamese or Sino-Thai ethnocultural identity is discursively impossible.[14] However, whereas Furnivall inferred from his "plural society" assumption that colonial Burma was incapable of nationhood, King Vajiravudh concluded that the only way to hold the Siamese uncommunity together was to let it be dominated culturally and politically by the Thai race.

The conclusive phase in the formation of Thai "official nationalism" took place under Prime Minister Field Marshal Plaek Phibunsongkhram. Having overthrown the Chakri absolute monarchy in 1932, he proceeded to take over and develop the legacy of Thai imagined uncommunity by deepening and expanding its residual racist, statist tendency to exclude culturally and politically not only the Chinese but also all other non-Thai ethnic groups. This resulted in the wholesale ethnicization of the Siamese polity as exclusively and monolithically Thai. Thus, beginning in 1939, a whole series of "Ratthaniyom" (cultural mandates) were issued by the Phibunsongkhram government. They decreed, among other things, that the country's name be changed from Siam to Thailand and that the national anthem be sung twice a day throughout the country. Its opening lines: "Thailand unites the Thai blood and race. A people's state, all parts belong to Thais."[15]

In order to maintain their achieved socioeconomic status and gain acceptance and membership in the Thai polity, members of non-Thai ethnic groups were expected to "assimilate" themselves culturally to the "Thai" identity. Formally, this involved the adoption of a Thai name, use of the officially standardized Bangkok-Thai language, a career in the state bureaucracy, and the search for a Thai political patron. Substantively, it entailed the adoption of a number of essentially "Thai" values, attitudes, and precepts, including "allegiance to the King of Siam" (according to King Vajiravudh),[16] "Love of National Independence, Toleration, and Power of Assimilation" (according to Prince Damrong, one of the king's uncles),[17] and "Thailand is a conformist and obedient nation," "Thais are excellent fighters," and "The country is the home, the military its fence" (according to Phibunsongkhram).[18]

Clearly, this "Thai" identity (or ethnoideology of Thainess) was based on a very selective reading of Thai traditional culture and history. It leaves out many of the values, attitudes, and precepts associated with highly independent, critical, dissenting, even rebellious, liberal or radical personalities and groups in modern Thai history, including Thianwan, Narin Phasit, Thawat Riddhidej, Siao Huadseng Sibunreuang, Kulap Saipradit, Pridi Banomyong, the Kekmeng party, the Workers' party, the Chino-Siamese communists, and even the left wing of the People's party itself. Based as it was on the elite's subjective and selective reading of traditional values, attitudes, and precepts of the Thai peasantry and bureaucrats, the ethnoideology of Thainess represented their attempt to coercively "assimilate," above all, the Chinese immigrant, urban, middle and working classes. These people constituted the most dynamic economic sector of the populace and the one in contemporary Thai civil society with the greatest potential for political autonomy and opposition to the conservative, authoritarian, militaristic, and clientelist political culture of the state and rural sectors.[19] The idea was to prevent them from transforming their economic power into political and thence state power.[20]

This goal is evident in the anti-Chinese writings of King Vajiravudh. He commented at one point that despite their many resemblances, there was nonetheless one major difference between the Jews and the Chinese: the Jews had no country of their own, whereas the Chinese still did. Consequently, the political activities, interests, and ambitions of the Chinese immigrants were oriented toward their homeland in China, rather than toward Siam, their temporary land of residence. This was fortunate, the king opined, because otherwise "they might prove very troublesome."[21] On another occasion, he composed a short political satire entitled "Rai-ngan kanprachum paliment siam" (Proceedings of the Siamese Parliament's meeting) that caricatured the call of Thianwan, a self-educated Thai commoner and reformer, for the establishment of a parliamentary system of government. In the noisy and chaotic parliament of his imagination, not a few members of parliament were Chinese who behaved in a disorderly fashion during the meeting, repeatedly shouting "Damn the government!" and being dragged out of the chamber by the police.[22]

Without the literary pretensions and dramatic flourish of his immediate predecessor, King Prajadhipok (1925–35) was blunter on this point. In 1927 he wrote a memorandum, entitled "Democracy in Siam," to Prince Damrong, his uncle and trusted aide:

> Now I am also inclined to think that a real democracy is very unlikely to succeed in Siam. It may even be harmful to the real interests of the people. One could readily imagine what a parliamentary form of government would be like in Siam,

and there is no need to go into details. I shall just mention one fact. The Parliament would be entirely dominated by the Chinese Party. One could exclude all Chinese from every political right; yet they will dominate the situation all the same, since they hold the *hard cash*. Any party that does not depend on the Chinese funds cannot succeed, so that politics in Siam will be dominated and dictated by the Chinese merchants. This is indeed a very probable eventuality.[23]

In that regard, the issue of "Thai-Chinese relationship" was actually a state-capital relationship shrouded in racist discourse, and the Thai state's widely acclaimed "cultural assimilation policy" toward the Chinese represented the political emasculation of capital and labor.[24]

But it was also the economic emasculation of the peasantry, for whereas the Thai bureaucratic state has always resisted the political power of the capitalist class, it has never deviated from the path of unequal capitalist economic development in which cheap labor and natural resources are extracted from the countryside to promote growth of both the urban economy and the state apparatus. This creates, on one hand, a patron-client relationship between the Thai state bureaucratic elite and the Chinese business class, and on the other hand, a yawning gap, a genuine—rather than imagined—socioeconomic structural uncommunity between the city and the countryside in Thailand. This situation has been the case especially since the launching of the first national economic development plan under the Sarit dictatorship in 1961. By 1972, Suguru Suyama, a Japanese economist, could make the following incisive comment on the economic plight of the Thais in his *The Economic History of the Overseas Chinese:*

> There is no merchant class among the Thais. The accumulation of national capital is almost impossible. These economically emasculated Thais have no choice but to end up being a peasant, or, if lucky, a well-to-do idler, or, if somewhat educated, a professional or government official.[25]

Thus, despite his virulent anti-Chinese discourse, King Vajiravudh had no qualms about incorporating the Chinese for economic reasons. Not only did the king have Chinese entrepreneurs as business partners, but he also helped them out financially time and again.[26] As a matter of economic policy,[27] he also preferred Chinese investors to Thais, since the former usually had more capital, business experience, and hence a better chance of success.[28] Much the same can be said of Field Marshal Plaek's subsequent economic nationalism. Research has revealed that while most, if not all, of the allegedly "nationalist" state enterprises set up under his authoritarian rule turned into lucrative sources of his henchmen's freewheeling corruption and embezzled personal wealth, almost all of these people interacted cordially with Chinese businessmen on the executive boards of many Chinese-owned or Chinese-operated companies or banks under their political patronage.[29]

Miraculously, the Thai nationalist elite's hypocrisy seemed to extend even into the netherworld. In his will, made on November 10, 1920, five years and sixteen days before his departure, King Vajiravudh, being of a clear and sound mind, dictated the following:

> During the seven days of alms-giving when my body lies in state and also in my cremation ceremony, a *gongtek* rite should be held.[30] If no one has faith in holding it for me, my heir should find priests of the Annamite or Chinese Sects to hold it for me.[31]

Alas, one could never be sure under which godly authority one would land in the otherworld!

HOW SOME *LOOKJIN* PLAYED THAIS — RIGHT AND LEFT

According to the laws of dialectics, every ideological subjection entails qualification, and every social structure is both a constraint on and an opportunity for action.[32] Under the cultural-political regime of Thai official nationalism, where the study of Chinese in formal educational institutions was severely restricted and actively discouraged, *lookjin* of alien Chinese parentage were barred from the Armed Forces' officer corps and had their voting and candidacy rights curtailed.[33] The *lookjin* learned to adopt (or, if one prefers, feign) the official nationalist "Thai identity" and play "Thai" according to the requisite political cultural code. During the decade after World War II, there were two interesting and contrasting examples of *lookjin* who adopted Thai names, learned the standard Thai language, and took "Thai" jobs for political purposes: Mr. Khow Tongmong and Mr. Chou Shoulim.[34]

Khow Tongmong

Khow Tongmong was born to Khow Huad (alias Chai Kanjanawat or Meun Suwansiriphong), a wealthy Chinese rice miller and ennobled village headman, and his Thai wife, Somjin, in Bang Khanak village, Bang Namprieo district, Chachoengsao province, on June 20, 1915. "Ti Noi Tongmong" ("Little Brother Tongmong," as he was called then) was sent by his father to attend the Kuomintang-founded, Teochiu-speaking Chinese Xinmin School in Bangkok, reputedly the best of its kind in the country at the time.[35]

Because of his knowledge of Chinese and English, he was recruited as a teacher by his alma mater after graduating around 1933. He quickly earned his Thai secondary education degree and rose to become the principal of another leading Chinese school, Huang-hun (later renamed, in Thai, Sahakhun Seuksa). Under the sponsorship of the Kuomintang government, Khow Tongmong and ten other Chinese teachers from Thailand were sent to receive further pedagogical training at Jinan University in Shanghai for a year and then on a study tour through northeastern China for another three months.

The promising teaching career of Khow Xiansheng (Teacher Khow) was cut short, however, when the nationalist Phibunsongkhram government closed Chinese schools in Thailand in 1939 and 1940.[36] Adapting readily to the changing times, Khow Tongmong enrolled in Thammasat University, got a new job as a translating clerk at the Department of Commercial Registration in the Ministry of Commerce, and changed his unfashionable, un-Thai name to an officially favored Thai one, Prasit Kanjanawat. Having graduated from Thammasat, Prasit resigned from his government job and set up a private law office called Manukij with a number of his Thammasat friends, the most important of them being Bunchoo Rojanasathian, a junior classmate at both Xinmin School and Thammasat University and now, in March 1994, head of the Palang Dharma party and a deputy premier of the Thai government.

While his law practice and joint ventures with Bunchoo and Chin Sophonphanich (on whom the novel *Lod Lai Mangkorn* was supposedly based) at the Asia Trust Company prospered, Prasit had his eye on something else. Partly to indulge his dilettantish literary and journalistic interests, but mainly to create a public relations instrument for his personal political ambition, he began to invest his money and engage his close business colleagues in some publishing and printing enterprises. Near the end of World War II, he founded and edited *Karnmuang,* a weekly newspaper; bought controlling interest in *Thai Mai,* a daily newspaper; owned a shop making woodblocks for use in fine printing, also called *Thai Mai;* and was deeply involved in establishing the Rungnakhorn Printing House, of which his friend Bunchoo was a co-founder and shareholder.[37]

Capitalizing on the regular public exposure he commanded as a newspaper owner, and deploying his editorial staff in his election campaigns, Prasit was elected, after three tries, as a pro-government member of parliament in his home province in February 1952. By no means a professional journalist, "Hia Sit," or "Elder Sit," as he was affectionately called by his newspaper employees, was a crafty politician who used his papers as mere stepping-

stones on his path to greater political power and higher governmental positions. These included member of parliament from Chachoengsao (1957, 1975,
1976), deputy minister of cooperatives (1958), member of the Bangkok
Bank's board of directors (1968), senator (1968, 1979), deputy director of the
Economic, Fiscal, and Industrial Division of the ruling military Revolutionary Group under Field Marshal Thanom Kittikachorn (1971), deputy minister of the economy (1971), deputy minister of commerce (1972), president of
the House of Representatives and the National Assembly (1975), vice president of the Bangkok Bank (1976), deputy minister of justice (1976), deputy
prime minister (1976), and president of the Bangkok Bank (since 1984).

Chou Shoulim

Born to a Chinese father and a Thai-Khamu mother in the northern province of Phichit, Chou Shoulim was sent to study in China as a child and then
went to Datong University in Shanghai.[38] Probably having been recruited
into the Chinese communist movement there, he later returned to Siam,
married a Thai woman, and continued his underground political activities.
Under the pseudonym "Piatoe," he was arrested with his comrades while
holding a meeting in a Chinese school in Phichit.[39] As the official investigators found him politically knowledgeable, he was told to write a testimony
on communism and Siam, and he duly complied.

The translation of his testimony, originally written in Chinese, was sent to
Prince Boriphat, the minister of the interior. After reading it, the prince
concluded that Piatoe was a full-fledged communist who, given a chance,
would incite the Thais against foreigners. Hence, he should be banished as
persona non grata. This was more easily said than done, however. Even
though this "full-fledged communist" had been brought up and educated in
China and could write his testimony only in Chinese, he was, having been
born in Siam and having married a Thai woman, nonetheless a Thai national
and could not be deported.

Unable to bring himself to believe that a Thai could also be a communist,
the prince submitted Piatoe's testimony to King Prajadhipok along with his
own report, part of which read:

> [People who believe in communism like Mr. Piatoe] are likely to cause a lot of
> trouble. It should not simply be taken for granted that he is a Thai by birth since
> his disposition is by no means Thai. . . . [He] should no longer be allowed to
> depend on His Majesty's merciful protection.[40]

The king wrote back that he agreed in principle with the report and the prince's suggestion that Piatoe be exiled. When the case came before the criminal court, however, the judge thought otherwise. Having successfully claimed his Thai nationality and thus prevented his deportation, Piatoe was sentenced to fifteen years in the Bangkhwang Penitentiary and a fine of 5,000 baht.[41]

In Area 6 of Bangkhwang Penitentiary, which was reserved exclusively for political prisoners, Chou Shoulim was neither lonely nor suffering. More than 100 of his Chinese and Vietnamese comrades were there, and soon 250 new arrivals joined them.[42] Yet these were not communists but so-called Bowaradej rebels, whose armed attempt to overthrow the People's party government and restore power to the monarchy in 1933 was bloodily crushed.[43]

These 350 prison inmates, who would spend up to six years together, were, both figuratively and literally, strange bedfellows indeed. Ethnically, the communists were Chinese and Vietnamese, while the Bowaradej "politicos" were mostly Thai. Sociologically, the former were teachers, merchants, and coolies, while the latter were mostly civil servants and military or police officers. In other words, the two groups were of low and high status, respectively, in Thai society. Perhaps most importantly, the two groups were at opposite poles ideologically, one composed of communist revolutionaries, the other of royalist counterrevolutionaries.[44]

Nevertheless, they now had many things in common. They were suffering the same ordeal, living in the same jail, being bound in similar chains, doing the same menial work, eating the same unsavory food, wearing the same blue uniforms, and enduring the grip of the same hostile government and jailers. Leading a life that was perforce largely collectivized and maddeningly leisured, they were gradually drawn to one another, especially the better educated and more experienced among them. After all, different as their backgrounds had been, they were politicized intellectuals whom the government saw fit to put together behind bars.[45] Therefore, it was plausible that they might find it convenient to share their diverse intellectual interests.[46]

Initially, they began their relationship by teaching foreign (non-Thai) languages to one another. The communists taught Chinese, Cantonese, and French to the politicos, who reciprocated by teaching them English and Japanese.[47] The teaching went on for several years, and judging from the circumstances, the linguistic medium of teaching must have been Thai. Then they moved on to politics, discussing, in both Thai and Chinese, communist ideology and doctrine, the strategy and program of communist

revolution in Siam, the "correct" conception and evaluation of labor, especially the menial type, the communists' personal feelings about imprison-
ment, and their ideological commitment, past experience, and future plans.
The exchange of ideas between the two groups of prisoners was serene,
pleasant, instructive, and fruitful enough when the communist interlocutors
were senior people of "leader or teacher ranks" (*chan huana* or *chan ajan*, in
Thai), with mature, educated, polite, and refined manners.[48]

One such communist inmate was Piatoe, whom Leuan Saraphaiwanich
(alias Captain Phraya Saraphaiphiphat, a former high-ranking aristocrat and
Bowaradej inmate) remembered as "a good friend," "of teacher rank," and
"polite and well-mannered." Piatoe, or Chou Shoulim, whose other Chinese
names included Mongji, Toe, and the derogatory Jek Tow, not only acquired
knowledge of the Thai language in prison but also found it politic to have
Leuan coin his first Thai name for him. Leuan chose Toe Jutharak (meaning
"Big Protector of the Crown or Head," which cleverly reflected both the
sound and the meaning of his Chinese names (Pia*toe* and Chou Shoulim,
because "Shoulim," or "Shouling" in Mandarin, denotes head, leader, or
chieftain).[49] Later he would also invent for himself such fanciful Thai noms
de plume and noms de guerre as Phayap Angkhasing ("Northwest Leonine,"
indicating his regional homeland in Siam), Phichit na Sukhothai ("Conquest
at Sukhothai," referring to his mother's home province of Sukhothai), and
Prapanta Virasakdi ("Writing with Honor or Courage"), the name he used
in public as spokesman for the Thai Communist party.

Why so much ado about names? One need only read another essay by
King Vajiravudh (1913), entitled *Priab namsakul kab cheusae* (A contrast of
family names with clan names), to gauge the immense political significance
of these nominal changes by Chou Shoulim and, for that matter, Khow
Tongmong. In that essay, the king aggressively called for the replacement of
Chinese clan names (*sae* in Teochiu, *xing* in Mandarin), still widely used
among Chinese immigrants and *lookjin* in Siam, with Thai family names. He
associated the latter with blood ties, love, modernity, civilization, social
hierarchy, national unity, and political obedience, while linking the former
to belligerent gangster solidarity, archaism, barbarism, group inclusion, national division, and political insubordination.[50] It followed from this fantastic Vajiravudhian cultural logic that a *lookjin* communist with a Thai family
name could only be a living discursive impossibility or a political contradiction in terms.

And yet, there he was, Toe Jutharak, alias Phayap Angkhasing, or Phichit
na Sukhothai, or Prapanta Virasakdi, a *lookjin* communist armed with not
just one but many Thai family names, stepping out of Bangkhwang and

going on to Yanan to help with the Chinese revolution, bringing Mao's thought back to Siam, publishing several books on communism and the Thai revolution *in Thai*, and becoming the first spokesman of the Thai Communist party.[51] Indeed, he could have been elected secretary at the second party congress in February 1952 if the majority of the party delegates had not objected to one seemingly trivial but politically damaging blemish on his Thai identity: he spoke unclear Thai with a Chinese accent.[52] Aiya, ik wok nok easie ak all to become a Thai khommunik![53]

THE *LOOKJIN* MIDDLE CLASS AND ITS INTELLECTUALS

As for the majority of *lookjin,* who did not deliberately play "Thai" politics, the state-centralized and supervised national education system, together with the rapid, state-planned, capitalist economic development launched by the military government of Prime Minister Field Marshal Sarit Thanarat in 1961, transformed them and their offspring into a significant plurality in the new multiethnic national urban middle class.[54] These *lookjin* have the following characteristics. (1) They are of Chinese descent but are basically illiterate in the Chinese language (especially when written). (2) They speak, read, and write Thai and therefore, paradoxically, are relearning Chinese culture, reviving their ethnic consciousness, and reimagining their Sino-Siamese identity through the medium of the Thai language. (3) They work in the most vibrant, dynamic, advanced, open, cosmopolitan, modern sectors of the economy and culture but remain subject to one of the most inefficient, corrupt, rigid, authoritarian, clientelistic, and outdated bureaucratic states in Southeast Asia. (4) They are generally civic-minded, patriotic, and apolitical; favor an open and accessible, pluralistic, parliamentary government to military dictatorship; hold the state bureaucracy in low regard; and have confidence in the private business sector. (5) They are gaining greater power as the largest group of entrepreneurs and consumers in the increasingly cohesive and unified national economic and cultural market, but they lack any genuine, adequate, elective representation in formal political institutions. And therefore (6) they cannot really control the state even though the survival and prosperity of their business enterprises and consumerist lifestyles are becoming more and more vulnerable to state policy.

Increasingly regarding the overcentralized but underunified power structure of the fragmented, pyramidal Thai bureaucratic state as the main impediment to their further economic prosperity and political freedom, the more politicized *lookjin* have been out on the streets and in the jungle waging battles, peaceful and armed, against the state since the early 1970s. These culminated in the uprising of October 14, 1973, the massacre and coup d'état of October 6, 1976, the communist-led armed struggle in the country-side, and, most recently, the uprising of May 1992 that overthrew the military government. Contrary to the middle class's somewhat naive expectations, however, the intransigent bureaucratic elites have steadfastly resisted and undermined any attempt to decentralize power and have clung to the old state structure despite the many courageous efforts and sacrifices of the May Democratic Movement in 1992. The *lookjin*'s political frustration has been further aggravated by the dismal performance of elected politicians, the lackluster achievements of the elected government, and the crisis-prone dysfunctionality of the existing parliamentary system. These frustrations are now being vented fully in the nation's booming print and electronic media by a new generation of middle-class intellectuals.

Broadly representing the middle class's interests and concerns, having a globalized outlook and broadly liberal-democratic political views, being well educated (in the country or abroad) and multilingual (in foreign and local languages), the new generation consists of (1) the state's economic and technical specialists, (2) the executives, consultants, researchers, developers, and creative designers of the private business sector, (3) intellectuals working in various kinds of media and in cultural, educational, and academic institutions, both public and private, and (4) intellectuals in nongovernmental organizations (NGOs) in urban and rural areas. They are armed with personal computers, cellular phones, fax machines, satellite dishes, cable televisions, compact disc and digital cassette players, videocassette recorders, laser disc players, packlinks, and electronic mail—all of which were used creatively and effectively in waging a guerrilla war in communications against the state's misinformation encirclement campaign during the May 1992 crisis.

In their published works, radio news commentaries, television advertisements, and talk shows, these people have since been imagining a new Thai national community that views itself in the following manner. (1) It is a multiethnic, multicultural community with the king as the center of the people's allegiance. (2) It is peaceful and calm because traditional social relations and cultures, whose continued existence had been threatened by socioeconomic changes, are securely restored. (3) It upholds Buddhism as the national religion but generously allows believers of other faiths to coexist peacefully. (4) It has bright prospects because its children are getting a good upbringing. (5) It is a member of the community of affluent nations. (6) It accepts economic inequality, yet the poor are happy because they are aided benevolently by the rich. (7) It is ruled by a modern, benevolent, compassionate, efficient, wise, visionary, and accessible national government that employs lenient methods to achieve national security, independence, sovereignty, and material prosperity. And (8) it either leaves out or deemphasizes the rule of law and constitutionally guaranteed rights and freedoms, as well as militaristic belligerence and values and rural farming.[55]

CONCLUSION

What is taking place in post–May 1992 Thai political culture, I believe, is the reimagining of the Thai nation as more pluralistic and genuinely nationalist (as against racist), more civil-society-centric, and more "democratic." Spearheaded by a renaissance of Chinese cultural awareness, the new Thai imagined community has the affluent and powerful middle class, composed largely of *lookjin,* as its social base, and their intellectuals as its vanguard. They have been busily turning the Thai national identity into a malleable, reimaginable object of cultural politics.

But having burst open the racist wall dividing the old imagined uncommunity, can the *lookjin* middle class hold the opening wide enough for long enough to let in other, less affluent, disadvantaged ethnic groups— be they Thais, Laos, Malays, or others—to join the new imagined community? This question is especially problematical given the real socioeconomic structural lack of community between the city and the countryside, between industry and agriculture, between Bangkok and the rest of the country, and between the awfully rich and the miserably poor. It may well be the burning question for the Thai nation as it enters the next millennium.

EPILOGUE

One night in mid-January, 1993, the annual banquet of the Machine Tools and Ironware Association of Thailand was held in a grand Chinese restaurant in downtown Bangkok. Despite having neither background in nor proclivity for this trade myself, I was invited by my cousins to join in the feast, only to find that most, if not all, of the more than one thousand guests at the banquet were ethnic Teochiu Chinese.

Typically of such gatherings, as anyone who is used to them can testify, there was a musical show to which hardly anyone paid attention. When I entered the banquet hall, a nicely dressed male singer was performing a song that was scarcely audible amid the noisy chattering and chaotic clattering of spoons and chopsticks. Having studied Mandarin Chinese in my youth—by no means a happy experience; my father forced me to do so—I happened to recognize and was struck by the words of the song, which, I found out later, was called "Wo shi zhong guo ren" (I am a Chinaman). The resounding final verse was:

> No matter where I was born
> I am a Chinaman.
> No matter where I die,
> I swear I'll be a Chinese ghost.[56]

And yet no one there seemed to hear, let alone be moved by, such a heartfelt patriotic call from the homeland.

Why not? Perhaps, first, because most of the guests, being literate in Thai and maybe the Teochiu dialect, but not in Mandarin, simply did not understand what "wo shi zhong guo ren" meant. And second, because, for better or worse, with regard to their life experiences, the spatiotemporal order they inhabited, and the particular cultural-political system to which they were subjected, they were not "Chinamen" but rather *lookjin* or *jek*—a derogatory term widely applied by Thais to Chinese in Thailand.

At the end of the two-hour eating marathon, the same singer reappeared onstage and announced to the well-fed audience that he was going to sing a song, this time in Thai, that was suited to such an auspicious occasion. Unlike the first time, there was a sudden and palpable hush when the song began. The audience listened attentively, as though something of crucial importance was being communicated to them.

The song turned out to be the title song of the "Lod Lai Mangkorn" television series. These were the words (according to my translation):

> From the Chinese land overseas
> on a small boat drifting afar
> penniless like a beggar
> arrives in the Gulf and land of Siam.
> Like a dragon in hiding
> flees away from the flame of war
> to a shelter one feels grateful for
> ever more determined to make good on this life.
> Builds a legendary business and romance
> to win public acceptance and reputation.
> Gives birth to a new generation
> the new wave of great energy.
> Fights the battle of the business world
> with flexible wisdom and nerve.

But, alas, as to the battle of love,
harsh wounds are inflicted on the heart.
Through the days and nights of toil
contemplates the coin of past struggling.
Dragon begins to spread its wings
pays back things it owes to this land.[57]

It struck me then that this was the long-missing anthem of their own imagined community.

NOTES

1. Thao Kae is a common Thai term for senior, wealthy, male Chinese. The spellings of Thao Kae's part in the dialogue are deliberately altered to convey the Chinese effects of his Teochiu accent. Without this, it would read: "People like you get every cent they have from their parents. Lazybones dares run after my daughter. Shame on you. Go away!"

2. In the television drama, Sa-ngiam is the name of a Thai university student who is running after Thao Kae's beautiful daughter.

3. "Yes, I have come to settle here. But this is Thailand, not your land. People like me are willing to kowtow to this land and to the Thais who are hard-working, but never to people like you."

4. Praphassorn Sewikul, *Lod lai mangkorn* [Through the dragon design] (Bangkok: Dokya Press, 1992). The successful adaptation of the novel for television owed much to the creative effort of the scriptwriter, "Wilasini" (Wichian Thangsuk), who actually managed to enliven it by "fully putting emotions into the story." See Sumali Wassana-achasakul and Adisak Nonthawong, "Samphas huajai willasini–wichian thangsuk phoo yoo beuanglang khwameuchao haeng siwika" [Interview with Wilasini–Wichian Thangsuk: The man behind the scandal of Siwika], *Matichon Weekend* 13:687 (October 22, 1993), pp. 70–71.

5. *Lookjin*, a Thai word literally meaning "Chinese descendants," is used here to denote people of Chinese blood who were born in Siam.

6. For more on the cultural-political significance of this television series, see the article "Lae lod lai mangkorn" in my *Lae lod lai mangkorn: Ruam Khokhian waduai khwampenjin nai siam* [Looking through the dragon design: Selected writings on Chineseness in Siam] (Bangkok: Kobfai's Publishing Work, 1994), pp. 13–18. When this article first appeared in *Phoojadkan Daily* (September 24, 1992, p. 17), it received keener attention and more favorable responses from a wider readership than usual and prompted a lively debate in the paper.

7. My use of "official nationalism" follows that of Benedict Anderson in chapter 6 of his *Imagined Communities: Reflections on the Origin and Spread of Nationalism* (London: Verso, 1991), which refers to "an anticipatory strategy adopted by dominant groups which are threatened with marginalization or exclusion from an emerging nationally-imagined community," "a means for combining naturalization with retention of dynastic power," and "a willed merger of nation and dynastic empire" (pp. 86, 101).

8. The following analysis of Thai official nationalism draws on my article "Pigtail: A Pre-History of Chineseness in Siam," *Sojourn* 7:1 (February 1992), pp. 95–122; Chai-anan Samudavanija, "State-Identity Creation, State-Building and Civil Society," in Craig J. Reynolds, ed., *National Identity and Its Defenders: Thailand, 1939– 1989* (Clayton, Victoria: Centre of Southeast Asian Studies, Monash University, 1991), pp. 59–85; Somkiat Wantana, "Song satawas khong rat lae prawattisatniphon thai" [Two centuries of the Thai state and historiography], *Thammasat University Journal* 13 (September 1984), pp. 152–71.

9. The term *interpellé* is derived from Louis Althusser's concept of "ideological interpellation." It denotes the process of subjection of the self and/or formation of subjectivity through ideologically addressing someone as a member of a particular category of people. See his "Ideology and Ideological State Apparatuses," in *Lenin and Philosophy and Other Essays* (London: New Left Books, 1971), pp. 121–73.

10. It is at this point that Chai-anan Samudavanija's incisive indictment of Thai official nationalism reaches its critical ceiling and loses its bite. Whereas he has no qualms about tearing to shreds Field Marshal Plaek's later monoethnic and statist version of Thai nationalism, he remains conspicuously silent about the openly negative, strongly anti-Chinese and hence primarily racist nature of its forerunner, King Vajiravudh's royalist nationalism. This consistent blind spot in Chai-anan's writings about the Chakri monarchs distinguishes his liberal conservative politics from that of, say, social critic Sulak Sivaraksa.

11. Asvabahu (King Vajiravudh), *Phuak yew haeng booraphathis lae meuang thai jong teun thoed phrom duai lai phra ratchahat khamplae phasa angklis* [The Jews of the Orient, and Wake up, Siam, with English translation in the king's handwriting] (Bangkok: King Vajiravudh Memorial Foundation, 1985), pp. 72–120.

12. J. S. Furnivall, *Colonial Policy and Practice* (London: Cambridge University Press, 1948).

13. Asvabahu, *Phuak yew,* p. 97, 113. Emphasis in original.

14. The term "uncommunity," obviously, is a play on Benedict Anderson's pivotal concept in his influential *Imagined Communities.* In addition, I use the word "imagining" here because the objective existence of such an uncommunity has never been conclusively proven, and it also runs completely counter to my childhood experience. On a narrow lane linking Yaowaraj and Jaroenkrung roads in the middle of

Bangkok Chinatown, there used to be a movie house called, outlandishly, "Texas," which my mother and I attended frequently. Totally unrelated to its namesake in the United States, it showed exclusively Indian movies dubbed in Thai. Its regular audience consisted mostly of Chinese, with some Indians and Thais, who all enjoyed themselves and applauded, laughed, and cried together peacefully and harmoniously for many years.

15. My translation. An alternative, semiofficial version is that of Mr. Phairoj Kesmankij, which reads: "Thailand, cradle of Thais wherever they may be. The homeland of our people, the whole land is the land of the Thais." Quoted in Montri Tramot, "Prawat phleng sansern phrabarami lae phleng chat" [The history of the royal anthem of Thailand and the Thai national anthem], *Sinlapakorn* 16:2 (July 1972), p. 93.

16. Asvabahu (King Vajiravudh), "Khwampenchat doi thaejing" [Real nationhood], *Pakinnakakhadi* [Miscellanies] (Bangkok: Khlangwitthaya Press, 1975), pp. 241–47. He "decreed" that "in order to determine someone's real nationality, one must consider to whom he pays his allegiance. If he pays his allegiance to the King of Siam, then he is a real Thai."

17. Prince Damrongrachanuphap, "Laksana kanpokkhrong prathes siam tae boran" [The character of the administration of ancient Siam], (Creation Volume of Mr Dao Buphawes, Rasbamrung Temple, Chon Buri, December 1, 1968), pp. 5–8.

18. Thaemsuk Numnon, "Meuangthai yuk cheua phoonam" [Thailand in the believe-the-leader age], *Thammasat University Journal* 6:1 (June–September 1976), pp. 144–45.

19. The Thai state's subjection of the urban Chinese middle and working classes to statist and clientelist political culture comes out clearly in the childhood experiences of many *lookjin* who grew up under the governments of Field Marshal Plaek Phibunsongkhram and Sarit Thanarat (1948–63). The late Yutthaphong Phoorisamban (1948–89), alias Rawi Domephrajan, a famous and fiery radical poet of the October 14, 1973, uprising, was a Hainanese *lookjin* who spent his childhood in the northern province of Phitsanulok under the Plaek and Sarit regimes. In the only lengthy interview he ever gave in Thai, shortly before his untimely death from cancer, he discussed in detail his early ardent Thai nationalist and anti-Chinese feelings, his unfulfilled wish to join the army, his love of peasant culture, and his aversion to the mercantile character and habits.

20. This point is succinctly formulated by Chai-anan Samudavanija in "State-Identity," pp. 67–68.

21. Asvabahu, *Phuak yew*, p. 86.

22. King Vajiravudh, "Rai-ngan kanprachum paliment siam" [Proceedings of the Siamese parliament's meeting], in Chai-anan Samudavanija and Khattiya Kannasut, eds., *Ekkasan kanmeuang kanpokkhrong thai (ph.s. 2417–2477)* [Documents of Thai

politics and government (B.E. 2417–2477)] (Bangkok: Siamese Studies Institute, Social Science Association of Thailand, 1989), pp. 150–55.

23. Quoted in Benjamin A. Batson, *The End of Absolute Monarchy in Siam* (Singapore: Oxford University Press, 1986), pp. 303–304. I am indebted to Dr. Batson for unearthing this revealing document from the Damrong papers.

24. Owing to the deliberate and consistent policy of successive Siamese monarchs of the Chakri dynasty since the early nineteenth century of encouraging Chinese coolies to immigrate en masse into the kingdom to satisfy the growing demand for wage—as against corvée—labor on the part of the Siamese absolutist state and its burgeoning market economy, there developed an ethnic division of labor in Siam in which Chinese were primarily merchants, artisan-craftsmen, and laborers, whereas Thais worked mainly in government and agriculture. See G. William Skinner, *Chinese Society in Thailand: An Analytical History* (Ithaca, New York: Cornell University Press, 1957), pp. 91–98, 117–18, 300–306.

25. Quoted in Suwinai Paranawaliai, *Borisat yipun kab kanpennik khong prathesthai* [Japanese corporations and Thailand's NICdom] (Bangkok: Faculty of Economics, Thammasat University, 1989), pp. 27, 29, my translation. Critical analyses of the growing class and sectoral disparities resulting from the unbalanced socioeconomic development are voluminous. The more political among them are Saneh Chamarik, "Problems of Development in Thai Political Setting," in *Democracy and Development: A Cultural Perspective* (Bangkok: Local Development Institute, 1993), pp. 219–67; and Chermsak Pinthong, "Prathesthai: kanphatthana thi khad khwamsomdul lae pentham" [Policy impact on rural incomes and poverty in Thailand: The case of inequitable growth], *Saranom* 47 (February 10, 1993), pp. 65–91. As for the latest figures on the distribution of income in the country, the governor of the Central Bank of Thailand, Vijit Supinit, reported recently that the average revenue per head of workers in Bangkok and its environs was 7.7 times that in the northeast, 5 times that in the north, 3.7 times that in the south, and 2.6 times that in the central area. "Central Bank Urges Economic Restructure," *Bangkok Post* (September 7, 1993), p. 21.

26. For example, several ennobled and commoner Chinese were among the major shareholders (three out of nine) and executive board members (two out of seven) of the Siam Commercial Bank, in which the Privy Purse held a 10 percent interest. The bank survived two financial crises caused by business slumps, panic among depositors, and massive embezzlement during the reign of King Vajiravudh, owing to generous support from the Privy Purse. See Sungsidh Piriyarangsan, *Thunniyom khunnang thai (Ph.S. 2475–2503* [Thai bureaucratic capitalism (B.E. 2475–2503)] (Bangkok: Chulalongkorn University Social Research Institute, 1983), pp. 55–61.

27. I say "economic policy" advisedly. The preference for Chinese is evident in the following excerpt from a letter from Chaophraya Yomaraj, then the minister of the capital (Nakhornban) to King Vajiravudh, dated March 1, 1916, in which he com-

mented on the economic value of the Chinese immigrant population in Siam: "The Kingdom of Siam is large, but her population is small, not to mention how lazy the people are. Without importing foreigners into the country, the population will not grow quickly enough, and consequently neither will the revenue. To develop the country, in both its military and its civilian terms, requires a great deal of public funds. If the revenue development does not progress at the same pace, development of the country will slow down accordingly and fail to catch up with the times. . . . To take a nearby example, the Privy Purse is now earning over 4,000 baht a month from its bazaar at Nakhon Pathom, and the money is from the Chinese vegetable growers. Without them, the bazaar would be left in ruins, not to mention the loss of the rent. As a matter of fact, if there were fewer Chinese in Bangkok, the rent income from the row houses would also decrease." Quoted in Seksan Prasertkul, "The Transformation of the Thai State and Economic Change" (Ph.D. dissertation, Department of Government, Cornell University, 1989), pp. 281–82, note 5p29133.

As it turned out, much more than rent from vegetables and row houses was at stake with regard to the Chinese "golden-egg-laying geese." According to data relating to the Siamese government's revenue from 1894 to 1902, the cumulative percentage of state revenues coming from Chinese-population-based taxes on opium, gambling, liquor, and the lottery amounted to 46.43 percent throughout the period. See Benedict Anderson, "Studies of the Thai State: The State of Thai Studies," in Eliezer B. Ayal, ed., *The State of Thai Studies: Analyses of Knowledge, Approaches, and Prospects in Anthropology, Art History, Economics, History, and Political Science* (Athens, Ohio: Ohio University, Center for International Studies, Southeast Asia Program, 1979), pp. 212, 221–23.

28. In 1923, for example, in response to King Vajiravudh's clarion call for greater participation by the Thais in "alien"-monopolized business activities, in his "Wake Up, Siam" essay, two Thai investors asked the king for a teak forest concession in Tak province. Much to the Thai patriots' dismay, the king decided to grant the concession to a Chinese firm instead. On top of that, it turned out that the Chinese owners of the firm were not even Thai citizens at the time, but French subjects. See Seksan Prasertkul, "The Transformation of the Thai State," p. 282n134.

29. Sungsidh's meticulously researched *Thunniyom* is the pioneering work and still the best on this issue. See especially chapters 3 and 4.

30. A *gongtek* rite is a Chinese religious rite for the dead in which paper miniatures of personal belongings, luxuries, money, mansions, livestock, vehicles, and even servants are burned so that they may be at the disposal of the dead in the hereafter.

31. The king's entire will was published in Prayut Sitthiphan, *Phramaha-thirarajjao* [King Vajiravudh] (Bangkok: Siam Press, 1972), pp. 414–41.

32. These notions are borrowed from Göran Therborn, *What Does the Ruling Class Do When It Rules?* (London: Verso, 1980), pp. 176–79, and from Anthony

Giddens's theory of structuration in his *Central Problems in Social Theory: Action, Structure, and Contradiction in Social Analysis* (Berkeley: University of California Press, 1979).

33. For details, see Richard J. Coughlin, *Double Identity: The Chinese in Modern Thailand* (Hong Kong: Hong Kong University Press, 1960), chapters 7–8. Currently, whereas state restrictions on Chinese education were abolished recently by the liberal Anand Panyarachum government, and there is a better chance for Thaified *lookjin* to get into the armed forces' officer corps, the restrictions on candidacy rights of a *lookjin* of alien parentage, in effect since 1933, still stand. To be qualified to run in a parliamentary election, he or she must have completed a secondary or university education. This regulation automatically excludes, among others, four of my own younger brothers from ever becoming a member of parliament, or a prime minister, for that matter. See Article 105 of the Constitution of the Kingdom of Thailand, B.E. 2534 and its B.E. 2535 Amendment, as well as Article 19 of the Election of Members of the House of Representatives Act, B.E. 2522 and its B.E. 2535 Amendment.

34. The following accounts of Khow Tongmong and Chou Shoulim are based on my "Commodifying Marxism: The Formation of Modern Thai Radical Culture, 1927–1958" (Ph.D. dissertation, Cornell University, 1992). The biographical profile of Khow Tongmong is based on "Prasit kanjanawat," *Phoonam Thurakij* 3:26 (February 1989), pp. 15–64. Biographical data on Chou Shoulim are drawn from interviews with, and memoirs of, some of his former comrades and friends, as well as a few secondary sources that made use of government documents on communist activities of the period, especially Suwadee Charoenphong, "Bot thi 5: Patikiriya khong ratthabal phrabatsomiej phrapokklaojaoyoohua to kankhleuanwai thang khwam-khid sangkhomniyom khommunit (Ph.S. 2468–2475)" [Chapter 5: The reaction of King Prajadhipok's government to the communist-socialist ideological movement, 1925–1932 a.d.], in Chai-anan Samudavanija and Suwadee Charoenphong, eds., *Kanmeuang-kanpokkhrong thai samai mai: Ruam nganwijai thang prawattisat lae ratthasat* [Modern Thai politics and government: A collection of research in history and political science] (Bangkok: Chulalongkorn University, 1979), and Thongchai Phuengkanthai, "Latthi khommunit lae nayobai totan khong ratthabal thai Ph.S. 2468–2500" [Communism in Thailand and government policy against communism, a.d. 1925–57] (M.A. thesis, Department of History, Graduate School, Chulalongkorn University, 1978).

35. Skinner, *Chinese Society,* pp. 159, 169. Skinner transliterated the name of the school as "Hsin-min."

36. Skinner, *Chinese Society,* pp. 267, 269.

37. Royal Thai Government, Department of Commercial Registration, Ministry of Commerce, "Rungnakhorn Company Limited," Registration Profile File no. 2349 (n.d.).

38. This according to Mr. Phin Bua-on, who worked closely with Chou Shoulim in the Thai communist movement during the late 1950s. From a personal interview with Phin Bua-on on his life and the history of the Thai communist movement, conducted by Somsak Jiamthirasakul, Bangkok, July 31, 1985.

39. Suwadee, "Patikiriya," pp. 315, 318, 332, 349; Thongchai, "Latthi khommunit," pp. 115–19, 121.

40. *Nangseu krab bangkhomthul khong kromphra nakhornsawanworaphinit* [Report to His Majesty from Prince Boriphat] (439/125116, January 6, 1930), quoted in Suwadee, "Patikiriya," p. 318.

41. Thongchai, "Latthi khommunit," p. 119.

42. The ensuing account of Chou Shoulim's life in prison is drawn from Leuan Saraphaiwanich (Captain Phraya Saraphaiphiphat), *Fan rai khong khaphajao* [My nightmare] (Bangkok: Bannakhan Press, 1959); Phimphawal Sethaputra, *Chiwaprawat kanthamphotjananukrom angklis-thai thai-angklis khong so sethaputra* [So Sethaputra and the making of his English-Thai, Thai-English dictionary: A biography] (Bangkok: Phimphawal Sethaputra, 1971); M. R. Nimitmongkhol Nawarat, "Chiwit haeng kankabot song khrang" [Victim of the two political purges], in *Meuangnimit lae chiwit haeng kankabot song khrang* [The sight of the future Siam and the victim of the two political purges] (Bangkok: Aksornsamphan Press, 1970); and Phayap Rojjanawiphat, *Yuk thamil* [Evil age] (Bangkok: Anthai Press, 1989). For a general, official history of Bangkhwang Penitentiary, see Somphop Jantharaprapha et al., *Prawat kanrajthan 200 pi* [200 years of history of the penitentiary] (Bangkok: Department of the Penitentiary, Ministry of the Interior, 1982), pp. 372–82.

43. For a general account of the Bowaradej rebellion, see Chaiwat Yonpiam, *Fan rai khong meuang thai* [Thailand's nightmare] (Bangkok: Chaophraya Press, 1985).

44. Leuan, *Fan rai,* pp. 34–36, 125–27, 155–56; Phayap, *Yuk thamil,* p. 63; Phimphawal, *Chiwaprawat so,* p. 170; Nimitmongkhol, "Chiwit," pp. 330–33, 336–37, 441.

45. Leuan, *Fan rai,* pp. 100–102, 149–58, 180, 185, 302; Phimphawal, *Chiwaprawat so,* p. 180.

46. Leuan, *Fan rai,* pp. 153–54; Phimphawal, *Chiwaprawat so,* pp. 168–69.

47. Leuan, *Fan rai,* pp. 153–54, 180–81, 301.

48. Leuan, *Fan rai,* pp. 154–58, 180–82, 195–96.

49. Pho. Meuangchomphoo (Udom Sisuwan), *Soo samoraphoom phoophan [phrom phak phanuak] pai meuang hang* [To the Phoophan battlefront, with an appendix: To the hang town] (Bangkok: Matichon Press, 1987), p. 210. Udom, another leader of the Thai Communist party and a close colleague of Chou Shoulim, was in charge of the party's publication department during the 1950s.

50. Vajiravudh, *Pakinnakakhadi,* pp. 79–94.

51. Leuan, *Fan rai,* p. 156; Phin, interview, July 31, 1985; Pho. Meuangchomphoo,

Soo samoraphoom, pp. 21, 46–49, 51–52, 132–33, 135, 141; Udom Sisuwan, personal interview on communism and literature in Thailand, conducted by Craig J. Reynolds, Bangkok, January 19, 1984.

52. One cannot stress strongly enough the political significance of clear Thai speech for recruitment into the Thai elite, whether "reactionary" or "revolutionary." Even today one can still (over)hear complaints, in both public and private, about the inability of, say, the rector of Thammasat University, the chairman of the board of directors of Bangkok Bank, or the president of the National Assembly to speak Thai clearly. The extent to which some *lookjin* elites are willing to go to confirm their Thainess is amazing. For example, a leading Chinese business tycoon was alleged to have had his Chinese-sounding name, Wan Sanseu, changed expediently to the Thai-sounding Van Chanseu once he was elected president of the Senate and hence ex officio president of the National Assembly. True or not, the allegation obviously upset him—so much so that whenever the opportunity arose, he reiterated his correct "Thai" name and explained its meaning to the Thai public in the following manner: "Van" = kind, "Chan" = steep, "Seu" = honest, therefore "Van Chanseu" = the kind of person with a high degree of honesty, QED! See Bunchai Jaiyen, *Ruai baeb jaosua 1* [Rich-tycoon style, volume 1] (Bangkok: Bunchai Press, 1990), p. 78.

53. For a Chinese of the Teochiu dialect group (which has been predominant among Chinese in Thailand), his inability to speak Thai clearly and articulately ("phood thai mai chad" in Thai) has a peculiar characteristic typical of all Teochius: the inherent absence of certain consonants (e.g., *d* and *r*) and vowels (e.g., *-euan, -n, -m*) from their original Teochiu speech and hence their replacement by other consonants (e.g., *l* for *d* and *r*) and vowels (e.g., *-ian* for *-euan; -ng* for *-n* and *-m*) in Thai speech.

54. Roughly speaking, the middle class in Thailand—broadly defined to include professionals, technicians, administrators, managers, businessmen, merchants, shopkeepers, clerks, and skilled salaried workers in both the private and public sectors—numbered around 900,000 in 1950, 1.8 million in 1970, and nearly 5 million out of a total population of over 54.5 million in 1991. See my *Lae lod lai mangkorn,* pp. 69–70; Benedict Anderson, "Withdrawal Symptoms: Social and Cultural Aspects of the October 6 Coup," *Bulletin of Concerned Asian Scholars* 9:3 (July–September 1977), p. 16. As for the Chinese in Thailand, one recent source estimates that they account for 10.5 percent of the total population; see Charles F. Keyes, *Thailand: Buddhist Kingdom as Modern Nation-State* (Bangkok: Editions Duang Kamol, 1989), p. 16. Although no precise figure is available, there is no doubt that the Chinese are considerably overrepresented in the middle-class population.

55. This outline of the new middle-class imagined community draws upon recent writings by Professor Nidhi Aeusrivongse, the most perceptive observer of and commentator on Thai nationalism and middle-class political culture. See his

"Chatniyom nai khabuankan prachathipatai" [Nationalism in the democratic movement], *Sinlapa-Wathanatham Monthly Magazine* 13:11 (September 1992), pp. 180–201; "Watthanatham khong khon chan klang thai" [The culture of the Thai middle class], *Thammasat University Journal* 19:1 (1993), pp. 31–41; "Kwampenthai nai khosana tivi" [Thainess in TV ads], *Phoojadkan Daily,* June 14, 1993, p. 33; "Latthiphithi sadej pho ro 5" [The cult of Rama V], *Sinlapa-Wathanatham Monthly Magazine* 14:10 (August 1993), pp. 76–98. Also see the debate on the current renaissance of Chinese culture in Thailand in Kasian Tejapira, Seksan Prasertkul, and Suphalak Kanjanakhundi, "Wiwatha: Lod lai mangkorn" [Debate on "Through the dragon design"], *Journal of Political Science* 18:2 (October 1992), pp. 101–27.

56. "Wo shi zhong guo ren" was composed by Liu Jia-chang and sung by Zhang Mingmian in 1988. See cassette-tape jacket information, *Wo shi zhong guo ren* [I am a Chinaman], Zhang Mingmian (Dragon Cassette, 1988, D-398).

57. The "Lod lai mangkorn" title song was composed by Suwinai Sornkhamkaew, arranged by Nukul Kiatklang, and sung by Prawit Preuang-aksorn in 1992. See the cassette-tape jacket information, *Teng neung chud lod lad mangkorn* [The favorite: Through the dragon design], Prawit Preuang-aksorn, et al. (Onpa Stereo, 1993, S.920907).

4 / "Pride and Prejudice" or "Sense and Sensibility"?

How Reasonable Was Anti-Semitism in Vienna, 1880–1939?

STEVEN BELLER

Considering what has happened in the twentieth century, it is more than understandable that the relationship between nationalism and Jews should generally be viewed as one between anti-Semites and their victims or targets. The Holocaust has meant that the Jewish role in modern European history has been teleologically construed as that of victim, of target, because that is what Jews ended up being. The focus on anti-Semitism has been so overwhelming in modern historiography that it, and not the history of the Jews themselves, is what is taught concerning Jews in modern Europe.

Because anti-Semitism and its consequences have proved to be among the most dangerous enemies of the liberal state, this focus is perhaps to be expected. In some instances, however, it has led writers to claim that it is not at all necessary to study the history of actual Jews to have a full and complete understanding of the history of anti-Semitism, and hence an understanding of the importance of the Jewish presence in Europe. All that is necessary, according to this sort of argument, is the internal analysis of the prejudice and its roots in the discursively anti-Semitic society. References to the externalities involved, especially to the position and behavior of the object of prejudice, European Jewry, are deemed unnecessary.[1]

Sources of the prejudice within the core society are sometimes allowed by this argument. Economic crisis can be accepted as a factor in bringing on an "attack" of anti-Semitism, and the usefulness of anti-Semitic prejudice as a tool of social control is often admitted. What is excluded from this sort of approach is any dependence of anti-Semitic prejudice on the actual role of Jews as a minority within the relevant (usually German) society. The causes and nature of anti-Semitism are held to lie so deep as to be beyond the influence of the reality of the Jewish presence.

Closely associated with this view of anti-Semitism is the widespread tendency to understand the phenomenon through the metaphor of disease.[2] There is a huge irony here, which, I suspect, is not accidental, for one of the most popular—and dangerous—ways in which anti-Semites understood the so-called Jewish question was through similar metaphors of disease. They spoke in terms of the Jewish "corruption" and "infection" of Christian-Aryan society and the need for a *cordon sanitaire* to protect native populations from the "degenerate" and "polluting" influence of Jews. In eerily similar language, anti-Semitism has been described as "endemic" to nineteenth-century Viennese society (I know, I wrote it).[3] It has "incubation periods," after which it spreads in "epidemics" that "infect" whole populations. By this seemingly unstoppable natural process, the scourge of anti-Semitism advances so that in times of economic and social distress, when a society's "immunity" is low, it falls prey to the plague in its most "virulent" form: racial anti-Semitism and events such as the Holocaust.

Usually the virus is traced back to its injection into the body of the early church, and it is the virus's deep-rootedness in the Christian heritage that is the source of the disease.[4] The illness is then exacerbated and made fatal by the perils of modernization and secularization and the crises that ensue. Europe succumbs to the virus almost despite itself, and in the horrible dialectic that leads to Europe's moral catastrophe the actual Jews play merely the role of horrified spectators, victims, and, ultimately, statistics.

It is "the Jew," and not the Jews, who plays a role in the nosology of anti-Semitism. It is the stereotype of what the anti-Semites took the Jews to be, not what their actual experience of Jews was, that is held to be the significant thing, because the interest is in diagnosing a pathological condition, not in explaining a historical ideology or political movement. In this view of anti-Semitism, "the Jew" is thus only target, and the Jews only victims. Indeed, the Jews themselves become "infected" by the syndrome, because they end up as victims of the double bind of self-hatred.[5] In this view everyone is part of a pathological situation because everyone is infected with the irrational prejudice of anti-Semitism, and the only way of dealing with it is through the equally irrational method of projection. Ultimately, even the non-Jews are not perpetrators but victims of this seeming force of nature, in which crazy people infect others with their madness and lead the whole of society to an irrational Armageddon. The remedy is to "immunize" society against its ever happening again, by teaching them that anti-Semitism is utterly mad in all its aspects, that it is based totally on lies and illusions, and that whatever the anti-Semites said about Jews being different from everyone else was by definition wrong, "irrational."

I do not deny that much of the content of the disease theory of anti-

Semitism is true. There was an anti-Jewish prejudice in Europe that did stem from the Christian heritage and was transferred into secularized society and culture. It was the basis for what came to be known as anti-Semitism. What I find unhelpful is the reliance on the dubious metaphor of disease, which makes anti-Semitism—and prejudice itself—a reified force of nature, operating on the irrational plane beyond any rational control.

It is much nearer the mark, I believe, to see anti-Semitism as the product of human beings who had their own motives—and hence reasons—for excluding Jews from the realm of the acceptable and who were able to convince others of the sense of their criticism of Jews because of the historical and social situation of those others and that of the Jews themselves.[6] In other words, what often decided whether anti-Semitism made sense or not depended on the presence of Jews in society and the role they played within it. Because of the power of the Christian heritage in European society, it would be wrong to insist that Jews always have to be present to have anti-Semitism; my point is that it helps. Anti-Semitism as a historical movement was clearly based on the cultural heritage of prejudice, but the role of Jews in Central Europe played a large role too.

In this essay I illustrate the relationship between Jews and anti-Semitism in Central Europe by considering two antinomies from the titles of novels by Jane Austen: *Pride and Prejudice* and *Sense and Sensibility*.[7] This might appear arbitrary and dilettantish, but the two novels do deal with issues at the heart of Jewish–non-Jewish relations in the modern era. *Pride and Prejudice* is a story about the experiences of strangers, and *Sense and Sensibility* is about the social consequences of the conflict between rationalism and romanticism. Both themes are central to my purpose, and this is not so surprising, because Jane Austen was writing at the turn of the nineteenth century when the problematic of Jewish emancipation and integration was crystallizing in both Western and Central Europe.

The relevance of the antinomies of *Pride and Prejudice* to the subject is self-evident. The "disease" school provides more than ample evidence to show that anti-Semitic prejudice abounded in nineteenth-century Central European discourse. Simply stating that there was prejudice, however, and tracing its subsequent development, is only part of the answer. It may have been a necessary cause, but it was not a sufficient cause of the success of political anti-Semitism in Vienna from the 1890s onward.

The role of prejudice or stereotyping in relations between groups, between "us" and "them," is too well worked over to need much discussion here. What is sometimes forgotten in the cataloguing of the terrible injustices made possible by prejudice is that it will always be with us, for it plays a necessary, indeed vital, role in group relations. We all take a preconceived notion of some sort to every encounter we have with others, whether of "our" group or not. What matters is whether the prejudice—literally, "judgment before"—is near enough the mark to be useful, or at least open to adaptation, or whether we are capable of dispensing with it and adopting a new way of understanding the person in front of us, or that person's group.

Pride and Prejudice's first title was "First Impressions," and an underlying theme of the novel is the necessity of first impressions, even if they are misleading.[8] They plainly can be, as the novel shows, and much of the plot consists of the heroine's struggles to overcome her initial, mistaken impressions of Fitzwilliam Darcy. This being a novel written by a sensible author in empirical England in the early years of the age of improvement, Elizabeth does overcome her prejudice, because her mind is open to counterargument and the factual evidence. Why, then, did something similar not occur in Austria, particularly in Vienna?

One argument would be that anti-Jewish prejudice was so deep-rooted that no amount of evidence to the contrary would have shaken it. The double-bind argument has some validity. The more Jews became like non-Jews, the more particular and far-reaching became the standards demanded of them. The finish line kept moving, and the Jewish hare never could catch up to the anti-Semitic tortoise, in the mind of the anti-Semite. And Christian-based prejudice against Jews was indeed deep. The Jews were the murderers of Christ, the Jew was the sexual co-conspirator with woman, he was a ritual murderer of Christian virgins. Such ideas went back to the early church and were still alive in the Central Europe of 1900, as the Hilsner affair shows.[9]

Added to this was the history of Jews in the corporate, feudal society of premodern and early modern Europe. Jews had been separate and different; they had served only particular functions in the economy, as moneylenders and merchants in particular trades, because Christians should not perform such immoral services and Jews, as deniers of Christ, should not be allowed to perform any others. The connection between Jews and money was thus a result of prejudice that had, however, resulted in a socioeconomic reality whereby finance, especially the finances of many Central European states, was often "in Jewish hands," to use a loaded phrase.[10] This situation could have been interpreted in terms of Jewish financiers' making possible some of the great Habsburg military victories of the late seventeenth century by their organizing and financing of military supplies, as Samuel Oppenheimer did, but usually it was seen simply as the potential threat of Jewish enslavement of the Christian monarch and state.[11]

The combination of the cultural baggage of Christianity and the historical experience of Jews in premodern society made possible the identification of "the Jew" with a much larger *Feindbild* (enemy image) that involved "nihilism" (secular rationalism), "money" (capitalism and the modern economy), and "corruption" (that is, the mere fact of being other in a society with pretensions to harmony and wholeness disrupts and hence corrupts it). The potential for "the Jew" to become a symbol and scapegoat for all that was felt to be wrong with modernizing Europe was plainly there and did not have to have much to do with actual Jews. But the question remains why this potential way of looking at the world became the dominant theme of political and social debate in Vienna at the end of the nineteenth century.

It was not the dominant tendency in all of Central Europe. Even in many sectors of Viennese non-Jewish society, the "discourse" of anti-Semitism, indeed racial anti-Semitism, though present, did not translate into social or political action. In Vienna, for instance, there was debate in the medical profession about the racial aspects of Jewish as opposed to Aryan males.[12] Yet this did not prevent a majority of the Vienna University medical faculty from being of Jewish descent.[13] In Prague, as Gary Cohen has shown, the German liberal political elite remained hostile to anti-Semitism and true to its liberal principle of acceptance of German Jews in the city, even though their counterparts in most of the rest of the Habsburg monarchy went over to the anti-Semitic camp.[14] In Budapest, similarly, the Magyar elite did not allow anti-Semitism any breathing room in the 1880s, and, with some ups and downs, the Jewish bourgeoisie enjoyed good relations with the Magyar elite—until 1918.[15] If anti-Semitism was an endemic prejudice throughout Central Europe, and indeed all of Europe, why did it take off only in particular places at particular times? Why not among Prague Germans, or in Magyar Budapest? Why Vienna?

If prejudice is only part of any answer, what about pride? The most obvious way in which pride has played a role in the debate over the causes of anti-Semitism is in the assertion, or accusation, by contemporaries and some later scholars that the Jews refused to mingle, to give up their Jewish loyalties, their Jewish selves, in order to assimilate fully and "disappear" into the host society. Given that the dominant assumption on which Jewish emancipation was justified was that the Jews would "cease to be Jews" and would become like any other members of their respective societies, the question of pride becomes one of whether Jews did consciously opt to be "humble," to practice "self-denial," and whether they were successful at it.[16]

In the eyes of the irredeemably prejudiced, the double bind always operated, and so it was impossible, a priori, for Jews to "cease to be Jews," because the finish line always shifted. But the irredeemably prejudiced are not interesting. Those who are interesting for us are that part of society who, for long periods of the nineteenth century, especially in the 1860s, seemed to be accepting Jews as fellow citizens, who seemed to be expecting the liberal predictions of the disappearance of any "pernicious" Jewish difference to be borne out, but who seem ultimately to have "succumbed" to prejudice by rejecting liberal claims about both the economy and the Jews. If liberalism's approach had been popular at one point, why was the anti-Semitic prejudice that it had rejected allowed to come back?

One of the reasons was that liberalism itself was shown to have failed large sections of the Austrian populace in the wake of the crash of 1873; it was seen to have betrayed the people's trust in it to produce overnight prosperity.[17] Another reason, however, specific to the "Jewish question," was that the way in which that question had been posed by the liberal camp—for whom success was measured by how far Jews had "ceased to be Jews," how far they had assimilated so as to be no longer a separate and distinct presence—made it far easier for the populace to answer in the negative than in the positive.

Here it was not simply a question of prejudice. The Jews did not disappear as predicted. They stayed together as a religious community in an Austrian state that, despite the constitution, remained de facto a Christian state.[18] Without conversion, Jews found it almost impossible to get on in the bureaucracy or the state-run educational system.[19] This led to severe distortion of the Jewish community's occupational structure, with large social repercussions. In any case, Jews remained a largely distinct socioeconomic community in Vienna. They remained concentrated in commerce and finance, branching out into the "liberal" professions (excluded as they were from the official equivalents).[20] Socially, they remained largely dependent on other Jewish families for their friendships, alliances, and marriage partners.[21] At one point around 1860, there may have been spatial mingling—Jews and Christians living in the same apartment blocks—but there is also evidence that the topological map of Viennese society in the later nineteenth century was one of Christian-Jewish distance rather than proximity.[22] Jews kept to Jews, Christians to Christians, even when they attended the same schools.[23] This seems to have resulted not only from anti-Semitism or Christian exclusivity but also from the Jews' own wish to be among their own kind.

It is also true that many Jewish individuals tried as much as humanly possible to "fit in," not to "stand out," to adapt entirely to prevailing Viennese modes of behavior. Many even converted. Such behavior, though, was not the norm and was often decried by Christians and Jews alike as, in essence, hiding. Jews saw conversion as self-serving cowardice, and Christians doubted whether anything but a superficial change, for career reasons, had taken place.[24]

The bulk of Viennese Jewry did effect a dramatic transformation in the collective "character" or "identity" of their community from the preemancipation, traditional original. The rationale of the emancipation, a quid pro quo whereby Jews' gaining of equal rights was conditional on their self-reformation, was one that the vast majority of Central European Jewry came to accept and act upon. They gave up their previous identity and changed their behavior and many of their practices and values, as both the German and Jewish Enlightenments, *Aufklärung* and *Haskalah,* had demanded. As such, the modernization of Central European Jewry was spectacularly successful.[25] The problem was that the new, modern, enlightened identity was not that of the rest of Viennese society.

This is perhaps not surprising, considering that the new identity was adopted for reasons partly internal to Central European Jewry and was basically a Jewish interpretation of the *German* Enlightenment's version of German culture. This emancipatory identity was supposed to have been compatible with that of Vienna, the seat of the Habsburgs. For a time it actually looked as though this supposition was not far-fetched, when the city was dominated by the German liberal values of Ringstrasse society. With the decline of German liberal hegemony, both political and cultural, in the last decades of the nineteenth century, however, the old, Catholic, Baroque city reasserted itself, and the new Jewish identity did not fit into it at all well. Jews had thus assimilated, had integrated, into a culture and society that existed more in their own minds and among other Jews than it existed in the rest of Viennese society.[26]

While some did their best to take on a completely Viennese identity of Baroque Catholicism, most Jews in Vienna remained wedded to their essentially German liberal identity, disdaining what to them seemed the inferior culture of the Viennese populace. They simply refused to give up on their liberal version of the city, even when the very "Viennese" Christian Socials swept to power on an anti-Semitic platform in 1895. After all, what was the point of giving up your previous Jewish identity if you could not replace it with a better version that preserved the "essence" of Jewish values, only better expressed and articulated in the superior form of German culture— the culture of Goethe, Schiller, and Lessing? In comparison, having to embrace the quasi-pagan world of Baroque hedonism and idolatry was no option at all.[27]

Underlying many Jews' response to the decline of liberalism in Vienna was the assumption, occasionally even stated in public, that the Jews were indeed superior as a group to the rest of Viennese society, especially in their level of education and their basic morality. Sigmund Mayer, a chronicler of Viennese Jewry, expressed this assumption in terms of Jews' having completed their side of the bargain, only to see the rest of society do nothing to improve itself.[28] Moreover, this sense of Jewish superiority, or pride, was in many ways completely justifiable. Jews were better educated, and they were much less liable to commit violent crimes or have illegitimate children. Much of this difference was explicable in terms of occupational structure, as was the higher propensity of Jews to commit fraud (so many Jews were involved in business).[29] Yet such an explanation was itself a reflection that the Jews as a group were, structurally, much more "bourgeois" than non-Jews, with much higher percentages of the self-employed and salaried among them. The vast bulk of non-Jewish Viennese were wage earners; only about a third of Jews were so classed.[30] In material terms Jews might have been poor, but in terms of education, social structure, and self-perception they were, on average, far more bourgeois than the rest of the populace.

The disparity, culturally and socially, between the predominant Jewish identity in Vienna and that of the rest of the populace had strong repercussions in the sphere of high culture. Jewish intellectuals and artists found themselves largely on the liberal or socialist left in Vienna, and much of the criticism of Viennese life at the turn of the century came from Jews. One should not let anti-Semitic claims about the Jewish intellectuals' corrosive attacks on Christian-Aryan Austrian society and values obscure the fact that Jewish writers and artists were indeed critical of many aspects of Viennese life, were not "humble," and refused to "fit in" to Viennese society by keeping quiet.[31] The proper response to the anti-Semites, it seems to me, is to say that these intellectuals were right to be critical. The fact of their refusal to submit to the Habsburg model of a Christian, aestheticized totality, their refusal to disappear on ethical grounds, can nevertheless be seen as a form of pride, and hence a source of friction.[32]

There was, therefore, a genuine cultural tension in the relationship between Vienna and its Jews. On the one hand, Jewish writers and intellectuals saw the superiority of the Jewish outsider's ethical truth over the superficially attractive but morally hollow blandishments of Viennese aesthetic harmony. On the other, many Viennese resented the disturbance by Jewish troublemakers of their cosy Viennese existence, and the Jewish intellectuals' forcing their ideas on them rather than leaving them to their Gemütlichkeit. There was a sort of Jewish "pride" here, and it would be prejudice not to acknowledge these genuine differences. Even so, there is no reason why the existence of these cultural tensions should have led to the Holocaust or even to a success-ful movement of political anti-Semitism. Cultural and ethnic tensions exist in almost any society where there is more than one identifiable group, and yet they do not always lead to the type of ethnically based political and social phenomena represented by Viennese political anti-Semitism.

Perhaps the other antinomy, "Sense and Sensibility," will help. When defined as the contrast between rationalism and irrationalism, the Enlighten-ment and romanticism, then this antinomy is almost as common as "Pride and Prejudice" in discussions of anti-Semitism.

On the one hand, whether one was anti-Semitic or, indeed, philo-Semitic, Jews were often seen as being on the side of rationalism. Anti-Semites tended to see Jews as abstract rationalizers of European traditions and "mystery." They could be attacked from both right and left: from the right because of their rationalist destruction of history and authority, and from the left because of their role in rationalizing economic relations in an ab-stract, "reified" capitalist system. Rationalism and capitalism, united in the concept of the rational actor, were both identified with the Jew and were seen by many as closely linked. The leveling, destructive power of capital and money went hand in hand with the leveling, destructive power of empiricism and utilitarian cultural relativism. Once poetry and pushpin were equatable, then all values could be calculated, and thus everything had a price, could be bought. It was precisely this fear of the demystifying power of modernity that powered romantic anticapitalism, and the identification of the Jew with these processes made a romantic anti-Semitism highly proba-ble, though not inevitable.[33]

On the other hand, from a Jewish perspective, or rather from the perspec-tive of the emancipated and assimilatory Jews, they were human beings like anybody else—or at least they had the potential to become so—and it was therefore highly irrational to exclude them from human society or from the national society by racial or religious arguments. This view, that anti-Semitism was a totally irrational response to the Jewish presence in Europe or to a process of modernization with which Jews were only tangentially associated, is essentially the same as the "prejudice" argument. The meta-phor of disease, when understood as mental disease, assumes the pathologi-cal irrationalism of labeling the Jews as "different."

What is interesting about this antinomy is that the two sides, anti-Semitic and Jewish, were substantially agreed on the main point. Jews were seen as on the side of reason or rationalism, whereas the anti-Semites were either proudly irrationalist or seen as irrational, unreasonable. There was also some basis to this dichotomy. The Jews' emancipation had been based squarely on the Enlightenment and liberalism. The rationale of emancipation had therefore been indeed rationalist, centered on the idea of *Mensch,* the rational, morally autonomous human being, the greatest expression of which was the Kantian intelligible self of the categorical imperative. It was no accident that perhaps the most influential German Jewish commentator on Jewish identity around 1900 was the neo-Kantian Hermann Cohen.[34] In Vienna as well, the power of man to overcome unreason and nature remained an article of faith. None other than Sigmund Freud had displayed in his office an etching of *Oedipus and the Sphinx,* showing Oedipus answering the riddle of Man and thus defeating the half-woman, half-beast of the sphinx.[35]

Nor was this championing of reason something that Jews were always shy of proclaiming. Cohen himself, following the example of Moses Mendelssohn, made it a major principle that Judaism was a rational religion.[36] In the 1860s, when anti-Semitism appeared dead, some Jewish writers had unselfconsciously written of the Jews' role in rationalizing German culture and modernizing the German economy.[37] Adolf Jellinek, the chief preacher in Vienna, claimed that modernity, in its embrace of individualism, was taking on Jewish "qualities" (*Eigentümlichkeiten*) and for that reason should be just to the Jews.[38] Theodor Herzl, for all his dislike of the Viennese Jewish bourgeoisie, thought of Jews (Central European Jewry) as being in the vanguard of modernity; Zionism was to make a modern people the most modern.[39] Jews, as supporters of German liberalism, often joined in attacks on the "irrational" institutions of organized religion, which were deemed to stand in the way of progress. As the "Kulturkampf" in Germany showed, "sense" could easily be the aggressor in the struggle with "sensibility."[40] Although Jews were generally reluctant to support what amounted to an assault on religious liberty in that instance, in Austria they were usually supportive of anticlericalism, even though Judaism could be included among its targets, because it was an ally against the forces of reaction.[41]

It was also evident that the traditional position of Jews in European society made them extraordinarily well placed for the opportunities presented by the new, modernizing economy. Restricted as they had been before, it was clearly in their interest to greet the opening up of the economy created by laissez-faire policies after 1850. Jews *did* go from being peddlers to merchants, court financiers to railroad and industry financiers.[42] If sense and sensibility are seen in terms of markets versus guilds, "Gesellschaft" versus "Gemeinschaft," then Central European Jews were, generally speaking, on the sense side, whereas large parts of the non-Jewish community were left on the other side.[43]

Note here that the Jewish siding with economic "sense" in Vienna led to

Jews being prominent both in the capitalist camp and as leaders of the socialist camp. This idea, often used by anti-Semites, of Jews being on both sides of the economic equation is often cited as evidence of the supreme irrationality of anti-Semitism, for, if Jews were plotting to take over society, why should they be on both sides of the dominant class conflict of modern society? This often-rehearsed argument misses a central point, blinded as it is by the crass Marxist assumption that capitalism and socialism were the only relevant interests in the modern economy and society, the only players that counted.

The real society in Central Europe included very large numbers in the lower middle class, in the *Mittelstand,* who, whether new or old, were threatened by a pincer movement of owners of capital, on one side, and a factory proletariat organized by a "scientific" and hence rationalist Marxist socialism, on the other, with no room for more traditional concerns of religious faith or status. Marxism, one should remember, embraced the modernizing, leveling effect of capitalism. Capitalism and socialism *were* "in league," for they were the two parts of a dialectic of modernization that was indeed eating away at more traditional economic forms. Similarly, that Jews were so prominent in the Viennese socialist leadership was no accident. Many were attracted to socialism precisely because it remained a rationalist movement that admitted Jews as rational human beings. Even if it identified the human being with the proletarian, he or she was still a rational actor, regardless of ethnic descent or customary status.

The fact is that in Vienna at least, Jews were indeed prominent as both capitalists and socialists. Anti-Semitic attacks on Jews as rationalizers of thought, society, and the economy were thus far from being as "irrational" as the capitalist-socialist argument might make it out.

On the other hand, not all anti-Semitic arguments against Jews took the approach that the Jews, or "the Jew," were the vanguard of rationalism. A substantial number of anti-Semites, especially in the radical right intelligentsia, argued the reverse. Eugen Dühring, one of the most prominent racial anti-Semitic ideologues, thought of Jews not as rationalists but as mystics, obsessed with atavistic superstition and ritual and hence unworthy of being part of progressive, scientific, modern German society.[44] Houston Stewart Chamberlain saw Jews as equally backward, as not really autonomous, rational beings. Following Kant, he saw the Jewish God as a source of heteronomous value, unlike the internalized Christian God, the true source of moral autonomy and real human freedom. Judaism for him was a combination of will and materialism, as opposed to belief and reason (*Verstand*); it was a slave religion, not a religion of modern, free beings.[45]

This sort of anti-Semitism led ultimately to the idea that Jews, though rationalists, were really using a lower form of reason, the sort of superficial reasoning behind the leveling tendencies of utilitarianism, "destructive" capitalism, and Marxist, cosmopolitan socialism. Jews, unlike Germans or Aryans, lacked the ability to think as *truly* rational beings and were therefore not *Menschen* but *Untermenschen*. Moreover, the way in which such assertions were "proven" was through the most up-to-date form of authority, scientific evidence, from the most prestigious field of science at the time—Darwinian biology.[46] Cranial measurements and the like fill us with bemusement and horror, yet a great many scientists and intellectuals were convinced that there were substantial racial differences that could be, in theory at least, scientifically researched and demonstrated.[47] Reactionary modernism thus had its counterpart in reactionary scientism—indeed, in a form of reactionary rationalism.[48] If, after all, certain races could be scientifically shown to be inferior, would it not be rational to treat them accordingly? And if eugenics was exploring the possibilities of selective breeding among humans, did this not have implications for the rational policy to be pursued in furthering the mental and bodily hygiene of the human race?

Such thoughts were largely limited to a select group of highly educated, mostly right-wing intellectuals, often in the medical profession. In Vienna, racial anti-Semitism was rather a minority interest, though very strong among university students.[49] "Reactionary rationalism" was more influential outside Vienna than inside it, so let us leave that topic to one side. A related question bears more thinking about: the question of the "rationality" of anti-Semitism in Vienna generally. Put another way: what happens when we reverse the antinomies of *Sense and Sensibility* and talk instead of Jewish sensibility and anti-Semitic sense?

In Austen's *Sense and Sensibility,* the representatives of sensibility are Marianne Dashwood and Willoughby. They court disaster not only because they let their feelings get the better of their sense but also because they allow their perception of reality to be clouded by their wishes and dreams. In other words, like all good romantics, they ignore the limits imposed by society on their conduct, and their neglect of social reality leads to disaster for both. The denouement is the triumph of common sense and society over imagination and the individualist. If the theme of *Sense and Sensibility* is the need for sensibility to recognize the constraints of common sense, of social reality, which group in Vienna was nearer to a proper understanding of, had a better sense of, the social reality in Vienna—Jews or anti-Semites? And who acted more "sensibly"?

On the Jewish side, there was clearly quite a gap between their general assumptions about European society and the reality of Viennese society. The predominant rationale for integration of Central European Jews was, after all, based on accepting Austrian society not for what it was but rather for what it could someday become. At the base of the emancipatory ideology was an idealistic vision of a future age: the educability of all humanity would lead to a humane and tolerant society in which everyone, Jews included, would be judged on their merits and could operate as *Menschen,* not as Jews.[50] Austrian society did not follow this path. Perhaps, in the mid-nineteenth century and the ensuing liberal era that ended in 1879, it was possible to persuade oneself that Viennese society was developing as liberals wished it to. But this was soon to prove an illusion, out of touch with a reality in which traditions and popular culture would prove extremely difficult to dislodge as effective roadblocks to progress and to the realization of the liberal utopia in which Jews were just human beings.

It is doubtful whether Jews were ever "just human beings" to a majority of the Viennese populace, and Jews did not just disappear into Austrian society. Many Jews might persuade themselves that they had assimilated, that they were indistinguishable from the rest of Viennese society, but even then they phrased this belief in contrast to other Jews they knew who were still recognizably Jewish in their behavior and attitudes. When confiding their thoughts to diaries or notebooks, many Jews would admit that the Jews in Vienna were not the same as everyone else, but they carried on their public lives *as if* they and their fellow Jews were so, because that is what they wished to be the case.[51] This could cause us no end of complications in terms of the understanding of self and the matter of Jewish identity, and it leads quickly to questions about Jewish self-hatred—another debate. What is clear is that German and Austrian society did not develop as the original emancipationists, in their idealistic optimism, had envisioned. Its "common sense," the set of rules by which it operated, was not even that of Austen's rather hidebound English society, let alone a liberal utopia, but does that make it less "sensible" in its own terms?

If Jews were still regarded by the rest of Viennese society as "other"—because that society had not developed along the liberal lines predicted, because it still thought and acted according to religious and ethnic, group identifications—it was also true, whether Jews admitted it or not, that Jews had an enormous impact on Viennese society, on its high and even its popular culture, and on the city's economy. The idea of Jewish predominance in many key areas of Viennese life was not merely the paranoid invention of febrile anti-Semitic imagination but was based on a social reality confirmed by a few facts and figures.

Most of the liberal press was either owned, edited, or written by Jews, the *Neue Freie Presse* and the *Neues Wiener Tagblatt* being the two outstanding examples. This was also true of the major cultural periodicals, including Karl Kraus's *Die Fackel*. Most of the influential writers of Vienna around 1900 were of Jewish descent, including Arthur Schnitzler and Richard Beer-Hofmann. Hugo von Hofmannsthal owed his noble surname to his Jewish ancestor Isaak Löw Hofmann, at one time leader of the Viennese Jewish community. Freud's nascent psychoanalytic movement was almost entirely Jewish in personnel. So was the Austromarxist group of socialist theorists, excepting Karl Renner. In music, Jews were also prominent, as composers but even more so as critics, theorists, performers, and librettists. In the plastic arts there was initially only a small Jewish presence among the artists themselves, but a correspondingly large presence among those artists' private patrons. Jews were indeed predominant as the creators and encouragers of the culture we now know as "Vienna 1900," that is to say, the liberal end of Viennese modern high culture.[52]

One main reason for this predominance was the heavy concentration of Jews in the "liberal" sectors of Vienna's socioeconomic structure. I have already alluded to the extraordinarily "bourgeois" character of the Jewish occupational structure there, with its strikingly small proportion of "working-class" Jews (under a third), when compared with the rest of the Viennese populace (over two-thirds). Jewish concentration in certain occupations was also significant. For various historic and structural reasons already alluded to, Jews were concentrated in commerce and banking and the "liberal" professions of law, medicine, and journalism.[53] Jews were thus "fated" to be on the "capitalist" side of any modernization debate, at least in terms of economic interest.

This large concentration in the modern sectors of the economy was matched by a remarkable overrepresentation of Jews in the educational sector. Jews, under 10 percent of the city's population, provided around 30 percent of the city's secondary schoolboys and an even higher percentage among girls receiving secondary education. What this meant, when combined with the previously outlined Jewish concentrations in the economy, for the Jewish presence in the educated part of Vienna's "liberal bourgeoisie" is in many ways remarkable. Based on school records, my calculations show that almost two-thirds of the boys from a "liberal bourgeois" socioeconomic background who received an elite education in Vienna around 1900 were Jewish. This large number seems at least partially to explain the similarly large presence of Jews in the modern high cultural elite.[54] Jewish concentration in certain parts of the occupational, educational, and social structure of the city thus not only gave Jews a markedly different social profile from the rest of society but also made many Jews extremely prominent in significant—one might say "exposed"—parts of Vienna's cultural life. In terms of sheer numbers, the identification between Jews and modernism was not at all fanciful—in Vienna.

Similarly, Jewish concentrations in various economic sectors in Vienna had the result that those sectors came to be seen as "Jewish," and not without some empirical reason. Half of Vienna's doctors were Jewish by religion, let alone by descent. Something over 60 percent of the city's practicing lawyers were Jewish by religion.[55] It is not hard to see why caricatures of "corrupt" physicians or shyster lawyers might have a Jewish physiognomy. In commerce and banking, the most "Jewish" realms, and in certain sectors of industry, textiles, railroads, and brewing, the Jewish presence was remarkably high. In commerce, Jews made up approximately a third of all the self-employed in Vienna in 1910. But the actual figure for the Jewish presence among full-scale merchants (as opposed to more traditional, *mittelständisch* tradesmen) seems to have been much higher. As William McCagg pointed out, most of the officers in the commerce section of the Viennese Chamber of Commerce around 1900 were Jewish or of Jewish descent, the apparent result of a majority of the section's membership's also being Jewish.[56] The officers of the Viennese Stock Exchange were also mostly Jewish, because apparently so were a majority of the members of the exchange. The stereotype of the Jewish stockjobber, however crudely it was drawn, was a reflection, nevertheless, of reality.

In the banks, according to McCagg, the Jewish founders and owners did their best to disguise Jewish control by giving Christian aristocrats and businessmen well-paid positions on the banks' boards, as high-class *Paradegoyim*. Meanwhile, the running of the banks was still in the hands of the right-hand men, almost all Jewish, of the respective banks' founders, similarly almost all Jewish—the most famous case being that of the Rothschilds' Credit Anstalt. The reasons for disguise were fairly obvious, given the anti-Semitic climate and the additional sensitivity caused by the banks' control of large segments of Austrian industry. Yet, McCagg cogently claims, Jewish bankers occupied the key administrative posts in almost every major Austrian bank, and hence Jews still ran the Austrian banking sector.[57]

The Jewish wish not to court trouble, not to "stand out," which this attempt to disguise the real financial situation displays, played right into the hands of anti-Semitic prejudice. After all, were Jews not hiding behind these fronts their actual control of Austrian industry and finance, and hence of Austria? Were they not, behind the scenes, plotting to increase Jewish wealth

and power? The strength of this rhetorical temptation is evidenced by
McCagg himself, who calls this period in the history of Jewish wealth in
Vienna the "manipulative" stage, as if Jews really were manipulating the
Austrian economy to their Jewish advantage.[58] I think this usage unfortu-
nate, for I do not believe these professional bankers were doing anything
other than being bankers, adding value to their investors' investments regardless of ethnic or religious loyalties. In this sense, these were banks, not Jewish
banks. Yet these strategies of disguise say something about the social climate
and also, if McCagg is right, about the huge financial power that the rich
Jews in Viennese high finance did wield.

At this point it is well to remember that there were only a few super-rich
Jews in Vienna, and many Jews who were very poor. Many could send their
children to secondary schools only on scholarships and were too poor to pay
the Jewish community's minimal religious tax.[59] Jews were shorter on average than the rest of the Viennese population, and thus, it is assumed, less
well nourished and poorer.[60] That said, for our purposes in figuring out how
sensible anti-Semitism was in Vienna, such considerations about the bulk of
Viennese Jewry, poor as it might have been, are irrelevant. Much more
relevant is the consideration that a very large proportion of the country's
economic wealth, and a very influential—and controversial—part of the
city's cultural and professional life, was "in Jewish hands." It is in this light,
the light of what could apparently be gained from the Jews if they were
somehow disenfranchised or even expelled, that the question has to be
asked, how "sensible" was anti-Semitism for the Viennese as a political
movement and even as public policy? In this light, the large presence of Jews
in the economic and cultural elite suggests that anti-Semitism could be very
sensible, at least in an immediate perspective, for those lower down the
totem pole or those competing for the goods and services and jobs "in
Jewish hands."

When I speak here of "rational," "sensible," or "reasonable" behavior, I
am not trying to lay claim to some all-embracing "reason." Clearly, if one
believes in a universal Reason that drives history ever forward, then anti-
Semitism is, by definition, irrational, even antirational. Yet it is not too
much, it seems to me, to claim that there are various levels of, and perspectives for, rational action and decision making. Individual decisions can be
eminently reasonable and yet lead to collectively irrational outcomes; any
student of economics or game theory knows this. It is not at all clear, then,
that on an individual or even societal basis anti-Semitism was not a rational
option in the pursuit of self-interest, the classic goal of the rational actor. On
this level of instrumental rationality the question is of self-interest, advan-

tage and disadvantage, costs and benefits. It is not so much Reason as reasons, and common sense, the sense held in common in a particular group or locality, that become our guide to what is "sensible." And it is on that level that the "reasonableness" of Viennese anti-Semitism can be judged: whether hostility to Jews was sensible on the basis of the individual or collective self-interest of the Viennese non-Jewish populace.

It should be recalled that the one period when Jews were relatively well received in Austria was during the liberal era's boom, when liberalism and its Jewish allies (Jews were extremely prominent as successful entrepreneurs and financiers during this period) seemed to a naively optimistic populace to be delivering on the promise of unending prosperity. The crash of 1873 and its aftermath thus had a devastating effect on the Viennese public's confidence in liberalism—and its Jewish allies—because it appeared that liberalism had reneged on its promise and was instead turning on the lower middle classes who made up such a significant proportion of the city's populace. The Viennese had been conned, it seemed; liberalism had failed to deliver, except to one prominent group of beneficiaries—the Jews.[61] The relative decline in the handicrafts sector and the rapid rise of Jews in the professions—the result of the respective socioeconomic positions of Jews and non-Jews in the modernization process—added to this picture, in which Jews "got on" at the expense of non-Jews. The Jewish position in the economy, culture, and society was therefore not to be admired as a result of achievement, but envied, even hated.

What made all this so explosive, though, was the fact that the Jews had never really been accepted as "the same." Even when they had been looked on benevolently, they had been looked on as a group apart. The envy the Viennese felt for rich and successful Jews was thus more an envy of "foreigners" than of "natives."

This response is not at all unique to Central Europe; indeed, it is here that the parallel with the experience of the overseas Chinese in Southeast Asia becomes all too close and all too relevant. The chapters in this volume describe a situation in most Southeast Asian countries in which, apparently without any suspicions of irrationality, overseas Chinese are viewed both as a clearly separate group and one with an economic predominance that exceeds present-day historians' most generous estimates of the parallel economic predominance of Jews in nineteenth- and twentieth-century Central Europe (except perhaps in Hungary). The resulting response from the "native" populaces and political leaderships is, for a historian of Central European Jewry, eerily familiar.

In Malaysia, the combination of separate·identity and economic power has led to policies to "correct" the "unfair" advantages enjoyed by the *comprador* Chinese over the "national bourgeoisie."[62] In other cases, paralleling Vienna in the 1870s and Hungary before the First World War, the response has been one of alliance with the Chinese, the ones "who know about business," for mutual economic benefit. Even in the latter response, however, there is the sense of a utilitarian contract in which one side expects the other to deliver. It is unclear what might happen in either case if the "disadvantages" are not overcome or the large expectations of economic well-being are not met.

The Central European parallel is not encouraging. There, Jewish success, the Jewish occupation of so many high positions in the economy and cultural life, could be tolerated so long as the "natives" could also expect success. But when those expectations were not met, then Jewish success was seen in terms of "natives"—real, *bodenständig* "Viennese"—being denied those positions, that success. An alliance of mutual benefit became a zero-sum game; the "foreigners" could be seen as having failed to deliver their side of the bargain.

Adding to the complications was the fact that there were really very few "natives" in Vienna around 1900. Many Jewish families had been native to Vienna much longer than most non-Jewish Viennese. A large proportion of the Viennese population in 1900 did not even come from German-speaking backgrounds. Up to a quarter, perhaps even a third, of the population was Czech in origin.[63] Everyone was assimilating into the city's culture, not just the Jews. In reality, the Jews were no more "foreigners" than everyone else. Yet, as the geologist and liberal politician Eduard Suess astutely remarked, this fact made anti-Semitism only more powerful and sensible, for it gave it a strong rationale.[64] In a city that was an imperial capital and in which nationalism per se did not operate very efficiently, there was no national identity around which to coalesce. But without any clear title to a "Viennese" identity, without any clear claim to "belong" to their adopted city, non-Jews could at least be sure of one thing—they were not Jewish. One of the most powerful reasons for supporting anti-Semitism in the big city was that it allowed for "negative integration," for defining yourself by identifying what you were not.[65]

It was thus "sensible" to identify Jews as *the* foreigners, and once that was done, it seemed "sensible" to see Jewish possessions as an unfair disadvantaging of "our kind." It was also undoubtedly sensible for a canny politician such as Karl Lueger to identify this sort of logic and exploit it to the utmost. In his hands, anti-Semitism proved a handy and thus sensible tool in the urban politics of Vienna.[66] Jews as "foreigners" could be politically attacked virtually with impunity, given the actually small number of Jewish votes in Vienna, and their apparent economic position made them plausible culprits for Vienna's economic problems, even if this were untrue. Such a strategy was mendacious, and thus immoral, but it was politically sensible and spectacularly successful.

Economic anti-Semitism in its Christian Social, Luegerite form had at least an instrumental rationality. But what about the racial anti-Semitism that is usually associated with the more radical politics of German nationalism? Here again, a racial anti-Semitic approach could make sense, depending on the circumstances. The leadership of the original German nationalist movement in Austria, which had sprung from the left wing of the German Liberals in the 1860s and 1870s, had many Jews in prominent positions. Victor Adler, Seraphin Bondi, and Heinrich Friedjung had been the main writers of the original draft of the Linz Program of 1882, and Friedjung had founded one of the movement's main media outlets. The turn from cultural to racial anti-Semitism can thus be partially explained as a convenient rationale for easing out "Jews" from such plum positions.[67] Racial anti-Semitism was "reasonable" when seen in terms of the self-interest of non-Jewish German nationalists.

The same applies to attempts to exclude Jews from the bureaucracy, from professorships, from student organizations, and so forth. It also helps to explain the attraction of economic boycotts of Jewish firms. In each case, the exclusion or boycott of a Jew meant that a non-Jew, "one of us," stood to gain, whether by keeping his exclusive job or by gaining more customers. Whether the exclusion was on religious or racial grounds could depend on the extent of penetration of the field by Jews. The racial anti-Semitism of many non-Jewish students at Vienna University can at least partially be explained by the competitive threat their Jewish colleagues posed to them in their potential careers as doctors and lawyers. With Jews comprising roughly half of the city's doctors and more of its lawyers in a very tight and competitive market, any form of advantage was to be seized. If a sizable part of the competition could be excluded—or customers lured away—by the argument of racial corruption or racial inferiority, then even this would do.

Comparison with the other Habsburg capitals, Prague and Budapest, is instructive here. In both of the other cities, among Germans in Prague and Magyars in Budapest, anti-Semitism made little sense in group-political terms. In Prague, Germans needed Jews to help keep their cultural and political heads above water in the face of overwhelmingly superior Czech numbers. So, unlike their Sudeten brethren, they did not become anti-Semitic.[68] In Budapest, the Magyar political leadership early on reasoned that the Jews represented both a powerful engine of economic growth, necessary for state power, and a marginal but crucial pocket of pro-Magyar support in a demographic situation where Magyars alone were just under half of the Hungarian kingdom's population.[69] In both instances, therefore, it made sense to be good to Jews, because politically they were useful allies. The result: no serious anti-Semitism before 1914. In Vienna, in terms of building group identity and political coalitions, and in terms of the economic interests of elites and constituencies alike, the reasons for not being anti-Semitic were far outweighed by reasons for being anti-Semitic. It was because anti-Semitism made sense in Vienna that it was so politically successful before 1914.

The proof of the pudding is in the eating. When, in 1934, the Ständestaat was declared, thus ending the period when socialist control of Vienna had ensured a relatively benign situation for Viennese Jewry, one of the first organizations set up was the Vaterlandsfront. With some exceptions, Jews were informally excluded from this organization. Because membership in the front was a prerequisite for promotion or appointment, this exclusion operated as a vehicle to keep Jews out of positions in academia and the professions, especially medicine, a long-term aim of Austrian anti-Semites.[70]

It was in 1938, however, with the *Anschluss,* that the full logic of the "sense" of anti-Semitism was allowed to unfold. Gerhard Botz has shown how much of the logic of the Final Solution itself was implied in the very practical way in which "native" Austrian Nazis and anti-Semites realized the full potential of Austrian economic anti-Semitism.[71] First, Jewish wealth was expropriated, either by the immediate methods of ransacking and looting, in March and then November 1938, or by more deliberate methods later on. Jobs also became free as Jews were sacked from academic and professional posts or their clientele was restricted. All this meant huge gains for individual participants, so bitingly satirized by Helmut Qualtinger's phrase from "Herr Karl": "I' hob' nur an Juden g'führt. I' war ein Opfer"—"I only led out one Jew; I was a victim."[72]

Second, unlike in Germany proper, where Jewish homes had largely been left alone up to this point, the Viennese authorities soon set about solving the pressing problem of a housing shortage at Jewish expense. There were approximately 60,000 apartments occupied by Jews, so Jews were turned out of them and crowded into a much smaller number of apartments. Then a concentration camp was proposed for them. Before it could be built, another solution—shipping the Jews to occupied Poland—was put forward and implemented.[73]

All this, in the Viennese context, made a great deal of policy and political sense. Social policy had to be at someone's expense, so why not at the expense of those who—as a large majority of the populace seemed to agree, or at least not to disagree—did not belong? When economic self-interest is at stake, "foreigners" are rarely given much consideration, and politicians who pay heed to interests other than those of their immediate constituency are often regarded as pitiably misguided. In Vienna in 1938, the "sensible" thing to do was to dispossess the hated and envied Jews and satisfy the demands for redistribution of wealth that way. Maybe not every Jew was a millionaire, but there was a substantial amount to be gleaned from their expropriation and sacking, which satisfied many at minimal cost.

The history of anti-Semitism in Vienna went the way it did not so much because anti-Semitism was an irrational ideology that had "infected" the minds of the non-Jewish populace and made them blind to the unreasonableness of their actions and policies. What happened did so more because there was too little moral *sensibility* of the terrible injustice being done, in either the 1890s or the 1930s. There was too little moral sensibility of the pathos of a universal humanity—of the liberal ideal—to combat successfully the powerful combination of prejudice and "sensible" self-interest that made Vienna the site for such successful and prevalent anti-Semitism.

Anti-Semitism, from our perspective, was wrong, evil. Yet given the benefits that could be seen to accrue in the short-term, politically and economically, and did in fact accrue for many in 1938, it was far from being "irrational" for large swathes of the Viennese population. No matter how much we argue about the objective wealth and influence of Viennese Jews, there was *enough* of a reality behind the anti-Semitic propaganda and mythology to make anti-Semitism pay off. If you were not Jewish, as most of the Viennese populace was not, anti-Semitism could "make sense" in personal and group terms.

Reason alone cannot guarantee virtue, for there is always, in Alexander Herzen's phrase, the potential for "rational evil."[74] Perhaps we should not be too proud to be sensible of that.

NOTES

1. See Sander L. Gilman and Steven T. Katz, "Introduction," in S. Gilman and S. Katz, eds., *Anti-Semitism in Times of Crisis* (New York: New York University Press, 1991), pp. 1–19, especially p. 18; Robert S. Wistrich, *Antisemitism: The Longest Hatred* (New York: Pantheon, 1991), p. xx.

2. See Gilman and Katz, *Anti-Semitism,* p. 15; Wistrich, *Antisemitism,* p. xxii;

Jakob Katz, *From Prejudice to Destruction: Antisemitism 1700–1933* (Cambridge, Massachusetts: Harvard University Press, 1980), especially pp. 245ff.

3. Steven Beller, *Vienna and the Jews, 1867–1938: A Cultural History* (Cambridge: Cambridge University Press, 1989), pp. 188ff. (Mea culpa.)

4. Gilman and Katz, *Anti-Semitism*, pp. 15–18; Wistrich, *Antisemitism*, pp. xx, 13ff.; Katz, *From Prejudice to Destruction*, pp. 13–22.

5. See Sander L. Gilman, *Jewish Self-Hatred: Anti-Semitism and the Hidden Language of the Jews* (Baltimore, Maryland: Johns Hopkins University Press, 1986).

6. See Peter Pulzer, *The Rise of Political Anti-Semitism in Germany and Austria* (London: Peter Halban, 1988, rev. ed.). This remains by far the best guide to the subject matter discussed in what follows. A similar view, concentrating on the interwar period, is that of Bruce F. Pauley, *From Prejudice to Persecution: A History of Austrian Anti-Semitism* (Chapel Hill: University of North Carolina Press, 1992). Also see Ivar Oxaal, "The Jews of Young Hitler's Vienna: Historical and Sociological Aspects," in I. Oxaal et al., eds., *Jews, Antisemitism and Culture in Vienna* (London: Routledge, 1987), pp. 11–38.

7. Jane Austen, *Pride and Prejudice*, edited by Tony Tanner (Harmondsworth: Penguin, 1972); Jane Austen, *Sense and Sensibility*, edited by Tony Tanner (Harmondsworth: Penguin, 1969).

8. See Tanner's "Introduction" in Austen, *Pride and Prejudice*, pp. 9ff.

9. See the chapter by Hillel Kieval in this volume; also Steven Beller, "The Hilsner Affair: Nationalism, Anti-Semitism and the Individual in the Habsburg Monarchy at the Turn of the Century," in Robert B. Pynsent, ed., *T. G. Masaryk (1850–1937), vol. 2: Thinker and Critic* (London: Macmillan, 1990), pp. 52–76.

10. On "court" Jews, see Selma Stern, *The Court Jew* (Philadelphia: Jewish Publication Society, 1950); Jonathan Israel, *European Jewry in the Age of Mercantilism, 1550–1750* (Oxford: Oxford University Press, 1985), pp. 123ff.

11. William O. McCagg, Jr., "Jewish Wealth in Vienna, 1670–1918," in Michael Silber, ed., *Jews in the Hungarian Economy, 1760–1945* (Jerusalem: Magnes, 1992), p. 55.

12. See Sander L. Gilman, *Freud, Race, and Gender* (Princeton, New Jersey: Princeton University Press, 1993).

13. Beller, *Vienna and the Jews*, p. 36.

14. Gary B. Cohen, *The Politics of Ethnic Survival: Germans in Prague, 1861–1914* (Princeton, New Jersey: Princeton University Press, 1981), especially pp. 178–83, 245–62.

15. William O. McCagg, Jr., *A History of Habsburg Jews, 1670–1918* (Bloomington: Indiana University Press, 1989), pp. 190–95; John Lukacs, *Budapest 1900: A Historical Portrait of a City and Its Culture* (London: Weidenfeld and Nicolson, 1989), pp. 187–204.

16. See Beller, *Vienna and the Jews,* pp. 123–24; George L. Mosse, *Germans and Jews: The Right, the Left and the Search for a Third Force in Pre-Nazi Germany* (Detroit: Wayne State University Press, 1987), pp. 39–40.

17. Arthur J. May, *The Habsburg Monarchy, 1867–1914* (Cambridge, Massachusetts: Harvard University Press, 1965), pp. 66–68; McCagg, *A History of Habsburg Jews,* pp. 156–57.

18. For the analogous phenomenon in Wilhelmine Germany, see Peter Pulzer, *Jews and the German State: The Political History of a Minority, 1848–1933* (Oxford: Oxford University Press, 1992). Pulzer shows how the legal structure of the German Empire facilitated the survival of discriminatory legislation at a state level, and hence the survival of the "Jewish question" despite ostensible legal religious equality at the imperial level.

19. Beller, *Vienna and the Jews,* pp. 189–90. See also Marsha L. Rozenblit, *The Jews of Vienna, 1867–1914: Assimilation and Identity* (Albany: State University of New York Press, 1983), pp. 47–70; Pulzer, *The Rise of Political Anti-Semitism,* pp. 5ff.

20. Beller, *Vienna and the Jews,* pp. 47–49; Oxaal, "The Jews of Young Hitler's Vienna," pp. 33–38.

21. Rozenblit, *The Jews of Vienna,* pp. 71ff.

22. Oxaal, "The Jews of Young Hitler's Vienna," pp. 25–26; Grafen Paul Vasili, *Die Wiener Gesellschaft* (Leipzig, 1885), p. 226.

23. Arthur Schnitzler, *Jugend in Wien* (Frankfurt am Main: Fischer, 1981), p. 77; Rozenblit, *The Jews of Vienna,* pp. 123–25.

24. Beller, *Vienna and the Jews,* p. 84; Rozenblit, *The Jews of Vienna,* pp. 127–45.

25. See David Sorkin, *The Transformation of German Jewry, 1780–1840* (Oxford: Oxford University Press, 1987).

26. Beller, *Vienna and the Jews,* pp. 144–87.

27. Beller, *Vienna and the Jews,* pp. 188–206.

28. Sigmund Mayer, *Ein jüdischer Kaufmann, 1831–1911: Lebenserinnerungen* (Leipzig, 1911), p. 91.

29. Leo Goldhammer, *Die Juden Wiens: Eine statistische Studie* (Vienna, 1927), pp. 44–48.

30. Oxaal, "The Jews of Young Hitler's Vienna," pp. 36–37.

31. Beller, *Vienna and the Jews,* pp. 207–37.

32. It might be noted that the plot of *Pride and Prejudice* also resolves itself into a dichotomy between ethical truth on the one hand and the deceptive immorality of the aesthetically beautiful on the other. It is the handsome charmer, Wickham, who is the deceiving reprobate, while it is the dour, difficult stranger, Darcy, the man who refuses to kowtow to social convention, who is the real, ethical hero.

33. See Pulzer, *The Rise of Political Anti-Semitism,* pp. 42ff.

34. See Beller, *Vienna and the Jews,* pp. 136–40.

35. Fritz Wittels, *Sigmund Freud* (London, 1924), p. 114.

36. Friedrich Heer, *God's First Love* (London: Weidenfeld and Nicolson, 1970), pp. 176–78, 224; Hermann Cohen, "Das Judentum als Weltanschauung," in *Öster-reichische Wochenschrift* 15:12 (March 25, 1898), pp. 221–23, and 15:13 (April 1, 1898), pp. 241–43. For a positive view of Judaism as a rational religion in 1870, see Simon Szanto's essay in *Die Neuzeit* (January 7, 1870), pp. 7–9.

37. See Richard Wagner, "Modern," in Wagner, *Sämtliche Schriften und Dichtungen,* vol. 10 (Leipzig: Breitkopf and Hartel, 1912), pp. 54ff. This essay was, according to Jakob Katz, a response by Wagner to an anonymous pamphlet, "Die Juden im Deutschen Staats- und Volksleben," apparently written from a Jewish perspective. See Jakob Katz, *The Darker Side of Genius: Richard Wagner's Anti-Semitism* (Hanover, Massachusetts: Brandeis University Press, 1986), p. 107.

38. Adolf Jellinek, "Der jüdische Stamm," *Die Neuzeit* 15 (December 13, 1861), p. 181.

39. Theodor Herzl, *Der Judenstaat: Versuch einer modernen Lösung der Judenfrage* (Vienna: Breitenstein, 1896), p. 74.

40. David Blackbourn, "Progress and Piety: Liberals, Catholics and the State in Bismarck's Germany," in D. Blackbourn, *Populists and Patricians* (London: Allen & Unwin, 1987), pp. 143–67.

41. May, *The Habsburg Monarchy*, pp. 47–49. Of special note on relations between church and state as it concerned Jews is the Kompert trial of 1864, which saw a basically liberal Jewish establishment in Vienna opposing a possible coalition of Orthodox Jews and the Habsburg state and strenuously arguing against state "protection" of Jewish "dogma." See *Die Neuzeit*, January 1, 1864, pp. 1ff.; especially March 4, 1864, pp. 110–14; September 2, 1864, pp. 413–15. On hostility to any idea of a "Concordat," see *Die Neuzeit*, January 7, 1870, p. 9.

42. Sorkin, *The Transformation of German Jewry*, pp. 107–10; McCagg, "Jewish Wealth," pp. 65ff.

43. Note that this does not apply so well to Galician Jewry, and especially not to the Hasidim, among whom organic community and tradition—"sensibility"—clearly played a huge role. There were tensions, in fact, between the more modernized *Westjuden* and the more traditional *Ostjuden*. Here, John M. Cuddihy's *The Ordeal of Civility* (Boston: Beacon Press, 1974) might have a point, based as it is on a model of East European Jewry. But the majority of Viennese Jewry did not come from Galicia, and many of those who did came specifically to make their fortune in the big city, in the market—to join the world of "sense." On this point, see the brilliant account by Klaus Hödl, *Als Bettler in die Leopoldstadt: Galizische Juden auf dem Weg nach Wien* (Vienna: Böhlau, 1994).

44. Katz, *From Prejudice to Destruction*, pp. 265–67.

45. Houston Stewart Chamberlain, *Die Grundlagen des neunzehnten Jahrhunderts*

(Munich, 1899), pp. 244, 410, 453–55; Katz, *From Prejudice to Destruction*, pp. 306–309; Pulzer, *The Rise of Political Anti-Semitism*, pp. 50–53 (on Dühring and Chamberlain).

46. Katz, *From Prejudice to Destruction*, p. 310; Pulzer, *The Rise of Political Anti-Semitism*, pp. 47–53, 286–87.

47. Such ideas in a modified form are not so far-fetched as we might like to think. The work of Eysenck on inherited intelligence and the recent advances in genetics make a return to racial theories intellectually likely, if morally unpalatable.

48. See Jeffrey Herf, *Reactionary Modernism: Technology, Culture and Politics in Weimar and the Third Reich* (Cambridge: Cambridge University Press, 1984).

49. Pauley, *From Prejudice to Persecution*, pp. 30–34.

50. For example, Heinrich Jaques, *Denkschrift über die Stellung der Juden in Österreich* (Vienna, 1859); also Beller, *Vienna and the Jews*, pp. 137–43.

51. For example, Theodor Herzl, *Briefe und Tagebücher*, vol. 1 (Berlin: Propyläen, 1983), pp. 158–60; H. Gomperz and R. A. Kann, eds., *Theodor Gomperz: Ein Gelehrtenleben im Bürgertum der Franz-Josephszeit* (Vienna 1974), pp. 104–105, 154, 168, 263, 382.

52. For details on the foregoing, see Beller, *Vienna and the Jews*, pp. 14–42.

53. Oxaal, "The Jews of Young Hitler's Vienna," pp. 36–37.

54. See Beller, *Vienna and the Jews*, pp. 43–70.

55. Beller, *Vienna and the Jews*, p. 37.

56. For this and the following, see McCagg, "Jewish Wealth," pp. 72–79.

57. McCagg, "Jewish Wealth," pp. 76–77.

58. McCagg, "Jewish Wealth," p. 79.

59. Rozenblit, *The Jews of Vienna*, pp. 79, 112.

60. John Komlos, "The Standard of Living of Jews in Austria-Hungary: The Anthropometric Evidence, 1860–1920," in Silber, *Jews in the Hungarian Economy*, pp. 127–34; see also Pulzer, *The Rise of Political Anti-Semitism*, pp. 13–15.

61. May, *The Habsburg Monarchy*, pp. 66–68; McCagg, *A History of Habsburg Jews*, pp. 156–57.

62. See K. S. Jomo's essay in this volume.

63. Monika Glettler, *Die Wiener Tschechen um 1900: Strukturanalyse einer nationalen Minderheit in der Grossstadt* (Munich: Böhlan, 1972), pp. 28–34, 268; Michael John and Albert Lichtblau, *Schmelztiegel Wien einst und jetzt* (Vienna: Böhlau, 1990), pp. 11ff.

64. Suess's remark is reported in *Die Neue Freie Presse* (morning edition), March 29, 1895, p. 5.

65. See Hans-Ulrich Wehler, *The German Empire, 1871–1918* (Leamington Spa: Berg, 1985), pp. 90ff.

66. On Lueger, see John W. Boyer, *Political Radicalism in Late Imperial Vienna* (Chicago: University of Chicago Press, 1981). For a less rosy view, see Richard S.

Geehr, *Karl Lueger: Mayor of Fin de Siècle Vienna* (Detroit: Wayne State University Press, 1990).

67. William McGrath, *Dionysian Art and Populist Politics in Austria* (New Haven, Connecticut: Yale University Press, 1973), pp. 202–207.

68. Gary B. Cohen, *The Politics of Ethnic Survival: Germans in Prague, 1861–1914* (Princeton, New Jersey: Princeton University Press, 1981), especially pp. 178–83, 245–62.

69. Silber, *Jews in the Hungarian Economy*, p. 21; McCagg, *A History of Habsburg Jews*, pp. 190–95; Lukacs, *Budapest 1900*, pp. 187–204.

70. Sylvia Maderegger, *Die Juden im österreichischen Ständestaat, 1934–1938* (Salzburg: Geyer, 1973), pp. 224ff.

71. For the following, see Gerhard Botz, "The Jews of Vienna from the Anschluss to the Holocaust," in Oxaal et al., *Jews, Antisemitism and Culture*, pp. 185–204.

72. Quoted in John and Lichtblau, *Schmelztiegel Wien*, p. 377.

73. Botz, "The Jews of Vienna from the Anschluss to the Holocaust," pp. 193–202.

74. Alexander Herzen, *Ends and Beginnings* (Oxford: Oxford University Press, 1985), p. 254.

5 / Jewish Entrepreneurship and Identity under Capitalism and Socialism in Central Europe

The Unresolved Dilemmas of Hungarian Jewry

VICTOR KARADY

The impact of Jewish entrepreneurship has proved to be much more important in postfeudal east-central Europe than anywhere else in the world. Jews formed either the main entrepreneurial class or a major component of it during the period when capitalist market economies were established in the region extending from Germany and Switzerland in the west to historic Russia in the east. This region includes almost all of the old Habsburg monarchy, Poland before its partition, and the Romanian principalities. However prosperous and successful they may have been, Jewish entrepreneurial groups (including traders, industrialists, professionals, and other "independent" members of learned classes) were condemned to elimination during the Shoah (the "catastrophe"), and then to social degradation or severe professional conversion in most countries subject to Stalinist rule after 1947–48.[1]

In this essay, I offer an account of these long-term socioeconomic developments with special reference to Hungary, the only country in the region where sizable sectors of local Jewry, including its entrepreneurial groups, survived the Shoah and have remained until today. I begin with a summary of the collective characteristics of Jews as minority entrepreneurs in east-central Europe during the first long period of "modernization," that is, from the eighteenth to the twentieth century.[2] Then I discuss the main sociohistorical causes behind Jewish preeminence in early and mature capitalism in east-central Europe.[3] Next, problems arising during the transition to communism in Hungary, stemming from the Shoah and official anti-capitalist policies, are discussed. Finally, a special section is dedicated to identifying the dilemmas peculiar to former Jewish entrepreneurial groups and the more general problems of integration and assimilation of Jews under state socialism.

HISTORICAL CHARACTERISTICS OF JEWISH
ENTREPRENEURSHIP IN EASTERN EUROPE

Despite their often spectacular economic achievements, Jewish entrepreneurs have never shed their pariah status to the degree that other successful ethnic aliens or upwardly mobile members of the lower strata have done. When and if they became economically dominant, they could not fully convert their assets into the political or social capital possessed by members of the traditional and newcomer elite. In most regions, they remained at best economically dominant pariahs, suffering from a permanent kind of status incongruity.[4] Jewish entrepreneurs could never achieve political power or public prestige that paralleled their economic success. Various militant anti-Semitic movements sought to ensure this, constantly challenging the positions of Jews, especially the entrepreneurs.[5] Such status incongruity was eased, in some cases, when Jewish entrepreneurs entered into class alliances with Gentile elites, as they did in pre-Trianon—that is, pre-1918 liberal—Hungary,[6] nineteenth-century German Prague,[7] and interwar Czechoslovakia.[8]

This situation stemmed from the hegemonic conservation—present in most countries until the arrival of state socialism—of a feudal value system and the survival of gentry elites as the sole legitimate holders of political office and representatives of elite social ideals. One can link this development to the generally insufficient embourgeoisement of east-central Europe. While most Jews were adopting the ideals of modernization, most non-Jews were not. This general modernization deficit was reflected in intellectual affairs (e.g., weakness of secularization), patterns of social mobility (overall scarcity of entrepreneurs), the overwhelming role of the state, continuing high birth and death rates, underurbanization, and economic underdevelopment as measured by the paucity of industrial capital when compared with capital immobilized in agriculture or invested in trade, communications, and, especially, public services.[9] Jews became uprooted bourgeois entrepreneurs in undercapitalized, semitraditional economic markets and backward, postfeudal social organizations.[10]

There were two consequences. First, the longer development was delayed or remained limited to large cities, the greater became the role of Jewish entrepreneurs in local economies and, second, because this increasing role exacerbated anti-Semitic sentiments, the more the Jews were "estranged." This was obviously the case in the easternmost fringe of the region, Romania and the Polish lands, with Hungary and Austria being intermediate cases.[11] Where and when indigenous modernization succeeded—as it did in Bohemia after the late nineteenth century—Jewish entrepreneurial functions were less eminent and disparities of social status between Jews and Gentiles tended to diminish.

In terms of size, the bulk of world Jewry was settled in east-central Europe before World War I, and probably up to the Shoah. Thus the reservoir of Jewish would-be entrepreneurs, relative to that in Western Europe or even the United States, was enormous. But the propensity for modernization and embourgeoisement varied considerably among Jewish groups. Jewish entrepreneurs and other professional elites could become economically dominant while the rest of Jewish society remained bogged down in traditional trade and crafts.[12] Hence the paradox: the participation of Jews in modern entrepreneurship was incomparably more important in the east, but in terms of modernization, East European Jewry generally lagged behind its West European and American counterparts. There were exceptions, notably in Bohemia, where modernization was a general feature in both Jewish and Gentile milieus and where the size and proportion of the Jewish population was limited and declining. There, Jewish entrepreneurship played a significant but not hegemonic role in the modern economy.

Jewish entrepreneurial groups differed significantly from their Gentile counterparts in terms of economic specialization, investment strategies, and recruitment patterns. More often than not, Jewish entrepreneurs behaved differently even when they pursued similar goals and were engaged in comparable activities. Sectoral investment differences were radical indeed. Jewish capital growth was directed primarily toward trade and finance and toward the manufacturing of finished or semifinished goods such as textiles.[13] In this sense, it remained somewhat "premodern." But Jewish investment in cultural production was highly modern and went into journalism, publishing, show business, the cinema, art galleries, and so on. The same was true of investment in education that led to the modern "independent" professions. Agriculture was of only marginal importance.

An essential feature of Jewish entrepreneurship in east-central Europe was the regular combination of very high monetary and intellectual investments. Whenever comparisons are made between Jews and Gentiles of the same socioeconomic class, Jews are found to have had more formal and informal education. They were much more frequently bilingual or multilingual than others were, for example, and often had a special interest in the control of information. Even when standardized by class, Jews had substantially higher levels of schooling than equivalent classes among the non-Jews. This resulted in a kind of "overinvestment" in education.[14]

A final characteristic of east-central European Jewish entrepreneurship was its demographic, occupational, and intellectual mobility. A good part of the Jewish entrepreneurial class originated in Austrian, Hungarian, and Romanian small towns. But Jewish capital and capitalists flowed primarily into economically developed urban centers and, most conspicuously, into regional or national capital cities such as Warsaw, Cracow, Lemberg, Czernovitz, Iasi, Bucharest, and Budapest. The geographic mobility of the Jewish entrepreneurial classes, once they left their ghettos, went hand in hand with their social mobility. Entry into Gentile social and economic markets required a measure of forced or strategic acculturation and assimilation, partial secularization, and, relative to their Gentile counterparts, greater intellectual mobility.[15]

The high level of education, combined with such high physical and social mobility and with continuing pariah status, explains why members or offspring of the Jewish entrepreneurial classes have so often enthusiastically espoused social or intellectual utopias over the past two centuries, especially "salvation ideologies" that promised to liberate Jews, together with other dominated groups, from their historical predicament. These included systems based on universalistic values, such as antireligious secularism, Freemasonry, liberalism, socialism, and communism, and those connected with secular forms of modern Jewish particularism, such as Bundism, folkism (cultural autonomism), and Zionism.[16]

AN INTERPRETATION OF JEWISH
ENTREPRENEURSHIP IN EAST-CENTRAL EUROPE

Jewish entrepreneurial success in this region can best be interpreted by reference to three sets of factors: the preemancipation socioeconomic situation of Jewry, the collective skills, incorporated virtues, and competencies Jews developed, often under duress, during the years of early capitalism after emancipation, and the maintenance of dual market arrangements throughout the period of modernization.

Jewish economic practice before civic emancipation was subjected to essentially negative influences that can be summarized under the following headings: pariah-type exclusion from the normal feudal economy and the feudal status system, prohibition of most kinds of long-term investments, especially in land, and locally negotiated forms of exploitation by the feudal hierarchy. These feudal restrictions undermined the Jews' prosperity and security in the short run, but they would ultimately provide advantages or indirectly generate assets for Jews in the markets of early capitalism.[17]

Exclusion from the feudal economy meant, among other things, that Jews were barred from craft and trade guilds and from attending markets or even staying in cities without special permission. Most industrial and agricultural activities were forbidden to Jews, as were economic privileges of the gentry and patrician burgher class. They could not, therefore, purchase real property. But however restrictive this situation was, it also offered some implicit liberties and economic advantages, including freedom from serfdom, freedom to fill the gaps in the feudal economy by methods such as some lucrative forms of international trade or money dealing, and significant competitive power in bidding for leaseholds and other feudal tenures for which competition was generally scarce. Altogether, they had greater geographic and sectoral mobility in the economy than all these restrictions would suggest.

The combination of exclusion and mobility, combined with the benefit of Jewish solidarity, forced Jews to rely on their international networks. Thus, they tended to be better informed about regional, national, and international markets as well as about financial conditions.

The restriction on buying land, even for a shop or synagogue, had two major economic consequences. First, Jews were excluded from agriculture and most other forms of capital immobilization. They could, of course, take landed leaseholds, and often did so in Poland, eastern Hungary, and Romania, but Jewish involvement in agriculture was limited to rather exceptional and specific kinds of entrepreneurial ventures. Thus, as capitalist markets expanded, prospective Jewish entrepreneurs were much freer to invest in the new, more profitable economic sectors. The second, more important consequence was that Jews were allowed to accumulate only mobile capital— cash, short-term investments, jewelry, credits, goods to stock for sale. This secured considerable market benefits for them in early capitalism, when credit was scarce and expensive and the banking system was underdeveloped or nonexistent. This was why so many of certain types of trading and banking activities fell into their hands, or why they were the only ones capable of developing them.

Exploitation by overtaxation was the usual condition required in order for feudal princes or landlords to "tolerate" or "protect" Jews. This was an obvious cause of the Jewish economic plight, frequently reinforced by anti-Jewish measures such as expulsion, restrictions on the settlement of family members, "letter killing" (organized refusal to honor debts), and blood-libel accusations.[18] Overexploitation was linked to the absence of civil rights and led to a considerable degree of Jewish self-exploitation, self-denial, hoarding of security assets, and underconsumption.

The sum total of these behaviors represented a truly inner-worldly asceticism directed toward economic performance and rationality. Such habits were quite exceptional in the feudal and early modern economy, which was largely regulated either formally by corporate rules in trade and crafts, informally by peasant household tradition, or by the display of status-oriented overconsumption, as in the case of the landed gentry. The competitive edge that such protocapitalist behavior gave to Jews once open markets emerged was substantial.

With this, we have broached our second main topic: the specific skills and competencies produced by the historical position of Jewry in the postfeudal societies of east-central Europe.

Jews had already been compelled to behave as protocapitalist entrepreneurs under feudalism. After emancipation, the characteristics they had acquired could be converted into market assets. Reviewing the effects of their traditional religion, educational striving, international connections, and pariah status shows how this worked.

The Jews' religious habits contributed to their successful entrepreneurial conduct in a number of ways. The most important was the discipline it imposed on them by insisting on strict functional organization, control of time and space, and the use of the body according to the requirements of *kashrut,* observance of Shabbat, fasting, and other prescriptions. Stress should be laid on the internal constraints that came with religious socialization, because these were more likely to be applied to spheres of activity such as the economy, education, and matrimony, where strategic conduct and rational choices were essential for success.[19]

Jewish educational propensities were equally important in making Jews successful. They originated to a large extent in religious practices grounded, at least for men, upon learning and active literacy. This was quite different from both Christianity and Islam, in which most theological knowledge remained the preserve of certified clerics. The most immediate result of traditional denominational learning was the spread among Jewish men of elementary literacy, a smattering of arithmetic, and an ability to acquire, formulate, and manipulate both large quantities of historical knowledge and rather abstract ideas.[20] Basic literacy and numeracy were extremely rare abilities in early modern Europe and were easily convertible into economic assets whenever market opportunities had to be quantified, calculated, or controlled. Furthermore, religious educational habits gave rise even more directly to secular learning propensities applicable to highly specialized knowledge used in the independent professions or in freelance, para-intellectual occupations such as journalism, editing, creative writing, and other cultural endeavors.[21]

The function of international networks has already been alluded to in connection with premodern entrepreneurship. Notwithstanding these networks' frequent stigmatization in anti-Semitic phantasmagoria as part of the "worldwide Jewish conspiracy," they played a major role in offering models of Western economic and cultural practices to Jews emerging from east-central European ghetto life. Effective patterns of entrepreneurial conduct were thus transferred. Aspiring young Jewish entrepreneurs were assisted in acquiring a high level of business know-how in some of the best Western European firms. This knowledge endowed Jews with a capacity for innovation that enabled them to act as mediating agents of modernization between East and West. Thus, a "cosmopolitan," Westernized, and internationally oriented style was bestowed upon Jewish entrepreneurship and investment strategies in east-central Europe.[22]

Finally, the postemancipation remnants of pariah status fulfilled a number of essential functions in successful Jewish entrepreneurship. The accumulation of capitalist wealth and economic leverage remained a path of compensation or revenge for the Jews' persistent pariah status. But it was also instrumental in pushing Jews toward overachievement in business, education, and other ventures. This need to overachieve proved to be effective not only in compensating for imposed handicaps but also in contributing to the development of a secularized Jewish elite consciousness, a collective characteristic that was much more striking in east-central Europe than in the West. This corresponded with and was a response to the traditional religious vocation of the "chosen people." The same kind of collective narcissism could operate like a self-fulfilling prophecy to boost entrepreneurial achievements.

For most emancipated Jews, however distinctive many of their cultural traits, assimilation into the modern Gentile world remained the ultimate goal. Whether Jews' assimilationist strategies, aimed at identity change, succeeded or not is a controversial issue.[23] What is important for our purposes is to understand how assimilationist attitudes manifested themselves as verbal or attitudinal conformism or perfectionism, as residential and social "mixing" tactics, and as adhesion to national goals or political aims that corresponded to the host society's value system. All of these could become sources of entrepreneurial or social success, especially in local trade, the liberal professions, and most of the learned or semi-intellectual occupations where mutual service relationships and intensive contacts with non-Jewish clienteles and associates were indispensable.

As for the conception of collective identity, even a partially successful assimilation of Jewish entrepreneurial or professional groups into the Gentile elite—which happened on a vast scale in liberal Hungary, imperial Vienna and German and Czech Prague—produced some "nationalization" of Jewish groups. This included a strong commitment by these sections of the Jewish bourgeoisie to local languages and cultures and to patronage of the "national" arts and sciences. There were also a growing number of mixed marriages, social mixing with the Gentile elites, participation in liberal political parties, and substantial support for "national causes."[24] All this helped to develop patriotism and a strong national consciousness in some countries that was detrimental to Zionism and other forms of cultural separatism. For these relatively assimilated groups, cultural and linguistic loyalty to the national elites went hand in hand with loyalty to nationalist governments and parties. Thus, in Hungary and Vienna, but also to some extent in Bukovina and Galicia during the late Habsburg era, assimilated Jews began to consider themselves not minority entrepreneurs but authentic representatives of the national or regional bourgeoisie, despite widespread local political and cultural anti-Semitism.[25]

The last major factor directly responsible for Jewish entrepreneurial success was the maintenance of dual markets. In most east-central European societies (including imperial Germany), this arrangement prevailed up to the very end of the old regime and, in some cases, even beyond. The dual market system was based on the assumption that the traditional elites—the national gentry, the patrician class and its clients, the propertied peasantry, and the petty bourgeoisie that had staffed the state during the transition from feudalism to capitalism—were entitled to further protection by the state in order to guarantee their survival in the emerging modern nation. Public jobs in the administration and the political bureaucracy at all levels, including publicly run or controlled industries and services, had to be reserved for these groups. New, competitive economic markets, therefore, were left open to newcomers such as Jews and other ethnic aliens.[26]

In some ways these limitations were detrimental to Jewish social mobility, which was more or less curbed in "public" markets. But there were benefits as well. The Gentile elite directed its mobility strategies toward public markets, where lower performance was actually demanded and benefits were better.[27] This left Jews free to pursue innovative and competitive careers in the private economy. For example, judges were Gentiles, but the bar was opened to Jews after emancipation, and by the early twentieth century more than one-half of the lawyers in Budapest, Vienna, and Warsaw were Jews. The situation was similar in medicine, journalism, and architecture. In a few places, notably liberal Hungary and interwar Czechoslovakia, Jews could attempt to make careers in public service, but their success usually required exceptional performance or, for higher positions, baptism.[28] The overall effect of the dual market system was to reinforce the Jewish predisposition toward high performance and innovation, while the average competitive capacity and propensity of their Gentile counterparts, whether intellectual or entrepreneurial, remained significantly lower. This was made evident by the differential success rates of the two groups in purely open markets, with education being perhaps the best example.

Understanding this background helps to explain the peculiarities of Jewish adaptation to communism in Hungary after World War II.

THE TRANSITION TO COMMUNISM: THE HUNGARIAN CASE

Several aspects of the Hungarian Jews' special situation—a high degree of assimilation, a commitment to national causes, and a disinterest in Jewish separatism (most typically Zionism)—have already been mentioned. The survival of Jews in Hungary was also unique in east-central Europe in many other respects.

The Jewish community that survived in Hungary after World War II was, to be sure, far from the largest surviving one in the region in either relative or absolute terms. By June 1946, there were approximately 200,000 "counted remnants" registered in Hungary,[29] whereas in Poland—although Polish Jewry survived in German-occupied territories only in fragments—the number of repatriates, a majority of whom returned from the Soviet Union, reached over 240,000 at that time.[30] In Romania, both the number and the proportion of survivors were higher, while in Bulgaria, where there had been a much smaller Jewish population (about 50,000),[31] all but a few were saved by the authorities. (This was not the case for Jews in Yugoslav and Greek territories occupied by the Bulgarians, who did not consider them "national" Jews.)

What was distinct about the Hungarian experience was the high proportion of Jews who remained in their birthplace. With the renewal of murderous anti-Semitism in Poland after World War II—tolerated, manipulated, and later even stimulated by the new regime—a large-scale emigration of Jewish survivors from there started immediately after the liberation.[32] Then, after the anti-Semitic purges of 1968, all but about 5,000 Jews left Poland. In Romania, Jewish emigration has continued, if intermittently, until the present, leaving fewer than 10,000 Jews, an insignificant portion of the 1945 total. In relatively hospitable Bulgaria, the large majority of the Jewish community left for Palestine in the years immediately after the communist takeover. The same was true of Czechoslovakia, where emigration of the few Jewish survivors peaked after the 1949 Prague coup, owing particularly to the officially sponsored anti-Semitic hysteria and Aryanization process that followed the 1951 Slansky trial.[33]

The reason for continuous emigration from most communist countries was linked, as it was everywhere, to the persistence of popular anti-Semitism and its often outspoken political exploitation by communist leaderships. Hungary remained, by and large, immune from this. Although implicitly anti-Semitic purges occurred there during Stalin's final years, public anti-Semitism was officially downplayed, and under János Kádár's rule from 1956 to 1988, it was suppressed outright. Better integration of Jews in the party apparatus, dissident circles, and society at large also explains why almost half of Hungarian-Jewish survivors remained in their birthplace and were joined by many from the formerly Hungarian territories of Slovakia, Transylvania, Carpathian Ukraine, and the Yugoslav Voyvodina. At present, Hungarian Jews (those with at least one parent of Jewish extraction) are estimated to number between 80,000 and 100,000 people.

Whereas in most neighboring countries, notably Romania, Poland, and Czechoslovakia, the "Jewish question" remained a major political issue until the collapse of communism, it tended to be systematically downplayed by officials in Hungary, even if this meant merely "sweeping it under the carpet."[34]

Hungarian Jewry was unique not only for its size—even though this was only one-fourth of the prewar figure—but also for its socioprofessional makeup and its prospects for further mobility within the newly established social hierarchies. A major factor in this evolution was the selective bias of the persecutions. Propertied and educated local Jews were somewhat protected by their Gentile friends and allies and even by the government. To a considerable extent this protection exempted them from the Final Solution prior to the Nazi takeover in 1944. Then, deportations to death camps uprooted almost all of the provincial half of local Jewry but only part of the urban, mostly Budapest half. The delay enabled an unprecedentedly high proportion of the latter to seek conversion in the panic-stricken months during the spring and summer of 1944. Although solicited under duress, the baptisms vastly modified the denominational composition of those who survived persecution. Those from some provincial cities (for example, Szeged and Debrecen) were deported to Austrian camps, where the risk of death was lower than at Auschwitz. Certified degrees of assimilation, if demonstrated by baptism or mixed marriage, entailed a measure of protection by social partners, officials, and churches. The wealthiest could sometimes buy their freedom, as was demonstrated by the notorious escape of the powerful Weisz family and by the "protected train" escorted by the SS to Switzerland.[35]

Thus, even if selectivity did not always operate to ensure the "survival of the strongest"—for example, women and the elderly in Budapest were less at risk—there was a bias in that direction. The result, paradoxically, was to enhance the upward mobility and modernity of the survivors both in terms of socioprofessional stratification and degree of secularization or assimilation. With the near elimination of provincial communities, Orthodox Jewry all but disappeared in Hungary. Rural Jews suffered much heavier losses than those in the capital city. The higher brackets of the urban middle class were generally less decimated than the lower class. Converts and those who assimilated survived more frequently. Generally, survivors represented the culturally more Magyarized and socially more integrated sections of Jewry in Hungary.[36]

The few indicators of social stratification among surviving Jews confirm the paradoxical embourgeoisement that resulted from the Shoah. A comparison of the Jewish populations of 1935 and 1945 shows that the percentage of independent entrepreneurs and professionals who survived was much greater than that of other groups. In Budapest, there were only 46 percent as many Jews in 1945 as in 1935. But the number of Jews who were self-employed in industry in 1945 was 89 percent of the 1935 total. The figure for those self-employed in trade was 56 percent of the 1935 total, and, because of flight into the city, it was 111 percent of the previous total for professionals.[37] Such data illustrate not only the socially selective nature of the genocide but also the selectivity of migrations into Budapest immediately after the Shoah, as well as some of the emigrations to the West and Palestine that started after the liberation.

Forced mobility produced by the anti-Semitic legislation of 1938–44 also played a role, because it caused many executives to transfer into "private practice" of some sort in order to escape the ban imposed on the employment of Jews (a maximum of 6 percent in any particular business, according to the Second Anti-Jewish Law of 1939).[38] Surviving Jewry, henceforth concentrated in Budapest, showed a markedly more entrepreneurial occupational profile than it had before the Shoah. Thus, it was the more "bourgeois" and "assimilated" Jews who faced the challenges and prospects of communism.

Liberation from the Nazis opened up new opportunities for social mobility and integration. The new regime immediately lifted the anti-Semitic legislation that had begun in 1938, and many Jews were tempted by the promise of a new start in which the rest of their particularistic identity would be abandoned.[39] As duly certified antifascists, the Jews were natural political supporters of the new regime, and many of them readily entered into the power structure. The "changing of the guard" required rapid replacement of the old regime's civil service. The need for reliable public servants and new political personnel put Jews, with their political and educational capital, in a good collective bargaining position in many of the traditional as well as the previously inaccessible bureaucratic markets of middle-class activity—the armed forces, the diplomatic corps, and the new party-state bureaucracy. These offered unprecedented prospects for complete social integration.[40]

The opportunity for professional success in the state apparatus proved all the more tempting because other, more traditional roads to middle-class careers began to be closed as the Communist party, after a brief "popular front" coalition in 1945 and 1946, began to nationalize the entire economy.

The full-fledged and increasingly hysterical antibourgeois drives that were launched as large capitalist enterprises and banks were nationalized in 1946 turned implicitly anti-Jewish that summer, in the form of a campaign against "speculators" and "profiteers of the black market," before inflation was stemmed and a new currency was introduced—thus ruining those holding cash, among whom Jews were disproportionately represented. In the wake of this, anti-Semitic pogroms were staged in several places, the most notorious of which, in Miskolc and Kunmadaras, claimed several victims.[41] By 1948 the new regime had virtually eliminated those independent "bourgeois" economic activities that the Jews had favored.

After the consolidation of Communist party rule in 1948, the surviving petite and middle bourgeoisie, traders, craftsmen, and industrialists were expropriated. All capitalist real estate was nationalized. Liberal professionals had either to become wage-earning employees in state-run institutions and firms or submit to outside control that drastically restricted their professional liberty. Thus, the appeal of the communist path was countered by its brutal rejection, indeed destruction, of earlier Jewish life-worlds and modes of economic existence. This made escapist strategies—above all, emigration to the West or Palestine—attractive to former members of the entrepreneurial class. Those who stayed had to face the destiny reserved for "class aliens" by the communist regime: the loss of productive property, social degradation, exclusion from educational opportunities, deportation to rural areas, compulsory professional conversion to (mostly) petty state positions, and sometimes even more ruthless persecution. The elimination of "entrepreneurial classes" meant the loss of a major source of particularistic Jewish identity in Hungary.

Hence, the bloody process of "restratification" during the old regime and the post-Shoah sociopolitical conditions in Hungary were only partly favorable to further Jewish social mobility. For many Jews they represented a new kind of economic and existential disaster. Yet there was also unprecedented objective assimilation that, for those willing to take the communist path, offered a new chance and an experience of social integration. Here were the ingredients for a classic identity crisis. On one hand, "objective" identity factors and interests often militated in favor of positive integration into the new regime. On the other hand, the "subjective" experience of the Shoah, combined with a new form of persecution ostensibly aimed only at "bourgeois" Jews, could lead to exactly the opposite attitude—a complete rejection of the regime's offer of assimilation.[42]

These divergent choices could all be satisfactorily legitimized. Consequently, post-Shoah Jewry in Hungary found itself in an exceptionally "open" situation—in a properly Promethean state in which history had created a variety of options whose appeal was approximately equal.

THE SHOAH AND IDENTITY DILEMMAS BETWEEN ZIONISM AND COMMUNISM

The trauma of the Shoah was the experience that defined all subsequent existential choices for surviving Jewry. Whatever other background variables were in play, it was the Shoah's paramount importance that consolidated the Jews' consciousness of their radical, collective otherness and thus limited their options to those that broke with the past.[43]

In earlier times, Hungarian Jewry had been strongly committed to Magyardom, in both political and cultural terms. This meant, among other things, that its majority and officialdom had successively espoused great national causes since the *Vormärz*. This nationalism excluded support for the Zionist or folkist type of anti-assimilationism. Indeed, the Jews' mother tongue in Trianon Hungary became almost fully Magyar, and even most Orthodox and Hassidic communities shared this national identification with the host country, although they firmly opposed any concessions to denominational laxity or secularization. Because of the Shoah, this "Jewish-Magyar symbiosis,"[44] which found its parallel in Western Europe but not in Poland, Romania, or other Eastern European counties, now collapsed. Unlike in Poland or the Nazi-occupied west, Hungarian Jewry had fallen victim to local "national socialism," even though this tragic fate required German occupation in March 1944 for its full realization.

Elsewhere, the Nazis had also been enemies of the nation-state and, for that matter, as in Poland, of the national elite and the remaining population. Even in a largely anti-Semitic society like Poland, this fact could unite Jews and non-Jews in the fight against fascism and make the liberation a common euphoric experience, even if only briefly. In Hungary there was neither a noteworthy movement of resistance nor much significant collective action taken to protect Jews, although there were individual acts of bravery by some church leaders, both Catholic and Protestant, and by some anti-Nazi officials. Thus, the defeat of the Third Reich and its Hungarian acolytes left the bulk of Jews and non-Jews as divided as ever.[45] This was like the Romanian situation. What was undoubtedly liberation for Jews appeared much more like another occupation for most non-Jews.[46] The Soviet "army of liberation" was received by most Hungarians as an instrument of foreign domination.

In due course, the public image of the new regime came to be identified with the earlier social underdogs, the Jews and the "proles." In such circumstances, the former Jewish-Magyar identification could not be maintained. All further identity choices included a marked distance from the national past, which survivors reinterpreted negatively.

No matter how objectively "assimilated" or "modern" Jewish identity had become, the memory of the persecutions and the mere idea that such monstrosities could occur forcibly stimulated the feeling of radical Jewish otherness. This was true, of course, not only in Hungary. Still, the post-Shoah pattern of otherness was probably an even more crucial existential experience in Hungary, where the survivors had been received with mixed feelings, where there was little organized public mourning, and where the authorities refused material compensation on the grounds that the country was too poor and, as a communist fellow traveler put it, "in the old regime, the whole working people had suffered." Petty Nazis also enjoyed far-reaching immunity under the communist "mass party," and the new regime's populist demagogy, whenever it was directed against the "exploiting classes," fostered collective manifestations of anti-Semitism after 1946.[47]

Thus, the consequences of the liberation enlarged the gulf between Jews' self-perception, basically of themselves as victims, and the social definition of Jews as undesirable aliens. The tension between the two gave rise to new patterns of Jewish identity that tended to bridge the gulf either by self-conscious acceptance of otherness (but of a kind qualitatively different from what anti-Semites suggested) or by minimization or dissimulation through adopting a communist or liberal-national value system. Whichever the choice, it must be stressed that each was a reaction to the emerging post-Shoah situation. With the advancement of "objective assimilation," the reconstruction of Jewish identity after 1945 could not draw upon traditional or inherited assets such as specific cultural goods, anthropological particularities, or socioeconomic competencies, as it had done in earlier times. In this respect, Hungarian Jewry could be regarded as fully "Westernized." Jewish self-definition in Hungary became, more than ever before, purely reactive or reflexive, with sole reference to collective perils and necessities in the recent past and, by implication, in the present. Beyond the variability of actual identity options, the essentially responsive character of Jewish-Hungarian self-understanding served as an implicit means for reunifying post-Shoah Jewry.

This reunification did little, however, to minimize conflicts between strategies for managing the self; indeed, reactions to the same collective trauma took three utterly different shapes: communism, Zionism, and the remodeling of earlier assimilationist options. In some cases, elements of these three could be either combined or adopted successively without ceasing to be conflictual. In this respect, conflicts emerged not only within families and circles of friends and allies but also within the choices one made at different stages of life. An identity crisis was raging within groups and within the self. Adults might join the Communist party and, at the same time, have their newborns baptized or enroll their children in the Zionist youth movement, at least as long as this was legally possible. Between 1945 and 1949, the heyday of both Zionism and communism among Jewish Hungarians, the rate of baptism was as high as it had been during the rise of fascism in 1932–33.[48]

The responsive character of the new and conflictual identity options also caused an often ambivalent, confused, or contradictory reaction to earlier "naive" (i.e., sincere) assimilationist options, which had proved illusory. The desire to "break away from the past" did not mean that earlier assimilationist schemes such as mixed marriages or baptisms were rejected outright. On the contrary, Jews sometimes consciously resorted to them as before, but for different reasons. Communist cadres, for example, might marry partners of working-class extraction to increase their families' "political capital." Even baptism was sought in a different way from before, since entry into a Christian church was not always preceded by a renunciation of Judaism. Nothing but the monstrous trauma of the Shoah, combined with the past high degree of assimilation to a Magyar identity, can explain the ultimately disorderly character of, and simultaneous recourse to, contradictory identity options that in earlier times would have been mutually exclusive.[49] By comparison, in Romania, which had also been a German ally during the war, up to three-quarters of Jewish survivors opted for a new identity by emigrating to Israel between 1945 and 1950. In Hungary, the majority remained in place.

However contradictory they were to each other, the options open to Hungarian Jewry entailed breaking away from the past. In this respect, Zionism and communism became, in the new regime's first years, strongly competitive, though functionally equivalent and not always mutually exclusive, options. Members of Hashomer Hatsair, to take an example, rightly felt that they had joined socialist ideals to Zionism. Indeed, both signified and guaranteed, however differently, the most radical departure from past practices, particularly those concerning basic Jewish attitudes about society and identity. Let me sum up some of the major similarities and dissimilarities between communism and Zionism in Hungary. In spite of appearances, the former seems to have carried as much weight as the latter.

First, both Zionism and communism were conceived as social utopias that would be built by several generations. In both, the burden of Jewishness in a hostile social environment would be fully removed and "Jewish alienation" radically done away with. This was the spiritual foundation upon which the functional equivalence of the two rested.

Second, both were based upon universalistic principles, albeit contrasting ones. Communism promised the "normalization" of the Jews' social condition through integration into a classless society ("the melting in the masses") that ignored racial, denominational, and ethnic discrimination. Zionism appealed to the universal principle of nationhood. Jews would be "normalized" as a separate people and an established nation-state among other peoples and states. Their secular character (religious Zionism was practically nonexistent in Hungary) confirmed the ideological kinship of Zionism and communism in this respect. Both, indeed, proposed an ideology of modernization along universal lines, although for Zionists such modernity had to be embodied in the new Jewish state that would serve as a home for Jews dispersed all over the world.

Third, as a consequence, universalism was a major component not only of communist and Zionist ideology but also of their political practices, through which they were trying to create ideal communities. For communists this community encompassed the whole "progressive" or "peace-loving" part of humanity as against the "imperialists," "reactionaries," and "warmongers." For Zionists it was limited to the Jews of the Diaspora. Yet despite their different forms, both options developed or legitimized a sense of belonging to a universal community that had hitherto been repressed. Heavily stigmatized "Jewish cosmopolitanism" could be positively reinterpreted in line with "proletarian internationalism," while the vehemently denounced manifestations of "Jewish solidarity" across borders won reappraisal as an asset in the overdue unification and resettlement of the Jewish people. This reappraisal was just as spiritual as it was practical. As interdependency was operationalized on the political, economic, and even military level among movements and countries of the "progressive world" (as defined by Moscow's interests), worldwide Jewish mutual aid made itself felt in Budapest and elsewhere in Eastern Europe through the philanthropic services of the Zionist organizations or the famous *Joint.*

Fourth, from a more historical and sociological view, both options were new for Hungarian Jews, considering that prior to World War II they had touched only a small minority among them. Communism, in spite of its ephemeral success in 1919, had all but disappeared from the political landscape of Hungary and the Jewish intelligentsia during the interwar years, partly because most of its leaders and activists fled abroad. And relative to the dominant assimilationist credo, Zionism had always been utterly marginal among modern Hungarian identity options. Officials in community organizations actively resisted it. It emerged as a major identity choice only from the Jewish resistance and the Shoah. Thus, with the general depreciation of established values, communism and Zionism each proposed a new start with uncompromised principles shrouded in the halo of heroic nonconformism.

Fifth, the very radical ideological standing of both communism and Zionism enabled and motivated a high level of intense investment in affective, moral, political, and even aesthetic values. The militant organization of communist and Zionist movements obviously added to this as it emphasized their collective rituals, the warmth of a militant community, and the fervor expected from their followers. So did Jewish hopes for these utopian choices. Jews expected higher symbolic and social rewards from communism than others did, since they were indebted to its salvationist ideology as Jews, not only as members of a "dominated class." Overcommitment in both Zionism and communism stemmed from an attitude of revenge against the tragic fate of Jewry and from eagerness to oppose the risk of renewed murderous anti-Semitism.

Sixth and finally, at the psychosociological level, communism and Zionism paralleled each other in reversing Jews' past relationship with society. Shameful Jewish submissiveness was eliminated by challenging the age-old attitudes of Gentiles who had at best merely tolerated Jews' existence. Thereafter, either as participants in the Communist party power structure or as would-be citizens of the state of Israel, Jews would self-consciously assert themselves, discarding former tendencies to fear others, avoid open conflict, and sidestep anti-Semitic provocations or challenges. The underdog syndrome was condemned to disappear from the Jewish repertoire. Communism and Zionism thus contributed to a kind of revolution in Jewish public behavior.

Such common features explain to some degree why the passage between Zionism and communism was often relatively easy. A Zionist in 1945 could become a fervent communist by 1949 and return to the ideals of the Jewish state after 1956.

JEWRY UNDER COMMUNISM: CHALLENGE, TEST, AND ORDEAL

But communism and Zionism also conflicted with one another in many ways. The former stressed purely universalistic values, while the latter insisted upon the particularistic nature of Jewish historical identity. Communism appeared from the outset to be incompatible with most Jewish cultural traits, religion above all, but many others as well. And whereas Zionism was determined to integrate Jews of all spiritual shades and social brackets, communism proved to be highly selective in its recruitment and, as we shall see, brought about drastic leveling and the forced dissimulation of everything Jewish among those whom it admitted.[50]

Given the highly problematic nature of both communist and Zionist identity choices, it is not surprising that a third option, more traditional on the whole, revealed itself as the choice of the "silent majority"—namely, the passive continuation of a revised form of the nationalist-assimilationist pattern. After the transitional years of the coalition government in Hungary from 1945 to 1947, Zionism was banned and harshly persecuted. Until 1957, no legal emigration to either the West or Israel was allowed. Zionist sympathies had to be kept hidden. But the majority of surviving Jews were not involved in communism either; most sought a simple modus vivendi with the Stalinist system. This was all the more so because, with the destruction of "bourgeois" living conditions, freedom of choice in matters of social identity was restricted. Religious practice was strictly confined to the synagogue, and the regime's official anticlericism affected the Jewish community notably through the forceful dissolution of the Zionist association and the equally arbitrary unification of the three Jewish religious organizational networks.[51]

Under these circumstances, political conformism was the common lot of both Jews and non-Jews. Regime pressure equalized economic conditions and survival strategies. Brutal relegation to underdeveloped rural areas was a fate shared by many Jewish and non-Jewish members of the well-to-do urban middle class, just as they shared the political purges that weeded them out of the ranks of public administration. The Stalinist predicament created common ground for uninvolved Jews and non-Jews, and this implicitly prepared them for further rapprochements. Mutual suffering had the same influence as had earlier focal points of community in the nation's history. The 1956 October Revolution and its aftermath, with a united "popular front" type of resistance to communism, proved to be a shared experience in this respect, comparable in importance to 1848 for constructing a new kind of Jewish-Hungarian understanding.[52] The strength of this neutral—that is, neither communist nor Zionist—identity option was made clear by the renewed increase in assimilation through mixed marriages inside and outside Communist party circles.

Because communism was undoubtedly the more dramatic of the new choices and offered a less orthodox chance for the reconstruction of post-Shoah Jewish identity, its implications must be assessed more closely. Even if it was not necessarily an option for most survivors, it did engage a good part of the younger generation and those who were interested in advancing their careers. Because the number of emigrants, whether Zionist or not, was less than 30,000 before the Iron Curtain went up (out of 190,000 to 200,000 registered survivors in 1946), and because the Shoah had dramatically reduced the size of Jewish families, entry into the *nomenklatura* affected most Jewish circles either directly or through family ties.

Most new cadres, to be sure, were not Jews, but the Jewish presence in Hungarian communism proved to be more notable than elsewhere because of the public visibility they maintained with their positions in the press, the upper echelons of the armed forces (especially in the secret police), and the political bureaucracy. The four main party bosses, among them Mátyás Rákosi, "the best pupil of Stalin," were of Jewish descent. Thus, from the early years of the regime, its public image was that of "Jewish rule."[53] If the realities of party policy often and cruelly invalidated this image, the Jewish commitment to communism continued to carry more weight because it appeared to be more compromising. This could only increase the aforementioned overcommitment to the Jewish-communist option. Here, we must turn to the practical implications of this borderline pattern of Jewish identity, which was based on a high degree of collective self-assertion, on one hand, and the forceful dissimulation, indeed suppression, of markers of particularism, on the other.

Ambivalence about its beginning and its outcome was from the outset a built-in component of Jewish-communist commitment.[54] Being a shareholder in the party-state apparatus offered considerable advantages, but it also demanded complete behavioral alignment and conformism, excluding, among other things, any manifestation of Jewish identity. It actually imposed the highest possible degree of assimilation. Jewish cadres were expected to adopt not only the political platform of the party but also its "populist" clothing, speech, and life-style. The party line was to transcend and annihilate the distinction between cadres of different social origins and mold them into a common form.

Jewish cadres self-consciously accepted the pattern. Their children were educated in a lay spirit so they could declare that, "being atheists and Communists," they belonged to no denomination. Voluntary silence about Jewishness became the rule, even inside families. Children were regularly brought up unaware of their own ancestry, the martyrdom of their parents and kin, the historical fate of Jewry, and the Shoah. Many learned about being Jewish only when faced with anti-Semitism at school, in sports associations, or at private parties.[55] Such a privately observed taboo on Jewishness was meant to act as a self-fulfilling prophecy, under the assumption that if one completely dissimulated the fact of being Jewish, that identity would cease to exist.

Communist doctrine also imposed a veritable public taboo on all matters Jewish after 1949. Until then, hundreds of books, articles, pamphlets, films, and plays had dealt with the Shoah. Suddenly, no explicit mention of it could be made, or even of historical anti-Semitism. The euphemistic Stalinist vocabulary mixed victims of the Final Solution with other "victims of fascism." State-controlled media portrayed the antifascist resistance as a popular experience and ignored Zionists and the role played by Jews. This taboo indiscriminately affected literary fiction, political discourse, and the social sciences. In a way, both the Shoah and the Jewish past in Hungary were expelled from the collective memory. Of course, references to other ethnic and denominational communities were jettisoned, too, if they did not fit into the evolutionist scheme of history as a result of "class struggles" dictated by official Marxism.

The Jewish past was not the only casualty of Stalinist historical revisionism; the Jewish present outside the country suffered the same fate. After the founding of Israel, which had been promoted through a joint effort by the United States and the Soviet Union, an anti-Zionist campaign was launched in the satellite states that led to the brutal suppression of all Zionist movements in the region. Since the line separating the fight against Zionism, which was now labeled a "hellhound of imperialism," from other anti-Jewish measures was difficult to distinguish, the campaign often took on explicitly anti-Semitic overtones, especially in Czechoslovakia, Poland, Romania, and Russia.[56] The same was true, to a more limited extent, in the Hungarian trial of László Rajk, which had several Jewish victims, and in the persecution of "Zionist leaders" in Hungary. Contacts of Hungarian Jews with family and friends in Israel and the West were severed, and official relations between the Hungarian Jewish community and world Jewry were forbidden. Yet overt anti-Semitism was not as great in Hungary as it was in the USSR or Czechoslovakia.

Nevertheless, because of their allegedly middle-class extraction, well-established Jewish cadres could not feel secure. As "bourgeois elements," they frequently became targets of party purges after 1949. More importantly, ideological conformism did not protect Jews from discrimination, because high members of the *nomenklatura* espoused principles that helped to exploit and manipulate potential divisions between Jews and non-Jews inside the hierarchy. Thus, instead of neutralizing background variables, the Communist party during the Stalinist purges accentuated their influence on political careers. Jews were assigned to control "non-Jewish lobbies," and vice versa, or were dispersed so that they would be less "visible." Consequently, rather than disappearing or weakening, a Jewish consciousness was gradually re-created under the cover of official nondiscrimination policies of the Communist party. The dirty tricks that Stalinism played on Jews as the mirage of liberation and the egalitarian utopia dissolved into terror added to the price of socioprofessional *déclassement* that many of them paid in the early 1950s.

The aftermath of the death of the "father of progressive humanity" in 1953 was marked in Hungary by the heavily "revisionist" June program of the first Imre Nagy government. Having been so emotionally committed to communism, some Jewish cadres were among the first to turn against the Stalinist predicament and reinvest their hopes in "democratic socialism." The fight against Muscovite despotism created a new type of Jewish attachment to collective national causes, since many Jews and non-Jews joined efforts during the years of the thaw and in the revolutionary "popular front" of October 1956. Together they suffered the ensuing neocommunist repression, both in and out of prison. They also stood the test of the burgeoning political dissident movements of the 1970s and 1980s. On the other hand, many former Jewish cadres maintained their earlier communist bonds— upon which their careers continued to depend—but this was less true of their offspring. Jews were indeed strongly overrepresented among the rebels of 1953–56, the intellectual heroes of the October Revolution, and the leaders of the subsequent anticommunist dissidence.

This long, tortuous history explains why Jewish-Hungarian identity choices can nowadays once again be enriched with renewed patriotic, even nationalist, engagement, and by liberation from the communist taboo on Judaism.

Well before communism's collapse in 1989, many Jews became prominent as champions of the Transylvanian-Magyar cause, as well as in the process of normalization of local Jewish community life.

This is the ultimate irony. The last substantial surviving Jewish community in east-central Europe now faces a problem of identity that has been at the heart of Jewish existence throughout this region since the early nineteenth century and has never been resolved. Assimilation into the Hungarian nation and the promotion of a distinct Jewish identity again appear as viable options, as they did a hundred years ago.

NOTES

1. See Peter Kende, ed., *Zsidosàg a 1945 utàni Magyarorszàgon* [The Jews in Hungary after 1945] (Paris: Cahiers Hongrois, 1984), especially the articles by András Kovacs, pp. 3–32, and V. Karady, pp. 39–180. See also François Fejtö, *Les Juifs et l'antisémitisme dans les pays communistes (entre l'intégration et la sécession)* (Paris: Plon, 1960).

2. The concept of modernization is used here in its simplest historical sense, with reference to three major developments that marked the disappearance of feudalism. First, there was the creation of open markets, accessible to all economic actors. This meant the abolition of corporate restrictions and feudal limitations on trade, industry, and finance (as they were enforced against serfs, Jews, ethnic aliens, etc.) and the expansion of free enterprise. Second, there was the lifting of restrictive, legally stipulated status-bondage of persons—those laws limiting the geographic, residential, social, and denominational mobility of serfs, burghers, Jews, and so forth. Equality before the law and equal political and human rights for all were the final outcomes of this process. Third, modernization completed the development of nation-states with collective international sovereignty, representative government, and a political system based on a measure of separation of executive, judicial, and legislative powers and on the vastly enlarged and ever-growing competence of the state in fields of collective welfare.

3. On Jewish preeminence in early capitalism, see Hillel Levine, *Economic Origins of Anti-Semitism: Poland and Its Jews in the Early Modern Period* (New Haven, Connecticut: Yale University Press, 1991); Michael Silber, ed., *Jews in the Hungarian Economy, 1760–1945* (Jerusalem: Hebrew University Press, 1992), especially pp. 3–22. The only attempt to account for the social history of most sectors of Central European Jewry during the period of modernization is that of William O. McCagg, Jr., *A History of Habsburg Jews, 1670–1918* (Bloomington: Indiana University Press, 1989). Various aspects of this history are discussed in the papers of the first conference ever

dedicated to the topic, held in Paris in 1985; see Yehuda Don and Victor Karady, eds., *Social and Economic History of Central European Jewry* (New Brunswick, New Jersey: Transaction Books, 1990). For a thorough overview of the Jews' situation, especially the political, in each major country in the region before the Shoah, see Ezra Mendelsohn, *The Jews of East Central Europe between the Wars* (Bloomington: Indiana University Press, 1983). For economic aspects of Jewish success, see Yehuda Don, "Patterns of Jewish Economic Behaviour in Central Europe in the Twentieth Century," in Silber, *Jews in the Hungarian Economy*, pp. 247–73; Victor Karady, "Jüdische Unternehmer und Prozesse der Verbürgerlichung in der Habsburger-Monarchie (19.–20. Jahrhundert)," in Werner Mosse and Hans Pohl, eds., *Jüdische Unternehmer in Deutschland im 19. und 20. Jahrhundert* (Stuttgart: Franz Steiner Verlag, 1992), pp. 37–52; Joseph Marcus, *Social and Political History of the Jews in Poland, 1919–1939* (Amsterdam: Mouton, 1983).

4. Victor Karady and István Kemény, "Les Juifs dans la structure des classes en Hongrie, essai sur les antécédents historiques des crises d'antisémitisme du 20è siècle," *Actes de la Recherche en Sciences Sociales* 22 (1978), pp. 26–60.

5. On militant anti-Semitic movements, see Mària M. Kovàcs, *The Politics of the Legal Profession in Interwar Hungary* (New York: Columbia University Institute of East Central Europe, 1987).

6. Andrew C. Janos, *The Politics of Backwardness in Hungary, 1825–1945* (Princeton, New Jersey: Princeton University Press, 1982), pp. 76–182; Karady and Kemény, "Les Juifs," pp. 28–36; Rolf Fischer, *Entwicklungsstufen des Antisemitismus in Ungarn, 1867–1939. Die Zerstörung der magyarisch-jüdischen Symbiose* (München: Oldenburg, 1988), pp. 115–16; László Gonda, *A zsidosàg Magyarorszàgon 1526–1945* [Jewry in Hungary, 1526–1945] (Budapest: Szàzadvég, 1988), pp. 162–64.

7. For a thorough study of the German-Jewish symbiosis in Prague, interpreted as a rampart against Czech nationalism, see Gary Cohen, *The Politics of Ethnic Survival: Germans in Prague, 1861–1914* (Princeton, New Jersey: Princeton University Press, 1981). On the broader Bohemian situation, see Hillel Kieval, "Caution's Progress: The Modernization of Jewish Life in Prague, 1780–1930," in Jakob Katz, ed., *Toward Modernity: The European Jewish Model* (New Brunswick, New Jersey: Transaction Books, 1987); Hillel Kieval, *The Making of Czech Jewry* (New York: Oxford University Press, 1988).

8. Ruth Kestenberg-Gladstein, *Neuere Gehscichte der Juden in den Böhmischen Ländern* (Tübingen: Mohr, 1969).

9. Janos, *The Politics of Backwardness*, pp. 112–18; Carol Iancu, *Les Juifs de Roumanie, 1866–1919, de l'exclusion à l'émancipation* (Aix-en-Provence: Editions de l'Université de Provence, 1978), passim; Gerhard Botz, Ivar Oxaal, and Michael Pollak, eds., *Jews, Antisemitism and Culture in Vienna* (London: Routledge and Kegan Paul, 1987), pp. 10–38.

10. These differences can be best understood by comparing Jewish and Gentile patterns of socioeconomic stratification in various countries. Whereas Jewish stratification was marked by a majority of independent entrepreneurs or professionals, disproportionate urbanization, and the presence of large educated groups, Gentile societies on the whole were overwhelmingly made up of peasants and other rural strata. For such comparisons, see Arthur Ruppin, *Soziologie der Juden,* 2 vols. (Berlin: Jüdischer Verlag, 1930–31), pp. 357–88; Karady and Kemény, "Les Juifs," pp. 40–43; Marcus, *Social and Political History,* pp. 5–121; Silber, *Jews in the Hungarian Economy,* pp. 42–49, 53, 67, passim.

11. For Romania, see the following recent studies: Leon Volovici, *Nationalist Ideology and Antisemitism: The Case of Romanian Intellectuals in the 1930s* (Oxford: Pergamon Press, 1991), especially pp. 1–44; Iancu, "Les Juifs," passim. For the Polish lands, see Marcus, *Social and Political History.* On Hungary, see L. Randolph Braham, *Hungarian-Jewish Studies,* vols. 1–3 (New York: World Federation of Hungarian Jews, 1966–73), passim; Braham, *The Politics of Genocide: The Holocaust in Hungary,* 2 vols. (New York: Columbia University Press, 1981), especially pp. 16–69. For Austria, see particularly Marsha Rozenblit, *The Jews of Vienna: Assimilation and Identity, 1867–1914* (Albany: State University of New York Press, 1983), pp. 5–6, 145–96, passim. For the sociological, intellectual, and political aspects of the development of Viennese Jewry after 1848, see, respectively, Botz, Oxaal, and Pollak, *Jews;* Robert S. Wistrich, *The Jews of Vienna in the Age of Franz Joseph* (Oxford: Oxford University Press [The Littman Library], 1889); Peter Pulzer, *The Rise of Political Anti-Semitism in Germany and Austria* (London: Peter Halban, 1988, rev. ed.).

12. Rachel Ertel, *Le stetl, la bourgade juive de Pologne* (Paris: Payot, 1982), pp. 113–26; Marcus, *Social and Political History,* pp. 51–72.

13. Don, "Patterns," p. 262.

14. Victor Karady and Wolfgang Mitter, eds., *Education and Social Structure in Central Europe in the 19th and 20th Century* (Köln: Böhlau Verlag, 1990), especially the chapter "The Case of Jewish Over-Schooling," pp. 141–246.

15. Peter Hanàk, "Problems of Jewish Assimilation in Austria-Hungary," in P. Thane, ed., *The Power of the Past* (Cambridge: Cambridge University Press, 1986), pp. 235–50; Béla Vago, ed., *Jewish Assimilation in Modern Times* (Boulder, Colorado: Westview Press, 1981), especially the contributions by N. Katzburg, pp. 49–55, and George Schöpflin, pp. 75–88; George L. Mosse and Béla Vago, eds., *Jews and Non-Jews in Eastern Europe, 1918–1945* (New York: Israel Universities Press, 1974), passim.

16. Steven Beller, *Vienna and the Jews, 1967–1939: A Cultural History* (New York: Cambridge University Press, 1989), pp. 111–13, 201–3; William O. McCagg, Jr., *Jewish Nobles and Geniuses in Modern Hungary* (New York: Columbia University Press, 1986, reissue of the 1972 edition); Pawel Korzec, *Juifs de Pologne, la question juive*

pendant l'entre-deux-guerres (Paris: Fondation Nationale des Sciences Politiques, 1980), pp. 30–67; Kieval, *The Making of Czech Jewry*, pp. 93–153.

17. For a subtle study of all these issues in pre-partition Poland, see Levine, *Economic Origins*, pp. 57–74. For other examples, see articles by Peter Hanàk and Vera Bacskai in Silber, *Jews in the Hungarian Economy*, pp. 23–49.

18. The infamous Familientengesetz, enacted by the Habsburg Emperor Charles III in 1726, was a conspicuous case of familial restrictions in the century of Enlightenment. In order to restrict the size of the Jewish population in Cisleithenian Austria (especially in Bohemia), only one male member in each Jewish family was allowed to marry and have a family.

19. McCagg, *Jewish Nobles*, passim; Karady and Mitter, *Education and Social Structure*, especially pp. 213–27.

20. Aron Moskovits, *Jewish Education in Hungary, 1848–1948* (New York: Bloch, 1964), passim.

21. On the social utility of education for Hungarian Jewry (and for further references), see Karady and Mitter, *Education and Social Structure*, pp. 222–27.

22. Peter Hanàk, "Das Judentum und die Modernisierung des Handels in Ungarn, 1760–1848," in Ferenc Glatz, ed., *Modern Age—Modern Historian* (Budapest: Institute of History of the Hungarian Academy of Sciences, 1990), pp. 97–109.

23. For in-depth sociological approaches to this matter in Vienna, see Rozenblit, *The Jews of Vienna*, pp. 126–74; Beller, *Vienna and the Jews*, pp. 206–36; Botz, Oxaal, and Pollak, *Jews*, pp. 59–74.

24. This happened most conspicuously in regions of the pre-1918 Hungarian territories, which were populated mostly by ethnic minorities. In "Upper Hungary"—Slovakia—and Transylvania (with a Romanian majority), the Magyarized Jewish intelligentsia and bourgeoisie represented Magyardom proper and behaved as committed Magyarizers, devoted to Magyar national ideals. This pattern of behavior prevailed after the 1848–49 revolution and the fight for independence, when most Hungarian Jews supported the Magyar cause against Austria and local national groups. Hence, the "Jewish-Magyar" symbiosis was a major ideological strand of Hungarian Jewry. Up to the Shoah, this weakened any political and cultural separatism or support for Zionism. See Fischer, *Entwicklungsstufen*, pp. 30–32; McCagg, *A History of Habsburg Jews*, pp. 136–39; Janos, *The Politics of Backwardness*, pp. 117–18; Gonda, *A zsidosàg*, pp. 162–69.

25. In this respect, the whole east-central European region can be divided according to whether there was an integrative or an exclusionary political culture. The Polish lands and Romania belonged largely to the latter category; Austria, Bohemia, and Hungary more to the former. The operative definition of the difference between the two can be based upon the degree to which Jews were admitted into national

political organizations and upon the scope of Jewish political separatism. Such separatism was practically nonexistent in Hungary throughout the period of modernization.

26. In some cases, as in interwar Poland, market discrimination affected Jews and sometimes even other ethnic aliens. See Marcus, *Social and Political History,* pp. 212–18. Elsewhere, as in both liberal (pre-1918) and interwar Hungary, Jews were exclusive targets of market discrimination within the civil service, while assimilated ethnic aliens were fully admitted to state-controlled markets. See Karady and Kemény, "Les Juifs," pp. 55–59.

27. The Hungarian civil service demanded six hours of work per day, whereas the figure was eight to ten hours in the private economy.

28. In imperial Austria, baptized Jews could reach ministerial rank. The Hungarian minister of defense during part of World War I, Baron Samu Hazai, was a baptized Jew. But it was only in the very last Hungarian governments of the Dual Monarchy, under the ephemeral rule of Emperor Charles in 1917–18, that a denominational Jew, Vilmos Vàzsonyi, could win appointment as minister of justice. Although Jews could be appointed to professorships after emancipation, baptism would still make career advancement much easier. See McCagg, *Jewish Nobles and Geniuses,* passim.

29. Kende, *Zsidosàg,* pp. 61–63.

30. Daniel Tollet, *Histoire des Juifs en Pologne* (Paris: Presses Universitaires de France, 1992), p. 298.

31. Institute of Jewish Affairs (n.a.), *European Jewry Ten Years after the War* (New York: Institute of Jewish Affairs, 1956).

32. On the new regime's role in anti-Semitism, see Marc Hillel, *Le massacre des survivants en Pologne après l'Holocaust (1945–1947)* (Paris: Plon, 1985); Christian Jelen, *La purge. Chasse au juif en Pologne populaire* (Paris: Fayard, 1974); Jean-Charles Szurek, "Shoah: De la question juive à la question polonaise," in *Au sujet de "Shoah," le film de Claude Lanzman* (Paris: Belin, 1990), pp. 258–75.

33. Fejtö, *Les Juifs,* pp. 66–68.

34. For Romania, see Raphael Vago, "The Communization of Jewish Life in Romania, 1944–1949," *Slavic and Soviet Studies* 1 (1977), pp. 49–67. For Poland, see Aleksander Smolar, "Jews as a Polish Problem," *Daedalus* 116:2 (1987), pp. 31–73; Szurek, "Shoah"; Marcin Kula, "A Postcommunist Problem or a Historically-Shaped Polish Problem? On Jews and Poles Once More," *Polish Sociological Bulletin* 2 (1992), pp. 95–114; Michel Wievorka, *Les Juifs, la Pologne et Solidarnosc* (Paris: Denoël, 1984). For Czechoslovakia, see Fejtö, *Les Juifs,* pp. 70–98; Vilma Iggers, *Die Juden in Böhmen und Mähren, ein historisches Lesebuch* (München: Beck, 1986), pp. 339–72. For Hungary, see Andràs Kovàcs, "La question juive dans la Hongrie contemporaine," *Actes de la Recherche en Sciences Sociales* 85 (1985), pp. 45–57; Victor Karady, "Some Social Aspects of Jewish Assimilation in Socialist Hungary, 1945–1956," in

L. Randolph Braham, ed., *The Tragedy of Hungarian Jewry: Essays, Documents, Depositions* (New York: Columbia University Press, 1986), pp. 73–131.

35. L. Randolph Braham, ed., *Studies on the Holocaust in Hungary* (New York: Columbia University Press, 1990); Braham, *The Politics of Genocide,* pp. 514–24.

36. Victor Karady, "Post-Holocaust Hungarian Jewry, 1945–1948: Class Structure, Re-Stratification and Potential for Social Mobility," *Studies in Contemporary Jewry* 3 (1987), pp. 147–60; Kende, *Zsidòsàg,* pp. 72–84.

37. Karady, "Post-Holocaust Hungarian Jewry," p. 150.

38. Yehuda Don, "The Economic Dimensions of Anti-Semitism: Anti-Jewish Legislation in Hungary, 1938–1944," *East European Quarterly* 20 (Winter 1986), pp. 447–65.

39. Kende, *Zsidòsàg,* pp. 134–37.

40. Kovàcs, "La question," pp. 48–49

41. For a classical study of this period, see István Bibó, "La question juive en Hongrie après 1945," in *Misère des petits Etats d'Europe de l'Est* (Paris: L'Harmattan, 1986), pp. 211–392, especially p. 377.

42. Kende, *Zsidòsàg,* p. 110; Kovàcs, "La question," p. 51; Karady, "Some Social Aspects," pp. 74–75.

43. Karady, "Some Social Aspects," pp. 110–11.

44. As the expression was cited in Fischer, *Entwicklungsstufen.* See also McCagg, *A History of Habsburg Jews,* pp. 132–34.

45. See Bibó, "La question," pp. 287–363 and passim, for a detailed discussion of the postwar Jewish-Gentile division that arose as a consequence of the "bad historical organization of relationships" between the two groups, especially the inadequate Magyar reactions to Nazism. This study is all the more important because it emanated from the most prominent Gentile political theorist of the new era. Bibó was briefly minister of state in the 1956 revolutionary government.

46. Kovàcs, in "La question juive," p. 47, duly stresses the divisive experience of the liberation.

47. On the dilemmas of identity options of formerly "bourgeois" Jews under communism, see Karady, "Some Social Aspects," pp. 108–10.

48. Kende, *Zsidòsàg,* pp. 69–71.

49. I have undertaken a number of empirical surveys about "remnant Jewry" in Budapest, Szeged, Kolozsvàr-Cluj, and elsewhere in order to clarify the social conditions underlying dissimilationist, dissimulationist, and assimilationist identity strategies between 1945 and 1951 or 1957. These surveys are based largely on contemporary public records or Jewish community archives concerning marriage choices (mixed vs. homogamous), patterns of baptism, the Magyarization of family names, schooling choices, and survivals of the Orthodox-liberal division in Jewish communities.

50. Kende, *Zsidòsàg,* pp. 142–43; Karady, "Some Social Aspects," pp. 117–18.

51. After the 1868 "Jewish Congress," which followed the Emancipation Bill of 1867, Hungarian Jewry was split into three nationwide community networks— Orthodox, "Neologue," and "status-quo-ante"—officially recognized by the state. Reform-minded "Neologues" were often termed "Congress Jewry" because their Orthodox counterparts walked out of the meeting at an early stage. This arrangement guaranteed a large measure of liberty for each Jewish group in religious matters and limited conflict among the different communities. The three networks were compelled to join a unitary organization created in 1951 under pressure from the Stalinist regime, which wished to consolidate its power over them.

52. Gonda, *A zsidosàg*, pp. 82–93; Fischer, *Entwicklungsstufen*, pp. 37–38; McCagg, *A History of Habsburg Jews*, pp. 134–35.

53. For a thorough investigation of this issue, which concludes that if Jews were prominent in the party apparatus, they by no means ruled as representatives of any kind of "Jewish interests," see Bibó, "La question," especially pp. 382–85.

54. On the following discussion, see Karady, "Some Social Aspects," pp. 111–19; Kovàcs, "La question juive," p. 51.

55. For a remarkable experimental study of this topic and a unique set of personal testimonies by young people of Jewish background born after 1945, see Ferenc Erös, Andràs Kovàcs, and Katalin Lévai, "Comment j'en suis venu à apprendre que j'était Juif," *Actes de la Recherche en Sciences Sociales* 56 (1985), pp. 63–68. The study is based on a selection of biographical interviews (out of 110) conducted under the direction of Erös and Kovàcs, which have so far been only partly used.

56. Fejtö, *Les Juifs*, pp. 34–56, 65–78.

6 / Anti-Sinicism and Chinese Identity Options in the Philippines

EDGAR WICKBERG

Four events of the early 1990s illustrate the promise and perils of the Philippine Chinese situation. For "promise," consider the first and second. In September 1992, a capacity audience of 2,500 expatriate Filipinos paid substantial prices to attend the Carnegie Hall concert of Jose Mari Chan. Chan, an ethnic Chinese born in the Philippines, is an immensely popular composer and singer of romantic ballads of the kind especially attractive to Filipinos. A longtime American observer of the Philippines has suggested that Filipinos consider Chan, although Chinese, "one of the authoritative carriers of contemporary Philippine popular culture."[1]

Shift the scene to Manila, where, in January 1993, at least 25,000 ethnic Chinese marched in an unprecedented protest demonstration against the Philippine government's alleged lack of vigorous action against kidnap-for-ransom gangs that particularly targeted ethnic Chinese. The protest march, led by an organization of young (under age fifty) ethnic Chinese professionals, intellectuals, and businesspeople, was joined by a variety of ethnic Chinese organizations, including some of the more traditional ones.[2]

Two other events seem to illustrate perils for the Chinese, along with the persistence of older attitudes and policies on the part of Philippine leaders. Six ethnic Chinese billionaires who accompanied President Ramos on a tour of China were told at the end of it that they should invest in Philippine infrastructural development. Subsequently, a government news release announced that the Philippine Bureau of Internal Revenue would target for investigation the tax payment records of these six citizens. While denying that only ethnic Chinese were targeted, a government spokesman was quoted, in response to the question "What do you want the Filipino Chinese to do?" as saying: "They're already in a position of advantage. They should invest more in the Philippines rather than outside. The country should not be a milking cow."[3] To the Chinese this must have sounded like just the latest version of the familiar "shakedown"—not, this time, on charges of illegal immigration or communist sympathies, but something more contemporary.

In early 1994 the government announced that the citizenship petitions of more than a thousand ethnic Chinese, pending for almost twenty years, would finally be considered. At the same time, however, it spoke of how much revenue the government might reap by doing so. And in public statements, the government mixed its discussions of the applications of these long-time residents with news about an amnesty declaration for illegal immigrants—most of them Chinese.[4] Thereby, legally resident Chinese who aspired to citizenship were put in the same category as illegally present Chinese.

These incidents seem to illustrate what George Weightman, writing in 1985, characterized as the transitional status of the Philippine Chinese, somewhere between that of aliens and that of cultural minority.[5] Most of today's ethnic Chinese population was born in the Philippines, and most are citizens. But they are not, so it appears, citizens with full rights and nothing to prove. Some of the episodes just described seem similar to experiences of German Jews, in particular. Jose Mari Chan may indeed be the voice of Filipino pop culture (though a Chinese publication insists that his first concern is with the family business),[6] but there are well-known dangers for the descendant of a "stranger" minority who seems to outdo the dominant majority on its own terms. The "something to prove" theme is also familiar.

In what follows, I treat the Philippine Chinese case historically. Many years ago my book *The Chinese in Philippine Life* dealt with part of that history, stressing inclusion. Here I use as a framework what I see as the alternating inclusion and exclusion of ethnic Chinese in Philippine society. I argue that the Chinese were a business community on the margins of Philippine society from 1570 to 1750, an integral part of that society in the century from 1750 to 1850, a remarginalized alien group from then until the 1970s, and a group existing somewhere between marginality and inclusion since then.

1570–1850: CULTURAL AND RESIDENTIAL DEFINITIONS

1570–1750: Cultural Definitions

Large numbers of Chinese first began to arrive in the Philippines with the onset of Spanish settlement and colonial rule. By 1600, some 20,000 to

30,000 Chinese resided in Manila and a few other sites, and for much of the seventeenth century those were typical figures. Most Chinese were sojourners, not settling as families but coming as single males intending at some point to return to their families in China. In other words, the social stability and devotion to cultural maintenance often found among family-based settlers were not so common in this case. Economically, the Chinese created new occupations and services. Besides handling the important trade between China and the Philippines, they engaged in most lines of commerce, artisanry, and services. Having created these occupations, they quickly established a monopoly over them.

Within a few years after 1570 the Spaniards had developed an antipathy for the Chinese in their midst. The entire Spanish colony was economically dependent upon the Chinese, and the number of Chinese was usually much in excess of the number of Spanish officials, settlers, and military personnel. Although the Chinese created wealth, it was argued that they also took or sent it away to China.[7]

Besides these economic considerations, with their political overtones, there were cultural reasons for Spanish antipathies. The Spanish experience of the *reconquista* in Spain was not that distant in time. The conquest of the Philippines was undertaken in part as a missionary effort to spread Catholicism, which was closely linked with Spanish rule. Residents of Spanish-ruled territories, if converted to the Catholic faith, became vassals or subjects of the Spanish king. In Spain, the conquering Spaniards had encountered Jews and Moors, culturally alien groups with useful economic skills, but difficult to convert to Catholicism—people whose conversion, and therefore political loyalty, was seen as questionable. Spaniards carried the same attitudes and doubts to the Philippines and expressed them in dealing with the merchant "strangers" there, the Chinese. They regularly applied the term "infidel" to Philippine Chinese who had not accepted the faith.[8]

The Spanish sense of cultural mission—to convert and transform the inhabitants of the Philippines—was so strong that over many decades when the colony was a losing proposition economically, arguments supporting its retention on cultural grounds helped persuade Spanish governments to stay the course.[9] Converting the inhabitants meant mostly the Filipinos. By the mid-seventeenth century, the majority of Filipinos had become Catholics, accepting the faith—and Spain's tutorial role—at least partly on their own terms.[10] The Chinese, mostly, did not, or did so on dubious grounds and with questionable results.

Ideally, these essential businessmen, aliens at the start, could be redeemed into reliable subjects of the king.[11] But in fact, the Chinese did not match the

Spaniards in their religious attitudes. Whereas the latter defined themselves in large part by religion, the former did not. Chinese defined themselves by social ethics and discipline—attributes that encouraged social harmony and familial success. Religiously, they were eclectic. Far from undergoing the agonizing experience of European Jews over converting to Christianity, Chinese simply added it as one of many religious beliefs that gave additional structure and personal effectiveness to their world. There was no sense of surrender about accepting the dominant power's faith, and nothing specifically anti-Chinese about Christianity.

Filipinos, on the other hand, came to take Catholicism as one of their defining characteristics. The more they did so, the more they defined non-Catholic Chinese as alien to them. Meanwhile, the Spaniards, perhaps with an eye to the Filipino consumer, freely catalogued Chinese cultural evils. One list of such can be obtained from the index to a collection of Philippine documents.[12] There, more than forty reprehensible characteristics of non-Catholic Chinese are listed—mostly of a moral and social behavioral nature.

In the Spanish colonial tutorial environment, Filipinos picked up many of these attitudes. In pre-Spanish times their relations with Chinese visitors had been amicable, by all indications. Under Spanish tutelage, Filipinos learned the term for Chinese that Spaniards used: *sangley*. That name, Chinese derived, apparently meant "Chinese merchant," but Spaniards' usage gave it pejorative overtones. Before long, the Filipinos' term for Chinese, *intsik*, originally a word with respectful connotations, became one of opprobrium. It was often used in tandem with the word *babuy*, or pig. The two together might, in English, be rendered "Chink pig." But though Filipinos often sided with the Spaniards against the Chinese, they and the Chinese also frequently found themselves united in common causes.[13] The relationship was not a simple one.

Besides their economic and cultural objections to the Chinese, the Spaniards had one other, perhaps the most important of all: the suspected alien political loyalties of the Chinese. The Philippines are not distant from China, and Philippine Chinese made frequent visits there. In the seventeenth century the Spaniards' greatest fear was an uprising by the numerically dominant Chinese of Manila, accompanied by assistance from China. Although their fears proved groundless, the anxiety was real and conditioned Spanish policies of that era.

Those policies included immigration limitations (often ill enforced and ineffectual) and, for those already in the Philippines, restraints on geographic mobility within the islands, residential segregation, and attempts at conversion to Catholicism. A segregated Chinese quarter, the Parian (a word suggesting pariah status but of undetermined origin), was established outside Manila; there, economic services were available but security maintained. Converted Chinese were separated from "infidels." A special settlement for the former, especially those who had married Filipinas, was established in Binondo (site of today's Chinatown), distant from the Parian, with a Chinese Catholic church.

Conversion led to advantages and opportunities. The headmen of the Chinese, recognized by the Spaniards, had to be Catholics. Only Catholics could legally marry Filipinas—an important consideration in this mostly "bachelor" group. Catholics were often given opportunities to reside away from Manila—opportunities usually denied to others.[14]

The Chinese who came to the Philippines, mostly small entrepreneurs and artisans and often illiterate, probably lacked a sophisticated understanding of Chinese culture. They saw themselves in terms of their home region on China's south coast and identified China and Chinese culture with that region. Though they had no sense of China as a nation, they were undoubtedly given to assuming, as Chinese generally did, the superiority of the Chinese way as they understood it. They also were no doubt aware that China had a great history and heritage, even if they understood little of it. Their cultural values emphasized the commercial side of Chinese popular culture, and their agenda in the Philippines was to use business to benefit their families at home as quickly as possible.

They presented themselves as businesspeople and readily perceived that neither Spaniards nor Filipinos were so oriented. The subordination of Filipinos to Spaniards was also not missed and must have contributed to their views of both. Recent developments in coastal Chinese urban popular values,[15] along with their own experiences in the Philippines, encouraged the self-definition of these would-be business-class Chinese as more industrious, frugal, and resilient in the face of adversity (including restrictive policies) than Spaniards or Filipinos. Their term for Spaniards and Filipinos was the common south Chinese word for non-Chinese: "barbarians"—in their local dialect, *huan-a*. So far as we know, there were no literary forms of expression among the Philippine Chinese in this period, but we do know that Chinese theater was performed in Manila almost from the beginning. Whether the "comedias chinas" that so agitated the Spaniards in the eighteenth century did so because of the way they depicted Spaniards and Filipinos, we cannot as yet tell.[16]

Though the sojourning character of Chinese immigration meant much population turnover, some sense of community must have developed. Spanish policies certainly treated the Chinese as a community. Headmen spoke for the

Chinese bloc, and there were segregated residences, Parians or otherwise, Chinese churches, and a missionary hospital for the Chinese. A community chest, paid for by Chinese taxes, provided for certain welfare and other expenses for the group. Chinese must also have felt a common resentment of Spanish restrictions that frustrated their attempts at rapid economic betterment.

Chinese, Spanish, and Filipino contacts and attitudes reached flashpoint on several occasions in the seventeenth century. There were three or four "uprisings" and "massacres" during that time. In some of these, as many as 20,000 or 30,000 Chinese were killed. Detailed explanations of them may never be possible, but it is clear that their origins lay in the attitudes I have described, attitudes that were exacerbated, on the Spanish side, by fears of an uprising aided by China, and on the Chinese side, by fears of a preventive massacre. In some of these incidents, China was involved, though indirectly; in others, it was merely part of Spanish anxiety. But clearly, anxiety about China was an important background to all of them. It is equally clear that despite these sanguinary episodes, Chinese always returned to the profits of business (despite restrictions) in the Philippines.

For the Chinese, ethnicity options centered on conversion, intermarriage, and residence, and on the opportunities and visibility they entailed. Conversion offered the economic and political opportunities referred to earlier. It also provided one with a baptismal sponsor, usually a Spaniard, who might serve as a protector, guarantor, and business associate.[17] But the more involved one became with Spaniards, the more visible one would become, too. This raised the likelihood of responsibilities and demands that were unwelcome and distracting. Legal marriage (there were many irregular unions) might offer strategic advantages in business, and the children of the marriage might continue the business. But it was also a complicating factor. Long residence, coupled with conversion and intermarriage, enhanced one's reputation for reliability and stability. That, too, however, could be an encumbrance. It is likely that only well-established businessmen with highly developed businesses would reach this point. By then, whatever term they might have used for themselves, they would have been called *sangleyes cristianos* (Christian Chinese merchants) by Spaniards and Filipinos.

Conversion could be more complicating than that. In the seventeenth century, it might have made it impossible to return to China. For a time during that century the Spaniards in the Philippines insisted that Chinese converts cut their hair, thereby removing their plaited queues. The queue had been imposed upon the Chinese by the Manchu rulers of Qing China as a symbol of Chinese vassalage, and its removal was an act of disloyalty punishable by death. A Philippine Chinese who cut off his queue effectively cut himself off from returning to China.[18] Clearly, conflicting claims of loyalty and sovereignty were involved here. By the third decade of the eighteenth century, hair cutting was no longer an issue. But by that time the Qing government had in place both laws against Catholics in China and laws prohibiting emigration from China. The latter carried severe penalties for those emigrants who returned. A returning Catholic was in double jeopardy.

1750–1850: Residential Definitions

In the 1750s and 1760s, the Chinese population of the Philippines was reduced to about 5,000 to 10,000, and it remained at that level for the next several decades. The process began with a Spanish decision to favor the interests of local Spaniards and rising Filipino and mestizo merchants by expelling most of the Chinese and concentrating those remaining in the Manila area. By design, most of those remaining were Catholics. Within a few years, the Spaniards were shocked to discover that their cultural policy of equating Catholics with reliability was a complete failure. During the Seven Years War in Europe, English forces from Madras occupied Manila from 1762 to 1764, driving the Spanish government into exile in the interior. The Chinese of Manila were not slow to accommodate themselves to the new politics. When the Spanish government was restored, all Chinese who had sided with the English were expelled, the Catholics being especially censured for their apostasy and defection.

This experience apparently convinced the Spaniards that conversion as a policy was less valuable than they had believed, and the emphasis now switched to long residence as an indicator of reliability. Already, in the 1750s, a new trading facility had been built to keep seasonal traders from China separate from the Chinese who were residents, whether Catholics or not. By the 1790s the Manila Parian was dismantled, and resident Chinese, whatever their religion, were allowed to live anywhere in the Manila area. Most settled in Binondo, which soon came to be Manila's Chinatown, the locus of a mixed population of Chinese, Filipinos, and mestizos and the center of business for the city as a whole.[19]

The Chinese now entered a period of stability and acceptance into the society as a minority. Their population was small and stable. Even when concentrated, as in Binondo, it was matched by the non-Chinese population around it. Moreover, China was no longer seen as a threat. During this period the Philippines opened up to international trade, including that of non-Spanish Westerners trading with China. By the 1840s, Spanish merchants and even diplomats were visiting China as never before. By then, with news of the Opium War, it was evident that China was not the military threat it had once seemed to be. It was also evident that prohibitions on Catholics in China and on emigration by Chinese had been relaxed. In the Philippines there were no more flashpoints in the relations between Chinese and non-Chinese. There were anti-Chinese riots in the 1820s, but these were nothing like the uprisings and massacres of the seventeenth and eighteenth centuries.

By this time, many decades of intermarriage had created a sizable group of mixed Chinese-Filipino mestizos. By 1800 they were ten times as numerous as the Chinese.[20] Culturally, they usually identified themselves with their place of birth, the Philippines, and with Catholicism. Their styles of dress and behavior expanded upon Spanish models to create a hispanicized Philippine culture that set the pace for the urban Philippines for over a century. Many mestizos were quite skillful in business and began with an inheritance of some sort from their Chinese parent.[21] As the number of Chinese was decreased by the expulsions, mestizos moved into occupations Chinese had once dominated. There can be little doubt that mestizo business success reduced the pressures on the Chinese in this period and also made it easier for non-Chinese to accept the continuing presence of a smaller number of Chinese, who were now overshadowed by mestizos.

By the 1740s, the mestizos had their own *gremios,* or sociopolitical-religious associations, wherever they were numerous. The Spaniards recognized these and in fact accepted and enforced a policy of cultural classification and organization that attempted to keep Malay Filipinos, mestizos, and Chinese apart from one another. These were also tax groups: Chinese paid the highest taxes, mestizos the next highest, and Filipinos the lowest rates, based upon assumptions about earning power and assets.[22]

The Chinese mestizos of the Philippines may be thought of as a "creolized Chinese" group broadly similar to the *peranakan* of Indonesia and the *baba* of Malaya. What is striking about them is their apparently unambiguous sense of themselves not as special Chinese but as special Filipinos. Because of this identification with the Philippines and with Filipinos of similar class, Philippine Chinese mestizos seem to have been generally accepted by the Filipino population, though not without a mixture of envy and resentment at times. Indeed, in the late nineteenth century they helped create both the urban culture of the Philippines and the very term "Filipino."[23] In cultural expression, too, it is likely that they manifested no great sense of ambivalence about identity. The subject has not been researched, but glancing at the nineteenth-century writings of mestizos, one does not perceive the sense of personal agonizing over identity and intermarriage found in early-twentieth-century *peranakan* writings from Indonesia.[24]

With a small and stable Chinese population and with strict limits on immigration, it is likely that those Chinese who remained were increasingly following the identity options associated with long residence, conversion, intermarriage, and *mestizaje*.

1850–1975: NATIONAL DEFINITIONS

1850–1900: *Toward National Definitions*

In the middle of the nineteenth century, Spain began—belatedly, in comparison with other Southeast Asian colonial powers—to try to make its Philippine colony economically profitable. One of the measures it initiated was almost unrestricted immigration of "industrious" Chinese. During the decades after 1800, the Philippine Chinese population had slowly increased to a level of 40,000. Now it suddenly ballooned to 100,000 by the 1890s. Not only were the Chinese more numerous, but they were also able to reside almost anywhere in the islands and to participate in any occupation. The "Chinese economy" in the Philippines became much larger and more diverse than ever before. Chinese reclaimed their preeminence in retail trade and took a substantial share in wholesaling away from the mestizos. They also became the principal collectors of produce for export and distributors of imported goods.[25]

We do not yet know how long-resident, acculturated Chinese reacted to this sharp influx of newcomer Chinese. We do know that mestizos had to give up their predominance in several areas and were forced to adapt economically. This they did by moving into agriculture, especially sugar growing (and milling, in some cases) and certain craft lines. The most affluent mestizos, by this time, were also taking advantage of new opportunities for higher education in Manila and in Spain, thereby becoming professionals and intellectuals in the Philippines. Socially, culturally, and politically they now joined the growing body of educated, middle-class Malay Filipinos to form both a new middle-class urban culture and a new native elite, one that demanded for "Filipinos," the term they now used for themselves, the rights of Spaniards—the same rights hammered out in nineteenth-century Spain over decades of political turmoil. Eventually, these demands led to a Philippine revolution for independence in the 1890s. Spain's cultural tutoring had been so successful that it had created what Spain feared most.[26]

These changes took place within a broader context of changing Spanish conceptions of the Philippine environment. Social, administrative, and fiscal changes led to the decline and disappearance of the *gremios*. Mestizos and

Malay Filipinos could not be kept apart. Municipal judges were being appointed to take over local administration from ethnic *gremios*. Ethnic-based taxation was replaced by business and other taxes based on earning and asset categories rather than on ethnic assumptions.[27]

National considerations and frames of reference also entered the picture. By this time, many non-Spanish Europeans were living in the Philippines. They were jealous of their rights and privileges as citizens of their home countries, and Spain had to recognize these. By the 1840s, China began to be thought of in the same way. Chinese in the Philippines, if long resident and Catholic, might become Spanish subjects.[28] This option was similar to that available to Chinese in British territories in Asia by this time. In the 1860s, Spain signed treaties with China by which both sides recognized the right of Chinese to go to the Philippines in any number and to receive fair treatment there. There were prolonged discussions between the two countries over the possibility of a Chinese consulate in Manila, but Spain was reluctant and the negotiations failed.[29]

China was now changing its attitude and policy toward its subjects abroad, moving from disinterest and suspicion to solicitation of their continued remittances to their relatives in south China and encouragement of their financial aid to China's early modernizing projects. To this end, the Chinese government was willing to establish consulates and to woo leaders of Chinese communities abroad with honors and titles for their efforts.

The leaders of Manila's Chinese community were well aware of these changes. It was they who took the initiative regarding the consulate—part of their response to the changes just described. But some other relevant changes included a rising wave of anti-Chinese sentiment in the 1880s. Mestizos and Malay Filipinos (the latter often displaced from labor gangs by newcomer Chinese laborers), as well as newcomer Spaniards seeking fortunes that somehow were not there, turned upon the Chinese as the cause of their difficulties.[30] The campaign itself achieved nothing in terms of any anti-Chinese expulsion or even changes in immigration or other policies. Nor did it deflect Filipinos agitating for reform in the colony, whose target continued to be Spain. What it did do was create a sense of community among the Chinese.

The Chinese now organized for themselves more elaborate self-ruled organizations than ever before. A hospital and cemetery of their own and a welfare association to run them were part of this movement. An apical, or "umbrella," association was also created that tried to unite all Chinese and speak for them to Spanish authorities and the outside world in general. It was this association that approached China about a consulate.[31] Since the consulate did not materialize during this period, these Chinese community associations, a form of self-designed and self-operated protection independent of any Spanish governing or proselytizing needs, were undoubtedly strengthened.

By the end of Spanish rule, some Chinese leaders had received honors from the Spanish government, as well as contracts to operate certain government monopolies. So far as we know, these may have been the first Chinese to approach "court Chinese" status in the Philippines. Interestingly, and somewhat ironically, one of them accepted honors from both the Spanish and the Chinese governments.

When the Philippine revolution took place, several Chinese adopted the revolutionary side, notably Jose Ignacio Paua (Hou A-pao), who became a general in the revolutionary forces and is recognized as a Philippine hero today. Others accommodated themselves to the changes in one way or another, or else fled to Hong Kong until the dust settled in Manila.[32]

1900–1930: The Reality of China

The result of the Philippine revolution was not independence but United States intervention and the replacement of a Filipino dream with an American one. The Philippines is unique in two ways among Southeast Asian societies with a colonial history: it has a dual colonial heritage, and both its colonial masters sought to transform it. Each had a sense of cultural mission, the Spaniards to Catholicize and hispanicize, the Americans to create a modern Philippine nation with popular education in English and with American democratic ideals and institutions. Whereas the Spanish emphasis had been religious, the American was sociopolitical. The Philippines thus entered a second period of tutelage, but this time there was to be a prescribed end: the reward for learning the lessons was to be independence. This combination of tutelage with promises focused Filipinos' attention upon learning the lessons and passing the test. Their attention was directed toward the Americans, not the Chinese.

American policies regarding the Chinese applied the Chinese exclusion law current in the United States, by which Chinese laborers were to be kept out. On the whole, the law was enforced loosely, and there were already so many nonlaborers in the Philippine Chinese population that between immigration by relatives of those already in the country and looseness in dealing with possible laborer immigrants, the Chinese population continued to grow at a steady pace, reaching at least 120,000 by the late 1930s. The official census figure for 1939 was 117,000. The actual figure may have been much greater. Whatever the case, the Chinese population was never more than 2 percent of the total Philippine population, except in Manila, where it might at times have been as high as 5 to 10 percent.[33]

Unlike other "creolized Chinese" groups in Southeast Asia, Chinese mestizos now disappeared as a separate group. Their separateness and prestige had been based upon their mastery of Spanish culture and their role in transforming it into an urban Filipino culture. After 1898, Spanish culture waned rapidly in the Philippines, and skills in it were no longer critically important. Instead, the language of high culture was now English, which— unlike Spanish in earlier times—was available through popular education to everyone. Unlike the Dutch in Indonesia, who worked to keep *peranakan* culture alive, or the British in Malaya, who supported *baba* culture in its uniqueness, the Americans did nothing to maintain mestizo uniqueness.[34] The very term "mestizo" now came to mean all kinds of mixed-bloods— American, Spanish, Chinese, or other—all with some prestige but without the specific attributes and status accorded earlier to the Chinese mestizos. Chinese mestizos, like everyone else, now learned their lessons and their new cultural rules and values in English.

Meanwhile, in China, the years from 1895 to 1911 were marked by radical reforms followed by the 1911 Revolution, which overthrew both the Manchu Qing dynasty and the long-standing imperial system. Chinese governments from the 1890s onward stepped up their efforts to woo the Chinese abroad and attach them to China if possible. Consulates were established in many overseas sites, the Philippine one appearing shortly after the beginning of American rule there.[35] In the first decade of the new century, Chinese governments and leaders began to use a new term, *huaqiao,* or "overseas Chinese." This term strongly implied that the Chinese abroad were all sojourners who intended to return to China and who were primarily concerned about the affairs of China.[36] A more formal claim on their loyalty was made in the promulgation of the 1909 nationality law, which established the principle of *jus sanguinis,* or citizenship by descent, in this case through the male line. Thus, ethnic Chinese anywhere in the world, whatever other citizenship they might claim, were deemed to be Chinese citizens, as would be all their descendants in the male line.[37] In this way, the mestizo children of Philippine Chinese were now regarded by China as Chinese. Finally, as a direct result of the 1911 Revolution, the queue was no longer to be worn.

These changes put Chinese-Filipino distinctions on a national basis as they had not been before. In the seventeenth century, hairstyles, implying cultural commitments, had been a basis for claims of sovereignty and loyalty: a Manila Chinese with a queue was a Qing subject; one with a haircut was a Catholic and thereby a subject of the Spanish king. Even after Spanish rule had ended, the presence of the queue worn by most Philippine Chinese had made it possible to spot a Chinese person at a glance. Once the queue was gone, it was not so easy; one had to guess from facial features and occupation. Without the queue, it was probably easier for ethnic Chinese who wished to blend into Philippine society to do so.

In another way, too, it might have seemed possible, despite formal legal distinctions, for Chinese and Filipinos to come closer together. Some ethnic Chinese were now finding Christianity more attractive than before. In Hong Kong and the coastal cities of China, many Chinese business leaders had adopted it as a mark of modernity, especially Protestant Christianity. Protestant movements in south China found their way to the Philippines, as did American-based Protestant missionaries working with Filipinos, and inroads were made among both Chinese and Filipinos.

But these changes did not bring Filipinos and Chinese closer to each other; if anything, they were growing farther apart. Chinese Christian congregations were Chinese versions and tended to be exclusive. Schools, like churches, widened the gap. Citizenship definitions came at a time when the number of families in Chinese society in the Philippines was beginning to grow, leading to demands for formal educational institutions for the children. Until this point, education and cultural preservation or maintenance had been ad hoc in Philippine Chinese society. Those with enough money to do so hired tutors from China or else sent their children to the mainland. Now, for the first time, at the urging of both parents and authorities in China, who saw schools as another way to bind "overseas Chinese" to China, there were to be Chinese schools, teaching a combination of occupational skills, literacy in Chinese, and the heritage and norms of Chinese culture.

But in China itself that heritage was now under radical reconsideration and revision in the interest of defining *modern* Chineseness. The teachers sent to the Philippines and what they taught reflected debates by intellectuals far removed from the south Chinese businessmen in Manila. The teachers themselves were often not from south China, and they spoke and taught in Mandarin, the proposed lingua franca of the new Chinese nation, not the Hokkien regional dialect of the Philippine Chinese.

It was Chinese nationalism, taking hold among Philippine Chinese at the same time Filipino nationalism developed, that kept the two groups apart. Most Chinese children in the Philippines attended Chinese schools. The long-term future they learned about and the old and new values they absorbed had to do with the future of China as a modern nation. Filipinos, on a different track with a different destination, were simultaneously learning the American version of civic values for a modern Filipino nation.

As the two groups seemed to grow apart, both as a matter of formal national definition and, more particularly, because of the educational consequences of these new national identities, some new terms entered the lexicon of discussion about the Chinese. By the nineteenth century, as the Chinese population had become more diverse and was increasingly seen as nationals of China, the term *chino* (in its Philippine language version rendered *tsino*) had largely replaced the old *sangley,* which referred more specifically to Chinese merchants. As English-language media appeared, *tsino/chino* was rendered *sino,* not as an adjective, as in "sinocentric," but as a noun, as in the newspaper headline "Sinos run drug ring." There also appeared the term "alien," referring not to all non-Filipino nationals but specifically to Chinese.

"Alien," I believe, was both a national and a cultural term, reflecting the marginal political status of this noncitizen group and the cultural alienness of a group that did not share the dreams and new values of the majority.[38] The Filipinos were quickly and skillfully adopting and adapting the American lessons and adding them to the stock of values by which they defined themselves. The Chinese, also in a tutorial situation, were learning another set of lessons and redefining their Chinese cultural values in the process. The gap that existed between the two peoples was no longer based on a religious difference; instead, it existed because Chinese seemed to Filipinos to be seeking different values and institutions in a different language with a different modern nation in mind.

1930–1975: Filipino Redefinitions

In the 1930s, the United States decided to withdraw from the Philippines, creating a transition government to prepare for independence. The American withdrawal would leave Filipinos and Chinese alone with each other. In the past, the American attitude seemed to have been that the Chinese were economically useful and probably an inevitable feature of the Philippines. On occasion the United States had acted as a kind of colonial referee when Filipino nationalism aimed at the Chinese seemed to threaten the status quo.[39]

Now, American withdrawal gave Filipinos both an opportunity and a responsibility to define the framework of their future. The instrument of action was the Commonwealth government, a home-rule institution subject to restraints from the United States. Under the Commonwealth, some economic nationalist legislation was passed, limiting certain opportunities to citizens of the Philippines. Citizenship was defined in terms that excluded the ethnic Chinese. The principle of *jus sanguinis* was chosen, departing from the modified *jus soli,* or citizenship by place of birth, imposed by the United States. Now, the children of a male ethnic Chinese in the Philippines were, as he was, not to be seen as Philippine citizens.[40]

These changes took place in a difficult international atmosphere in Asia. In China, the Kuomintang (KMT) political party had recently established the most ambitious and assertive government China had had in many decades. This government had immediately reconfirmed the *jus sanguinis* principle of citizenship. Beyond that, it sought much closer relations with Chinese citizens abroad. An Overseas Chinese Affairs Commission was established in the government at cabinet level. Its tasks were to monitor the doings of Chinese residing abroad and to give aid to their educational and other needs, hoping thereby to encourage overseas Chinese financial investment in, and aid to, China and support for China's government and the party.

The politics of China now came to the Philippines as never before. Two visions of a modern China had crystallized: the KMT vision, stressing assertive nationalism, social harmony, welfarism, and respect for tradition; and the communist one, arguing for modernity, nationhood, and prosperity for all through radical sociopolitical and cultural revolution. Factions of "left" and "right" appeared in Chinatowns outside China, though the two poles were as often as not symbolic, and the real issues local ones of Chinatown politics.

In 1931, Japan invaded Chinese territory. Overseas Chinese communities around the world now came under severe pressure to put patriotic support of China ahead of all other considerations. Schools were particularly subject to pressure. Anyone who saw the local Chinese school as primarily a device for job training and general cultural maintenance found it hard to resist the outside representatives and their local supporters, who wished China-referent patriotic activities to take precedence over all else. Thus, the Philippine Chinese, while faced with new nationalist policies that would reconfirm them as noncitizens of the Philippines and exclude them, were being drawn ever closer to China.[41]

In China, the Japanese invasion led some families in the south to decide it was time to join their relatives already in the Philippines. As a result, the number of Chinese families in the Philippines increased significantly, the number of "bachelors" decreased, and, in all likelihood, the number of intermarriages also declined somewhat. The larger number of families probably also led to increased attention to family rituals at home, such as regular ancestral observances, and perhaps to more public manifestations of religion in the form of temple building as well.[42]

The Japanese occupation of the Philippines, from 1942 to 1945, was a frightening time for ethnic Chinese. Those who had participated in anti-Japanese patriotic activities in the 1930s had to go into hiding. Others, less visible, simply collaborated or remained as neutral as possible. Those in hiding included some who fought in all-Chinese guerrilla units throughout the occupation. Although Chinese and Filipino guerrilla forces sometimes cooperated, the common struggle against the Japanese does not seem to have brought the two peoples closer together.[43]

It was not long after the end of the occupation and the achievement of independence in 1946 that new nationalist laws and policies were put into effect by the Philippine republic. The three areas of focus of these policies and laws illustrate Filipinos' greatest concerns about Chinese economic preeminence. First, retail trade, the classic Chinese field, was limited to Philippine citizens. Second, all levels of the basic food-grain business were also nationalized. And third, in an interesting act of anticipation, the government, rather than reversing an existing situation, ruled that professions were to be open only to citizens. The anticipation lay in recognizing that higher educational facilities were rapidly expanding in the Philippines and that ethnic Chinese, true to their traditions, would be quick to take advantage of the opportunity.

These laws and policies are interesting also for what they did not exclude: other areas of economic life. It was as if the policymakers were saying to the Chinese that they were not to be evicted from the economy—their presence might even be wanted—but only from these three areas. Thus, by implication, they were encouraged to do what many able Chinese now did: move into wholesaling, light manufacturing, and, by the 1960s and 1970s, financial services and property development. Although the nationalist policies caused great hardships for many Chinese, many others, possessing or able to obtain the resources to do so, were able to move from one economic sector to another and to become more prosperous than ever.[44]

Because the laws were written in terms of citizenship, acquiring citizenship now became a prime goal. But for Chinese, the procedures were troublesome, lengthy, and financially exhausting. Some simplification and acceleration were possible, depending upon financial contributions. This procedure not only limited citizenship to the relatively few able to pay, but it also set up yet another rehearsal of a morality play that reinforced long-standing Philippine stereotypes, dating back to the seventeenth century, about the Chinese and bribery: of course a Chinese would bribe to get what he wanted; what else would one expect from a Chinese?[45]

Another way to deal with nationalist laws and policies during the 1950s and 1960s was to reorganize the Chinese community. At the top, a new set of leaders replaced the older heads of the Manila Chinese Chamber of Commerce. Their new vehicle was called the Federation of Chinese Chambers of Commerce (now the Federation of Filipino-Chinese Chambers of Commerce and Industry), and, as a federation, it more effectively represented all chambers within the archipelago. It acquired more power and control over the community than any predecessor organization had possessed. On the one hand, it used that control to maintain unity within the community: continued "left" differences with the hegemonic "right" were suppressed. On the other hand, it used unity to aid in negotiating with the Philippine government to mitigate the effects of nationalist policies.

The Federation, as it was called, was also closely in touch with Philippine representatives of the Republic of China (ROC) government in Taiwan. The civil war in China had left two claimants to legitimacy as "China" competing against each other for the support of overseas Chinese throughout much of the 1950s and the early 1960s. The Republic of China on Taiwan was the China recognized by the Philippines, within the context of the cold war alliance of Taiwan with the United States. The Philippine government now became closely associated with the Taiwan government, both of them as junior partners of the United States in alliance against mainland communist China.

Taiwan, the Philippines, and the United States all had an interest in maintaining the stability and noncommunist or even anticommunist character of the Philippine Chinese. On the basis of agreements made in the late 1940s, the Philippine government gave over to the Republic of China and its agencies responsibility not only for the behavior of the Philippine Chinese as citizens of the ROC but also for the curriculum and supervision of Chinese schools.[46] The school lessons, insofar as they were about Chinese culture and ideals, taught Taiwan's version of Chineseness.

Indeed, Chineseness in the Philippines was now of two kinds: good and bad. Bad Chineseness could be defended against by teaching good Chineseness, which helped ensure that the local Chinese would remain not only stable and nonthreatening but also suitably Chinese and thereby marginal, particularly at a time when nationalist laws were threatening them. Indeed, in the context of the perceived threat from mainland China and the possible resistance of local Chinese to nationalist laws, it is difficult to see how those laws could have been implemented without some arrangement of this kind. One China had become a real threat, not because it was China but because it was communist. The United States had helped bring in the "good China," or Taiwan, and the two of them helped the Philippines so that it was not facing its greatest fear, invasion from China, alone—especially while implementing nationalist policies against the local Chinese.

The closeness of the Taiwan and Philippine governments was matched by the unusual degree of influence the Taiwan government had over the Philippine Chinese community. The high degree of organization that took place in that community during the 1950s was assisted and mentored, at times, by local representatives of the Republic of China government.[47]

1975–1995: CITIZENSHIP DEFINITIONS

In the early 1970s, the situation of the Philippine Chinese was still much as Weightman had described it in the 1950s—that of a marginal trading community.[48] It seemed that the status quo of the early 1950s had been frozen for almost twenty years. But changes were already under way, from two sources: the breakdown of the cold war in Asia and the rise of a new and different generation of Philippine Chinese.

In the late 1960s, younger Filipinos began to question the United States' war in Vietnam. As the 1970s began and the Americans signaled both a withdrawal from that war and willingness to make peace with communist China, it became obvious that international relationships in the area were changing. It was time to move the Philippines closer to other Asian countries, including mainland China.

The generation of Philippine Chinese that came to maturity in the 1960s and 1970s was the first postwar and postindependence generation of Chinese born in that country. It was also, because of the influx of families in the 1930s, the largest generation in some time. It had other distinctions, too. It was the first ethnic Chinese generation to grow up in the Philippines lacking significant contact with the "home" areas in south China. Because of the cold war, these areas had been closed to visitors from the Philippines. There also had been only a trickle of immigration, legal and otherwise, from those areas to Manila during the 1950s and 1960s. Members of this generation had opportunities to visit Hong Kong and Taiwan and to study in the latter. But that was not the same as living in an ancestral locality as a regular resident for a prolonged period. That was the experience that was missing.

This was also the first generation to have among its members a disproportionate share with university educations—an experience that put them not only in touch with ideas beyond Chinatown, China, and the Philippines but also in personal contact with non-Chinese of their own age group. A significant number of these younger Chinese, riding on their educational backgrounds and on the country's general prosperity in the 1950s, became part of a new middle class in the Chinese community. Their interests and cultural skills overlapped with those in the broader Filipino middle class, with whom they often interacted.[49]

The appearance of this group manifested the diversity now characteristic of the Chinese community. The old identity of "Chinese" and "business" began to break down. Some of the new generation's members were, by training at least, professionals. Others were in business, but, whether in Chinese or non-Chinese firms, in modern organizational terms—not in the traditional Chinese way. There was even, by the 1970s and 1980s, a group of ethnic Chinese intellectuals of a kind not seen earlier. For some decades there had been Chinese journalists and teachers who also wrote essays, fiction, and poetry, in Chinese, about themes relating to China and its culture and, by the 1950s, about the survival of the Philippine Chinese community as well. The new writers expressed themselves in English, the dominant literary language of the country. They wrote about personal identity and problems, as *peranakan* writers had done for so long in Indonesia.[50]

The growing diversity of the community made it difficult for the Federation to maintain the unity it had preserved for so long. Because of the near closure of immigration for so many years, the majority of the Chinese population by the 1970s was Philippine-born.[51] Their experiences were Philippine, and they questioned the interpretation and even the relevance of the Chinese culture they were being taught. In the 1950s, members of Filipino political and intellectual circles had asked rather pessimistically whether the ethnic Chinese could be assimilated. By the 1960s, within the Chinese community itself, serious questions were being asked about whether the younger generation was already about to be assimilated. Out of these discussions, the possibility was raised that integration—close identification with the Philippines but retention of Chinese culture—might be possible and desirable. Further, in the context of discussions about a new constitution for the Philippines, questions were asked about whether the citizenship principle of *jus sanguinis* could somehow be changed to that of *jus soli*. For all the Philippine experience and orientation of this new generation, its members were still, unavoidably, citizens of the Republic of China on Taiwan.[52]

That would soon change. In 1975, acting under martial law, Ferdinand Marcos transferred diplomatic relations from Taipei to Beijing. In preparation for the consequences this move would have for the status of the Philippine Chinese, he suddenly facilitated citizenship for them. Almost overnight, the overwhelming majority of Philippine Chinese became citizens. At about the same time, he moved to Filipinize the Chinese schools, greatly reducing the number of hours of instruction in Chinese language and culture courses.[53] The schools, like the population, had now been brought under control. Relations with mainland China—no longer a threat—were now set at arm's length and stressed trade issues. The same was true for relations with Taiwan, which continued on an unofficial basis. One could say that Marcos had finally "nationalized" the "Chinese problem" in the Philippines.

These dramatic changes, therefore, redefined the ethnic Chinese as no longer marginals but as citizens, and so at least nominally a part of Philippine society. In his 1973 constitution, Marcos recognized as citizens those whose fathers—or mothers—were Philippine citizens. The Aquino constitution of 1987, after Marcos fell from power, continued this provision and made it retroactive to persons born before the 1973 constitution came into effect. Moreover, both the 1973 and 1987 constitutions stated that Filipino women who married non-Philippine citizens did not thereby lose their Philippine citizenship, as had been the case before 1973. Clearly, the intent of these documents was to put an end to dual citizenship as it affected Chinese in the Philippines and to facilitate access to Philippine citizenship for all Philippine Chinese who wanted it. It is clear, also, that the intention was to regard all Chinese mestizos (since, in such cases, it was usually the mother who was a Philippine citizen) as Philippine citizens.[54]

By this time, a new organization of younger ethnic Chinese professionals and businesspeople, mostly university educated, had emerged, devoting itself to the case for integration as opposed to assimilation. This organization, Kaisa para sa Kaunlaran, was the culmination of many years of organization and discussion. From the early 1970s onward, members of the new generation experimented with names for themselves that might express their sense of ethnicity as both Chinese and Filipino. They tried amalgams such as *sinpino* (from *sino* and *pinoy,* the Philippine language slang term for Filipino) and *pinsino* (the same reversed). Finally, in the 1980s, they settled on the North American hyphenated version of identity, Chinese-Filipino, still more recently rendered *tsinoy* (from *tsino* and *pinoy*).

The sequence of words is critical, as Kaisa members explain. "Filipino," the noun, expresses the basic sociopolitical commitment; "Chinese," the adjective, speaks of the cultural heritage that, it is hoped, can be preserved. By this formulation Kaisa implicitly argues that, contrary to traditional Philippine belief, an interest in Chinese culture and its preservation does not imply less than exclusive political loyalty to the Philippines. Even on cultural grounds, it is made clear that the heritage to be preserved is not only Chinese but both Chinese and Philippine.

Kaisa sees several roles for itself, not only that of promoting the acceptance of ethnic Chinese as Chinese-Filipinos. Its publications program, primarily in English and Chinese, publicizes community news and viewpoints and teaches readers about the history of Chinese in the Philippines. Its award-winning television show for children in the early 1990s was directed at non-Chinese as well as Chinese. The show shared Chinese culture and taught simple words in Chinese.

One of Kaisa's concerns is the loss of Chinese culture that seems possible as the schools teach fewer hours of Chinese subjects than before. Students also pay less attention to Chinese courses than they once did. When most job opportunities were in the Chinese community, it was necessary to do well in Chinese subjects. With the achievement of citizenship, all fields are now open to ethnic Chinese. As more of them attend university and go on to occupations away from Chinatown, Chinese skills become less important than those needed to secure admission to university. Not surprisingly, then, it is the English-language courses that receive most student attention. Accordingly, skills in Chinese language and culture have deteriorated.

Kaisa members see this happening among their own children. They themselves have become the "in-between" generation—between the less acculturated Chinese of the "older generation" and their own children, the new younger generation, who are seen as excessively acculturated. Kaisa sees itself as a bridge between Filipinos and Chinese but also between Chinese generations, and it appears to adopt a kind of tutorial role toward all of them, urging the "older generation" not to be so Chinese and the younger to be more so. Kaisa also takes the lead when it sees ethnic Chinese not being given due treatment as citizens, as in the protest demonstration referred to at the beginning of this chapter.[55]

All the changes since the 1970s have obviously altered the identity options available to Philippine Chinese. Community unity and pressures now have less to do with identity choices than they did in the century from the 1870s to the 1970s. The range of individual choice is broader, and individuals are free to draw on many sources to construct their own ideas of Chineseness. The decline of the Chinese schools has reduced the pressure of formally prescribed definitions, but it has also left people less informed in an organized way about Chinese culture. Recent developments relating to China and Chinese immigration are also relevant. Opportunities to visit "home villages" in south China, to trade with that region, and to invest there now exist.

Meanwhile, since the late 1960s, opportunities have opened up for ethnic Chinese, wherever they are, to migrate to the United States, Canada, Australia, New Zealand, and elsewhere. Many already overseas have moved to a second or even a third overseas destination. They become part of the global Chinese, with relatives scattered in cities around the world. The Chinese in the Philippines are part of that network. They are also aware of the discussions about "greater China"—to include Taiwan and Hong Kong and perhaps the Chinese abroad—and the term "cultural China," signifying a putative tie that binds all ethnic Chinese, wherever they are, not to China so much as to each other. Hence, Philippine Chinese ethnicity options are now considered not just within the definition "citizens of the Philippines" or in relation to mainland China, Taiwan, or Hong Kong. There are also the other contexts—with their business implications—of global networks of kin and possible cultural affiliates.

CONCLUSION

I organized the foregoing in terms of definitions, believing as I do that the way groups are defined by others has much to do with the options they consider open to themselves. I stressed the interaction of definitions with limitations on economic opportunities, and thereby with the shaping of possibilities of self-definition. My argument is that the keys to understanding anti-Sinicism and Chinese identity options in the Philippines are, on the one hand, the tutorial nature of Philippine colonialism and its consequences, and, on the other, the physical proximity of China and its consequences.

The combination of these two factors early in Philippine history resulted in the long-term association of interest in Chinese culture with suppositions about loyalty to a nearby and threatening China. Tutorial colonialism, and the adeptness of Filipinos in absorbing and modifying the lessons it presented, created an environment in which Filipinos were encouraged to distrust those among them—the Chinese—who did not share in the lessons they were accepting. From the sixteenth to the nineteenth century, those lessons were religious. In the first three-quarters of the twentieth century, they were civic. In the latter period, unlike in the former, both Chinese and Filipinos sought values appropriate to a commonly held goal—modern nationhood. But the values sought, and those taught, differed. When, as before, distrust over differences was associated with anxiety about nearby China, the Philippine formula was again activated.

In stressing tutorial colonialism, I wish to distinguish the Philippine Chinese situation and experience from those elsewhere in colonial Southeast

Asia. In the rest of that region, mistrust and suspicion of the ethnic Chinese were also characteristic. I believe, however, that the Philippine pattern is more deeply rooted and more specifically associated with China. Throughout Southeast Asia, cultural differences and the economic position of the ethnic Chinese had given rise to mistrust and suspicion, but the Philippine pattern began earliest. It was also associated not simply with basic differences between Southeast Asian cultural patterns and Chinese ones but with the exacerbation of these differences by contrasts during a long history of learning and accepting new values.

Elsewhere in Southeast Asia, European colonialism did not become tutorial until the twentieth century, if it did at all. In the Philippines, it was so from the moment the first missionary friar stepped ashore in the sixteenth century, and it continued in new directions under the Americans. It was not just basic cultural differences but differences in the direction of cultural change—of what outside ideas would be accepted—that made the Philippine situation different. When Chinese nationalism came to Southeast Asia at the turn of the century and local nationalisms were also developing, clashes elsewhere in the region were similar to that in the Philippine case. But in the Philippines, three hundred years of experience of induced change and contrast already underlay the twentieth-century clash.

The relationship between the Philippines and China was also different. Geographically, the Philippines is one of the closest countries to south China. China's continental neighbors to its immediate south maintained stable relations and reduced anxiety about China's intervention in their affairs by sending tribute to the Chinese court. In this way, they and the Chinese each thought they were managing the other. Other Southeast Asian countries, such as Malaya and Indonesia, were sufficiently distant to worry less about China's intervention in their affairs. Parts of what became the Spanish Philippine colony had sent tribute to China, but Spanish colonial rule interrupted most of that process. From that point on, Philippine leaders have felt the country peculiarly exposed to action by China. In the course of things, contrasts with Chinese values and intentions in the Philippines have been linked to anxieties about what nearby China might do, and loyalty has become the principal doubt about Philippine Chinese—not just possible disloyalty, but specifically loyalty to nearby China. Although such fears are common elsewhere in Southeast Asia, I believe that in the Philippine case they are more deeply rooted and more directly associated with the nearness of China than is true anywhere else.

Definitions of the Chinese as non-Catholics, nonresidents, or noncitizens limited their economic opportunities in the Philippines. On the other hand, many things about Philippine society offered individual cultural opportunities. Intermarriage, with or without benefit of clergy, and nominal acceptance of Catholicism were possible and common. Besides the queue, there was an obligatory dress code for Chinese in the seventeenth and eighteenth centuries, but by 1800 it clearly was unenforceable.[56] Even in Parian times, segregation was incomplete. Non-Chinese were always able to go to the Parian to purchase goods and services. Personal ties of reciprocal obligation common in the Philippines were not so different from those used in China and were rather easily formed. Chinese surnames and personal names could be modified at will.[57] In the twentieth century, even some unmodified Chinese surnames, such as Tan and Lim, became accepted as proper Filipino surnames.

The price for this relative ease of transit was that second- and third-generation mestizo descendants often felt obliged to distance themselves from their Chinese ancestors. This distancing might be expressed, for example, by mestizo politicians in the twentieth century when they sponsored anti-Chinese legislation, or simply by people's laughing references, made in social situations, to having had "an ancestor with a pigtail."[58] Opportunity, past a certain point, meant denial of ethnicity.

Until 1850, the available identity options might be defined as (1) Chinese in the Philippines, the sojourners, (2) Philippine Chinese, long-term residents, (3) Chinese Christian merchants, and (4) mestizos.[59] From 1850 to 1930, they might be called (1) sojourning Chinese in the Philippines, as before, (2) Philippine Chinese, now found in Chinatowns, in small towns, and on the frontiers around the islands, (3) *huaqiao*, "overseas Chinese," who were more or less permanent residents of the Philippines but were involved in the affairs of home localities in China and deeply concerned about China's future, and (4) Filipinos of Chinese background. During the period from 1930 to 1975, category (1) disappeared as the Philippines and mainland China were cut off from each other and sojourning was no longer possible; category (2), Philippine Chinese, were now concentrated in Chinatowns; and categories (3) and (4), the *huaqiao* and Filipinos of Chinese background, continued as before.

Since 1975, the situation has been as follows, with five identity options recognizable. (1) The "Chinese in the Philippines" have resurfaced, but these people are not now sojourners hoping to return to China. Instead, they are part of the global Chinese, or international cultural Chinese, called in Chinese language *huaren*. They happen to be in the Philippines, but they may move elsewhere. (2) The Philippine Chinese are concentrated in Chinatowns as before, especially in Manila's, and are focused upon Chinese community affairs. (3) The *huaqiao* are now a small and declining group. (4) Filipinos of Chinese background are a growing group. (5) There are now also Chinese-Filipinos, or *tsinoys*, who are mostly middle class and born in the Philippines. These integrationists are a growing group. In Chinese they are generally known as *huayi,* or "Chinese descendants."

The organization of Chinese descendants or Chinese-Filipinos known as Kaisa is significant in several ways besides those already discussed. Its middle-class, intellectual-professional members are classifiable as new "leaders from the periphery." Although Kaisa recognizes the Federation's leadership in general, it takes the lead in protesting publicly whenever the civil rights of Chinese-Filipinos are abridged, situations in which, typically, the Federation negotiates quietly, if it does anything.

Kaisa members' "in-between" status, as neither part of the Chinese community core nor an invisible part of the general Philippine society, makes them seem like the mestizos of old. The commitment to the Philippines is there, as is the use of the dominant literary language—in this case, English. But the differences are greater than the similarities. Kaisa members include both Chinese mestizos and fully Chinese descendants; their exact racial background is not what defines them as a group. It is their identification of themselves in part with Chinese culture but not with China, along with their efforts to promote and preserve Chinese culture, stripped of any loyalty connotations, that unites and defines them.

Similarly, Jose Mari Chan, in expressing and helping define Filipino pop culture, is doing a mestizo kind of thing. But he is not a mestizo and therefore is not eligible for the recognition of cultural creativity that Filipinos readily give to mestizos. He is an ethnic Chinese with full bicultural skills.

There probably are serious limits, at least in the short run, to how many of its goals Kaisa can achieve. First, its arguments for civil rights are based upon citizenship considerations, but there remain serious doubts in Philippine society about the validity of Chinese citizenship. It can easily be seen as having been purchased in the 1950s and 1960s and given by Marcos as a strategic maneuver in the 1970s. It was never the result of a demonstrated change of heart on the part of Malay Filipinos, even if, in the long run, it comes to be accepted by them.

Second, the long-standing association of interest in Chinese culture with loyalty to China will not be dissipated overnight. Few Filipinos of non-Chinese background are interested in studying or promoting Chinese culture. Third, although Kaisa does not explicitly argue for multiculturalism as a national policy, it is obvious that the integration solution they propose is best achieved, and perhaps is achievable only, in an environment of official multiculturalism. It is not clear that the Philippine government is about to adopt such a policy.

Finally, Kaisa's arguments may be falling on deaf ears. Faced with a multitude of problems and a population half of which lives below the poverty line, Philippine leaders and ordinary Malay-Filipino citizens have many other pressing issues on their minds. Economically, the ethnic Chinese, on the whole, do better than most non-Chinese Filipinos. The latter may well ask why they should care whether this prosperous group feels left out and wishes to be accepted at last into Philippine society on its own terms.

NOTES

1. T. R. McHale, personal communication, September 26, 1992.

2. *Tulay* (monthly Chinese-Filipino digest) 5:8 (February 14, 1993), especially pp. 3, 8–9; Teresita Ang See, personal communication, December 10, 1993.

3. *Asiaweek* (October 20, 1993), pp. 57–58. See also *Forbes Zibenjia* (Hong Kong Chinese edition of *Forbes*) 28 (January–February 1994), pp. 42–45.

4. *Tulay* 6:10 (March 7, 1994), p. 3, and related material on pp. 6, 11, 15.

5. George H. Weightman, "The Philippine Chinese: From Aliens to Cultural Minority," *Journal of Comparative Family Studies* 16:2 (Summer 1985), pp. 161–79, especially pp. 170–71.

6. *Forbes Zibenjia* 26 (November 1993), pp. 60–62.

7. Edgar Wickberg, *The Chinese in Philippine Life, 1850–1898* (New Haven, Connecticut: Yale University Press, 1965), chapter 1 and pp. 234–35. See also Victor Purcell, *The Chinese in Southeast Asia* (London: Oxford University Press, 1965, 2d. ed.), p. 524–25.

8. Wickberg, *The Chinese in Philippine Life*, pp. 8–9, 11–20, 154–55. See also Margaret Wyant Horsley, "*Sangley:* The Formation of Anti-Chinese Feeling in the Philippines" (Ph.D. dissertation, Columbia University, 1950).

9. William Lytle Schurz, *The Manila Galleon* (New York: Dutton, 1939), pp 43–44; and Wickberg, *The Chinese in Philippine Life*, pp. 8, 15–16.

10. Vicente Rafael, *Contracting Colonialism: Translation and Christian Conversion in Tagalog Society under Early Spanish Rule* (Ithaca, New York: Cornell University Press, 1988); John Leddy Phelan, *The Hispanization of the Philippines: Spanish Aims and Filipino Responses, 1565–1700* (Madison: University of Wisconsin Press, 1959).

11. Wickberg, *The Chinese in Philippine Life*, pp. 8–20.

12. See the index to Emma H. Blair and James A. Robertson, eds., *The Philippine Islands, 1493–1898*, 55 vols., especially "Characteristics: Mental (Positive)" and "Char-

acteristics: Mental (Negative)" in vol. 54, pp. 195–96 (Cleveland: Arthur Clark Co., 1903–1907). Victor Purcell drew on this index to create a list of more than forty negative qualities of Philippine Chinese as specified by the Philippine Spaniards, pointing out that in the Spanish documents negative qualities assigned to the Chinese greatly outnumbered positive ones. See Purcell, *The Chinese in Southeast Asia*, p. 522.

13. Wickberg, *The Chinese in Philippine Life*, p. 36. Note also the nineteenth-century children's rhyme in Spanish: De donde vienes? / De Emuy / Y que traes? / El Chino babuy (From where do you come? / From Amoy / And what are you bringing? / The Chinese pig). In the 1990s some highly acculturated ethnic Chinese in the Philippines sometimes spoke of unacculturated "Chinatown Chinese" as "G.I.s"— "genuine *intsik*s."

14. Wickberg, *The Chinese in Philippine Life*, pp. 10–41.

15. Wickberg, *The Chinese in Philippine Life*, chapter 1. On hard work and long-term family strategies for "getting ahead" as developed in coastal urban China in this period, see David Johnson, Andrew Nathan, and Evelyn Rawski, eds., *Popular Culture in Late Imperial China* (Berkeley: University of California Press, 1985).

16. On Chinese self-definitions developed in a comparable environment, see Collin Abraham, "Manipulation and Management of Racial and Ethnic Groups in Colonial Malaysia: A Case Study of Ideological Domination and Control," in Raymond L. M. Lee, ed., *Ethnicity and Ethnic Relations in Malaysia* (DeKalb, Illinois: Center for Southeast Asian Studies, Northern Illinois University, Occasional Paper no. 12, 1986), pp. 1–27. For twentieth-century views, drawing on earlier experiences, see George H. Weightman, "The Philippine Chinese Image of the Filipinos," *Pacific Affairs* 40:3–4 (Fall–Winter 1968), pp. 315–23. "Comedias chinas" are the subject of several documents in the Philippine National Archives.

17. Wickberg, *The Chinese in Philippine Life*, chapter 1 and pp. 176, 191–92.

18. Wickberg, *The Chinese in Philippine Life*, p. 191.

19. Wickberg, *The Chinese in Philippine Life*, pp. 15–23.

20. Wickberg, *The Chinese in Philippine Life*, pp. 24–25.

21. Wickberg, *The Chinese in Philippine Life*, pp. 19–36.

22. Wickberg, *The Chinese in Philippine Life*, pp. 7–10, 136–37.

23. Wickberg, *The Chinese in Philippine Life*, chapter 9; Wickberg, "The Chinese Mestizo in Philippine History," *Journal of Southeast Asian History* 5 (March 1964), pp. 62–100.

24. See Leo Suryadinata, "The State and Chinese Minority in Indonesia" and "From Peranakan Chinese Literature to Indonesian Literature: A Preliminary Study," in L. Suryadinata, ed., *Chinese Adaptation and Diversity: Essays on Society and Literature in Indonesia, Malaysia and Singapore* (Singapore: Singapore University Press, 1993), pp. 79–86 and 101–19.

25. Wickberg, *The Chinese in Philippine Life,* chapters 2–4.

26. Wickberg, *The Chinese in Philippine Life,* pp. 128ff., especially pp. 139–45.

27. Wickberg, *The Chinese in Philippine Life,* pp. 135–45.

28. Wickberg, *The Chinese in Philippine Life,* pp. 154–56.

29. Wickberg, *The Chinese in Philippine Life,* chapter 8.

30. Wickberg, *The Chinese in Philippine Life,* pp. 146–53. Note the general Southeast Asian phenomenon at this time of rising and economically ambitious local groups in contestation with the Chinese. See Go Gien Tjwan, "The Changing Trade Position of the Chinese in South-East Asia," *International Social Science Journal* 23:4 (1971), pp. 564–75.

31. Wickberg, *The Chinese in Philippine Life,* pp. 179–99 and chapters 8–9.

32. Wickberg, *The Chinese in Philippine Life,* pp. 113–19, 130, 191–203.

33. Purcell, *The Chinese in Southeast Asia,* pp. 493–505. See also George H. Weightman, "Changing Patterns of Internal and External Migration among Philippine Chinese," *Crossroads* 3 (1985), pp. 84, 90.

34. On *peranakan,* see Suryadinata, "The State and Chinese Minority," p. 79. On *baba,* see Koh Tai Ann, "Literature in English by Chinese in Malaya/Malaysia and Singapore: Its Origins and Development," in Suryadinata, *Chinese Adaptation and Diversity,* pp. 120–68.

35. Wickberg, *The Chinese in Philippine Life,* pp. 201, 233. On the late Qing efforts, see Yen Ching-hwang, *Coolies and Mandarins* (Singapore: Singapore University Press, 1985), and Michael Godley, *The Mandarin Capitalists from Nanyang; Overseas Chinese Enterprise in the Modernization of China, 1893–1911* (London: Cambridge University Press, 1981).

36. On *huaqiao,* see Wang Gungwu, *China and the Chinese Overseas* (Singapore: Times Academic Press, 1991), chapters 1 and 2 and pp. 240–46.

37. Wang Gungwu, "The Origins of Hua-Ch'iao," in his *Community and Nation: China, Southeast Asia and Australia,* new ed. (St. Leonards, New South Wales: Allen & Unwin, 1992), pp. 1–10.

38. Compare my earlier view of this in *The Chinese in Philippine Life,* pp. 166–67.

39. For example, the Bookkeeping Act, passed by the Philippine legislature, was appealed by the Chinese all the way to the U.S. Supreme Court, which declared it unconstitutional. For details, see Huang Xiaocang, ed., *Feilubin Minlila Zhonghua Shanghui Sanshi Zhounian Jinian Kan* (Thirtieth anniversary commemorative publication of the Manila Chinese Chamber of Commerce, 1936); Liu Chi Tien, *Zhong-Fei Guanxi Shi* [History of Chinese-Philippine relations] (Taipei: Zhengzhong Shuzhu, 1964), pp. 589–97; and Purcell, *The Chinese in Southeast Asia,* pp. 543–44.

40. Chester L. Hunt and Lewis Walker, "Marginal Trading Peoples: Chinese in the Philippines and Indians in Kenya," in C. L. Hunt and L. Walker, eds., *Ethnic Dynamics: Patterns of Intergroup Relations in Various Societies* (Holmes Beach, Florida:

Learning Publications, Inc., 1979), pp. 105–106; Cornelius J. Peck, "Nationalism, 'Race' and Developments in the Philippine Law of Citizenship," *Journal of Asian and African Studies* 2 (January–April 1967), pp. 128–43; Purcell, *The Chinese in Southeast Asia*, pp. 544–51.

41. Antonio Tan, *The Chinese in the Philippines, 1898–1935: A Study of Their National Awakening* (Quezon City: R. P. Garcia, 1972), pp. 279–375. For Southeast Asia in general, see Yoji Akashi, *The Nanyang Chinese National Salvation Movement, 1937–1941* (Lawrence: University of Kansas, Center for East Asian Studies, 1970), and Wang Gungwu, *China and the Chinese Overseas*, pp. 198–200.

42. Shi Zhenmin (Chinben See), "Feilubin Huaren Wenhua de Zhixu: Zhongqin yu Tongxiang Zuzhi zai Haiwai de Yanbian," [Persistence and preservation of Chinese culture in the Philippines], *Zhongyang Yanjiuyuan Minzuxue Yanjiusuo Jikan* [Bulletin of the Institute of Ethnology, Academia Sinica, Taiwan] 42 (1976), p. 127. The Seng Guan Temple, the major Chinese Buddhist institution in the Philippines, dates from this period. If intermarriage became less frequent, it may have done so only temporarily. Hunt and Walker report high rates for the late 1950s; see their "Marginal Trading Peoples," p. 102.

43. Antonio Tan, *The Chinese in the Philippines during the Japanese Occupation, 1942–1945* (Quezon City: University of the Philippines Press, 1981).

44. Chinben See, "Persistence and Preservation," pp. 128–29.

45. Wickberg, *The Chinese in Philippine Life*, p. 166n.

46. James Blaker, "The Chinese in the Philippines: A Study of Power and Change," (Ph.D. dissertation, Ohio State University, 1970), p. 252; Liu Chi Tien, *Zhong-Fei Guanxi Shi*, pp. 785–806.

47. Blaker, "The Chinese in the Philippines," pp. 206ff.; Chinben See, "Persistence and Preservation," p. 173. See also issues of the newspaper *Huaqiao Shang Bao* (Chinese commercial news, Manila), 1948–72.

48. George H. Weightman, "The Philippine Chinese: A Cultural History of a Marginal Trading Community," (Ph.D. dissertation, Cornell University, 1961).

49. Edgar Wickberg, "Some Comparative Perspectives on Contemporary Chinese Ethnicity in the Philippines," *Asian Culture (Yazhou Wenhua,* Singapore) 14 (April 1990), pp. 96–97.

50. For brief historical treatments, see Susie L. Tan, "Chinese Language Literature in the Philippines: Past and Present," *Asian Culture (Yazhou Wenhua)* 17 (June 1993), pp. 73–82, and Teresita Ang See, "Philippine-Chinese Literature in English and Filipino: An Introduction," *Asian Culture (Yazhou Wenhua)* 17 (June 1993), pp. 83–90. Paul Stephen Lim and Charlson Ong are the best known of the writers in English. See especially Ong's collection *Men of the East* (Manila: Kalikasan Press, 1990) and his essay "China Is in the Heart," *Solidarity* 133–34 (January–June 1993).

51. By 1990 there were an estimated one million ethnic Chinese in the Philippines,

the count apparently including first, second, and third generations. But that figure still amounted to less than 2 percent of the total population of the Philippines.

52. Chen Lieh-fu, *Feilubin de Minzu Wenhua yu Huaqiao Tonghua Wenti* [The national culture of the Philippines and overseas Chinese assimilation] (Taipei: Zhengzhong Shuzhu, 1968), especially pp. 118–57; Liu Chi Tien, *Zhong-Fei Guanxi Shi,* pp. 803–6, 845–59; Teresita Ang, "Citizenship Discussion in the Constitutional Convention: The Case for Qualified Jus Soli," in Charles J. McCarthy, S.J., ed., *Philippine-Chinese Profile: Essays and Studies* (Manila: Pagkakaisa Sa Pagunlad, 1974), pp. 184–211.

53. Wickberg, "Some Comparative Perspectives," p. 26; Antonio Tan, "The Changing Identity of the Philippine Chinese, 1946–1984," in Jennifer Cushman and Wang Gungwu, eds., *Changing Identities of the Southeast Asian Chinese since World War II* (Hong Kong: Hong Kong University Press, 1988), pp. 189–90; Chinben See, "Education and Ethnic Identity among the Chinese in the Philippines," in Theresa Carino, ed., *Chinese in the Philippines* (Manila: DelaSalle University Press, 1985), pp. 37–38.

54. Wickberg, "Some Comparative Perspectives," pp. 26–27. By 1980, mainland China had formally rejected dual citizenship. In its nationality law of that year, as in various agreements with Southeast Asian countries with ethnic Chinese minorities, China made it clear that it had no political claims on ethnic Chinese with local citizenship. For some relevant texts, including that of the 1980 law, consult the appendixes in Leo Suryadinata, *China and the ASEAN States: The Ethnic Chinese Dimension* (Singapore: Singapore University Press, 1985). See also Wang Gungwu, *China and the Chinese Overseas,* chapter 16.

55. Teresita Ang See, "Integration and Identity: Social Changes in the Post World War II Philippine Chinese Community," *Asian Culture* (*Yazhou Wenhua*) 14 (April 1990), pp. 38–46; issues of *Tulay* from 1988 forward; Wickberg, "Some Comparative Perspectives," pp. 29–30. See also *China Currents* 4:4 (October–December 1993), published by the Philippine-China Development Resource Center.

56. Wickberg, *The Chinese in Philippine Life,* p. 191.

57. On baptismal sponsorship and Chinese name change, see Wickberg, *The Chinese in Philippine Life,* pp. 32, 176, 191–92.

58. But for a time during the Aquino presidency (1986–92), it was quite acceptable and almost fashionable, or faddish, to have "Chinese roots." See Wickberg, "Some Comparative Perspectives," p. 27. Aquino not only expressed pride in her Chinese ancestry but also made a visit, unprecedented among the many Filipino political leaders who have had Chinese backgrounds, to her "ancestral home" in China; see *Asiaweek,* April 29, 1988, pp. 8–10. The major Catholic figure in the Philippines, Cardinal Jaime Sin, for a time also spoke freely of his Chinese background; see *Tulay,* October 16, 1988, pp. 1, 12. At a roundtable discussion in February

1992, a participant remarked: "Time was when even Claudio Teehankee (chief justice of the Philippine Supreme Court) refused to acknowledge his Chinese roots. Now that we're entering the Asia Pacific century, with focus on the success of this dragon, everybody starts claiming Chinese ancestry." See "Culture, Development and Democracy . . ." *Solidarity* 133–34 (January–June 1992), p. 71. Expressions of this kind seem to be less frequent since the election of President Ramos.

59. In the analysis of options presented here, terms such as "Chinese in the Philippines" and "Philippine Chinese" are used as analytical categories rather than as self-applied terms. The definitions given these terms are my own.

PART THREE

The Modernization of Ethnic Perceptions and Conflicts

7 / Anti-Sinicism in Java's New Order

TAKASHI SHIRAISHI

Violent, popular anti-Sinicism came to Dutch Java in the early 1910s. As late as 1908, W. Boekhoudt, author of a report on police reorganization, saw no real nationalist threat to the Indies state and the public order from among the natives; he observed that among Javanese, the national sense was "fast asleep."[1] He noted instead a growing sense of solidarity and nationality among Java's Chinese, and he pointed out that Chinese private schools, supervised by school inspectors sent by the Qing government, were providing education in the Chinese national language (*kuo-yu*) and in English. He also reported that a recent police raid at a *kongsi* (literally, union or company) gathering in Pemalang on Java's north coast had led to the confiscation of firearms and the discovery of Javanese participation in the "Chinese" *kongsi*. Neither "native" nationalism nor anti-Sinicism was a cause for alarm, in his view, but the rise of Chinese nationalism and native participation in *kongsi* were.

Within a few years, however, violent anti-Sinicism had become a reality. The Sarekat Islam (SI), the first popular native national movement, was born in late 1911 and early 1912 in Surakarta, Central Java, out of a racially mixed Chinese-Javanese *kongsi* that disintegrated amid widespread street fights between its Javanese members and their former Chinese *kongsi* brothers. Racial violence was not restricted to Surakarta alone. In the wake of the Chinese market strike in Surabaya in February 1912, hostility between Chinese, on the one hand, and Arabs and Madurese, on the other, flared up in rioting, and riots spread on Java's north coast from Surabaya and Bangil in East Java to Cirebon, West Java.

With the enormous expansion of the SI movement all over Java from late 1912 to early 1914 (by the time the second SI congress was held in Yogyakarta in May 1914, its total membership had reached more than 440,000), wild rumors circulated: the coming of Ratu Adil (the Just King), imminent war,

187

and the establishment of a new realm. Tensions mounted between SI members and Chinese, as well as between SI and non-SI natives, leading to numerous killings. "Tussles" (*relletjes*) took place not only in major urban centers such as Surabaya, Semarang, and Surakarta but also in small towns and villages. On Java's north coast, Chinese residents in the countryside sought refuge in Tuban and Lasem after anti-Chinese violence took place in some villages in August 1913.[2]

The rioting, street fights, disturbances, and rumors that accompanied the expansion of the SI alarmed the Indies government. So did the growing influence of revolutionary republicanism among Java's Chinese after the Chinese revolution in late 1911. But no longer did native participation in "Chinese" *kongsi,* let alone an anti-Dutch united front of Chinese and natives, alarm the Dutch. Whereas the Indies government had taken every measure to "protect" natives from Chinese exploitation in the 1890s and 1900s, it made many concessions to the Chinese from the late 1910s onward. The hated pass system, which required Chinese people to obtain passes to travel, was completely abolished. Dutch civil law was extended to the Indies Chinese. The legal basis for the Chinese quarters was ended. And Chinese were admitted to advisory councils at the central and local levels.

The danger of racial mixing, once feared by the Dutch, had now passed. A new order was in place, built along racial lines and based on deeply ingrained racial antagonism. As if to remind the Chinese of this new reality, a massive anti-Chinese riot took place in Kudus in 1918, the year when the quasi-parliamentary Volksraad was opened, its members nicely representing the different racial communities that made up the Dutch East Indies.

Clearly, something happened in the early 1910s that radically changed racial relations in the Indies and offered excellent opportunities for the Dutch East Indies government to adopt a new colonial strategy. What was it that occurred? Why did anti-Sinicism emerge as it did in the early 1910s?

Dutch officials offered two explanations. First, they argued that the Chinese had become "arrogant" after the Chinese revolution of 1911, had treated natives badly and haughtily, and had invited a native anti-Chinese backlash. There is good reason to believe that the Chinese did behave differently after the revolution. Excited about it, they demanded that natives treat them as they treated the Dutch, and so invited native resentment. Sharing anti-Chinese sentiments with the natives, Dutch officials, not surprisingly, argued that it was all the fault of the Chinese.[3] This hardly explains, however, the surge of widespread anti-Chinese violence and the breakdown of racially mixed *kongsi* in Java in the early 1910s. In Siam, King Vajiravudh's call for reactionary anti-Sinicism after the Chinese revolution found no popular echo, and Malays seem hardly to have noticed the event, even though Chinese nationalist associational politics was far more active in British Malaya than anywhere else in Southeast Asia.

Second, Dutch officials argued that the SI was established as an organizational instrument with which the native bourgeoisie could fight the increasingly intense commercial competition from the Chinese, and therefore they took native anti-Sinicism as something natural.[4] This explanation, which has been inherited by historians, looks plausible but is not entirely convincing. Certainly commercial competition intensified in the 1900s and early 1910s, because after the revenue farms were dismantled in the 1890s the Chinese sought new investment opportunities in *kretek* (clove) cigarettes, batik, and other industries hitherto dominated by the native bourgeoisie. Thus they came into direct conflict with a native class for the first time in their history in the Indies. But anti-Sinicism was not confined to centers of native industries such as Surakarta and Kudus. Nor can the breakdown of racially mixed *kongsi* be explained by intensified commercial competition. In any case, it is too simplistic to see the SI as an instrument of the native bourgeoisie, even in its early days.

The major problem with these explanations is that they tend to see the development of anti-Sinicism in isolation and to ask the wrong question— why the SI emerged as anti-Chinese. The rise of the SI and the surge of anti-Sinicism among natives were symptoms of more profound structural changes then taking place in Dutch Java. Something did happen in Java in the early 1910s, but we need to understand this "something" without being fixated only on the violent anti-Sinicism of the SI.

Hannah Arendt's brief discussion of the violent popular hatred of Jews in Poland and Romania is enlightening in this context. She writes:

> The governments . . . tried halfheartedly to encourage a middle class without liquidating the nobility and big landowners. Their only serious attempt was economic liquidation of the Jews—partly as a concession to public opinion, and partly because the Jews were actually still a part of the old feudal order. For centuries they had been middlemen between the nobility and peasantry; now they formed a middle class without fulfilling its productive functions and were indeed one of the elements that stood in the way of industrialization and capitalization.[5]

We can readily note several important structural differences between Dutch Java, on the one hand, and Poland and Romania, on the other. Whereas the feudal aristocracy in Poland and Romania succeeded in maintaining its political dominance, its counterpart in Java, whether feudal or not in the first place, was turned into a bureaucratic elite subordinate to the

Dutch in the nineteenth century and became dependent on the Indies state for maintaining its power. And whereas the feudal aristocracy successfully prevented the rise of a normal middle class in Poland and Romania, in Java it was not the native aristocrat-turned-bureaucratic elite but the development of Dutch-dominated modern corporate capitalism after 1870 that stunted the rise of a "normal" native middle class.

Yet the Chinese, or, more precisely, the "farm" Chinese ("farm" in the sense of concessions giving the purchaser the rights to future revenues), had formed a part of Java's old colonial order. The government dismantled their privileged position toward the end of the nineteenth century, and for a time seriously tried to liquidate them economically at the turn of the twentieth century. The Chinese survived the government's onslaught, but in the twentieth century they could fulfill only some of the functions of the middle class, as shopkeepers and traders between the powerful, Dutch-dominated, corporate capitalist sector and the native agrarian classes. Thus they came to stand in the way of the rise of a native middle class.

Herein lies a crucial and revealing combination of differences and similarities. Once a privileged social group and part of the old colonial order, Java's Chinese had not only become useless for financing the state by the early twentieth century but had also come to be seen, along with the native aristocrat-turned-bureaucratic elite, as a major obstacle to the progress of the Indies by the Dutch Indies reformist government. The government was well aware that it would be impossible to transform the Indies from a "medieval" to a modern bureaucratic state unless a "native awakening" could dismantle the privileged position of the native bureaucratic elite as well as of the Chinese. The rise of the SI and the native awakening it signified clearly marked the last phase of this transformation.

In this sense, the Dutch "ethical" project (their term for what they were doing) from above and the native awakening from below were two driving forces in the creation of a new order. In it, the Chinese would find themselves in a position vastly different from the one they had occupied in the nineteenth century. They were no longer needed as the state's financiers, they became vulnerable to violent popular hatred, and they were politically powerless even as they became an economically prosperous "middleman" minority in a society neatly structured along racial lines and dominated by a modern bureaucratic state and modern corporate capitalism.

What happened, then, in the early 1910s? Since the major contours of the SI movement in its early days are well known, it will suffice to note its development briefly.[6] The SI evolved out of the Rekso Roemekso, an organization established in Surakarta by Haji Samanhoedi and other batik manufacturers and traders as a Javanese "secret society" after they split from the racially mixed Chinese-Javanese *kongsi* Kong Sing, shortly after the revolution in China. In late 1911 and early 1912, the Rekso Roemekso was what its name, "the guard," signified—an organization for mutual help against "bandits" (*kecu*). After its establishment, many tussles took place between its members and their former Chinese Kong Sing brothers.

Soon, however, the Rekso Roemekso drew the attention of the local authorities, who inquired about its legal status. Haji Samanhoedi and other leaders consulted with Martodharsono, then editor-in-chief of the Javanese language newspaper *Djawi Kanda* and the Malay language newspaper *Djawi Hiswara,* who was also known for his esoteric knowledge of invulnerability and his extensive connections with Solonese officials and the Surakartan underworld. On his suggestion, the Rekso Roemekso leadership invited R. M. Tirtoadisoerjo, Martodharsono's mentor, who was then editor-in-chief of Java's most successful native newspaper, *Medan Prijaji,* and president of the Bogor-based Muslim cooperative Sarekat Dagang Islamijah (Islamic Commercial Association), to act as an advisor. He drew up new statutes for the Rekso Roemekso to win it legal recognition, and he announced that it was a branch of his own Sarekat Dagang Islamijah.

Thus was the Rekso Roemekso transformed into a modern association, the SI, with its statutes and, at least on paper, a clearly defined organizational structure. Nor did the SI remain just an organization for mutual help against bandits. Though not very successfully, it published its own organ, *Saro Tomo,* and under Martodharsono's leadership it was also turned into a boycott organization against Chinese firms. Street fights ensued, not only between SI members and Chinese Kong Sing members but also more generally between Javanese and Chinese.

In the tense atmosphere created by boycotts and street fights, the SI began to expand rapidly in June and July 1912. In early August, the Dutch assistant resident of Surakarta (the official responsible for administration of the city) estimated that the SI's membership had reached thirty-five thousand. Moreover, the SI began to expand into the countryside in July, and the "improper," "highly offensive" attitudes and behaviors SI members showed to Dutch and Javanese officials invited official anger. The Dutch resident of Surakarta (the official responsible for administration of the residency of the city) decided that the SI was threatening the *rust en orde* (quiet and order) and in August banned its activities in his region.

This ban marked the second turning point in the transformation of the SI. It forced the organization to expand outside the residency of Surakarta.

Within less than a year it had expanded all over Java, and SI branches had mushroomed everywhere. The key to this expansion was no longer vigilant action and boycott but newspapers and rallies led by journalists turned professional SI leaders.

Along with this expansion came riots, street fights, and runaway rumors. In the private estate areas of Batavia (now Jakarta), rumors said that in the near future all land under the control of foreigners would be returned to the natives, and in the coming war all the Chinese would be killed and the Europeans driven from Java. In Banyumas, Central Java, rumors circulated that Javanese who were not SI members would obtain no help when they got into trouble during the coming war between the Javanese and the Dutch kings, and that once sufficient numbers of people had joined the SI, it would make its own law and its members would no longer be required to obey the law of the country.

In some places, upon joining the SI, people refused to perform corvée labor for the state and showed "improper" attitudes toward Dutch and native officials. In other places, the religious sense of Islam was suddenly heightened, and attendance at the communal Friday prayers at the mosque increased greatly. SI members no longer wanted to exchange labor with non-SI members or to invite them to ritual meals. Village religious officials who joined the SI refused to offer funeral services for those who died without joining the SI. In many places, street fighting broke out between SI members and Chinese and between SI and non-SI members. Beatings and, in some cases, killings of Chinese took place in Surabaya, Bangil, Rembang, Semarang, Cirebon, Batavia, and other towns. Sometimes SI members "undermined state authorities" by arresting thieves themselves and handing them over to the police. They threatened those who abused SI members and "intervened in administrative affairs." In the early days of the SI movement, its central leadership had no intention of challenging Dutch rule, but whatever its program, the very expansion of the SI brought hitherto contained forces to the surface and threatened the old bureaucratic order.

The breakdown of racially mixed *kongsi* also took place in this setting. The Surakartan Kong Sing was the first casualty. The Kong Sing in Rembang, Central Java, also collapsed in early 1913. In Cirebon, a Macaonese *kongsi*, Hong Gi Hong, fell apart. Sometime in 1912, the Chinese weekly *Hoa Tok* observed:

> While earlier the natives were not ill disposed to the Chinese here in this country, and indeed native Solonese had even established an association with members of Chinese secret societies there for mutual help, change has come since the Chinese

revolution. The Chinese have become proud of belonging to the Kik Bing Tong [Revolutionary party] and treated the natives haughtily. They [natives] then broke away and established a Javanese party with tens of thousands [of members]. This led to unrest in Solo [Surakarta] in October last year, which was hushed up by Susuhunan [head of the major royal house in Surakarta] and Dutch officials. Since then, the party has spread steadily, thanks to the protection of a certain government [the Indies]. The purpose is no doubt driving the Chinese [from the Indies]. This is clear from the tussles in Tjilamaja [Cilamaya, West Java] and the killing of Chinese in Semarang after the agitation in Solo.[7]

Here *Hoa Tok* is expressing Chinese nervousness about the SI and the "protection" the Indies government accorded to it. It is important, however, to note the weekly's observation about the passing of an era when the Chinese and Javanese were friendly and joined in the same secret societies.

The breakdown of racially mixed *kongsi* did not take place everywhere. Now, however, the mixed ones emerged as part of a larger counterattack against the SI. As the SI expanded all over Java, anti-SI organizations were created in many places with the overt and covert encouragement of local administrative officials. In Surakarta, Mangkunegaran princes (of the minor royal house in Surakarta, often in rivalry with the royal house of Kasunaran) organized and financed the Darma Hatmoko, whose members aggressively engaged in fights against both SI members and the Chinese. In Cirebon, the Cirebonese sultan established a rival organization, Sarekat Iman, which was financed in part by Chinese and worked hand in hand with the *kongsi* known as Kong Gi Hing.[8] In the private estate areas of Batavia, it was the Kong Dji Hing, another *kongsi,* that emerged as a major anti-SI vigilante organization. And in many places, local Dutch and native officials also actively intervened in the internal affairs of the SI.

The first SI branch in Batavia was established in March 1913, and within less than a month, additional branches were founded in nearby Purwakarta, Tanggerang, and Bogor under the leadership of R. Goenawan, chairman of the Batavia SI. These branches attracted tens of thousands of members, especially in the private estate areas in suburban Batavia, with Islamic leaders and pious Muslims (mosque officials, hajis, Koranic teachers, and Arabs) as local leaders. As in many other places, the expansion of the SI was accompanied by rumors and fights, but in this region tensions also mounted because of the timing: the penetration of the SI took place in March and April when native tenants were negotiating land rent and corvée services with Chinese landlords.

Kong Dji Hing was established by Chinese landlords and expanded in the

region during these tense months. With the approval of the assistant resident of the Meester Cornelis district, the chief (*wedana*) of the subdistrict of
Bekasi also encouraged his subordinates (*oppasser* and *politiemandoer*) to
join the Kong Dji Hing and to dismiss or transfer officials who had joined
the SI. Kong Dji Hing members often gathered at gambling dens and spearheaded street fights with SI members. Whenever such battles took place, the
subdistrict chief blamed the SI and arrested SI members.[9]

Although Dutch officials reported that the Kong Dji Hing was "established" in early 1913, social networks of Chinese landlords, native local officials, native traders, and local toughs must have been there even earlier. The
situation must have been like that of the Kong Sing in Central Java, which,
as the resident of Rembang reported, had been around for at least fifteen
years. What is curious is that old social networks could be successfully
activated against the SI in suburban Batavia while racially mixed *kongsi* fell
apart in many other places, especially in Central and East Java. This was
undoubtedly because of conditions peculiar to the private estates where
landlords, mainly Chinese, continued to act as petty, quasi-feudal lords.
They maintained their rights to native tenants' corvée services and kept local
toughs in their pay to control the tenants, particularly in places where Dutch
and native administrative officials had to rely on them and their toughs to
maintain *rust en orde*.

To put it another way, old, racially mixed *kongsi* fell apart with the rise of
the SI in areas where old social networks of Chinese, local toughs, and the
local Dutch and native bureaucratic elites had been seriously undermined
and fragmented by the early 1910s.

What had the old order been like in nineteenth century Java? Though any
attempt to delineate Java's colonial society before the turn of the century
runs the risk of making it appear too static, it is useful for our discussion to
point out its major structural features. As studies by Onghokham, James
Rush, and Cornelis Fasseur demonstrate, at its apogee it was based on the
cultivation system and on opium and other revenue farms.[10]

The basic idea of the cultivation system, which was introduced in 1830 and
remained the principle of colonial exploitation until 1870, was simple and
straightforward. Instead of taking land rent in cash, the government required villagers to devote a portion of their land and labor to the production
of commercial crops such as sugar, indigo, and coffee. Regents (native
district chiefs), together with Dutch residents and assistant residents, were
responsible for supervising the villagers' fulfillment of this obligation. Both
European officials and Javanese, from regents down to village chiefs, re-

ceived a percentage of their territory's output as an incentive to push for higher production. The Indies government then shipped commercial crops to the Netherlands for sale at great profits to the state-owned Nederlandsche Handelsmaatschappij (NHM), which monopolized the shipment.

Just as the cultivation system was a refinement of the earlier system under the old Dutch East India Company, so were the revenue farms and monopoly concessions for running local markets, collecting fees, selling salt and opium, running pawnshops, and so on. The most important of these from the 1850s to the 1880s were the opium farms. Such a farm was granted by the Indies government to a concessionaire or farmer for a limited period of time, and the grant applied to a strictly defined territory. Chinese merchants paid dearly for this privilege and thereby yielded great sums of revenue to the government.

The cultivation system and the revenue farms were highly profitable for the Dutch. From 1830 to 1840, the first ten years of the cultivation system, the total value of Indies exports increased from 12.8 million guilders to 74 million, the value of coffee from 4.6 million guilders to 37.4 million, and that of sugar from 1.6 million guilders to 13.8 million. Two-thirds of the total exports from Java were handled by the NHM by 1840. Apart from profits from the cultivation system, revenue increased from 18.5 million guilders in 1831 to 44 million in 1840, of which the revenue farms and monopoly concessions contributed 25 to 30 percent. Remittances ("contributions") to the Netherlands government averaged 9.3 million guilders from 1831 to 1840 and 14.1 million from 1841 to 1850, and reached 15 million guilders in 1851.[11]

The Dutch depended on local elite intermediaries, above all Javanese aristocrats turned bureaucrats (*priyayi*) and Chinese farmers, for the day-to-day running of the cultivation system and the revenue farms. As late as 1883, fewer than 300 Dutch administrative officials—22 residents, 93 assistant residents, and 151 *contrôleurs,* to be precise—were responsible for the internal administration of Java, whose population in the 1870s was 18 million, including 27,000 "Europeans" (most of them mestizos) and 190,000 "Chinese."[12] As James Rush nicely put it, "the Dutch Colonial Service was an administrative head which was fitted upon the broad shoulders of the Javanese priyayi, who continued to govern their provinces and districts under Dutch command."[13]

The regents provided the main point of access for the Dutch to the native population, supervising the villagers to fulfill the obligation of the cultivation system and maintaining *rust en orde* in Java's interior. Wealthy, Javanized *peranakan* Chinese merchants ran the revenue farms and monopoly concessions.[14]

The Dutch, therefore, did not care about the working of these money machines, and even if they did, they could do little about them. They remained content so long as the machines made money for the government and for their personal gain. Javanese *priyayi* and Chinese farmers needed access to the village world from which produce and labor were siphoned off by the cultivation system and revenue farming. But neither the formal native bureaucratic apparatus headed by the regent nor the formal farm *kongsi* organization penetrated deeply into this world. Instead, the interface between the formal state structure and the village world was inhabited by informal social networks of native administrative officials, village chiefs, Chinese farmers and traders, local toughs, teachers of esoteric knowledge (*guru weri*), vagabonds, peddlers and artisans, musicians and theater folk, prostitutes, floating coolies, and so on. The regent relied on his informal networks of *weri* (spies), *jagabaya* (police), and *jago* (toughs; literally, fighting cocks), as well as his regency and village officials for maintaining order and supervising the smooth and profitable running of the cultivation system.

The success of an opium farm depended on its monopoly access to the village world provided by informal distributional networks of smaller shops, opium dens, and door-to-door peddling. The opium farm *kongsi* employed informers, spies, and local toughs to police its monopoly against black market competition. James Rush described this twilight zone inhabited by spies, police, informers, and thugs:

> Jagabaya distinguished themselves from ordinary villagers by their supravillage experience and an aptitude for intrigue.... Their metier was crime, its perpetration and detection, and their services were for hire. Thus they frequently appear alongside other local functionaries as village police (kapetengan), appointed by headmen to protect villages from banditry and arson, and as detectives and "secret police" in the service of headmen, priyayi officials, and Dutch administrators.... The social environment of the jagabaya was much broader than that of the ordinary villager. Jagabaya gathered in opium and gambling dens and consorted among the fringe elements of Javanese society: dancing girls, prostitutes and pimps, traveling show folk, magicians and con-men, brigands, fences, and thieves. It was their familiarity with the village world that made them such valuable resources. Jagabaya were, therefore, enlisted in the service of not only the native and Dutch authorities, but also a variety of other individuals and groups whose interests penetrated the village world.[15]

So long as the Dutch were content with making money, they could remain comfortably unconcerned about this twilight zone in which the formal state structure dissolved imperceptibly into the informal village world. Indeed, they were part of it. From 1870 onward, however, the old order was increasingly undermined and began to break apart, and the pace of fragmentation quickened after the depression of the 1880s.

The engine of change was capital. The age of private capital and of a new, liberal colonial policy was formally ushered in with the passing of the agrarian law in 1870, marking the end of the cultivation system. In the same year, the first railway in the Indies was built to link Semarang on Java's north coast with Surakarta and Yogyakarta in the interior. The east line linked Surabaya and Surakarta in 1884, and the west line connected Batavia and Yogyakarta in 1894, completing the through line linking Batavia, Bandung, Yogyakarta, Surakarta, Semarang, and Surabaya. Telegraph lines were built all over Java from the mid-1850s to the 1880s. Telephone lines went up in Batavia in 1882 and in Semarang and Surabaya in 1884, followed by long-distance telephone lines between Batavia and Semarang and between Batavia and Surabaya in 1896. Java was fast becoming smaller.

In those same last three decades of the century, Dutch society in the Netherlands was also changing fast. In the 1860s, one generation earlier than in the Indies, all the major towns in the Netherlands had been linked by the railway system. A new type of secondary school, the *hogere burgerschool,* was introduced, the state was made responsible for public health, medical practice was standardized, and anyone without a medical degree was excluded from the medical profession. The notion that the state should watch over and regulate all aspects of its citizens' lives found further institutional expression during the 1870s. The industrial employment of children under twelve was banned, the work of females was limited to a maximum of eleven hours a day, factory inspectors were appointed to enforce these provisions, an all-male association to fight prostitution was established by the government, and, in 1879, compulsory registration of all brothels and prostitutes was enacted. The twilight zone that had existed on the edges of society was coming under direct state policing in the Netherlands.

The Dutchmen who came to the Indies toward the end of the nineteenth century, therefore (and increasingly, Dutch women, too, in the early twentieth century), were of a different breed from the Dutch royal cronies and Javanized European mestizo elites who had dominated the Indies state in the mid-nineteenth century. Now they were not only administrative officials but more often officials in technical services, private planters, and executives and administrators of large-scale private plantations and trading companies. In the small administrative centers in Java, Europeans clustered in the *societeit* (club), spending their time in drinking, card games, and gossip. They ignored the native world but demanded more of the state. They wanted schools for their children, medical attention for their families and coolies, irrigation for their fields, and railways for their produce. They expected the Indies government (locally represented by the Dutch resident and assistant resident) to attend to their difficulties—supply of water, supply of labor, carting of produce, and control of mischief and petty thefts. They complained that the natives of "our" colony were being exploited by the Chinese and abused by native officials. They demanded that the natives be protected.

Dutch officials whose bible was Multatuli's novel *Max Havelaar,* which exposed the sins of the old colonial system, shared with Dutch private citizens this new notion of the need for a protective state. And they were more confident of their power to get things done.

In the past, when they had not been terribly concerned with the native world, Dutch officials had accepted outward signs as adequate proof of a sufficiently ordered society. The neatness of a village was equated with its security. There had been regulations on the heights and thicknesses of the fences that could be built around houses or along the roads. Cattle had to be put in communal stables at night and guarded. Villagers had been required to take turns on night watch, patrolling the village, the roads, and the waterworks.

Now, Dutch officials were imbued with a new spirit and began to expect much more. Toward the end of the nineteenth century, a spirit of imperial self-confidence possessed the Dutch as well as other colonial powers. As Onghokham put it:

> Cultural complacency and their growing numbers drew the Europeans together in a world of their own surrounded by an opaque Javanese society. Yet greater Dutch power did not still their sense of unease.... [T]he Dutch were nagged by the thought that the natives might not calculate as rationally as Europeans the impossibility of defying Dutch rule. Consequently, the colonial administrators were only too sensitive to any hint of disaffection—by "fanatical" Muslims, "treacherous" native chiefs, or the "rebellious" peasantry.... What weighed heavily on the resident who was ultimately accountable for law and order was the haunting thought that all might not be well beneath [the surface]. [His resources] were few, and the growth of the local European community had both distracted his attention from Javanese affairs and brought great pressure to react strongly to every imagined threat.[16]

Nor was this haunting thought confined to overworked Dutch officials. More widely, it found its popular expression in that dark and amorphous fear of *guna-guna* (black magic), Islam, white turbaned hajis, *jago,* and sexual Indies women in Dutch and Batavian Malay stories at the turn of the century. Thus, along with increased expectations and confidence in their ability to carry out reforms, officials were faced with new dangers and insecurities as they perceived that the order they had once accepted as sufficiently stable was actually a superficial cover hiding a turbulent reality.

This mood of heightened Dutch imperial self-confidence and perception marked the dawning of a new colonial era. After the depression in the 1880s, Dutch corporate business activities expanded rapidly. The Indies state was increasingly rationalized and centralized and its activities expanded. *Volkscredietwezen,* government pawnshops, a government opium monopoly, an agricultural information and extension service, a people's health and medical extension, a post, telegraph and telephone service, railways, government schools, a forestry service—all became part of state activities.

The revenue farms were a major casualty of this new development. In the 1890s, the old opium farms, pawnshops, and other revenue farms were gradually dismantled and replaced by the state opium monopoly (*Opiumregie*), government pawnshops, and other state institutions. The loss of farms deprived the Chinese of their access to Java's rural market, and their freedom of economic activity was further restricted by more rigorous application of the pass (1897) and residential (1900) regulations. Ethically minded Dutch officials blamed the Chinese for the declining welfare of the natives and for a time seriously tried to destroy their economic position. Banks were created to provide Javanese peasants with agricultural credit and to break Chinese moneylenders' control over the peasant economy. And for effective policing of black market competition, which was needed for the success of the government's opium monopoly, the smaller the Chinese presence in the village world, the better. With the freedom of their commercial activities restricted, Chinese traders sold fewer goods and could not collect the debts of villagers that had customarily been paid in rice and other produce. Deprived of their financial mainstay on the revenue farms, once vast *kongsi* networks, formal and informal, were shattered.

Dutch reformist attention was also directed toward the informal social networks that inhabited the interface between the formal state structure and the village world. Dutch officials unearthed and exposed the internal workings of Java's native administration in the 1900s in their massive studies for administrative and police reforms.[17]

In the absence of a modern police apparatus, the regent and his native officials continued to rely on their informal social networks of local toughs, informers, and spies for policing the village world.[18] Now, however, Dutch officials watched more carefully over their shoulders, often bypassing the regent and running the local native bureaucracy directly. For the Dutch, nonbureaucratic networks above the village level were not only of no use but were sometimes seen as sources of trouble to be neutralized by the new police apparatus.

While the government was transforming the state and dismantling the corrupt system infested by European and Chinese mestizo and native elites and their informal networks, modern politics also arrived in the Indies in the early twentieth century in the form of newspapers, associations, rallies, and boycotts. The development that triggered the rise of modern Chinese politics in the Indies was the Dutch recognition in 1899 of the Japanese as equal with Europeans in legal status. In the eyes of the Indies Chinese, who were in serious trouble because of the dismantling of the revenue farms and the rigorous application of the pass and residential systems, the reason for the continuing discrimination against them was clear. The strong, modernized Japanese state could protect and improve the position of Japanese in the Indies, whereas the weak, not-yet-modernized, dynastic Qing state could not. The key to improving the position of the Indies Chinese, therefore, had to be to push for faster progress and greater state protection.

In 1900, the Tjong Hoa Hwe Koan (THHK, Chinese Association) was established by Dutch-educated Chinese, and the next year it established the first Western-style THHK school. Within a few years, THHK schools were in operation all over the Indies. The advice, assistance, and protection of the Qing government were eagerly sought, and the Qing government, seeing a chance to tap the wealth of the Indies Chinese, responded positively. From 1906 onward, Qing dignitaries visited the Indies every year. With their advice, Chinese chambers of commerce were established in commercial centers and their officers were given Qing official ranks.

To raise funds for its schools, the THHK taxed Chinese business transactions such as commercial shipments and cotton and tobacco sales. Chinese chambers of commerce organized boycotts of European firms to protect Chinese commercial interests. Chinese journalism flourished with the publication of newspapers and magazines in Chinese and Batavian Malay. Along with the expansion of THHK schools, Chinese republican revolutionaries supporting Sun Yat-sen's cause also came to the Indies as THHK schoolteachers, and in 1909 they began to establish *soe po sia*, Chinese reading clubs, where lectures were held and books and periodicals were made available to the Chinese public. In 1907 and 1909, when two Chinese warships visited Indies ports, the Indies Chinese jubilantly welcomed them and demonstrated their new Chinese solidarity.

The rise of Chinese journalism and modern associational politics clearly signified the arrival of Chinese nationalism among the Indies Chinese. They were no long "anak Senen" (kids in Senen), "anak Grodok" (kids in Grodok), or Macaonese, as they had been identified in the late nineteenth century. They were becoming "Chinese" and establishing political ties with China. This alarmed the Indies government, which began to give them concessions to keep them as Dutch subjects. The new Dutch Chinese school system (Hollandsche Chineesche Scholen) was introduced in 1907 for the Dutch language education of Chinese children, although the Batavian Chinese elite preferred that the European elementary school system be opened to them. The pass system was relaxed in 1904 by the grant of passes valid for a year instead of for a single journey, in part because the tough pass system had led to mounting bankruptcies of Chinese firms that in turn caused losses for large Dutch trading companies doing business with them. In 1910 the right of free passage along the main highways without a permit was granted.[19] The Chinese, this time not just the farm Chinese but all of them, gained freedom of commercial activity and sought to place their money in sugar plantations and local industries such as *kretek* cigarettes and batik, as well as in small shops and commerce.

Then, in October 1911, came the Chinese revolution. The Qing dynasty collapsed and the republic was born. Indies Chinese saw this event as a sign of the emergence of a strong, modernized Chinese state, and the sense of Chinese power was all the more heightened. Though Chinese were not allowed to wear Western-style clothing or cut off their queues, they began to do so anyway after the revolution. The Chinese officer system, the main institutional device for Dutch control over Java's Chinese in the nineteenth century, also came under attack. With the dismantling of the revenue farms in the 1890s and the rise of modern Chinese politics in the 1900s, the Chinese officer system had already lost much of its prestige by the early 1910s. The revolution was the final blow.

In late 1911 and early 1912, Chinese officers were attacked for their ignorance of Chinese. A poster that appeared on walls in Batavia's Chinese quarter asked, "[O]f what nationality is the Majoor [a Chinese officer with the rank of major]? Answer: Chinese and still not Chinese; native and still not native; in reality [he is] of mixed race! This bastard cannot return to China and cannot be named a European."[20] In Surabaya, Chinese officers were forced to cut off their queues, and Cantonese broke into the house of a Chinese officer. In Semarang, a group of Cantonese tore down the Dutch flag from the house of a Chinese officer and trampled it. They were no longer what they used to be. They were Chinese who were conscious of being Chinese and who appeared in public like Europeans. They were no longer part of the social order but somewhere outside it.

Undoubtedly the Dutch regarded such acts as "arrogant." But Dutch officials' reports saying so bore some relationship to the changed reality. The Chinese did become "arrogant" after the revolution. The resident of Surakarta reported in May 1913 that after the revolution some Chinese had dared to say to natives that the new republic would soon drive away the Dutch, and the Chinese would become their rulers and masters. They demanded, the resident continued, that natives address them as *toean* (master) and show due respect as they did to the *priyayi* and the Dutch.[21]

In Surabaya, during the Chinese New Year celebration in February 1912, a Dutch ban on hoisting the new Chinese republican flag led to disturbances between Chinese and police. In protest against tough police measures, the whole Chinese community in Surabaya closed down its shops for several days. The inconvenience caused by the market strike angered natives who could not buy the rice they needed. The Dutch resident ordered the police to arrest all Cantonese in Surabaya in an effort to stamp out Chinese unrest. This was a clear enough go-ahead sign. Natives, especially Madurese, and Arabs attacked Chinese and beat them up.

Though Boekhoudt had reported that the natives' sense of nationalism was "fast asleep," signs of the arrival of modern politics were already there in the native world when he wrote his report in 1906 and 1907. Educational expansion since the 1890s was producing a small, native, salaried middle class, mobile but essentially urban, sharing a common Western-style education and called *kaum muda* (the young). Together with Western-educated European and Chinese mestizos, these people formed the reading public for Batavian Malay publications. In the 1890s and early 1900s—especially after 1906, when the new press law substituted postcensorship for precensorship—the number and circulation of Malay and other vernacular periodicals expanded greatly, from eight in 1890 to eighteen in 1905 and thirty-six in 1910.

Native journalism and modern politics developed with the *kaum muda* as their social base. The person who spearheaded this development was R. M. Tirtoadhisoerjo. In 1903, Tirtoadisoerjo, already a star reporter, started his own newspaper, *Soenda Berita*, the first newspaper financed, managed, edited, and published by natives. In 1906 he founded an association, Sarekat Prijaji (Association of Priyayi), to promote native education. In 1907 he started a hugely successful new weekly, *Medan Prijaji* (Forum of Priyayi), as an organ of "the Sons of the Country" (Anak Negeri), in which he attacked Dutch and native officials for bureaucratic abuses. And in 1909 he established the Sarekat Dagang Islamijah, an association of Muslim traders in Bogor, as an association of *kaoem mardika* (free people)—a Malay translation of the Dutch *vrije burgers* (free citizens).[22]

The rise of native journalism and modern politics offered new political opportunities for the *kaum muda* and for Java's supravillage informal social networks. Nothing illustrates this point more clearly than the transformation of Martodharsono from a *guru weri*, a traditional practitioner of esoteric knowledge, into a central leader of the Surakarta SI in its early days. A former official of the Surakartan royal house, Martodharsono was well known for his secret knowledge of invulnerability and his extensive connections with Solonese aristocrats and the Surakartan underworld. According to resident Harloff, he was arrested and banished to Lombok in 1894 on the charge of forgery. Soon, however, he escaped and returned to Surakarta with the help of his disciples, only to be arrested again and this time sent to Sumatra.

After serving his term, Martodharsono came back to Java, settled down in Bandung, joined Tirtoadisoerjo to work as an editor of *Medan Prijaji,* and then returned to Solo. When the Kong Sing fell apart and Samanhoedi formed the Rekso Roemekso, Martodharsono was in Surakarta working as editor-in-chief of the newspapers *Djawi Kanda* and *Djawi Hiswara.* His knowledge of native journalism and modern associational politics, as well as his reputation as a *guru weri* and his connections with the Surakartan underworld, were crucial in transforming the Rekso Roemekso, an association for mutual help against "bandits," into the SI, a modern association with legal status. The SI thereby also became an effective organization for boycotting Chinese firms.

In the early days of the SI, hundreds of Tirtoadisoerjos, Samanhoedis, and Martodharsonos emerged in many places and activated hitherto informal, supravillage social networks for the expansion of the SI in a new political way. The social networks activated (or rather their combinations) varied from place to place. Muslim commercial networks, native underworld networks of *jago,* informers, spies, and *guru weri, santri* networks of Islamic teachers, hajis, and religious students, *kaum muda* networks built on modern education, old patronage networks linking native officials and the village world—all these combinations made SI branches different from one place to another. But one thing was clear: hidden forces that had haunted the Dutch were now out in the open, and the old order that had managed to contain those forces had come to an end. Racially mixed *kongsi,* which had been fragmented and undermined since the 1890s at the latest, were casualties of this development. But they were not the only ones. Indeed, the regime of informal networks on which the whole nineteenth-century order had been built was now thrown into serious crisis.

> When the carriage approached [the Chinese quarter], they [the Chinese] rose and remained standing, respectfully. The Javanese for the most part—those who were well brought up and knew their manners—squatted. . . . [W]hen the carriage drove into the Arab quarter—a district of houses like any other, but gloomy, lacking in style, with life and prosperity hidden away behind closed doors, with chairs on the verandah, but the master of the house gloomily squatting on the floor, following the carriage with a somber look—this quarter seemed even more mysterious than the fashionable part of Labuwangi and seemed to radiate its unutterable mystery like an atmosphere of Islam that spread over the whole town, as though it were Islam that had poured forth the dusky, fatal melancholy of resignation that filled the shivering noiseless evening.[23]

Thus Louis Couperous, in his Indies novel *The Hidden Force,* describes the scene of an outing the resident's family made by carriage in Labuwangi, a small East Javan residency capital, at the turn of the century. From the window of the carriage, with his imagining eyes, Couperous watches Chinese, Javanese, and an Arab. Seeing them watching him, he can no longer be sure that the outward signs of order, such as the Chinese standing respectfully or the Javanese squatting, signify real quiet and order. He sees mystery hidden behind the propriety of their outward demeanor. Couperous thus says, in effect, that the Dutch are on stage and being watched, and that being on stage, they do not belong to the Indies as the Chinese, natives, and Arabs do, even though the Indies are "our" colony.

It was this Dutch on-stage mentality, their awareness of being watched by Chinese, Javanese, and Arabs, and their watching them and seeing mysteries behind them that informed the new Dutch colonial policy. It led the Indies government to want to "educate" ignorant and superstitious natives and make them decipherable, to reform the administrative "mess," to watch over Islamic schools, teachers, and hajis, to want to "protect" the natives from Chinese exploitation and Javanese official corruption and abuse of power, and to begin policing Java's interior with an apparatus under its direct control. All this was to establish a more rational and thorough order. But Dutch attempts to pacify Java in a new way were not entirely successful, and the hidden forces that came to the surface through modern and increasingly radicalized native associational politics were never brought fully under control.

The rise of modern politics and the emergence of hidden forces onto the surface, however, provided an opportunity for the Dutch to fashion a new order. Under Java's old order, the real distinctions among Europeans, Chinese, and natives were not a matter of race and custom. In the nineteenth century, mestizo *peranakan,* Europeans, Chinese, and natives shared blood, customs, and language. Yet legally one was either European, native, or Chinese. One's legally defined racial status determined where one could live, what taxes one paid, to which laws one was subject, before which courts one was tried, and, if found guilty of a crime, how and with what degree of harshness one was punished. In everyday life, it also determined what a person could wear. A native could not dress as a European, nor could a Chinese male cut off his Manchu braid.[24] Just as the neatness of a village had been equated with its security in nineteenth-century Java, neat racial distinctions had to be displayed openly, precisely because real racial distinctions were not even skin deep.

The rise of modern politics provided an opportunity for the Dutch Indies state to adopt a new strategy. It signified the "awakening" of the Chinese as Chinese and of "natives" as natives, and led to the breakdown of racially mixed *kongsi.* This assured the Dutch that anti-Sinicism would henceforth be firmly in place in the native mind and that Chinese and natives would go their separate ways without mixing. It was no longer necessary to require Chinese and natives to wear their own distinctive dress. It became perfectly permissible for Chinese and natives to appear in public in European dress, for the new politics quickly implanted racial distinctions in everyone's mind.[25]

No wonder, then, that the Indies government made "concessions" to the Chinese in the late 1910s. Under Java's new order, the Chinese were relegated to the position of pariahs—no longer part of the regime, without any real power to threaten the Dutch, and vulnerable to popular native antagonism. This position was fundamentally based on and underwritten by the new, violent form of native anti-Sinicism.

NOTES

1. W. Boekhoudt, *Rapport Reorganisatie van het Politiewezen op Java en Madoera (Uitgezonderd de Vorstenlanden, de Particuliere Landerijen en de Hoofdplaatsen Batavia, Semarang en Soerabaja) 1906–07* (Batavia: Landsdrukkerij, 1908), p. 3. If he had done his study in 1907–1908, Boekhoudt would not have said that the national sense was "fast asleep" among Javanese, for the establishment of the Boedi Oetomo, calling for native progress, in 1908 was seen as a sure sign of "native awakening" by Governor General Idenburg and his "ethical-minded" officials.

2. D. A. Rinkes, adviser for native affairs, to Governor General A. W. F. Idenburg, October 4, 1913, Mr. 2059/1913.

3. See, for instance, Resident of Surakarta van Wijk to Governor General Idenburg, November 11, 1912, Vb. 28–5-13–9.

4. See, for instance, Rinkes to Idenburg, August 24, 1912, included in S. L. van der Wal, ed., *De Opkomst van de Nationalistische beweging in Nederlands-Indie* (Groningen, Netherlands: J. B. Wolters, 1964), p. 86.

5. Hannah Arendt, *The Origins of Totalitarianism* (New York: Harcourt Brace Jovanovich, 1979, 3d ed.), p. 29.

6. For the early days of the SI, see Takashi Shiraishi, *An Age in Motion: Popular Radicalism in Java, 1912–1926* (Ithaca, New York: Cornell University Press), pp. 27–79.

7. Quoted in the report sent by B. A. J. van Wettun, the adviser for Japanese and Chinese affairs, to Governor General Idenburg, dated May 8, 1913. See van der Wal, *De Opkomst*, p. 170. This issue of *Hoa Tok* must have been published sometime in 1912, for the unrest in Solo took place in late 1911 to early 1912.

8. Rinkes to Idenburg, March 4, 1914, Vb. 15–3-15–8.

9. For more on Kong Dji Hing, see J. C. Bedding, assistant resident of Krawang, to Idenburg, April 21, 1913, Vb. 9–8-13-B13; Resident of Batavia Rijksnijder to Idenburg, May 27, 1913, Vb. 9–8-13-B13; Assistant Resident of Tanggerang Vernet to Rijksnijder, May 31, 1913, in Sartono, *Sarekat Islam Local* (Jakarta: Arsip Nasional, 1972); resident of Batavia to Idenburg, August 5, 1913, Mr. 1651/13; Notulen: Rapat S.I. di Cibarusa, November 16, 1913, Mr. 184/14, in Sartono, *Sarekat Islam Local,* pp. 27–29; Assistant Resident of Meester Cornelis Feith to resident of Batavia, July 28, 1914, in Sartono, *Sarekat Islam Local,* pp. 45–59; resident of Batavia to Idenburg, March 15, 1915, Mr. 2029/15, Vb. 8–3-16–50; adviser for native affairs to Idenburg, June 14, 1915, Mr. 2030/15, Vb. 9–3-16–26.

10. For the cultivation system, see, above all, Onghokham, "The Inscrutable and the Paranoid: An Investigation into the Sources of the Brotoningrat Affair," in Ruth T. McVey, ed., *Southeast Asian Transitions: Approaches through Social History* (New Haven, Connecticut: Yale University Press, 1978), and Cornelis Fasseur, *The Politics of Colonial Exploitation: Java, the Dutch, and the Cultivation System,* translated by R. E. Elson and Ary Krall, edited by R. E. Elson (Ithaca, New York: Cornell University Southeast Asia Program, 1992). For opium farms, see James R. Rush, "Social Control and Influence in Nineteenth Century Indonesia: Opium Farms and the Chinese of Java," *Indonesia* 35 (April 1983), pp. 53–64, and his *Opium to Java: Revenue Farming and Chinese Enterprise in Colonial Indonesia, 1860–1910* (Ithaca, New York: Cornell University Press, 1990).

11. J. S. Furnivall, *Netherlands India* (Cambridge: Cambridge University Press, 1939), pp. 128–34.

12. James Rush, *Opium to Java,* pp. 13, 17.

13. Rush, "Social Control and Influence," p. 53.

14. An opium farm *kongsi,* for instance, usually employed professional managers to conduct its business in a residency—manufacture of opium products, distribution of products to some fifty local stores, and collecting and auditing of opium receipts as they made their way from tens of thousands of customers up through the *kongsi* organization to the top. This operation involved hundreds of people, from clerks and coolies in local stores to technicians and chemists in manufacturing facilities. See Rush, "Social Control," p. 55.

15. Rush, "Social Control," p. 59.

16. Onghokham, "The Inscrutable and the Paranoid," p. 138.

17. See, for instance, W. Boekhoudt, *Rapport Reorganisatie;* see also *Onderzoek naar de Mindere Welvaart der Inlandsche Bevolking op Java en Madoera: VIIIb. Overzicht van de Uitkomsten der Gewestelijke Onderzoekingen naar het Recht en de Politie en daaruit gemaakte gevolgtrekkingen. Deel II. Slotbeschouwingen* (Batavia: Ruygrok & Co., 1912).

18. Modern police organizations were introduced in Java's three major urban centers, Batavia, Semarang, and Surabaya, in 1911. It was not until 1920 that a new police regime, led centrally by the prosecutor general and locally by the resident, was created to cover the rest of Java.

19. Dutch import houses in Surabaya lost 1.14 million guilders in 1896 because of the bankruptcies of their Chinese retail dealers, and imports to Surabaya declined 10 percent from 1895 to 1897. See Lea E. Williams, *Overseas Chinese Nationalism: The Genesis of the Pan-Chinese Movement in Indonesia, 1900–1916* (Glencoe, Illinois: Free Press, 1960), p. 31.

20. The poster, dated March 1, 1912, is quoted in Williams, *Overseas Chinese Nationalism,* p. 129.

21. Resident of Surakarta van Wijk to Idenburg, November 11, 1912, Vb. 28–5-13–9.

22. For the rise of native journalism and new associational politics and Tirtoadisoerjo, see Shiraishi, *An Age in Motion,* pp. 27–35.

23. Louis Couperous, *The Hidden Force,* translated by Alexander Teizeira de Mattos (Amherst: University of Massachusetts Press, 1985 [1901]), pp. 72–73.

24. Rush, *Opium to Java,* p. 14.

25. See Tan Boen Kim, *Peroesoehan di Koedoes* (Batavia: Drukkerij Goan Hong & Co., 1920), in which Tan Boen Kim imagines himself to be a Muslim native mingling with Arab entrepreneurs. They are jealous of the more successful Chinese entrepreneurs and intent on taking revenge on them for the economic losses they have suffered through their own fault.

8 / Middleman Minorities and Blood

Is There a Natural Economy of the Ritual

Murder Accusation in Europe?

HILLEL J. KIEVAL

In 1974, in a study of German anti-Semitism before the First World War, Stefan Lehr attempted to list all documented accusations of ritual murder against Jews that occurred during the last two decades of the nineteenth century.[1] He counted 128 incidents from 1873 to 1900; all but five occurred in the single decade from 1891 to 1900. Presumably, if he had chosen to continue to the Beilis affair of 1911–13, he would have found at least a half-dozen more. Whether the final count was 128 or 138 is hardly the point, however, since Lehr did not claim that the list was exhaustive. Nor did he make any effort to distinguish between a rumored accusation, such as might have appeared in a small corner of a newspaper page on a single day, and an event of major proportions, such as a protracted murder trial or the outbreak of riots. Indeed, his list seems merely to have quantified what all students of Central European affairs at the turn of the century already knew: that between 1880 and 1914, the theme of "Jewish ritual murder" occupied a prominent place in a number of intersecting discourses and enjoyed a salience it had not been seen for two centuries or more.

It is possible that what appears to have been a resurgence in the "culture" of ritual murder accusation was in reality no such thing, but simply the by-product of a popular press that had not been in place before this time. Mass-market newspapers, in other words, eagerly reported "sensations" of this kind both in the name of journalistic thoroughness and in order to sell newspapers. I would be inclined to accept this objection if the distribution of reported cases was relatively constant over time. But although the publishing of mass-market newspapers began in Germany and the Habsburg monarchy in the 1860s with the liberalization of press and censorship laws, interest in Jewish "ritual criminality" was hardly visible before the 1880s.

More remarkable is the degree to which the topic of ritual murder saturated popular culture in Central Europe in the following decade. It is of particular interest to me that formal murder trials played a part in the new cultural preoccupations. Between 1882 and 1901, magistrates and prosecutors in Germany and Austria-Hungary broke with nearly three centuries of legal and political precedent by reintroducing the charge of Jewish ritual murder to the criminal and legal proceedings of the state, thereby not only investing heavily in resources and time but also raising questions about their own bureaucratic ethos, as well as about the rational foundations of the state itself.

The formal trials in question took place in Tiszaeszlár, Hungary (1882–83), in Xanten in the Prussian Rhineland (1891–92), in Polná, Bohemia (1899–1900), and in Konitz, West Prussia (1900–1901; after 1918, this became Poland). These trials, as it happened, were sandwiched between two others held in the Russian Empire: in Kutaisi (1878–79) and in Kiev (1911–13)—the famous Beilis affair.[2]

Analysis of the modern ritual murder trial in Europe provides an excellent opportunity to consider the role of competing systems of knowledge and power in the elaboration of social conflict. On one level, the trials and ensuing debates seem to argue for the convergence of myth, irrationality, traditional wisdom, and rational discourse in the production of social knowledge. At the same time, the events in question offer a rare perspective on the social relations between Jews and Gentiles in the decades following political emancipation. Confrontations between Jews and their accusers appear to have impinged unexpectedly upon the political and cultural landscape, disrupting the equilibrium of Jewish social and communal life, revealing a significant domain of cultural misunderstanding and suspicion, and calling into question the very premises on which Jewish emancipation had rested: the basic humanity of the Jews, their status as Europeans, and the fundamental resemblance of Jews to non-Jews.

Beginning with Howard Paul Becker in the 1940s, sociologists have offered various versions of "middleman minority" theory to explain the sometimes dangerous instability of Jewish existence in Central and Eastern Europe.[3] Irwin Rinder introduced the concept of "status gap" in order to establish a structural explanation for Jewish economic specialization, an explanation that equated the situation of the Jews in Europe with that of other ethnic groups in other parts of the world and in other historical periods.[4] Most noteworthy in "status gap" theory, I think, is its tendency to ascribe cultural or psychological motives to one group of economic actors (e.g., feudal, imperial, and colonial elites) and pragmatic motives to another (usually the entrepreneurial minorities). Thus the premodern European aristocracy eschewed trade and commerce because of psychological hubris or cultural inhibitions, whereas groups such as Jews, who entered the economic wilderness, did so because they did not suffer such cultural disabilities. Their choice, in other words, was rational.[5]

Similarly, mainly psychological factors seem to be at play in relations between entrepreneurial minorities and their economic clients near the bottom of the social hierarchy. Groups who entered the "status gap" are said to have earned the enmity and resentment of those whose economic needs they met. Rinder stresses an additional, crucial factor in the condition of entrepreneurial minorities: their lack of rootedness in the host society. Ethnic groups occupying the "middle" were understood, fundamentally, to be strangers:

> They are different; they have had little part in the long and glorious history of patria; and their very manner of making a living marks them as ignorant, or even worse. . . . [N]o matter how successful these newcomers may be, they cannot buy belongingness for all their wealth.[6]

The ethnic middleman's supposed quality of unrootedness received verification by any number of other indications of "difference" with which he or she was marked: language, dress, religion, physical appearance, and so forth. And it was largely by virtue of his or her visibility that the ethnic "man in the middle" became a quintessential target for scapegoating in times of major social and economic change.[7]

Edna Bonacich's work on "middleman minorities" has sought to bring together issues of culture, ethnicity, and class, and, in doing so, to demonstrate that ethnic antagonisms can reflect the collision of incompatible economic interests and goals.[8] She argues that when trading minorities have come into conflict with members of other ethnic groups, the conflict usually has been experienced along class lines and—equally important—has derived from observable economic and cultural behavior. If entrepreneurial immigrants came into conflict with business rivals from a different ethnic group, it may have been not only because of ordinary competition but also because members of the immigrant group employed practices or enjoyed cultural traits that placed them in a relatively advantageous position. They may have been able to undercut their rivals by making use of their credit institutions, by restraining competition within their community, or by employing family members as cheap or unpaid labor. Immigrant minorities also may have had "real" interests that collided with those of their customers, tenants, and clients—people who stood apart from the "middlemen" both culturally and in terms of social class.[9]

In sum, much, if not most, of the hostility expressed by host societies toward entrepreneurial minorities can be said to have had a "rational" basis in the conflict between incompatible economic goals. Bonacich also has characterized entrepreneurial minorities as highly ethnocentric "sojourners" inclined toward cultural separatism.[10] In doing so, she manages not only to accept at face value the complaints of their antagonists but also to suggest that much of the responsibility for the hostility that exists between majorities and compact minorities rests with the behavior, the cultural traits, and even the psychological profile of the minority group.

In a response to Bonacich, Jack Kugelmass accepts as virtually unassailable the applicability of the middleman minority model to the Jews of Poland but takes issue with her characterization of the cultural implications of this status. The political and economic situation of the Jews in the Polish countryside, Kugelmass argues, promoted modes of exchange and lines of communication with the Gentile world that indicated anything but "alienation." The dominant pyschological process was one of intimacy, and in day-to-day business encounters, much more than currency was "exchanged."

> The economic interdependence of Jew and peasant did not always produce a significant degree of social unease or a diminution of social distance. . . . Whether or not friendly relations prevailed between Jew and peasant, on a cultural level the inevitable result of continued trade and prolonged proximity was an exchange of language and folklore that goes well beyond the apparent yet deceptive dissimilarity of religion, language and social status. Indeed the very act of haggling, so characteristic of Jewish/peasant market relations, introduced into that relationship a vehicle of exchange beyond the proper confines of money.[11]

More recently, in an attempt to reconcile conflicting middleman theories, Bonacich and Jonathan Turner have offered a more elaborate model of "middleman–host society" hostility. They posit three preconditions for the outbreak of unfriendly relations:

> The more an ethnic group (a) comes from a highly ethnocentric culture; (b) moves into a society with a low level of pluralism, or a high concern over national integration; and (c) shows a high degree of social, cultural, and/or physical contrast with the receiving society, the more likely is it to face initial hostility from the society of immigration.[12]

It seems noteworthy that one set of factors concerns the cultural behavior of the ethnic minority, one refers to the proclivities of what the authors refer to (uncritically) as the "host," or "receiving," society, and one highlights what are taken to be "objective" distinctions between the two populations. Fundamental problems of interpretation rest with each point. How does one determine that a "high degree of ethnocentrism" in the culture of origin promotes hostility in the new society? One method would be to compare the careers of diaspora minorities who display varying degrees of ethnocentrism. I see no evidence that such a comparative study has been carried out, nor is it clear to me what analytical criteria could produce reliable distinctions on the issue. Another approach—which I fear is the one more often taken—is to read the record of complaint against the minority in question without accounting adequately for the tendentious nature of the source. What would be truly desirable, however, would be an acknowledgment of the difficulty of disentangling sociological description from contending systems of knowledge.

The assertion concerning the strength or weakness of "pluralism" in the host society begs the question of whether "host" societies themselves exist in any objective sense. In the European context, the role of "host" or "native" often amounts to little more than a cultural construct arrogated to one group or another as an act of political will. The Jewish presence in the Czech lands, for example, is at least as old as that of the Slavs and certainly older than that of the Germans. In the nineteenth century, much ink was spilled in an effort to "prove" the antiquity of one group or another. Under such circumstances it seems doubtful that distinctions between host and sojourner, native and immigrant, are of much descriptive use.

I have questions, moreover, concerning the predictive possibilities of the pluralism–national integration dichotomy. Medieval and early modern Poland-Lithuania comprised a highly plural society, as did modern Hungary. Yet important ritual murder accusations against Jews were played out in both of these settings. Modern France, on the other hand, can (with some hesitation) be characterized as a unified nation-state, yet it witnessed no such agitation against Jews after the seventeenth century. To the contrary, of all of the countries in continental Europe, it was precisely in uninational France that Jewish integration appeared to make the greatest inroads after 1789. One could, justifiably, point to late-medieval Spain as a unifying country that found the presence of Jews intolerable and eventually expelled or forcibly converted the entire Jewish population. But Spain was hardly a uniform society. And notwithstanding Bonacich's denial that "host hostility" is self-generated, Spain presents a clear case in which a radical intolerance for Jews had everything to do with the internal dynamics of majority culture and almost nothing to do with "competing interests."[13]

Finally, to contend that a high degree of "social, cultural, and/or physical contrast" is likely to increase host hostility toward ethnic minorities is to risk underestimating the power of the imagination in the construction of difference in ethnic confrontations. In some of the fiercest cases of ethnic conflict in Europe—Germany in the first half of the twentieth century, Spain in the fifteenth and sixteenth centuries, and the countries of the former Yugoslavia today—no obvious physical, linguistic, or social distinctions can be said to have existed between the parties involved. The struggles in question did not represent an acknowledgment of fundamental divisions but, rather, exercises in boundary drawing, in the *discovery* of "difference" and the clarification of cultural ambiguity. Spanish elites created "purity of blood" statutes—the first example of racial legislation in European history—precisely because no cultural markers other than the notion of "lineage" separated new Christians from old.[14] Similarly, the racial legislation of Nazi Germany occurred in the aftermath of more than a century of Jewish acculturation and assimilation; the problem for German racialists was not that the Jews stood out, but that they did not.[15] And while the Muslims of Bosnia are physically and linguistically indistinguishable from Orthodox Serbs, their mutual incompatibility is no less real simply because it derives from the ethnic imagination.

It seems to me that even in situations in which an ethnic minority does possess physical or cultural characteristics that are distinct from those of the majority, the real question to ask is when, under what circumstances, and why does a group choose to notice those distinctions or proclaim them to be significant? It may be true, as Ernest Gellner argues in *Nations and Nationalism,* that ethnic minorities who occupy intermediate positions in preindustrial societies—often performing specialized bureaucratic as well as economic functions—are selected precisely because they are culturally distinct. The functions these groups perform may be considered too close to positions of real power or too ambiguous in terms of status and pollution to be entrusted to members of the dominant ethnic group.[16] I fear, however, that such a description ascribes too much conscious motivation to social processes.

A more reasonable scenario would be one that posits a plural universe made up of multiple allegiances and cultural styles, some of which will also correspond to the division of labor in society. Normally, cultural traits that are simultaneously ubiquitous to a particular group and secondary to its economic status are perceived by others as part of the natural landscape. Thus, to a Ukrainian-speaking peasant in the seventeenth century, the fact that the landed nobility spoke Polish and French and practiced the Catholic religion, whereas the innkeepers, moneylenders, and estate managers spoke Yiddish (and Polish) and were Jews, amounted to little more than an obvious description of the world. At crucial points in time, though, a sea change in consciousness occurs, as a result of which the very same traits are radically reinterpreted (or interpreted for the first time). By definition, they now are no longer "natural," and their main significance may also now be understood to lie in the realm of economics, although this is not the only possibility.

Some of my objections to middleman minority theory correspond to criticisms that have already been made by Donald Horowitz and Walter Zenner, among others. Horowitz questions the degree to which ethnic conflict can be said to rest on "realistic economic competition." He argues that ethnic occupational specialization in the context of preindustrial and colonial societies—what he calls the "ethnic division of labor"—tends not to exacerbate but to mitigate intergroup tensions. Such specialization inhibits competition among ethnic groups while it molds group aspirations in separate directions.[17] Ethnic groups, he concludes, "often have distinctly preferred occupational paths that are related to the structure of opportunities and to differences of culture and history."[18] As far as relations between traders and their customers are concerned, peasants, Horowitz points out, far from resenting "alien" traders, often prefer them to members of their own ethnic group, and participants in ethnic violence frequently go out of their way to avoid inflicting injury on middleman minorities.[19]

Surprising as it may appear at first glance, Horowitz's argument brings to mind remarks made by Gellner on the "dual ethic" of entrepreneurial minorities. In Gellner's view, a double standard has existed in the business practices of such groups, but it is the opposite of what many sociologists— including Weber—have supposed. Interpersonal relations *within* the group could be conducted on the basis of instrumental rationality and moral ambiguity; relations with the host society, however, were predicated on good performance, reliability, and trust. The very survival of "diaspora nations" such as the Jews hinged on their ability to establish a reputation for reliability and flexibility.

> This was quite different from the relations prevailing inside a *moral* community, where a commercial deal between two individuals was inevitably always far more than a mere commercial deal. . . .
>
> The advantage . . . of dealing with a minority, one with whom you could not eat, marry, or enter into political or military alliance, was that both parties could concentrate on a rational cost-benefit analysis of the actual specific deal in question, and expect, on the whole, to get what they bargained for, neither more nor less. Within the minority community, of course, relationships were once again many-stranded, and hence deals were less rational and reliable, and more many-sided.[20]

A retelling of economic encounters between Jews and peasants in the Polish town of Biala Podlaska, quoted at length by Kugelmass, adds interesting detail and local color to Gellner's contention that inside a moral community, "a commercial deal between two individuals was inevitably always far more than a mere commercial deal." If one can believe our Jewish informant in this account, Christians from the countryside actually preferred to deal with Jewish merchants.

> In the Christian store the customer had to remove his hat, he could not touch the merchandise but had to wait to be helped by the employee, he had to take what he was given and pay whatever the asking price was without bargaining. The Christian customer could not endure the tension and the Christian merchant did not understand the psychology of the customers, whom one had to let bargain and bring down the price.
>
> In the Jewish store the Christian felt free to select the merchandise, test it, haggle and bargain down the price, get credit, and in general have a talk with the Jewish merchant, who was not pompous like the Christian storeowner. The Jewish merchant was quite familiar with the habits of the Christian customers and knew how to cater to them. The Jewish storeowner would also take the agricultural produce which the peasant brought to town, and consequently the peasant felt more tied to the Jewish storeowner than to the non-Jewish one.[21]

Even if we acknowledge the tendentiousness of the testimony—that is, the likelihood that it was intended to counter anti-Semitic stereotypes and encourage a certain nostalgic yearning for pre-Holocaust Poland—we must concede that it is anthropologically rich and rings true in many of its details. Accounts such as this remind us of the cultural complexity of situations of economic exchange and ought to discourage all one-dimensional analyses. They ought, moreover, to suggest that outbreaks of anti-Jewish hostility may represent not the natural outcome of traditional entrepreneur-client relations but a significant disruption of conventional patterns and outcomes.

In Zenner's view, what middleman minority theory lacks most is room for the interplay of autonomous cultural factors in conflict situations—for agents such as stereotypes and ideologies that are not tied to local circumstances. Zenner characterizes such agents as "outside agitators" whose development and diffusion over time and space owe more to the internal history of ideas than to specific socioeconomic realities.[22] He wonders, for example, whether one can adequately assess Southeast Asian attitudes toward ethnic Chinese without taking into account the importation by European colonialists of classical Western, anti-Jewish stereotypes. Such attitudes conveyed crucial cultural information about an ethnic group that did not exist so far as Javanese or Thais were concerned, but they learned from European colonial administrators and scholars to assign the specific moral evaluations of anti-Semitism to the local ethnic context. Early Thai nationalists, then, were able to see the Chinese in their midst as the "Jews of the East" by first learning to visualize Jews.

Hillel Levine's *Economic Origins of Antisemitism* represents the most interesting attempt in recent years to relate the problem of hostility toward Jews in Eastern Europe to structures of socioeconomic existence.[23] Though he does not refer specifically to middleman minority theory, Levine does argue that Jews' participation as intermediaries in the autarkic economy of early modern Poland rendered them doubly vulnerable to popular animosity and attack. One hears echoes of Rinder and Bonacich in his analysis of the Jewish role in the *arenda* system, through which Jews acted as lessors and managers of noble estates and monopolies. Whether willingly or by necessity, Jews implicated themselves in an exploitative economic system and, in the process, earned the animosity of the peasants with whom they came into contact day in and day out. And the failure of the Polish nobility, or *szlachta*, to "modernize"—that is, their refusal to emulate the transition of Western European societies to open-market, free-labor economies—only served to increase Jewish vulnerability. Rather than sacrifice traditional power and privileges, Polish elites in the eighteenth century offered a moral reevaluation of social and economic life that placed the blame for entrenched poverty, low productivity, and drunkenness on the deleterious impact of Jews on peasant society.[24]

Following the lead of other Jewish historians, Levine also contends that eighteenth-century Poland witnessed a resurgence of the ritual murder accusation.[25] The "blood libel," he suggests, although religious in expression, may well have been economic in structure or essence. He offers into evidence a number of explanations for the recourse to this type of accusation against Jews—for example, it was a psychological resolution of the problems of infanticide and child abuse in Polish society—before discarding them for being, in the final analysis, insufficient. What rendered the blood libel so compelling to the early modern Polish imagination, Levine feels, was the very web of Polish-Jewish interaction, based on Jewish leaseholding and manifested especially in the *propinacja*, the lord's monopolistic right to the manufacture and sale of vodka.[26]

> The plausibility of the blood libel was strengthened by Polish anticommercialism and by the suspicion and envy evoked by the Jews through their business and managerial successes. . . . The intuitive sense and tenacious conviction with which the "primitive idea" that someone's profit is someone else's loss was held in Poland may have led to such primitive enactments as the blood libel.[27]

The ritual murder accusation, in Levine's words, "dramatized the discrepancy between the religiously ascribed definition of Jews as lowly and perfidious and their achieved position as privileged and powerful." It underlined a profound tension in Polish society between the symbolic and the utilitarian roles of the Jews.[28] Middleman minority theory clearly reverberates in judgments such as these. They bear the same sense of timelessness, the same emphasis on economic structures, the same assumptions of Jewish power and wealth. At the same time, the eighteenth-century libels were historically and culturally contingent, that is to say, distinctively "Polish." What rendered them so, in Levine's opinion, were the *propinacja,* as institutional context, and the inn, as the locus of events.

Levine's analysis here moves between theory and empiricism. The specific evidence he offers for the link between the Polish blood libel and Jewish innkeeping emerges from an accusation made in Zhitomir, Ukraine, in 1753. A Catholic priest, Kajetan Soltyk, who played an important part in rousing popular opinion against the Jews, wrote in a letter to the archbishop of Lwów that when the body of a dead child was moved past a tavern, "it began suddenly to bleed profusely from its left rib."[29] Soltyk's depiction of the event conformed in two important respects to traditional ritual murder discourse. It bequeathed to the dead youth a "miracle"—the sudden bleeding from the rib, an act recapitulating the sufferings of Jesus at Golgotha and revealing the circumstances of the child's death—and it situated the miracle in a location that indicated clearly who the perpetrators of the crime were. In medieval accounts, similar miracles typically happened in the vicinity of the synagogue or outside the home of a rabbi or sexton.[30] Soltyk clearly chose the tavern for the same effect: to indicate an unambiguously Jewish locale. Whether he intended thereby a criticism of Jewish innkeeping is another matter. It would require an even greater leap to conclude from all this that a specific economic occupation (innkeeping) encouraged a particular form of ethnic persecution (ritual murder accusations).

Levine insists, nevertheless, that the *propinacja* provided the Polish imagination with an indispensable frame of reference without which the eighteenth-century blood libel would have been impossible. In this drama, the "real" and "symbolic" elements of daily life received expression: grain, as sustenance; blood, as vitality; and wine, as an indication of joyfulness, spiritual elevation, and freedom:

Grain-based intoxicants, provided by the Jews, were enjoyed by the peasants but reinforced the bonds of their serfdom. The alcohol made from the grain, produced by serf effort, did not contribute to serf sustenance and vitality. Jews involved in the propinacja siphoned off surplus serf profit; that profit represented the economic and metaphorical link between blood, as expended effort, and money, as reserve sustenance. The economic activities of these Jews, so productive in relation to the interests of the gentry, were perceived to be leechlike and parasitical to the Polish body politic. . . .

The growing recognition of the harmful effects of an economy that promoted alcoholism for economic and political purposes took on additional symbolic meaning. Alcohol, in accordance with Slavic folklore, was experienced as a facilitator of contact with other worlds, including the netherworld to which Jews were commonly believed to have close links. An integral part of the representation of that netherworld in the world of everyday Polish life was the belief that the Jew, by providing alcohol, was eager to bring about the serfs' debasement and ruination.[31]

This is a breathtaking interpretation, but it suffers from some of the same weaknesses as middleman minority theory in general. Its logical operation consists of imputing causal properties to an economic structure without paying much attention to the empirical record. Little regard is taken for the specific, local circumstances under which "knowledge" of Jewish ritual murder was constructed, nor is sufficient sensitivity displayed to the question of authorship. Is the Catholic priest, Soltyk, transmitting Polish folklore? Is his a "peasant" voice? On the basis of the little evidence we have been given, a stronger case can be made linking Soltyk to a traditional—and more universal—discourse of Jewish ritual murder.[32] He may also be giving expression to the self-serving reform rhetoric of the eighteenth-century nobility, who were prepared to censure Jewish economic behavior while maintaining the imbalance of power in society. In any event, *propinacja* criticism belonged to elite discourse and cannot be said to have reflected the opinions of the burghers and peasants who came into daily contact with Jews at the level of the local tavern. In the end, a case has not been made for the ambitious, symbolic associations of grain, alcohol, money, and blood.

In general, my objections to prevailing attempts to assign a natural economy to ethnic conflict, and to accusations of Jewish ritual murder specifically, are as follows: (1) Arguing exclusively from the perspective of structure, they lack appreciation for the dynamics of local cultural exchange and for the generation of knowledge at the local level. (2) They tend not to acknowledge the problem of "point of view" in the sources they cite, accepting, instead, what are often tendentious accounts as empirical descriptions of the behavior or characteristics of a minority group. (3) Middleman minority theories deal in a partial way with psychological factors, but they assume a very limited range of emotional responses based on a narrow conception of interpersonal relations. (4) Empirical tests do not provide sufficient support for a backdrop of socioeconomic crisis; at a minimum, the disjuncture between general economic trends and local circumstances needs to be addressed, and variations among localities explained. (5) Room is not provided for the interplay of independent cultural factors such as Christian doctrine and teachings from the pulpit. (6) A question remains as to whether or not Jewish communities that found themselves at the center of ritual murder accusations fit the conceptual category of middleman minority. (7) Last, there is a historically static quality to such theories that does not account adequately for change over time, even on the single question of the reception of entrepreneurial minorities in the host societies.

The cases of ritual murder trials in the nineteenth and twentieth century that I have studied confirm the difficulty of tying discrete events in the realms of culture and politics to broad economic trends. The Jewish defendants often appear not to fit the formal category of middleman, or entrepreneurial, minority—in some cases because their occupational profiles are not sufficiently distinct from those of their Gentile neighbors (Tiszaeszlár, Polná), in others because the phenomenon itself has ceased to exist in the societies in question (Xanten, Konitz). The cases also reveal the central role that local cultural exchange and local knowledge play in the genesis of this ethnic libel and, hence, the need always to be aware of the interplay between structure and local action.

The Hungarian trial, which involved the disappearance and apparent murder of a fourteen-year-old peasant girl named Eszter Solymosi, offers a strong challenge to the presumption of economic or political crisis as a necessary background to such events.[33] It also suggests that it was not necessary to have hostile interethnic relations to produce an accusation of ritual murder. Of all of the territories of east-central Europe in the 1860s, 1870s, and 1880s, Hungary was quite possibly the least conducive to serious anti-Jewish agitation. The economic and political institutions of the state—as well as the reigning political culture of the Magyar gentry—encouraged economic specialization among Jews (now, however, in the areas of industrial capitalism and the liberal professions), rapid acculturation, and social integration, while restraining expressions of anti-Jewish hostility.

William McCagg has written in this regard of a "collaboration" between Hungary's "Jewish capitalists" and the "nobiliary old regime."[34] Andrew Janos locates the defining features of the economic and political order in post-1867 Hungary in what he calls the "ethnic division of labor," in which the Magyar gentry dominated the bureaucracy, parliament, and the judiciary, and Jews monopolized the liberal professions and fed the capitalist economy.[35] The most likely sources of anti-Jewish feeling, according to C. A. Macartney, were to be found in the Catholic church, among the lesser gentry—who began to see some of their lands "pass into Jewish hands"— and in the towns. Magnates may have looked upon the Jews "with that benevolent and contemptuous patronage which was the traditional relationship between the two classes."[36] On the whole, however, Jews and Magyars in Hungary had established a firm political and economic relationship that offered both security and opportunity for Jews. The general position of Jews in Hungarian society compared favorably with that in any other European country before 1914.

Those historians who would claim that anti-Semitism assumed a greater role in Hungarian affairs before World War I invariably point to 1875 as a turning point. In April of that year, the nominally liberal deputy Gyözö Istóczy delivered a speech to the Hungarian parliament that called for restrictions on Jewish immigration and warned of the certain, deleterious effects of prolonged Jewish influence in the country.[37] Yet Istóczy's speech comprised an isolated, if jarring, event and was received by both the political establishment and the vast majority of deputies with anger and derision.[38] Thus, while it is true that by 1882 there may have been interested parties who would have jumped at the opportunity to exploit "damaging news" about the Jews, such individuals or groups stood at the margins of the political system, and there is no evidence to suggest that they had either the opportunity or the foresight to "create" Tiszaeszlár.

An alternative to an instrumentalist argument is to seek the emergence of the Tiszaeszlár accusation in the constellation of *local* cultural, social, and religious factors that operated in isolation from modern politics and its practitioners. Fundamentally, the charge of Jewish ritual murder derived from the "social knowledge" of Hungarian villagers, constructed at the local level and directed at the mysteries of criminality and social deviance.[39] To say that "knowledge" of Jewish ritual criminality was the product of local memories and understandings is not to suggest that the peasants of northeastern Hungary were anti-Semitic in a political sense or that Jews and non-Jews in Hungarian rural settings acted in their daily lives on the basis of mutual hostility and suspicion. It acknowledges, rather, that ethnic groups who live in close proximity simultaneously know and remain woefully ignorant of the other.

In the village of Tiszaeszlár, relations between the mixed population of Calvinists and Catholics and the Jews appear to have been friendly— according to some accounts, "intimate"—though defense attorney Károly

Eötvös took pains in his memoirs to add that Christians tended to look down upon the Jews with "a certain old-fashioned, accustomed sense of superiority."[40] The report offered by Paul Nathan, a Berlin-based journalist, in 1892 was more nuanced but basically positive: relations between the two groups seem to have been cordial and cooperative on an everyday level, as would befit life in a village. Tiszaeszlár had no Jewish quarter or ghetto. Jews lived side by side with their Gentile neighbors, and social contacts between the two groups were marked by familiarity and even affection, as well as by jealousy, resentments, and petty conflicts.[41] Only Andrew Handler insists on characterizing the Hungarian peasant as implacably hostile to Jews, though he offers only ambiguous folk proverbs in defense of this view and does not differentiate between regions of the country.[42]

Finally, the ethnic struggles that undermined Hungarian stability in the decades leading up to World War I cannot be said to have been a direct factor in the Tiszaeszlár case. Unlike western Hungary, where the German-oriented and, later, Magyar-oriented acculturation of Jews at times incensed the Slovak-speaking population, and where violent demonstrations against Jews periodically broke out, the northeast was populated mainly by Jews of Galician origin whose acculturation to Magyar norms was relatively rapid and whose political loyalties were not at issue.

Clearly, one does not need to presuppose the existence of fundamentally antagonistic relations between Jews and peasants to understand that the social-psychological dimension of their encounters could be fraught with ambiguities and misunderstandings. And if one were to retrace the steps by which "knowledge" of ritual murder was produced at the local level, one would navigate a field cluttered with collective memories, personal fears and desires, and cross-cultural misfirings. Even to address the elementary question "Who initiated the idea of ritual murder in this case?" is problematic, because the records of the criminal investigation and trial contain internal inconsistencies. On the whole, however, it appears that the earliest elaboration of a *theory* of ritual murder occurred in the context of a set of local cultural exchanges. The weight of the evidence also suggests that, in the first instance, it was the victim's mother, Mária Solymosi, and aunt who built the case for a "ritual murder," and it was they who pressed the matter before the police.[43]

Mrs. Solymosi relied on the convergence of chance occurrences, interpersonal exchanges, and memories, both personal and collective, to arrive at her construction of events. Two days after her daughter's disappearance, she paid two visits to the *bíró*, or local magistrate, of Tiszaeszlár, requesting that he organize a search for the missing girl; on the second visit she indicated specifically that the Jewish synagogue should be examined. Encountering resistance from the local official, Mária Solymosi pressed her case before the district magistrate (*foszolgabíró*) in Vencsellö. This official reacted with incredulity and advised Solymosi to "put such thoughts out of her mind and refrain from giving credence to those who should spread such rumors."[44] Although he refused to conduct an investigation on Solymosi's terms, the district magistrate did dispatch a messenger to Tiszaeszlár instructing the local official to initiate a search for the missing girl.

For three to four weeks, the state's intervention in what was still the case of a missing person failed to turn up any new information: no sign of Eszter or of her body, and no evidence of "foul play" on the part of the Jews. At the same time, a sequence of interactions on the part of a widening circle of women in the village began to produce (or "uncover") the narrative evidence for a meaningful ritual murder accusation.

First, several women came forward to offer testimony that they had seen and heard strange occurrences in the vicinity of the synagogue on the day of Eszter's disappearance, including the muffled sounds of a child's shouts or cries.[45] Subsequently, four women, including the sister of the *bíró* of Tiszaeszlár, insinuated themselves into the company of the younger son of one of the main defendants, József Scharf, a lad named Samu, not yet five years old. There is only vague evidence concerning the terms and scope of this interaction, beyond the fact that the women—singly or collectively—succeeded in joining Samu in play for certain periods of time. Toward the end of April and the beginning of May 1882, the women began to relate snippets of conversation they ostensibly had had with the young boy. One announced that she had heard Samu tell some peasant children that his father had enticed Eszter into the synagogue and bound and washed her, and that a *schochet* (Jewish ritual slaughterer) had "cut" her. Another said Samu's father had called the girl into the synagogue, where she was forced into a chair. Móric, the older brother, held Eszter's hands, József held her feet, and the *schochet* "cut" her leg.[46]

In early May, Mária Solymosi made a second trip to the district magistrate in Vencsellö, this time armed with the collected revelations of the past weeks, which amounted to the beginnings of a plausible theory of conspiracy. And this time her complaint could not be dismissed as the rantings of a distressed mother. Within a few days, the administrative involvement of the state expanded to include not only the district magistrate but also the assistant royal prosecutor and the president of the Nyíregyháza court. The last, Ferenc Korniss, ordered a full-scale investigation into the disappearance of Eszter Solymosi. The affair had begun.

The reconstruction of the Tiszaeszlár accusation calls to mind Walter Zenner's appeal for due consideration of the role of autonomous cultural factors and "outside interventions" in anti-middleman agitation. In my view, however, the picture is a good deal more complex than one of an emotionally neutral social setting that is "polluted" or "corrupted" by forces from the outside. For six weeks, no one in Budapest, Vienna, or Berlin knew about the events that had taken place in Tiszaeszlár. Like politics, perhaps, all ritual murder accusations are local. To the extent that "extraneous" ideologies or beliefs were involved, they stemmed predominantly from religious teachings and folk wisdom and, by this time, formed an inextricable part of local tradition.[47] Up to the arrival in Tiszaeszlár of the investigating magistrate, József Bary, evidence of manipulation or interference by politicians, national organizations, or provocateurs is extremely hard to come by.

With his involvement, however, the mystery surrounding the fate of Eszter Solymosi began to be taken up by the public imagination at large. Newspapers—Hungarian at first but eventually foreign—started to cover the story; clergymen spoke about it from the pulpit; individuals composed letters to editors and public officials; and Géza Ónody, an impoverished nobleman and Tiszaeszlár's representative to the Hungarian Diet, stood on the floor of the house to denounce this "Jewish crime."[48]

Ónody himself seems not to have taken part in the local elaboration of "knowledge" of ritual murder before some time in May. His main role thereafter consisted of occasionally escorting the investigating team around the village and of selectively feeding reports of what were supposed to have been the secret investigative proceedings of the Nyíregyháza court to the main Hungarian anti-Semitic newspaper, *Függetlenség,* which began to report in earnest on the affair on May 24.[49] *Függetlenség,* as the first major paper to disseminate "news" of the criminal investigation, was able to dictate for a period of time the type of knowledge that the Hungarian public had of the affair.

Ónody thus mediated in an important way among fragmented strands of knowledge, opinion, and expertise. His public status was simultaneously complex and authoritative: nobleman, local resident, parliamentary deputy, self-proclaimed student of Jewish customs, advisor to Istóczy—a leader of the Hungarian anti-Semitic party—and occasional confidant of the investigating team headed by Bary.[50] He could observe and appropriate local cultural negotiations over the meaning of Eszter Solymosi's disappearance, translate these meanings into the idiom of party politics, and carry the symbols (even in a literal sense) of Jewish ritual murder to the international domain of contemporary political discourse. As one of the few private individuals who was privy to details of the pretrial criminal investigation, he was also in a unique position to dictate much of the form and content of public knowledge of the affair. His dispatches to *Függetlenség*—rewritten by the editor, Verhovay—laid down the essential terms of the antiliberal position in the renewed debate about ritual murder and grounded this knowledge in the authority of the police and the courts.

By the summer and fall of 1882, the main contours of a public discussion were well in place, as were the vehicles for its dissemination. The Hungarian publicist Georg von Marczianyi—Ónody's principal translator into German—issued the first mass-circulation brochure on Tiszaeszlár, published in Berlin and composed of translated selections from the *Függetlenség* exposés.[51] The first International Congress of Antisemites, meeting in Dresden, made room in its deliberations for the renewed ritual murder charge alongside more conventional complaints about Jewish influence in economic and political life and about the hatred of Jews in general for Christians. Ónody himself helped introduce not only the iconographic elements of the modern libel but also its narrative interpretation, with the publication of his booklet *Tißa-Eßlár in der Vergangenheit und Gegenwart.*

Eventually, even this contribution to social knowledge was overshadowed by a whole panoply of interventions and appropriations, ranging from academic treatises to public theater. August Rohling, professor of Old Testament studies in the Catholic Theological Faculty of the German University in Prague, placed himself in the middle of a public debate that was raging in Vienna over the meaning of the Talmud for Jewish-Christian relations. By May 1883, he was offering his services to the court in Nyíregyháza as an expert witness on Judaism as well as on Talmudic prescriptions for ritual murder.[52] Rohling's hundred-page pamphlet *Meine Antworten an die Rabbiner, oder: Fünf Briefe über den Talmudismus und das Blut-Ritual der Juden* sold in the tens of thousands throughout Bohemia in the spring of 1883, both in German and in Czech translation.[53] A few weeks after the close of the criminal trial, in August 1883, the Chomutov (Komotau) summer theater produced a five-act play about the affair, translated from the Hungarian and advertised in posters around the city as a "great sensation from the most recent past." The same advertisements referred to the Tiszaeszlár trial as "the most sensational event . . . which has captivated and claimed the attention of the entire world."[54]

During the nine years that intervened between the disappearance of Eszter Solymosi in 1882 and the death of five-year-old Johann Hegmann in Xanten in 1891, a complex, multidimensional, yet cohesive public discussion of Jewish ritual murder injected itself into numerous spheres of Central European cultural life.[55] Beginning with the Xanten case, it becomes extremely difficult to disentangle locally constructed social knowledge of Jewish criminality and ritual murder from outside interventions or the wider context of public discourse. Local knowledge in a "pure" sense, one is tempted to conclude, does not really exist. When the *Jewish Chronicle* of London, for example, mentioned the Xanten accusation for the first time, it did so in the context of a report on the general diffusion of ritual murder claims by German anti-Semitic newspapers:

> The anti-Semitic Press in Berlin, finding that all other weapons are unsuccessful, are trying to incite the German Christians against the Jews by a dose of "blood accusation." The *Kreuz-Zeitung* publishes a telegram from Constantinople reporting the murder at Mustapha Pacha of a girl eight years old by Jews, and also of a Christian butcher who had discovered the first crime. The *Volk* improves on the method of its contemporary by reporting the perpetration of a murder by Jews for ritual purposes in Germany. The scene of the alleged tragedy is at Xanten, a town in Rhenish Prussia, and the victim is said to be a boy four [*sic*] years old.[56]

It bears repeating that neither the *Kreuz-Zeitung* nor the *Volk* "invented" its story. Each picked up the report and sought to exploit it, endowing it with a particular set of meanings, a coherent interpretation of the newspaper's own making. At the same time, the newspapers—together with politicians and a handful of magistrates and prosecutors—were responsible for creating an environment of public debate that was becoming increasingly receptive to charges of gross criminality on the part of Jews. For this reason, I concur with Hillel Levine's suggestion that the first task of the historian of anti-Semitism ought to be to uncover the "structures of plausibility" that underlie particular clusters of attitudes.[57] With regard to the *modern* discourse of Jewish ritual murder, the question that ultimately is most relevant is not why it *emerged* but why it *worked* (at least until World War I). How is it that consensus about the meaning of things was achieved? What rendered images of Jewish ritual murder "plausible" among key groups at the turn of the century?

The answer to this last question, it seems to me, lies not only in the lasting power of myth and premodern stereotypes but also, and more importantly, in the ability of the modern knowledge of Jewish criminality to speak in the idiom of contemporary cultural authority. Modern ritual murder discourse rested on the expertise of medical science, criminology, and social psychology while it both drew on and added to the storehouse of imagery and rhetoric of the new political anti-Semitism. In the events of 1882 to 1914, priests, theologians, and confessors took a back seat to physicians, forensic specialists, and criminologists. Explanations of the Jewish danger referred not so much to the errors of Judaism as to the depravity of Jews, and the evidence was to be found less in the Talmud or in the miracles performed by martyred children than in autopsies and the latest theories about the impact of the environment on the criminal mind. The discourse worked for as long as it did because it was modern, not despite the fact that it was medieval. Nevertheless, it had little enough to do with "real" Jews. And in the light of everything that it entailed, its connection to premodern economic exchange seems almost to have been trivial.

NOTES

1. Stefan Lehr, *Antisemitismus—religiöse Motive im sozialen Vorurteil: Aus der Frühgeschichte des Antisemitismus in Deutschland 1870–1914* (Munich: Chr. Kaiser Verlag, 1974), Anhang A, pp. 239–43. Lehr essentially reproduces the list found in Georg Kalckert, *Die Haltung des deutschen Katholizismus zum Judentum im 19. Jahrhundert* (n.p., n.d.), which, in turn, was based on Friedrich Frank's *Der Ritualmord vor den Gerichtshöfen der Wahrheit und Gerechtigkeit* (Regensburg, 1901). The cases are limited for the most part to Germany, Austria-Hungary, and the Balkan countries; the Russian and Ottoman empires receive some attention, but Western Europe is not represented.

2. Although monographs and article-length studies have been published for individual cases, there is to date no comprehensive study of the modern ritual murder trial in Europe. On the ritual murder accusation generally, see Daniil Khvol'son, *Die Blutanklage und sonstige mittelalterliche Beschuldigungen der Juden: Eine historische Untersuchung nach den Quellen* (Frankfurt am Main, 1901), and Hermann L. Strack, *Das Blut im Glauben und Aberglauben der Menschheit mit besonderer Berücksichtigung der "Volksmedizin" und des "jüdischen Blutritus"* (Munich, 1900, 8th ed.) (published in translation as *The Jew and Human Sacrifice*, London: Cope and Fenwick, 1909). For the accusation in its medieval context, see Gavin Langmuir, *Toward a Definition of Antisemitism* (Berkeley: University of California Press, 1990): chapter 9, "Thomas of Monmouth: Detector of Ritual Murder," pp. 209–36; chapter 10, "The Knight's Tale of Young Hugh of Lincoln," pp. 237–62; chapter 11, "Ritual Cannibalism," pp. 263–81; and chapter 12, "Historiographic Crucifixion," pp. 282–98.

3. Howard Paul Becker, *Man in Reciprocity* (New York: Praeger, 1956), pp. 225–37. A useful survey of middleman minority theories can be found in Walter P. Zenner, *Minorities in the Middle: A Cross-Cultural Analysis* (Albany: State University of New York Press, 1991), pp. 1–26.

4. Irwin D. Rinder, "Strangers in the Land: Social Relations in the Status Gap," *Social Problems* 6 (1958–59), pp. 253–60.

5. A good example of this distinction can be found in the following paragraphs from Rinder, "Strangers in the Land," pp. 254–55:

> To maintain distance, members of the dominant group must never engage in any demeaning activity which could reduce their prestige, their "face," their aura of superiority. Since trade relations require that buyer and seller play complementary and interdependent roles, members of the upper strata must consider trade beneath their dignity. *Thus the status gap produces an economic gap which persists until filled by a third party* [emphasis in the original]. Those recruited as third parties serve as economic liaison between those who might service the population massed in the lower strata but choose not to, and the lower strata members who cannot perform these services for themselves.
>
> The people entering the gap become the wholesale and retail merchants, the industrial entrepreneurs, the pioneers in whatever happen to be the unstaked frontiers of venture capital. And they become the bankers, ranging up and down the spectrums of size, prestige, and legitimacy from usurers, rice-crop forestallers and engrossers, money lenders and money changers, pawnbrokers, mortgage bankers, and masters of commercial and investment banking houses that have, in certain historical instances, become the unofficial state treasuries. As outsiders, the people entering the gap may engage in those economic activities which have been traditionally proscribed for the in-group; and as outsiders, they may enter those activities looked upon with disdain by the upper strata, or those beyond the ken of the lower.

6. Rinder, "Strangers in the Land," p. 257.

7. Rinder, "Strangers in the Land," pp. 257–58. To the fundamental "visibility" of entrepreneurial minorities, Rinder adds their vulnerability to the "whims and caprices of the superior status groups" and their general accessibility as factors that explain their being cast in the role of scapegoat.

8. Several formulations can be found in Edna Bonacich, "A Theory of Middleman Minorities," *American Sociological Review* 38 (1973), pp. 583–94; Bonacich, "A Theory of Ethnic Antagonism: The Split-Labor Market," *American Sociological Review* 37 (1972), pp. 547–59; and Jonathan H. Turner and Edna Bonacich, "Toward a Composite Theory of Middleman Minorities," *Ethnicity* 7 (1980), pp. 144–58.

9. Bonacich, "A Theory of Middleman Minorities," pp. 586–92.

10. Bonancich, "A Theory of Middleman Minorities," pp. 585–86.

11. Jack Kugelmass, *Native Aliens: The Jews of Poland as a Middleman Minorty* (Ph.D. dissertation, New School for Social Research, 1980), pp. 39–40.

12. Bonacich and Turner, "Toward a Composite Theory," pp. 151–52.

13. Bonacich's denial of the primacy of internal cultural concerns is made in "A Theory of Middleman Minorities," p. 589. The case for the expulsion of the Jews of Spain hinged ultimately on the perceived crisis involving the country's large population of new Christians, or *conversos,* which numbered between 100,000 and 200,000.

The argument that ultimately held sway in the councils of state was that so long as a distinctive Jewish community remained in Spain, the *conversos* would not assimilate into society at large. Although a ritual murder accusation stood at the center of these debates as well, economic grievances against Jews were not expressed. And they would not have made much sense in this context, since the Jewish *conversos* to Christianity maintained a generally Jewish economic profile without the accompanying discriminatory restrictions. In other words, "ethnic" Castillians and Aragonese gained nothing economically from either the expulsion of the Jews or their forced conversion. See Haim Beinart, *Conversos on Trial: The Inquisition in Ciudad Real* (Jerusalem: Magnes Press, Hebrew University, 1981); Henry Kamen, "The Mediterranean and the Expulsion of the Jews in 1492," *Past and Present* 119 (May 1988), pp. 30–55; Stephen Haliczer, "The Castilian Urban Patriciate and the Jewish Expulsions of 1480–92," *American Historical Review* 78 (1973), pp. 35–62; and Maurice Kriegel, "La Prise d'une décision: l'expulsion des juifs d'Espagne en 1492," *Revue Historique* 260 (1978), pp. 49–90.

14. See Yosef Hayim Yerushalmi, "Assimilation and Racial Anti-Semitism: The Iberian and the German Models," *The Leo Baeck Memorial Lecture* 26 (New York: Leo Baeck Institute, 1982).

15. On German racial legislation, see Michael Burleigh and Wolfgang Wippermann, *The Racial State: Germany, 1933–1945* (Cambridge: Cambridge University Press, 1991), pp. 44–73. On the acculturation of German Jews, see David Sorkin, *The Transformation of German Jewry, 1780–1840* (New York: Oxford University Press, 1987), and George L. Mosse, *German Jews beyond Judaism* (Bloomington: Indiana University Press, 1985).

16. See Ernest Gellner, *Nations and Nationalism* (Ithaca, New York: Cornell University Press, 1983), pp. 102–103.

17. Donald L. Horowitz, *Ethnic Groups in Conflict* (Berkeley: University of California Press, 1985), pp. 107–13.

18. Horowitz, *Ethnic Groups in Conflict*, pp. 111–12.

19. Horowitz, *Ethnic Groups in Conflict*, pp. 120–21.

20. Gellner, *Nations and Nationalism*, pp. 103–104.

21. *Sefer Biala Podlaska* (Tel Aviv, 1961), p. 151; reprinted in English translation in Kugelmass, *Native Aliens*, p. 38.

22. Zenner, *Minorities in the Middle*, pp. 46–60.

23. Hillel Levine, *Economic Origins of Antisemitism: Poland and Its Jews in the Early Modern Period* (New Haven, Connecticut: Yale University Press, 1991).

24. Ultimately, in Levine's view, it was the members of the *szlachta* who refused to adopt the economic transformations of the West, who constructed a defensive ideology of Polish uniqueness and "disorder" to justify a weak state and a disintegrating

economy, and who put forth unflattering images of Jewish exploitation and unpro-
ductiveness to "reconcile rather than resolve" Poland's contradictions. See Levine,
Economic Origins, p. 17. On the "rhetoric of reform," in the eighteenth century, see
pp. 152–90.

25. Levine, *Economic Origins*, pp. 137–38. His assessment appears to coincide with
those of M. Balaban, *Letoldot ha-tenuah ha-frankit* [On the history of the Frankist
movement], 2 vols. (Tel Aviv: Dvir, 1934–35), and Bernard Weinryb, *The Jews of
Poland: A Social and Economic History* (Philadelphia: Jewish Publication Society,
1973), and is based on tables published in the Weinryb study (pp. 152–53). Judging
from the data presented by Weinryb, I would take issue with the conclusion that
incidents of "blood libel" were on the rise in the eighteenth century. He lists eleven
ritual murder charges for the second half of the sixteenth century, twenty-three for
the seventeenth century, and twenty-one for the eighteenth century. To me, the
evidence suggests a relatively unchanging rate of accusation over the two and a half
centuries in question. The flatness of the curve is important when one attempts to
relate the frequency of the ritual murder accusation to major economic transitions.

26. Levine's analysis of the ritual murder accusation in eighteenth-century Poland
is to be found in his *Economic Origins*, pp. 183–91.

27. Levine, *Economic Origins*, p. 187.

28. Levine, *Economic Origins*, p. 187.

29. Quoted in Levine, *Economic Origins*, p. 183.

30. On the construction of traditional, medieval accounts of Jewish ritual murder,
see Gavin Langmuir, "Thomas of Monmouth: Detector of Ritual Murder," and "The
Knight's Tale of Young Hugh of Lincoln," in his *Toward a Definition of Antisemitism*,
pp. 209–62.

31. Levine, *Economic Origins*, p. 188.

32. We are informed, interestingly, that Soltyk was later imprisoned and exiled by
the Russian government "for his Catholic zeal and his incitement of rebellion against
the granting of religious rights for Russian Orthodox peasants." See Levine, *Economic
Origins*, p. 183.

33. The Tiszaeszlár investigation into the disappearance and presumed murder of
Eszter Solymosi lasted for fourteen months, from April 1882 to June 1883, and was
followed by a criminal trial against fifteen Jewish defendants held in the nearby town
of Nyíregyháza. During his summation, the state prosecutor, Ede Szeyffert, took the
unusual step of recommending that the defendants be acquitted of the charge of
ritual murder. On August 3, 1883, the three-judge panel handed down a verdict of not
guilty.

General accounts of the Tiszaeszlár affair can be found in the following works:
Andrew Handler, *Blood Libel at Tiszaeszlár* (Boulder, Colorado: East European Mono-

graphs, 1980); Nathaniel Katzburg, *Antishemiyut be-hungariya 1867–1914* [Antisemitism in Hungary 1867–1914] (Tel Aviv: Dvir, 1969), pp. 106–55; and Paul Nathan, *Der Prozess von Tisza-Eszlár: Ein Antisemitisches Culturbild* (Berlin: F. Fontane, 1892).

34. William O. McCagg, *Jewish Nobles and Geniuses in Modern Hungary* (Boulder, Colorado: East European Monographs, 1972), p. 223. Similarly, in his *A History of Habsburg Jews, 1670–1918* (Bloomington: Indiana University Press, 1989), McCagg describes the "alliance between the Magyar-speaking nobility and the reformer Jews" that was cemented in the 1860s (p. 135).

35. Andrew C. Janos, *The Politics of Backwardness in Hungary, 1825–1945* (Princeton, New Jersey: Princeton University Press, 1982), pp. 112–18.

36. C. A. Macartney, *Hungary* (London: Ernest Benn, 1934), pp. 216–17.

37. See, for example, Andrew Handler, *Dori: The Life and Times of Theodor Herzl in Budapest (1860–1878)* (University, Alabama: University of Alabama Press, 1983), pp. 109–10. See also, Katzburg, *Antishemiyut,* pp. 53–55; Jacob Katz, *From Prejudice to Destruction: Antisemitism, 1700–1933* (Cambridge, Massachusetts: Harvard University Press, 1980), pp. 237–42.

38. As Handler acknowledges, Istóczy's speech was frequently interrupted by catcalls and sarcastic remarks. Some questioned his sanity, and the prime minister, Wenckheim, rejected the notion of a "Jewish question" out of hand (Handler, *Dori,* p. 110).

39. My use of the term "social knowledge" stems from the view that what an individual or group understands and remembers about an event (particularly one that has been designated a "mystery") results from knowledge that is produced and transmitted in social settings. Such "knowledge" differs from both empirical observation and received tradition, though the two can serve as ingredients in its production. At the same time, the very concept of "social knowledge" calls into question the possibility of capturing either observed fact or received tradition that is unmediated by interpretation or lines of social communication.

I am indebted to recent work in both the sociology of knowledge and cultural anthropology. I part company, however, with Peter Berger and Thomas Luckmann, *The Social Construction of Reality* (New York, 1966), to the extent that they subordinate socially constructed knowledge to the *mechanisms* and institutional contexts of its distribution. Rather, my thinking on this subject is more closely attuned to that of Clifford Geertz, who writes in "The Way We Think Now: Ethnography of Modern Thought" (in his *Local Knowledge: Further Essays in Interpretive Anthropology* [New York: Basic Books, 1983], p. 153), that the true task of the sociology of knowledge "is a matter of conceiving of cognition, emotion, motivation, perception, imagination, memory . . . whatever, as themselves, and directly, social affairs." That is, the task is "to analyze symbol use as social action." To do so "is to attempt to navigate the plural/unific, product/process paradox by regarding the community as the shop in which thoughts are constructed and deconstructed, and history as the terrain they seize and surrender, and to attend therefore to such muscular matters as the representation of authority, the marking of boundaries, the rhetoric of persuasion, the expression of commitment, and the registering of dissent."

40. Handler employs both terms in describing Jewish-Gentile relations (*Blood Libel*, p. 36). It is he who provides the quotation from Eötvös. Katzburg combines the two sentiments when he describes relations as "friendly, even if [they] contained a small measure of superiority" (*Antishemiyut*, p. 107).

41. Nathan, *Der Prozess*, pp. 93–97 and passim.

42. Katzburg, *Antishemiyut*, p. 107; Handler, *Blood Libel*, pp. 23–24.

43. Nathan quotes at length from German translations of both the investigation and trial protocols (see Nathan, *Der Prozess*, pp. 98–312). See also the (incomplete?) German translation of the trial proceedings: *Der Blut-Prozeß von Tisza Eszlár in Ungarn. Vorgeschichte der Anklage und vollständiger Bericht über die Prozeß-Verhandlungen vor dem Gericht in Nyiregyháza. Nach dem amtlichen, stenographischen Protocollen aus dem Ungarischen übertragen* (New York: Schnitzer Bros., 1883). Both the district magistrate, Bary, who believed in the guilt of the accused, and the defense attorney, Eötvös, agreed that the original impulse to accuse the Jews of a violent crime came from Ezster's mother and aunt. See Handler's frequent references to the memoirs of Károly Eötvös, *A Nagy Per, mely ezer éve folyik s még sincs vége* [The great trial that has been going on for a thousand years], 3 vols. (Budapest: Révai Testvérek, 1904), and József Bary, *A Tiszaeszlári Bünper. Bary József Viszgálóbíró Emlékiratai* [The criminal case of Tiszaeszlár: The memoirs of investigating magistrate József Bary] (Budapest: Magyar Élet Kiadása, 1941, 2d ed.). On this point, the references are to Eötvös, vol. 1, pp. 82–88, and Bary, pp. 39–50.

44. Handler, *Blood Libel*, p. 43.

45. Handler, *Blood Libel*, pp. 43–44.

46. Handler, *Blood Libel*, pp. 44–45, based on Eötvös, *A Nagy Per*, vol. 1, pp. 89–96, and Bary, *A Tiszaeszlári Bünper* pp. 51–60.

47. In a tantalizing allusion to the types of collective memories that both Jews and non-Jews carried—but did not really share—Mária Solymosi (the girl's mother) intimated on at least one occasion that a chance encounter with the main defendant, József Scharf, led her to suspect that he was hiding information about her daughter's whereabouts. The incident in question involved a clumsy effort on the part of Scharf to offer consolation to the mother. Drawing on his own childhood memory, he is said to have offered advice approximating the following: "Don't worry, neighbor. Your daughter will be found. She probably just wandered off somewhere. Something like this happened also in Hajdunánás. There, too, a child got lost and the people already started saying that it was the Jew who got hold of her. But then the child came home. She'd been sleeping among the tussocks" (Eötvös, *A Nagy Per*, vol. 1, p.

82, quoted in Handler, *Blood Libel*). It is possible that Scharf's recollection of unjusti-
fied collective accusation triggered Mária Solymosi's own memories of esoteric
knowledge about Jews. See Handler in this regard: "Desperately searching for answers and having exhausted logical alternatives, Mrs. Solymosi could no longer resist
the lure of the past. Scharf's consoling words unlocked her tormented mind, releas-
ing age-old rumors, accusations, hatreds, suspicions, and fears" (*Blood Libel*, p. 42).

48. For this section I follow the description in Handler, *Blood Libel*, pp. 52, 55–56;
Katzburg, *Antishemiyut*, pp. 112–16; and Nathan, *Der Prozess*, pp. 7–25. Ónody delivered his speech during a parliamentary debate on an unrelated matter on May 23,
1882. Nathan quotes from the parliamentary record on p. 8.

49. There was an earlier, but isolated, journalistic report of the Tiszaeszlár
"crime." József Adamovics, the Catholic priest of the village, published an article in
the clerical paper *Magyar Állam* on May 20 under the headline "The Mysterious
Disappearance of a Young Girl," in which he gave voice to Mária Solymosi's suspicions concerning the Jews and complained of the slow pace of the official investigation. But this single, barely read piece had minimal impact on the general, social
knowledge of the event, which is more appropriately connected to the reportage in
Függetlenség and the debates in the Hungarian Diet. See Katzburg, *Antishemiyut*, p.
112.

50. On Ónody's purported expertise in Jewish matters, see Handler, *Blood Libel*,
pp. 31, 212–13, and Nathan, *Der Prozess*, pp. 26–27. Ónody's 1883 portrait of the
Tiszaeszlár case (the pamphlet *Tißa-Eßlár in der Vergangenheit und Gegenwart*) bore
the subtitles "Über die Juden im Allgemeinen.—Jüdische Glaubensmysterien.—
Rituelle Mordthaten und Blutopfer.—Der Tisza-Eszlárer Fall."

51. *Esther Solymosi oder Der jüdisch-rituelle Jungfrauenmord in Tißa-Eßlar. Autori-
sirte deutsche Uebersetzung aus dem Ungarischen. Nebst einer Abbildung der Synagogue
in T.-E.* (Berlin: M. Schulz, n.d. [apparently summer or fall 1882]).

52. On Rohling's role in the Talmud debate in Vienna, his self-promotion as an
expert on Jewish behavior, and his desire to intervene in the Tiszaeszlár affair, see
I. A. Hellwing, *Der konfessionelle Antisemitismus im 19. Jahrhundert in Österreich*
(Vienna: Herder, 1972), pp. 71–183; and Joseph S. Bloch, *Erinnerungen aus meinem
Leben*, vol. 1 (Vienna: R. Löwit, 1922 [translated as *My Reminiscences* (Vienna, 1923)];
and *Acten und Gutachten in dem Prozesse Rohling contra Bloch* (Vienna, 1890).

53. The Praesidium of the Bohemian governor's office received numerous reports
of the pamphlet's circulation, together with worried predictions of popular violence
such as had already occurred in the Hungarian city of Pozsony (Bratislava). The
governor's office ordered the work confiscated toward the end of May 1883 (Státní
Ústřední Archiv, Prague, PM 1881–1890 [8/1/9/1]).

54. Státní Ústřední Archiv, PM 1881–1890 (8/1/9/1), pp. 7194.

55. In the Xanten case, a Jewish butcher and stonecutter, Adolf Buschhof, was put

on trial for the ritual murder of Johann Hegmann, a five-year-old boy who had been found brutally murdered in the barn of the innkeeper and town councilor, Wilhelm Küpper. Buschhof was acquitted. For general accounts of the investigation and trial, see Paul Nathan, *Xanten-Cleve: Betrachtungen zum Prozess Buschhof* (Berlin, 1892), and Julius H. Schoeps, "Ritualmordbeschuldigung und Blutaberglaube: Die Affäre Buschhoff im niederrheinischen Xanten," in *Köln und das Rheinische Judentum: Festschrift Germania Judaica 1959–1984* (Cologne: J. P. Bachem, 1984), pp. 286–99.

56. *Jewish Chronicle,* July 24, 1891, p. 15.

57. Levine, *Economic Origins,* p. 17.

PART FOUR

Chinese Businesses in Contemporary Southeast Asia

Are There Parallels?

9 / A Specific Idiom of Chinese
Capitalism in Southeast Asia

Sino-Malaysian Capital Accumulation
in the Face of State Hostility

K. S. JOMO

In recent years, much has been written about the economic boom in East Asia. Attention was focused first on Japan and the newly industrializing countries (NICs) of South Korea, Taiwan, Hong Kong, and Singapore. By the early 1980s, culturalist explanations were touting Confucianism as the common element responsible for these economic miracles.[1] This is particularly ironic because as recently as the 1970s, Western culturalists, among others, were blaming Confucianism for the economic backwardness of the Chinese. In any case, many Chinese dismiss the term Confucianism as a Western reification of their mixed cultural heritage, which includes Daoism, Buddhism, and various other influences. And while acknowledging the profound impact of Chinese culture on their own, few Japanese or Koreans have ever reduced this culture to Confucianism. Nevertheless, because of the hegemonic influence of Western academia, a generation of culturalists has been rediscovering Confucianist influences throughout East Asia, often to the amusement of East Asians themselves.

With the rapid growth of most economies in the Association of South East Asian Nations (ASEAN) since the 1970s, including Vietnam since the late 1980s, there has been much talk about a second generation of Southeast Asian NICs and fresh speculation about the factors responsible for the East Asian economic miracles. With the dominant role of ethnic Chinese business minorities in most Southeast Asian economies and the sustained boom in China since the 1980s, there has been increasing speculation about an emerging Chinese economic zone and renewed emphasis on Confucianist explanations, even though most first-generation immigrant Chinese businesspeople in Southeast Asia have modest (and hence unschooled and "uncultured") social backgrounds.[2]

The increasingly blatant encouragement of "overseas Chinese" investments by China's authorities has resulted in increased investments from

Southeast Asian Chinese. This has led to increased official and renewed popular resentment—encouraged by ethnopopulist politicians—against Chinese economic dominance in Southeast Asia. Consequently, greater public attention has been focused on the apparently ethnically exclusive Chinese business networks that are believed to be responsible for Chinese business success in Southeast Asia and elsewhere.[3]

In this essay I argue that a distinct idiom of Sino-Malaysian capitalism has developed in Malaysia in response to perceived anti-Chinese hostility from the colonial and, especially after it promulgated the New Economic Policy (NEP) in 1971, the postcolonial state. The NEP was intended, among other things, to achieve economic parity between the politically dominant Malays and the commercially ubiquitous Chinese by "restructuring society to eliminate the identification of race with economic function." I also consider whether and to what extent the Malaysian experience may be generalizable to the rest of Southeast Asia.

COLONIALISM AND ETHNICITY

The demographic history of colonial Malaya is reasonably well known. Except for the irrigated rice plains of Kedah and Kelantan and the colony of Malacca, most of the peninsula was relatively sparsely populated before the advent of British colonialism in the last quarter of the eighteenth century. Although the population was composed primarily of Muslim Malays, there were also small colonies of other ethnic groups, including Chinese and Indians, that dated back at least to the fifteenth century, when the Malacca sultanate linked China to India and lands beyond.[4]

British imperialism's initial interest was to break Dutch and other mercantilist control of trade through the Straits of Malacca and in the Malay archipelago. This was done by establishing "free" ports in what became known as the Straits Settlements of Penang (1786), Singapore (1819), and Malacca (in the last case, twice: first during the French occupation of Holland during the Napoleonic wars, and again as part of the post-Napoleonic division of "Malay" Southeast Asia into English and Dutch "spheres of influence"). Commercial expansion through free trade attracted merchants from near and far, including southern Chinese—mainly Hokkiens from Fujian, as was the case in much of archipelagic Southeast Asia. Chinese commerce, as well as the settlement of Chinese and Malay agricultural workers, followed British imperialism and in some cases, such as early-nineteenth-century Kedah and Johore, even extended beyond the sphere of direct colonial control.

With a growing demand for tin, both the decline of tin mining in Cornwall and Dutch control of tin in Bangka and Billiton in the Dutch East Indies made the tin deposits on the west coast of central Malaya irresistible to the British. Fighting between rival Malay chiefs and their Chinese miners provided a sufficient pretext for British intervention in 1874 to secure control of the tin-rich states of Perak, Selangor, Negri Sembilan, and Pahang—which later became the Federated Malay States—although the illusion of Malay authority was maintained. Colonial law and order created conditions favoring further agricultural settlement by Chinese, as well as by Muslim "Malays" from the northern states under Siamese suzerainty and from the neighboring Dutch East Indies. British capital, however, failed to wrest control of tin mining from Chinese miners, whose position was strengthened by the use of labor-intensive mining techniques. Only with the introduction of capital-intensive dredging in the early twentieth century did Britain's superior access to mining land become decisive for securing its control of the industry.

Shifting Anglo-Siamese relations at the beginning of the twentieth century finally defined British Malaya's northern borders as Kedah, Perlis, Kelantan, and Trengganu. They came under indirect British rule and formed the Unfederated Malay States, along with Johore, Singapore's hinterland after Raffles's "discovery" of the island in 1819 and its "secession" from the Riau sultanate in 1885.

In the meantime, the rubber boom was beginning as the latex-producing plant, which had been smuggled out of Brazil, took root on the peninsula, especially in the foothills of the west coast. In support of British capital, the colonial government broke Chinese employers' hold over Chinese labor by restricting indenture and banning secret societies and the "truck" employee-consumer credit system. The British sought to secure their own pool of labor from south India, much as their predecessors had done in colonial Ceylon. Although colonial advantage secured most of the best land (in terms of access, fertility, and infrastructure), British capital continued to have difficulties controlling workers and wages. With high attrition rates among their predominantly Indian laborers, British planters often had little choice but to purchase land cleared and planted by Malay and occasionally Chinese agricultural pioneers.

It was not until the early 1930s that several related developments converged to establish the notion of a "nation of intent" while still under colonial rule.[5] The Great Crash of 1929 reverberated throughout the colonial economy. Nationalist movements in China, Indonesia, and India led ethnic communities to support "patriotic" anticolonial causes. Indian nationalists protested the use of their country as a labor sponge that supplied workers when needed and then, as happened during the depression, was obliged to take them back when demand slackened. Consequently, male labor emigration from India was restricted, while female emigration was allowed in order to encourage permanent settlement in colonial Malaya.

Meanwhile, nascent radical nationalists discovered their own nation in the British colony. Part of the Nanyang Communist Party, founded in 1928, became the Communist Party of Malaya in 1930 after the failed communist uprising in the Dutch East Indies during the late 1920s sent political refugees into British Malaya. As their upper-class counterparts received an English "public school" education at the Malay College, Kuala Kangsar (MCKK), in preparation for service at the intermediate levels of the colonial administration, students of peasant origin, training at the Sultan Idris Training College (SITC) in Tanjung Malim to teach "their own kind," discovered a common Malayness that transcended local and state identities. Thus, radical Malay nationalism was born as SITC graduates formed the Young Malay Union (Kesatuan Melayu Muda) in the early 1930s.[6]

Debates among the British over the desired nature of colonial rule, taken together with the 1931 census finding that there was a slight non-Malay majority in Malaya (including Singapore), resulted in immigration restrictions and a "freezing" of the colony's demographic profile. This reduced mobility must surely have contributed to a greater sense of permanence in conceiving the "nation." Occupational segregation, however, conspired with residential, cultural, religious, educational, and language differences to maintain strong ethnic identities that inevitably limited any deep sense of national identity. Ethnic identities were strengthened and shaped by colonial policies toward the various communities, and the identities were in turn reinforced by ethnic mobilizations. Japanese occupation policies, while different in crucial ways, did not deemphasize or undermine ethnic distinctions. Instead, they strengthened them for their own purposes.

The foregoing summary reminds us of the weakness of the Malayan nationalist tradition. Though not unaware of this difficult heritage, the communist-led radical nationalists of the postwar era apparently did not know how to surmount such a formidable challenge. They often chose instead to coordinate ethnic mobilization initiatives covertly.

Increased repression of radical nationalist anticolonial agitation after 1948 initially involved only the police and military forces. The failure of these efforts, however, forced a more comprehensive "hearts and minds" approach to counterinsurgency beginning in the early 1950s. This approach involved a whole range of reforms, including the introduction of electoral politics and labor reforms. The Employees Provident Fund (EPF), moderate unions (notably for plantation workers), a trade union center (the MTUC), and a labor party were all established. There were also new rural development initiatives such as the Rural Industrial Development Authority (RIDA), the rubber replanting fund, the Federal Land Development Authority (Felda), the encouragement of agricultural cooperatives, and legal reform to limit rice land rents.

Perhaps most importantly, the notion of ethnic "special privileges" was officially accepted, ostensibly to rectify historical socioeconomic inequalities. During the late colonial era, however, the colonial authorities' commitment to improving the lot of Malays was limited. The main agency set up for this purpose, RIDA, was run by Onn Jaffar, who resigned as president of the United Malays National Organization (UMNO) when the party rejected his demand that it be transformed into a multiethnic party and thus qualify—in British eyes—to take over the reins of government after independence. While enabling Onn to retain some credibility among the Malays, RIDA's efforts were not enough to ensure that he could lead the country to independence. Instead, his successor as UMNO president, Tunku Abdul Rahman, forged an electoral coalition with the British- and Kuomintang-sponsored Malayan Chinese Association (MCA), which performed well in the first Kuala Lumpur municipal elections.[7] The coalition later formed the Alliance, which included the Malayan Indian Congress as well, and which won an overwhelming victory in the first general election in 1955 and thus qualified to lead the country to independence two years later.

ETHNICITY AND STATE INTERVENTION

The constitution of the new Federation of Malaya established special privileges for Malays, notably the provision of scholarships and government employment. It has always been unclear whether the privileges were accorded to rectify historical economic inequalities or because of the Malay claim to being indigenous. Considering that the constitution provided for a review of these provisions fifteen years after independence, the original intent was probably to overcome inequalities. Both the constitution and the electoral arrangements of the newly independent nation, however, ensured that the political influence of Malays would far exceed their slight demographic majority. This influence, in turn, has protected and broadened the scope of the original ethnic privileges. With the formation of Malaysia in September 1963, these privileges were nominally extended to all indigenous peoples, collectively known as Bumiputeras, or "sons of the soil."

Although Bumiputeras include the various indigenous peoples of Sabah and Sarawak, as well as the Orang Asli (aboriginal people) of the peninsula, whereas non-Bumiputeras include ethnic Indians and "others," who constitute almost one-tenth of the population, the primary divide is between Malays and Chinese.[8] It is said that the constitution and the postcolonial political settlement deliberately favored Malays because of their claims to indigenous status and the need to compensate them for Chinese economic dominance. Demographically based arguments have changed considerably over time. When the Malay majority was slimmer, bias was said to be necessary to provide them greater political clout. By the late 1980s, the growing Malay majority—which resulted from higher fertility and lower emigration rates—was being invoked to claim an equivalent share of the country's economic wealth.

Under Tunku Abdul Rahman, the first prime minister, Malay special privileges were most pronounced in the official disbursement of scholarships, business licenses, and government employment. In the first years after independence, Malays experienced considerable upward mobility in the civil service as they replaced the colonial expatriates who had previously been dominant. By the mid-1960s, the civil service was thoroughly Malay-dominated, which limited prospects for further upward mobility.

Malay civil servants and politicians turned their attention to the business sector, organizing the first Bumiputera Economic Congress in 1965. This, in turn, led the government to establish Bank Bumiputera and Perbadanan Nasional (Pernas, or National Corporation), as well as to reorganize and expand RIDA, which it renamed Majlis Amanah Rakyat (MARA), officially translated as the Council of Trust for Indigenous Peoples. All of this was done ostensibly on behalf of the Bumiputera community. These gains strengthened rather than weakened demands for Malay economic advancement and led to mounting criticism of the Tunku administration's efforts toward this end and its laissez-faire policies and fiscal conservatism.

The transition to independence and the nature of the postcolonial regime ensured that British interests were not threatened. Occasionally they were even consolidated. For example, Malayan-style import-substituting industrialization privileged firms with dominant market shares willing to assemble, process, or package their products in the newly independent country. British firms that were already well established benefited most from this. But Chinese business gained even more as the colonial constraints that had favored their British rivals were eroded. Grateful to the MCA for bankrolling the ruling coalition's expenses since the early 1950s, Tunku appointed MCA leaders to the key economic ministries, including finance and trade and industry.

While politically favoring Malays, Tunku's Alliance government generally avoided stifling the growing Chinese business activity in the postcolonial economy. Sometimes it even favored Chinese business interests—for example, by protecting Chinese manufacturing as part of its import-substitution policy and by awarding banking licenses.

This honeymoon for Chinese business came to an abrupt end in May 1969, when the majority of the population, especially the Chinese, voted against the Alliance in the country's third general election. It appears that the Chinese community at large had been alienated from the Alliance by growing unemployment, deteriorating conditions in the cities and new villages (set up in the early 1950s as part of the counterinsurgency campaign), and limited expansion of political, cultural, and especially educational rights. Although the MCA had never enjoyed much support in the Chinese community, this was its worst performance.

Yet a gerrymandered electoral system and a divided opposition allowed the Alliance to retain majorities in the federal parliament and all but two state legislative assemblies on the peninsula (it lost Chinese-dominated Penang to the opposition Gerakan). The ensuing race riots resulted in the creation of a de facto extraparliamentary government, the all-Malay National Operations Council (NOC), led by Tunku's longtime deputy, Tun Abdul Razak. By 1971, however, parliamentary rule had been restored, with Razak taking over as prime minister, and crucial reforms, including the New Economic Policy, were in place.[9]

Ostensibly designed to achieve national unity by reducing poverty and ethnic economic inequality, the NEP has increasingly been viewed as benefiting Malays through various types of state intervention, including expansion of the public sector.[10] Poverty reduction measures have been oriented primarily toward the predominantly Malay peasantry. They include heavy government spending on rural infrastructure, agricultural extension, subsidies, health services, schools, Muslim religious facilities, and special programs designed to strengthen UMNO's political patronage at the village level.

Access to educational opportunities, especially at the tertiary level, is rationed to favor Malays. There has been a similar bias in recruitment and promotions in government service, in public enterprises, and, increasingly, in the private sector as well, especially where government influence exists. This "middle-class" privilege has probably generated the most interethnic animosity, but the area of business privilege is almost equally contentious. Since the 1970s, most business regulation in Malaysia—whether pertaining to the allocation of licenses, permits, shares, and other business opportunities or to the award of tenders and contracts—has favored Malays.

But there have also been important variations in the NEP's implementation. In the early 1970s, government spending remained modest, constrained by the fiscally conservative finance minister and MCA head of the Tunku period. His replacement, along with increased petroleum revenues—coming with the discovery of oil off peninsular Malaysia's east coast, the 1973 price hikes by the Organization of Petroleum Exporting Countries (OPEC), and the 1974 Petroleum Development Act, which transferred jurisdiction over oil from the states to the federal government—led to significantly greater government spending from the mid-1970s onward. Heavy spending continued and was justified in the early 1980s by the need to ride out the global recession through expansionary deficit spending.[11]

The NEP remained the primary rationale for public spending and for expanding state intervention, especially during the 1970s. But of the NEP's two "prongs," interethnic redistribution, or "restructuring," has always been more important, both politically and in the public consciousness, than its other aim, alleviating poverty. "Restructuring" accounted for an increasing proportion of NEP expenditure at least until the mid-1980s, when public sector expansion, ostensibly on behalf of the Bumiputeras, began to decline.

By the 1990s, the NEP's objectives seemed largely to have been achieved, although it remains unclear to what extent this can be ascribed to the NEP's implementation, let alone to the cost-effectiveness of its redistributive measures. According to official measures, poverty in the peninsula fell from 49 percent in 1970 to 15 percent in 1993. Although sectoral employment patterns still reflect the ethnic division of labor from colonial times and the government's pro-Malay recruitment policies since then, occupational distribution has improved considerably for Malays. Arguably, though, this has come largely at the expense of ethnic Indians. Malays occupied 32 percent of the most lucrative professional positions in 1992, up from 6 percent in 1970. This trend is likely to continue.[12]

Attention remains focused, however, on the distribution of wealth, especially corporate stock. As table 9.1 shows, the Bumiputera share of corporate stock at par values jumped from 1.5 percent to 15.6 percent between 1969 and 1982, before climbing more modestly to 19.3 percent in 1990 and 20.6 percent in 1995. The Chinese share grew from 22.8 percent in 1969 to 33.4 percent in 1982, and then to 45.5 percent in 1990, before falling to 40.9 percent in 1995. Hence, at least until the early 1980s, the Malay share rose much faster in relative terms and even faster in absolute terms as domestic ownership replaced foreign control. Since then, Chinese ownership seems to have remained just slightly more than twice as important as Bumiputera ownership,

TABLE 9.1

Ownership of Shares of Limited Companies in Malaysia,
by Percentage of Total Par Value

Ownership group	1969	1982	1990	1995
Bumiputeras[1]	1.5	15.6	19.3	20.6
Chinese	22.8	33.4	45.5	40.9
Indians	0.9	0.9	1.0	1.5
Others	0.0	1.6	0.3	1.0
Local entities[2]	12.7	13.8	8.5	8.3
Foreign entities and residents[3]	62.1	34.7	25.4	27.7

SOURCES: Data are from the Second (1971), Mid-term Fourth (1984), and Seventh (1996) Malaysia Plans (Kuala Lumpur, Malaysia).

[1]Including trust agencies.

[2]State and federal governments and other locally controlled companies; nominee companies only from 1990.

[3]In 1969 these were mostly British, but they are now increasingly Japanese. The rise of foreign-controlled capital in the 1990s accounts for a recent decline of both the Bumiputera and the Chinese shares.

though of course the Bumiputera population is about one and a half times as great as that of the ethnic Chinese.

Because the market value of the shares is much greater than the par value, and because this is disproportionately more the case for Bumiputera-controlled companies, which benefit from political favoritism, the actual share of indigenous ownership relative to Chinese ownership is greater than table 9.1 indicates. Fong Chan Onn has claimed that the distribution of corporate wealth among Bumiputeras, Chinese, and foreign residents in 1988 was about even after adjusting for market values.[13]

After Prime Minister Mahathir's April 1982 electoral victory, he announced an austerity drive that began to alter the policy of aggressive favoritism through government intervention for the Bumiputeras. In order to pursue Mahathir's heavy-industrialization strategy, the government continued to guarantee loans taken by public enterprises from Japan. But Mahathir also began undertaking initiatives to strengthen the private sector over the long run. Aware that reversing pro-Malay policies could have adverse consequences, Mahathir proceeded slowly but surely with a program of economic liberalization until he announced in 1986 that the severe economic recession made it necessary to suspend the NEP. Then he made liberal amendments to legislation controlling, among other things, investment and foreign property ownership. The cessation of growth in the Bumiputera share of stock ownership and the spurt in foreign ownership since 1990 reflect these new policies.

In February 1991, Mahathir made a remarkable speech in which he claimed that by making growth, modernization, and industrialization the national priorities over the next three decades, Malaysia would be a developed country by 2020. While not explicitly abandoning the NEP redistributive agenda entirely, Mahathir has certainly deemphasized it. Indeed, because the NEP has been closely identified with the Outline Perspective Plan (OPP) for 1971–90, there is some uncertainty about whether it remained operative after 1990. Perhaps owing to the buoyant economic conditions that have prevailed since 1987, Mahathir has not lost much support from the Malay community.

Thus, whereas Chinese business interests in Malaysia complained bitterly about ethnic discrimination during the OPP years, they warmed considerably to Mahathir's economic reforms of the mid-1980s and especially those of 1991. While political and civil liberties have continued to erode under Mahathir, his economic liberalization has been accompanied by some cultural liberalization. This includes his discreet promotion of the English language and greater tolerance of non-Malay culture, especially when politically expedient. For example, he opened an international lion dance competition and loosened travel restrictions to China just before the 1990 elections.

There is some evidence that such policies encouraging capital repatriation and greater domestic investment have worked to keep more Sino-Malaysian capital at home. Not all domestic investment has been in industry, however, which many consider crucial for capital to be truly "progressive."

THE STATE AND INDUSTRIALIZATION

British colonial policy in Malaysia encouraged manufacturing activity only for the processing of raw materials such as rubber and tin. Processing requirements and transportation costs encouraged the location of the relevant facilities in colonial Malaya. Similarly, transportation costs, market location, and related considerations ensured that some industries which catered to local markets (e.g., beverage bottling) enjoyed "natural protection." Moreover, manufacturers, most of them Chinese, often produced goods and services (e.g., food processing, construction materials, engineering materials) for the domestic market that countered government preferences.[14]

Unlike many "intermediate" nationalist regimes in postcolonial Africa and Asia and populist alliances in Latin America during the 1930s, which promoted state-directed industrialization, the Tunku administration encouraged private enterprise and foreign investment. This policy created tariff barriers and low taxes, which enabled foreign, especially British, firms to preserve and expand their market shares. Unlike the policies of Northeast Asian regimes, however, which forced their import-substituting industries to produce for export (thus improving quality and efficiency), the Malaysian government's protectionism made infant industries dependent and incapable of competing internationally.

After an awkward transition during the second half of the 1960s, when investment, industrial relations, and labor laws were reformed and infrastructure improved, foreign-dominated, exported-oriented industrialization developed rapidly in the 1970s. In this regard, Malaysia followed the East Asian NICs that, lacking hinterlands (Singapore and Hong Kong) or significant natural resources (Taiwan and South Korea), had begun manufacturing for export in the 1960s. These new export-oriented industries, located in Malaysia to enhance their competitiveness, have generated profits in a very different manner from the import-substituting industries.

Partly in response to declining foreign investment in Malaysia, Mahathir initiated an ambitious, state-led, heavy-industrialization campaign with Japanese government assistance. This was tantamount to a second round of import substitution, although with a different array of industrial products. The heavy-industrialization program was aborted in the mid-1980s when Malaysia's fiscal and debt crises reached alarming proportions. Primary commodity prices had fallen, the yen had appreciated sharply against the Malaysian ringgit, and the pioneer heavy industries had encountered slack domestic demand (cement, cars), severe international competition (cement dumping), and design failure (steel).

The deep crisis of the mid-1980s accelerated the economic liberalization tentatively begun by Mahathir; in 1986, the government quietly "suspended" its New Economic Policy (meaning a reduction of redistributive measures to benefit Malays) and inaugurated a range of measures to liberalize the investment climate. With more advanced Asian countries suffering from currency appreciation and labor shortages, a good deal of manufacturing capacity moved to Southeast Asia. Malaysia succeeded in attracting much of this new investment. The economic liberalization of the mid-1980s has been complemented by a cultural thaw that has reassured skeptical Chinese that changes have not been made just to attract foreign investment. Tax exemptions and more liberal capital repatriation laws have also enhanced Chinese business confidence in the Mahathir regime, especially in the early 1990s.

Nevertheless, these five phases of development—colonialism, import substitution, export-oriented manufacturing, heavy industrialization, and the liberalization that revived the export industries—have led to a certain economic dualism. The manufacturing sector is divided between export industries and protected domestic industries, which may obstruct its becoming more coherent and dynamic.

THE CHINESE ROLE

There is some controversy over the nature and extent of Chinese participation in the Malaysian manufacturing sector. According to some studies, Chinese manufacturers play a minor role in comparison with Malays and foreigners, at least in terms of ownership.[15] The evidence is problematic, however, because it refers only to large projects, which, under the Industrial Coordination Act, require at least 30 percent Bumiputera participation in order to gain official approval. In fact, most Malaysian manufacturing enterprises are Chinese, but the majority of them are small, family owned, and enjoy little if any government support. Indeed, they are often harassed by the authorities for violating laws concerning intellectual property rights, land use, labor, and the environment.

The problem is that these nascent industrialists are involved in a kind of "guerilla capitalism" that, despite the romantic imagery, limits growth, technological innovation, the achievement of economies of scale in production and marketing, and international competitiveness. "Small" is unlikely to be "beautiful" when it comes to worker remuneration, industrial safety, occupational health, or environmental protection. One might argue that this is a price worth paying for the emergence of industrial capitalism. Ethnic considerations and the political influence of big business, however, especially outside manufacturing, make it most unlikely that the Malaysian government will start favoring the Chinese. Hence, while they may represent Malaysia's best chance for domestic-led industrialization, it is doubtful that they will be granted the opportunities necessary for expansion.

There are some politically influential Chinese manufacturers who have entered lucrative, protected, import-substitution industries such as cement, flour, sugar, and automobile assembly. But the few who are significant exporters of manufactured goods enjoy little state support. Thus, while manufactured exports hold promise for improving international competitiveness, the state has generally not favored the most dynamic Chinese entrepreneurs.

The consequence of government intervention in the manufacturing sector has been to promote short-term thinking, because, despite long-term regime stability, policies fluctuate considerably, especially in regard to ethnic matters. Not surprisingly, then, Chinese capital has gravitated toward finance and real estate, investments that offer fairly rapid, attractive returns and relatively easy exit.[16]

Under such interventionist conditions, "know who" has determined business success more than "know how." Hence, the very nature of investments has been greatly affected. In this environment, corruption, patronage, and generally legal "political" contributions have usually been crucial for gaining access to business opportunities. Because such a process of resource and opportunity allocation must be nontransparent, there is no real auctioning process at work, and it is not necessarily the highest potential bidder who secures whatever is being offered.

Thus, not only does the state fail to capture the full "rents" from disbursing such privilege, but those who allocate such business opportunities often fail to maximize rent capture for themselves, owing to the absence of forces compelling efficiency. This may reduce some business costs for those who secure the relevant opportunities, but it also correspondingly reduces the incomes of those capturing the rents. Moreover, there is no imperative for them to invest their incomes in ways that may contribute to growth.

There is also a crucial ethnic dimension to such transfers of wealth and resources. Those seeking opportunities are largely Chinese, whereas those who wield political influence are mainly Malay. While this disparity may serve official efforts to redistribute wealth among ethnic communities, it also inadvertently creates a business culture that can undermine the development of an internationally competitive national economy.

The economic liberalization under Mahathir and former finance minister Daim has shifted the emphasis from state accumulation—ostensibly on behalf of indigenous communities—to private accumulation by Malays and others who are politically favored.[17] This shift has substituted a more dynamic, aggressive Malay business community for one that operated under the pretense of serving its ethnic community's larger interests, a result that has deprived Malays of an important justification for their state-allocated privileges. It is not yet clear whether Mahathir's policy reversal will allow politically favored Malays to take over businesses previously dominated by Chinese.

The NEP's logic has led to attempts at "ethnic bypass," in which Malays collaborate with foreign partners in order to avoid dependence upon Chinese. Ethnic bypass tactics have also been employed by the government. The major example is Mahathir's national car project. It deliberately did not incorporate the existing Malaysian automobile assembly firms, dominated by Chinese, even though this strategy undermined the government's bargaining position in joint-venture negotiations with Mitsubishi and extended the new firm's "learning curve" unnecessarily.

The recent emphasis on private accumulation, however, could also force "know-who" Malays to collaborate in some ways with "know-how" Chinese. With "know-how" Malays scarce and therefore expensive, "know-who" Malays will be likely to prefer "know-how" Chinese who are both cheaper and more likely to remain subordinate. This preference will be strengthened by suspicions among all ethnic groups that the achievements of "know-how" Malays are mainly the product of political connections.

It is tempting to consider Chinese capital collectively, especially in Malaysia, because of the country's preoccupation with interethnic wealth distribution and the apparent exclusiveness of Chinese business. Indeed, there do seem to be business networks based on specifically Chinese cultural resources, including language, education, and social organizations such as clan associations (especially those based on patrilineal kinship), trade guilds, chambers of commerce, school boards, temple committees, and local community associations. Such frequent interaction has undoubtedly generated considerable "cultural" or "social" capital, which is crucial for explaining business trust, risk sharing, informal contracts, and information as well as transaction cost reduction.[18]

Yet the existence of a particular Chinese business idiom that has been successful in Malaysia and much of Southeast Asia does not necessarily mean that it is correct to treat Chinese business as a monolithic bloc, especially in historical analyses. The specific idiom of Chinese businessmen can be traced historically to the fact that they could not rely on the colonial state to provide the legal enforcement necessary for successful business transactions. Thus, social relations based on trust became important. Small business units were organized around kinship networks, whether real, created (e.g., through marriage), or fictive (e.g., by adoption, legally or socially). Similarly, credit and labor, as well as job-contracting relations, developed in distinctive ways on the basis of mutual trust rather than of formal contracts enforced by the colonial state. Even when the state and the legal system became more accessible to Chinese business interests, this Chinese business idiom persisted and evolved, with extralegal (and occasionally illegal) activities complementing the legal ones. Unencumbered by the legal system's often burdensome requirements, this extralegal realm of Chinese business often allowed for faster and cheaper transactions.

This business idiom has been seen as discrimination against non-Chinese. For a long time, even peak organizations—those transcending family and kin ties—still operated within the boundaries of dialect-group or provincial affiliations. This happened, for example, when three Hokkien banks merged to form the Overseas Chinese Banking Corporation during the interwar period. Thus, if collective action requires cooperation beyond the family level, such imagined communities provide the preferred basis for trust.

At the same time, the generally undifferentiated treatment of Chinese by the colonial and postcolonial state, the cultural influence of nationalist movements in China on Chinese emigrés, and the spread of Mandarin as the accepted Chinese language have all contributed to a growing sense of "Chineseness" that transcends provincial and linguistic loyalties. Residential proximity, especially in rural areas and small towns, and common business interests also probably contribute to this relatively new sense of "Chineseness." "Subethnic" patterns of settlement and occupational specialization may have mitigated this pan-Chinese tendency in the past, but these are now of declining importance.

It has been suggested that "Chineseness" is an especially useful analytical category for postcolonial Malaysia because of the significance and consequences of official ethnic discrimination. But although such discrimination has generated various communitywide responses, business interests have often adopted individual coping strategies. The first major pan-Chinese efforts at business reorganization in Malaysia took place only in the mid-1970s. They were initiated by the Malaysian Chinese Association, whose political fortunes were waning with the implementation of the NEP.[19] The existence of a collective voice does not mean that all responses are collective. Even exit—in the form of capital flight or emigration—is usually an individual response, albeit one with cumulative consequences.

The diverse responses and strategies undoubtedly also reflect the different opportunities, capacities, perceptions, and information that individual businesspeople have. Thus, while it is possible to speak on one level of a Chinese business idiom in Malaysia, this idiom does not determine the behavior of a specific business. Hence, it is rarely meaningful to speak of Chinese capital in an aggregated sense, even, in most cases, in relation to the state. Discriminatory measures directed at Chinese businesses, however, ultimately stimulate unintended collective action such as the MCA-initiated modernization and corporatization movement in the mid-1970s. Subsequent initiatives by the

All-Malaysian Chinese Chambers of Commerce and Industry (for example, the establishment of Unico Holdings) were also responses to perceived increased discrimination and exclusion.

Sino-Malaysian capital has collaborated intimately with the state in some cases and pursued extralegal ventures in others. Those Chinese businessmen whose access to the state creates opportunities for them are usually obliged to build on the "rents" so derived. This obligation does not preclude business initiative and innovation, but it does steer entrepreneurship in a distinctive, and not always maximally efficient, direction. The same can increasingly be said of the "new breed" of Malay businessmen, those reportedly patronized by former finance minister Daim. In their case, the greater access to politically determined rents tends to encourage them to rely even more heavily on favoritism.

On the other hand, the "ethnic bypass" strategies of the Malaysian state have prompted most Chinese businesspeople to create "guerilla" business practices in the gray economy, based largely on trust. Such activities and enterprises tend to be small and therefore more likely to escape the state taxing agencies' attention. But such evasion also involves violation of laws concerning overtime regulations, workers' compensation and protection, occupational health and safety requirements, and building codes. Libertarian attitudes thrive in these circumstances and are often expressed as political opposition to the state.

Insofar as such attitudes toward states have long been found in China—during the Manchu Empire, the corrupt Kuomintang regime, and the rule of the Communist party, and even now, under "market socialism"—as well as in Chinatowns all over the world, one could suggest that they tend to be a distinct idiom of Chinese capitalism. In Southeast Asia, the high incidence of Chinese commercial success has triggered considerable resentment among business rivals and political elites. The latter have therefore tended to mobilize against "alien" Chinese capital by invoking a cult of indigeneity. The Chinese, moreover, have facilitated this mobilization by alienating themselves from native communities. Yet not unlike the administrators of fiscally conservative colonial regimes, the indigenous postcolonial political elites—reluctant to strengthen their opponents—have generally tolerated, if not encouraged, those Chinese willing to "get things done" in ways that serve the state's interests. Hence, the indigenous elites' attitudes toward Chinese business are profoundly varied and even contradictory, and are often determined by local developments and exigencies rather than by a consistent grand design.

Malaysia is generally considered to have had the most hostile policies toward Chinese business of any country in Southeast Asia. Nevertheless, all Southeast Asian Chinese business cultures share some, though certainly not all, of the characteristics of their counterpart in Malaysia. Although Singapore has a Chinese majority, the state has largely dominated the economy there, often to the chagrin of Chinese entrepreneurs, especially smaller ones. This dominance has probably contributed to the retention of a Chinese business culture in Singapore similar to that in Malaysia, despite the presence of a Chinese-dominated state. Sinophobia is supposedly less significant in Thailand and the Philippines, although it is important to note that anti-Chinese actions have been officially encouraged in both countries in the postwar period.

The Indonesian situation probably most closely parallels that in Malaysia. Indonesia has had no official policy such as the NEP to redistribute ownership of capital, but this has not prevented the emergence of a substantial indigenous business community. This community is increasingly likely to come into conflict with the dominant Chinese businessmen and to try to use the state against them. That the present Indonesian regime has been supportive of large Chinese businesses in the past does not mean it will continue to be so in the future.

Despite variations in Southeast Asia, it may be possible to speak more generally of a Chinese business idiom, or culture, based on a kind of resistance to state control and the sense that ethnic discrimination is either an existing or at least a potential threat.

NOTES

1. One of the more sophisticated versions of this argument can be found in S. G. Redding, *The Spirit of Chinese Capitalism* (New York: de Gruyter, 1990). For nuanced and comparative perspectives, see Joel Kotkin, *Tribes: How Race, Religion and Identity Determine Success in the New Global Economy* (New York: Random House, 1993); Tania Li, *Malays in Singapore: Culture, Economy and Ideology* (Singapore: Oxford University Press, 1992); Tan Chee-Beng, "Culture and Economic Performance: The Chinese in Southeast Asia," *Chinese Currents* 3:1 (January–March 1992), pp. 3–13; 3:2 (April–June 1992), pp. 8–12.

2. On talk of an emerging Chinese economic zone, see Linda Lim, "The Emergence of a Chinese Economic Zone in Asia?" *Journal of Southeast Asia Business* 8:1 (Winter 1992), pp. 41–46. On the role of ethnic Chinese business minorities in Southeast Asian economies, some of the main compendia include those of Linda Lim and Peter Gosling, eds., *The Chinese in Southeast Asia*, 2 vols. (Singapore: Maruzen

Asia, 1983); Ruth McVey, ed., *Southeast Asian Capitalists* (Ithaca, New York: Cornell University Southeast Asia Program, 1992); and Jennifer W. Cushman and Wang Gungwu, eds., *Changing Ethnic Identities of the Southeast Asian Chinese since World War II* (Hong Kong: University of Hong Kong Press, 1988). A more ideological and poorly informed perspective is to be found in Wu Yuan-li and Wu Chun-hsi, *Economic Development in Southeast Asia* (Stanford, California: Hoover Institute Press, 1980). For a more historical perspective, see Victor Purcell, *The Chinese in Southeast Asia* (London: Royal Institute of International Affairs, 1965, 2d ed.). For an excellent case study, see G. William Skinner, *Chinese Society in Thailand: An Analytical History* (Ithaca, New York: Cornell University Press, 1957). To get a sense of the contribution of accumulation in Southeast Asia to capitalist development in China, see M. R. Godley, *The Mandarin-Capitalists from Nanyang: Overseas Chinese Enterprise in the Modernization of China, 1893–1911* (Cambridge: Cambridge University Press, 1981).

3. Some of the more interesting items in the vast literature on this subject are works by Gary Hamilton, *Overseas Chinese Capitalism* (University of California, Davis, Institute of Governmental Affairs, East Asian Business and Development Working Paper Series, 1992); Linda Y. C. Lim, "Chinese Economic Activity in Southeast Asia: An Introductory Review," in Lim and Gosling, *The Chinese*, vol. 1, pp. 1–29; Victor Simpano Limlingan, *The Overseas Chinese in ASEAN: Business Strategies and Management Practices* (Manila: Vita Development Corporation, 1986); J. A. C. Mackie, "Changing Patterns of Chinese Big Business in Southeast Asia," in McVey, *Southeast Asian Capitalists*, pp. 161–90; J. A. C. Mackie, "Overseas Chinese Entrepreneurship," *Asia-Pacific Economic Literature* (May 1992), pp. 41–64.

4. Some of the more important socioeconomic studies of the Chinese in Malaysia include those of Lee Poh Ping, *Chinese Society in Nineteenth-Century Singapore* (Kuala Lumpur: Oxford University Press, 1978); Carl Trocki, *Princes and Pirates* (Singapore: Singapore University Press, 1979); Yen Chinghwang, *A Social History of the Chinese in Singapore and Malaya* (Singapore: Oxford University Press, 1986); and Edwin Lee, *The Towkays of Sabah* (Singapore: Singapore University Press, 1976).

5. For discussions of the relationship between business ethnic minorities, the colonial condition, and economic nationalism, see W. F. Wertheim, "The Trading Minorities in Southeast Asia," in his *East-West Parallels* (The Hague: van Hoeve, 1964), pp. 38–82; and Frank Golay et al., *Underdevelopment and Economic Nationalism in Southeast Asia* (Ithaca, New York: Cornell University Press, 1969). For more polemical discussions about the role of business minorities in the rural economy, see K. S. Jomo, *A Question of Class: Capital, the State and Uneven Development in Malaya* (Singapore: Oxford University Press, 1986); Tan Tat Wai, *Income Distribution and Determination in West Malaysia* (Kuala Lumpur: Oxford University Press, 1982); and L. A. P. Gosling, "Chinese Crop Dealers in Malaysia and Thailand: The Myth of the Merciless Monopsonistic Middleman," in Lim and Gosling, *The Chinese*, vol. 1, pp.

131–70. For a more nuanced and historical perspective, see T'ien Ju-K'ang, *The Structure of Sarawak: A Study of Social Structure,* Monographs on Social Anthropology, no. 14 (London: London School of Economics and Political Science, 1953).

6. My discussion rejects the suggestion made by William Roff in his classic *The Origins of Malay Nationalism* (Kuala Lumpur: Oxford University Press, 1994 [1967]), that the pan-Islamic reformist Kaum Muda and the privileged Malay "administocrats" of the MCKK type were nascent nationalists. Not unlike their leader, the Egyptian Muslim modernist Muhammad Abduh, the Kaum Muda's emphasis on pan-Islamic reformism compromised its patriotism and anticolonialism. While perhaps discovering their common Malayness through colonial institutions such as the MCKK, Malay aristocrats were generally privileged only as members of the colonial-dominated administration within the context of their respective Malay states. This undermined both their pan-Malayness and their anticolonialism.

7. On the MCA, see Heng Pek Koon, *Chinese Politics in Malaysia: A History of the Malaysian Chinese Association* (Singapore: Oxford University Press, 1988).

8. There is an extensive literature on this subject. See, for example, Martin Brennan, "Class, Politics and Race in Modern Malaysia," *Journal of Contemporary Asia* 12:2 (1981), pp. 283–338; Hing Ai Yun, "Capitalist Development, Class and Race," in S. Husin Ali, ed., *Malaysia: Ethnicity, Class and Development* (Kuala Lumpur: Malaysian Social Science Association, 1984), pp. 296–328; Donald Horowitz, *Ethnic Groups in Conflict* (Berkeley: University of California Press, 1985); Hua Wu Yin, *Class and Communalism in Malaysia: Politics in a Dependent Capitalist State* (London: Zed Books, 1983); Jomo, *A Question of Class.*

9. A great deal has been written on the economic impact of the NEP. See Bruce Gale, *Politics and Public Enterprise in Malaysia* (Singapore: Eastern Universities Press, 1981); Horii Kenzo, "Disintegration of the Colonial Economic Legacies and Social Restructuring in Malaysia," *The Developing Economies* 29:4 (December 1991), pp. 281–313; Onozawa Jun, "Restructuring of Employment Patterns under the New Economic Policy," *The Developing Economies* 29:4 (December 1991), pp. 314–29; Torii Takashi, "Changing the Manufacturing Sector, Reorganizing Automobile Assemblers, and Developing the Auto Component Industry under the New Economic Policy," *The Developing Economies* 29:4 (December 1991), pp. 387–413; Ozay Mehmet, *Development in Malaysia: Poverty, Wealth and Trusteeship* (London: Croom Helm, 1986); Kamal Salih and Zainal Aznam Yusof, "Overview of the New Economic Policy and Framework for the Post-1990 Economic Policy," *Malaysian Management Review* 24:2 (1989), pp. 13–61; Saruwatari Keiko, "Malaysia's Localization Policy and Its Impact on British-Owned Enterprises," *The Developing Economies* 29:4 (December 1991), pp. 371–87.

10. Literature dealing with the impact of the NEP on Chinese-Malaysian business includes Hara Fujio, "Malaysia's New Economic Policy and the Chinese Business

Community," *The Developing Economies* 29:4 (December 1991), pp. 350–70; Eddie C. Y. Kuo, "Ethnicity, Polity and Economy: A Case Study of the Mandarin Trade and the Chinese Connection," in Gary Hamilton, ed., *Business Networks and Economic Development in East and Southeast Asia* (Hong Kong: University of Hong Kong Centre of Asian Studies, 1991), pp. 155–75; and Yasuda Nobuyuki, "Malaysia's New Economic Policy and the Industrial Co-ordination Act," *The Developing Economies* 29:4 (December 1991), pp. 330–49; The most detailed study of the MCA-initiated Chinese corporatization movement between the mid-1970s and mid-1980s is that of Yeoh Kok Kheng, "A Study of the Malaysian Chinese Economic Self-Strengthening (Corporatisation) Movement, with Special Reference to MPHB, Other Communal Investment Companies and Cooperatives" (M.Ec. thesis, Faculty of Economics and Administration, University of Malaya, Kuala Lumpur, 1988).

11. See K. S. Jomo, *Growth and Structural Change in the Malaysian Economy* (London: Macmillan, 1990). The best study of the Malaysian economy from a dependency perspective is that of Khor Kok Peng, *The Malaysian Economy: Structure and Dependence* (Kuala Lumpur: Maricans, 1983).

12. There are many studies of the distributional consequences of Malaysian economic development. See K. S. Jomo, *Beyond 1990: Considerations for a New National Development Strategy* (Kuala Lumpur: University of Malaysia Institute of Advanced Studies, 1989). A partial review is offered by Charles Hirschman, "Development and Inequality in Malaysia," *Pacific Affairs* 61:2 (1989), pp. 72–81. A comparative perspective is offered by Pang Eng Fong, "Race, Income Distribution and Development in Malaysia and Singapore," in Lim and Gosling, *The Chinese*, vol. 1, pp. 316–35.

13. Fong Chan Onn, "Malaysian Corporate Economy Restructuring: Progress since 1970" (paper presented at the meetings of Malaysian Social Science Association, Kuala Lumpur, July 24–26, 1989). Also see Sally Cheong, *Corporate Groupings in the KLSE* (Kuala Lumpur: Modern Law Publishers, 1990); Lim Mah Hui, *Ownership and Control of the One Hundred Largest Corporations in Malaysia* (Kuala Lumpur: Oxford University Press, 1981); and Tan Tat Wai, *Income Distribution.*

14. Some of the better studies on the subject of the state and industrialization include those of Heng Pek Koon, "The Chinese Business Elite of Malaysia," in McVey, *Southeast Asian Capitalists,* pp. 127–44; Lim Mah Hui, "Ownership and Control of the One Hundred Largest Corporations in Malaysia: The Role of Chinese Businessmen," in Lim and Gosling, *The Chinese*, vol. 1, pp. 275–315; Sieh Lee Mei Ling, "The Transformation of Malaysian Business Groups," in McVey, *Southeast Asian Capitalists,* pp. 103–26; and Hara Fujio, ed., *Formation and Restructuring of Business Groups in Malaysia* (Tokyo: Institute of Developing Economies, 1993). For a fine example of the contribution of business journalism to our understanding of this phenomenon, see Jonathan Friedland, "Kuok the Kingpin," *Far Eastern Economic Review* (February 7, 1991), pp. 46–50.

15. There have been several major studies of the consequences of the NEP's apparent ethnic bypass policy, including those of Alisdair Bowie, *Crossing the Industrial Divide: State, Society and the Politics of Economic Transformation in Malaysia* (New York: Columbia University Press, 1991); and James Jesudason, *Ethnicity and the Economy: The State, Chinese Business, and Multinationals in Malaysia* (Singapore: Oxford University Press, 1989). Other studies offering different perspectives include those of Wong Tai Chee, "Industrial Development, the New Economic Policy in Malaysia and the International Division of Labor," *ASEAN Economic Bulletin* 7:1 (July 1990), pp. 106–19; Paul M. Lubeck, "Malaysian Industrialization, Ethnic Divisions, and the NIC Model: The Limits to Replication," in Richard Appelbaum and Jeffrey Henderson, eds., *States and Development in the Asian Pacific Rim* (London: Sage Publications, 1992), pp. 176–98; and Richard Doner, *Driving a Bargain: Japanese Transnationals and the Automotive Industry in Southeast Asia* (Berkeley: University of California Press, 1991). For a different view of Chinese business under apparently hostile political conditions, see Danny Kin-Kong Lam and Ian Lee, "Guerilla Capitalism and the Limits of Statist Theory: Comparing the Chinese NICs," in Cal Clark and Steve Chan, eds., *The Evolving Pacific Basin in the Global Political Economy* (Boulder: Lynne Rienner, 1992), pp. 107–24.

16. See Hing Ai Yun, "The Financial System and Industrial Investment in West Malaysia," *Journal of Contemporary Asia* 21:4 (1987), pp. 409–35; K. S. Jomo, ed., *Industrialising Malaysia: Problems, Potential, Prospects* (London: Routledge, 1993).

17. See Bruce Gale, *Politics and Business: A Study of Multi-Purpose Holdings Berhad* (Singapore: Eastern Universities Press, 1985); E. T. Gomez, *Politics in Business: UMNO's Corporate Investments* (Kuala Lumpur: Forum, 1990); E. T. Gomez, *Money Politics in the Barisan Nasional* (Kuala Lumpur: Forum, 1991); and E. T. Gomez, *Political Business: Corporate Involvement of Political Parties in Malaysia* (Cairns: James Cook University, Southeast Asia Studies Centre, 1994). Some of the better-known regional studies include those of James Clad, *Behind the Myth: Business, Money and Power in South East Asia* (London: Unwin Hyman, 1989); and Yoshihara Kunio, *The Rise of Ersatz Capitalism in South-East Asia* (Singapore: Oxford University Press, 1988).

18. Several studies, mainly anthropological, have contributed to understanding this idiom of Chinese-Malaysian capitalism. See, for example, Chia Oai Peng, "Trust and Credit among Chinese Businessmen in Kelantan," *Southeast Asian Business* 14 (Summer 1987), pp. 28–31; Maurice Freedman, "The Handling of Money: A Note on the Background to the Economic Sophistication of Overseas Chinese," *Man* 89 (April 1959), pp. 64–65; Donald Nonini, "The Chinese Truck Transport 'Industry' of a Peninsular Malaysia Market Town," in Lim and Gosling, *The Chinese*, vol. 1, pp. 171–206.

19. Yeoh Kok Kheng, "A Study."

10 / Ethnicity and Capitalist Development

The Changing Role of the Chinese in Thailand

GARY G. HAMILTON AND TONY WATERS

Why are the Chinese so successful in business? This question has been asked again and again in reference to the Chinese in virtually every location outside of China where they have settled in any substantial numbers in the past 150 years. Many anthropological and historical accounts of the Chinese in this or that location suggest answers to the question, but the answers often end up being either too broad or too narrow. The broad answers are usually sociological, and the narrow answers are either historical or cultural. In this chapter, we steer a middle course between the two extremes. Rather than asking *why* the Chinese are economically successful, we will examine the organizational contexts of their success.

In order to frame our organizational approach, it is important to distinguish it from conventional sociological interpretations. Many sociologists argue that some ethnic minorities, the Chinese being one, naturally excel in commerce and trade. The reasons for minority success, they contend, are to be found in five advantages conferred by the conditions of ethnicity and minority status.

Three of these advantages come from the nature of minority status itself. The first is market objectivity. In his famous essay "The Stranger," Georg Simmel maintained that minority status makes persons into ever-present strangers, people "who are here today and stay tomorrow" but who do not quite fit into an established social framework.[1] Because they are socially marginal, minorities are able to maneuver in the marketplace with an objectivity unavailable to people who are more deeply entangled in the social order and more invested in the status quo.

A second advantage comes from the experience of being sojourners, temporary migrants whose journeys may extend across generations.[2] Sojourners, defining their migration as temporary, choose not to, and perhaps cannot, socially integrate into a host society. Their mobility blocked, migrants look inward. As a group of long-term temporary settlers, they create sets of institutionalized motivations and practices that favor hard work, maximum savings, and reluctance to invest in social status activities in the host society.[3]

The third advantage is that ethnicity nurtures the ability of people in relatively small, well-bounded groups to create close-knit networks. Scholars have examined such networks in some detail and find that they increase trust and predictability among economic actors, a condition that reduces economic risk and enhances economic success.[4]

The two other sources of economic advantage arise, as an interaction effect, from the minority group's relation to the host society. This host-minority relationship sometimes creates an "opportunity structure" that provides two sources of minority economic advantage.[5] First, advantage ensues from the fact that the economic system in the host society has a differentiated occupational structure that allows members of minority groups to monopolize selected economic roles and niches that are important for the overall economy but are otherwise difficult to fill. In occupying such niches, minority entrepreneurs become dependent on an economic order in which minority status and host hostility combine to create a stable "middle-man minority."[6] The second and related source of advantage arises when a dominant political group actively bestows economic privileges on minority groups. In effect, political elites ethnicize key economic roles while simultaneously denying ethnic groups access to political power. In this context, groups such as the Jews in medieval Spain or the Chinese in colonial Southeast Asia become "pariah capitalists."[7]

These five interrelated explanations for minority economic success are so often mentioned in the sociological literature that they appear to be propositions applicable to all ethnic groups and not just a few. In fact, the sociological literature on minority capitalism concentrates more or less exclusively on only a handful of groups, with the Jews, the overseas Chinese, the overseas Indians, and more recently the Koreans in the United States being the most prominently mentioned. Other groups are cited only rarely and then in special social and historical circumstances.

So commonly mentioned are these few groups that the question may not be simply why minorities succeed in business but rather why some minorities succeed so widely and not others. This latter question has some importance in both Southeast Asia and Central Europe because only a few groups are really prominent in either location. Other groups in a particular locale or niche have, on occasion, achieved economic success, but overwhelmingly the Chinese and the Indians are *the* economic minorities of Southeast Asia and the Jews were *the* economic minority of east-central Europe until World

War II. Why not other groups? Why primarily only these few? The sociological literature does not address these questions very well.

If the sociological interpretations are too broad and overgeneralized, then the historical and cultural explanations go to the opposite extreme. They focus on extraordinary qualities of particular groups or particular people within a group. Explaining Chinese success in Southeast Asia, for instance, some writers select cultural traits that Chinese traditionally have, such as a high regard for education, hard work, and obedience,[8] a precocious ability to handle money,[9] and a Confucian emphasis on self-discipline and family welfare.[10] Other writers prefer more specific explanations that border on mere historical particularism. Chinese success in a particular location is explained through a succession of events and the accomplishments of key entrepreneurs. The inference drawn from cultural and historical explanations is that Chinese success is to be explained in terms of either endogenous, predetermined traits or idiosyncratic events and personalities. Such explanations single out the Chinese and by implication suggest that other groups simply do not possess the same cultural traits or produce such extraordinary individuals.

Without a doubt, the sociology, history, and cultural traditions of the overseas Chinese have significant bearing on their economic success, but explanations for their success going to either extreme do not tap the institutional and organizational variations that the Chinese have encountered historically and cross-culturally in the many societies to which they have migrated. Moreover, when such variations are examined closely, one must question and qualify the extensiveness and historical continuity of Chinese entrepreneurship. Most Chinese migrants were unsuccessful, and many died penniless in places distant from their homeland. More importantly, even the most successful Chinese did not succeed in just one way but rather in many ways, ways as numerous as the institutional and organizational contexts of the societies in which they lived and worked. It is this ability to be flexible, to adapt their businesses to strikingly different contexts, that the Chinese have demonstrated repeatedly.

In this chapter we examine the institutional and organizational variations that Chinese have encountered historically within a single society, and the adaptations they made to these variable conditions. Specifically, we analyze three distinct institutional "situations" the Chinese have confronted in recent Thai history and to which they responded by reconstructing the nature of Chinese ethnicity vis-à-vis the Thai majority. For each situation, we examine, first, the institutional context and, second, the entrepreneurial strategies used by Chinese who successfully adapted to change. We illustrate these situations by looking closely at one leading, highly successful Chinese family in each period.

The Chinese have been the prominent economic minority in Thailand for hundreds of years.[11] Many chroniclers of this fact have stressed the continuity of Chinese entrepreneurship without also noting the changing nature of their entrepreneurial involvements.[12] Although it is true that the Chinese have been successfully engaged in the Thai economy for a long while, that economy has changed drastically several times. In the twentieth century alone, the Thai economy has gone through two substantial organizational transformations, the first concomitant with a change in government in the 1930s and the second with rapid globalization of the economy in the 1970s and 1980s. Throughout all periods, Chinese have occupied crucial economic roles, but there has been little continuity in their involvement over time. Different sets of Chinese, operating in organizationally distinct ways, have dominated the economy in each period. Moreover, in each period the Chinese in Thailand have reconstructed themselves as an ethnic group.

The first period dates from the eighteenth century and ended abruptly in 1932. It was the period of strong patrimonial rulership by the Thai kings, centralized control over portions of the economy, and an economically privileged and politically powerful Chinese minority. Its transformation began in the middle of the nineteenth century, when Thailand opened to Western traders and Western influence, and culminated in 1932 with the creation of a Western-style state.

The second period began with a coup d'état. In 1932, junior military officials and civil servants forced the Thai king to accept comprehensive reforms that created a constitutional state. The king became a figurehead in an authoritarian regime led by military and bureaucratic arms of the government. The factionalized government created an economy that looked like a patchwork quilt; every agency had its economic preserve and every top official his connections for gaining wealth. During this period, a combination of political harassment and Thai xenophobia created a cohesive, embattled, yet economically significant Chinese minority.

The transformation to the third period began gradually in the late 1950s and early 1960s, when the pace of global economic development quickened and gradually transformed the Thai domestic economy into an export-oriented, trade-based economy closely linked with global capitalism. The new period, however, became fully engaged only in 1973, when the military elites relinquished their hold on the government and civilian-led governments took over. During this third period, which is still very much in the process of formation, the People's Republic of China (PRC) returned to global prominence, some Japanese business groups moved significant portions of their manufacturing capabilities to Thailand and elsewhere in Southeast Asia, and Chinese overseas capitalism, centered in Hong Kong, Singapore, and Taiwan, became a major economic force throughout East and Southeast Asia.

The Chinese in Thailand linked themselves to these economic movements, and in the process they have significantly refocused themselves. No longer members of a harassed, inward-looking minority group, the Chinese in Thailand have embraced the outside world and reaffirmed their Chinese identity, as well as maintaining their Thai identity. Some Thai Chinese have become highly successful global economic actors and members of a world community of "Chinese overseas," loyal both to China as a civilization and to the political state in which they live.

PATRIMONIAL RULERSHIP AND DEPENDENT CAPITALISM

Before the middle of the nineteenth century, the kings of Siam ruled the territory of what is now Thailand as a patrimonial regime. Like rulers of patrimonial regimes elsewhere, the Thai kings had to establish an independent base for their personal power in order to offset the authority of decentralized traditional elites.[13] They centrally administered their regimes through agencies of the royal household staffed by dependent subjects, often Chinese. This independent power base provided leverage against the Thai hereditary aristocracy, which controlled much of rural society through a complex system of patron-client relationships.[14] The royal household did not tax the lands of the aristocracy directly, but rather maintained its hegemony vis-à-vis the aristocracy by creating reliable streams of revenues coming from royal monopolies, in-kind tax farming, and tributes of local products ranging from tropical lumbers, tin, rice, and spices to luxury goods such as birds' nests (for bird's nest soup) and ivory. The royal household then exported these products in the monopolized tributary trade with China.[15]

The Thai kings were able to maintain their hegemony only with the help of Chinese who ran the tributary trade and staffed key positions in the royal household. The use of aliens to enhance one's political power is common in most patrimonial regimes,[16] but the rulers of Siam went considerably beyond this strategy. Chinese privileges began in the early eighteenth century when the rulers of Siam at the time cultivated a small Chinese minority in Bang-kok to run the tributary trade with China.[17] At this time, imperial China, the celestial empire, had high status in Southeast Asia, as did the Chinese traders who traveled to Siam. Living at court and largely serving the kings, a few Chinese became trusted allies in the kings' struggle for power with the aristocracy and with neighboring kingdoms.

The position of the Chinese, however, changed greatly in the last half of the eighteenth century, when Taksin, a descendant of a Chinese trader and a Thai mother, became king. Taksin came to the throne during a period of intense warfare in 1766–67, when the Burmese captured the imperial city of Ayutthaya. A trusted aide to the king at the time, Taksin fled the capital city, regrouped the Thai forces, and led them to victory. He recaptured Ayut-thaya and defeated the Burmese decisively. Then he took the throne and held it for fourteen years, until 1782. During his reign, he transferred the capital city to the site of present-day Bangkok and encouraged migration from the Teochiu dialect area in southeastern China, his father's native home. Taksin was later deposed, but his successor, whose reign title was Rama I and who started the present Chakkri dynasty, was also half Chinese and was married to Taksin's daughter. He was "invested under an authentic Chinese name, Cheng Hua."[18]

The Bangkok period that began with the reign of Rama I marked the high point in the tributary trade with China.[19] A large portion of the royal revenues derived from the royal trading monopolies. Wanting to increase their wealth and political position, the Chakkri kings encouraged Chinese migration, so much so that Bangkok became a predominantly Chinese city.[20] Initially, the Chinese migrants were not embedded in local society. Being distant from the Thai aristocracy, the Chinese were more loyal to the king and the royal household than to anyone else. Moreover, as relationships with particular families deepened, the kings granted to those Chinese with whom they had the closest ties licenses for tax farming and for trading monopolies. Favored Chinese became court household officials with admin-istrative duties. Chinese elites and members of the Thai royal household regularly intermarried.

The inward-directedness of this patrimonial kingdom ended with the Bowring Treaty in 1855. In the middle of the nineteenth century, the Thai rulers realized that Western powers were going to conquer and colonize every possible location in Southeast Asia in the name of free trade. Unlike other Southeast Asian states, Siam escaped colonialism and maintained its independence by allowing Westerners and Western modernizing practices into Thailand.[21] In the 1850s, tributary relations with China ended, as did the royal monopolies on overseas trade. Western merchants established trading houses in Bangkok and opened the Thai economy to international influences. With the increased economic opportunities offered by Western commerce, Chinese began to migrate to Thailand in still greater numbers and to shift their loyalties.[22] A few prominent Chinese families continued their linkage with the royal household, serving primarily as tax farmers, but many Chinese merchants also developed connections with Western traders and increasingly became the compradores for Western trading houses. These compradores focused initially on the export of teak and rice but soon began to organize extractive industries such as tin mining as well.

By the 1890s, income for the royal household, primarily from tax farming and overseas trading, had fallen. The fiscal basis of the state was in jeopardy and in need of reform.[23] The king and his household officials began to search for new ways to create the wealth needed to preserve the political and economic privileges of the royal family. In the 1890s, the Chakkri kings began to modernize the state structure and, as earlier kings had done, relied on Chinese dependents to make the new strategy work. Using Chinese capital, expertise, and labor, the royal household began to create and establish monopoly ownership over a group of capitalist enterprises. Through these enterprises, the state began construction of Thailand's infrastructure and systematically extracted primary resources. The core of these patrimonially rooted enterprises was the Privy Purse Bureau, which later became the Crown Property Bureau, the largest landowner and infrastructure conglomerate in Thailand today.[24]

In the late nineteenth century, under direct control of the king, the Privy Purse Bureau began to invest heavily in railways, tramways, shipping, mining, banking, and construction, starting one or more firms for each endeavor.[25] In each such venture, the royal household pooled its investments with money raised from Chinese who had previously been associated with the royal household, as well as from foreign sources. Among the most important enterprises to begin this way were the Siam Commercial Bank and Siam Cement, founded, respectively, in 1906 and 1913. By the time of the 1932 revolution, the royal household had effective control over, and partial ownership of, most of Thailand's significant infrastructure.

At the same time that the royal household was using Chinese capital and expertise to create modern enterprises, the structural situation of the Chinese in Thailand began to shift decisively. No longer a small, privileged minority, they were becoming far more numerous, and their influence was spreading. Not only were the Chinese no longer the kings' dependents, but by the early twentieth century they were becoming his competitors. They worked for Westerners, for the aristocracy, and, especially, for themselves.

This was the period when Thai kings first began to Westernize their political practices and to justify their rule by using the political vocabulary of the Western nation-state. Siam, the kingdom, became Thailand, the nation-state, which encompassed all of the Thai people. In this redefinition of political legitimacy, the Chinese rather suddenly became ethnic strangers instead of privileged insiders. By 1914, King Rama VI saw Chinese economic power as unearned and undeserved, and using a European analogy, he accused the Chinese of being the "Jews of the East."[26] This change in attitude among the Thais regarding the Chinese soon became widespread as a consequence of the 1932 coup d'état.

EXAMPLE ONE: ROYAL PATRONAGE AND THE KHAW FAMILY

Exercising their patrimonial position at the top of the aristocratic hierarchy, the Chakkri kings claimed large portions of the Thai economy that were not strictly controlled by local elites. Throughout the period, the kings and their officials in the royal household controlled access to the key routes by which wealth could be generated, especially tax farming and licensed trading. The kings and the kings' officials, some of whom were Chinese themselves, favored appointing Chinese for these economically privileged roles. Accordingly, from the Chinese point of view, one of the primary routes to enrichment was to court the royal prerogative. Strategies to accomplish this goal were many, but they generally included demonstrations of loyalty and economic prowess. To illustrate these strategies, we look at one of the best-known Chinese families of this period, the Khaw family, whose success illustrates concretely the structure of opportunities and the constraints that the Chinese faced in the nineteenth and early twentieth centuries.

The Khaw family, according to Jennifer Cushman, achieved a position of preeminence "equalled by few others in the kingdom" of Siam.[27] The founder of the family, Khaw Soo Cheang (1799–1882), an immigrant from the Hokkien region of southeastern China, arrived penniless in Penang in 1822. Shortly afterward, he moved to Ranong in southern Siam, where he found a job trading tin between the Muslim principalities of the Malay peninsula, in what were then vassal territories of the Siamese king in Bangkok. His early success earned him sufficient wealth to bid successfully in the royal household for the tin mining concession for Ranong. This role permitted him to organize tin mining in the region and to collect in-kind taxes from tin miners. He then sold the tin on the international market for cash and used the cash to make his tax payments to the royal household in Bangkok. In order to expand his profits, as well as those of the king, he recruited a large number of immigrant Chinese laborers for tin mining. This effort was so successful that in 1854 he was appointed governor of Ranong, and in 1862 he was awarded the title of *phraya,* the second highest rank in royal service.[28]

Serving the king loyally and well, Khaw Soo Cheang was able to obtain similar privileges for his sons. One son, Khaw Sim Kong, succeeded him in 1877 and remained in charge of the administration of Ranong province until 1895. Other sons obtained Thai appointments in other provinces of the south, including Krabi, Trang, and Phuket.[29] At the same time that he sought high positions for his sons, he was actively involved in establishing shipping and mining businesses based in Penang. Under the direction of his surviving sons, the family developed an extensive set of firms known as the Khaw group.

The control the family had over both politics and the economy in southern Siam was fairly typical of the way the Siamese empire was administered during the nineteenth century.[30] Such a system demanded a great deal of trust between the royal household, centered in Bangkok, and the administrators and tax farmers in the peripheral regions. Failure to remit tax payments could threaten the fiscal stability of the crown, and for this reason the alien Chinese proved somewhat more reliable than locally based aristocrats, who had their own followers to support.

The Chinese position, however, had always been precarious, for they served at the whims of the kings. To consolidate their position in the new economic climate that was emerging in the second half of the nineteenth century, the Khaw family, like other Chinese families, began to establish alliances with aristocratic families located in their region in southern Thailand and began to engage in economic endeavors on both sides of the emerging Thai-Malay border. In Siam, the Khaw family married into families of the minor Thai nobility, including the naNakhon family, which controlled the area immediately north of Ranong, and the Bunnag family, members of which controlled the Thai crown during the minority of King Rama V and the Ministry of the South during his majority. At the same time in Malaysia, where the Malay rajahs were in the process of severing tributary relationships with the Thai crown in exchange for British protection, the Khaw family began to arrange marriage alliances with the elite Chinese trading houses of Penang.

These connections, arranged through marriage, business, and political patronage, gave the Khaw family a great deal of leverage when European interests began to focus on the tin mines of the isthmus at the turn of the century. Western industrialists had developed dredging equipment that could be used to exploit the area's alluvial tin deposits more completely than Chinese mining techniques had been able to accomplish. This equipment, however, required more capital and different expertise than the Khaw family possessed. Accordingly, during the period when British interests were opening the closed trading system throughout the Malay peninsula, the Khaw family began to enter into agreements with British and Australian adventurers who could provide the capital to purchase dredging equipment and ships to transport the tin ore to smelters. They established the Tongkah Mining and Dredging Company and the Eastern Shipping Lines, both under the leadership of Khaw Sim Bee, youngest son of Khaw Soo Cheang.[31]

In 1913, when he was head of the family during its period of greatest influence and wealth, Khaw Sim Bee was assassinated. Thereafter, the family began to go into decline. After a few years of only modest success in Western-oriented commerce, the Khaw family began to sell off its key businesses and tried to revive its alliance with the Thai king. In an effort to maintain the family's economic interests, Khaw Sim Bee's nephew, Khaw Joo Tek, was able to reestablish a link to the royal household by building a special relationship with Prince Damrong, minister of the interior. For a short time this linkage stabilized the family's influence in Thailand's southern periphery, but when the military revolted in 1932, the patron-client relationship on which the family's influence was based disappeared. The family's distance from the center of influence in Bangkok, as well as its inability at a crucial moment to maintain its commercial position and wealth, originally obtained through political patronage, led to its decline. As a consequence, what was in the early days one of the most influential Sino-Thai families in terms of both economic power and political authority waned during the transition to a new era.

The strategy of obtaining an official position in the patrimonially organized economy was also used by many other Chinese families. It worked only so long as the kings and the royal household actually organized the economy. Once their prerogatives ended with governmental reforms in 1932, the strategy no longer worked. Although some Thai-Chinese families continued to serve the royal household, notably the Sarasin family,[32] their roles shrank and their numbers dwindled. Only a few Chinese were able to continue as managers in the kings' Western-style companies and as political brokers. Moreover, those previously privileged families who were able to make successful transitions into the new economic climates did so primarily as Thais rather than as Chinese, and as politicians rather than as entrepreneurs. These families assimilated ethnically into Thai society and no longer played a role in the entrepreneurial elite that became the driving force in the industrialization of the Thai economy.

MILITARY REGIMES, FACTIONAL POLITICS, AND ETHNIC OPPRESSION

Southeast Asia in the late nineteenth century had come to serve as an important source of primary products for the industrialized Western countries. Metal ores such as tin, tropical lumbers, tropical oils, tea, and rice were the area's key primary exports. But even though the trade-based economies of the late nineteenth and early twentieth centuries had been directed largely by Western colonial interests and core Western merchant houses, large portions of that economy had actually been controlled by Chinese.[33]

In the middle of the nineteenth century, a mass migration of Chinese from south China, mostly from the area of Teochiu (Ch'ao Chou), arrived in Bangkok. Connected through various types of trading associations, fellow-regional clubs, secret societies, and surname associations, Chinese merchants and petty traders quickly became prominent players in the new trade-based domestic economy. This situation was similar to what was going on elsewhere in Southeast Asia, because even though Thailand was not colonized, it underwent an economic transformation much like that which took place in the colonial parts of the region.[34]

Following lines of existing economic opportunity, these Chinese quickly established themselves in small, commercially oriented businesses such as selling sundry goods, rice trading and milling, native banking, and simple manufacturing (alcoholic beverages, soft drinks, bottling plants, etc.).[35] These small businesses were not dependent on royal concessions or other favors from the patrimonial state. This wave of migration created a substantial concentration of Chinese in Bangkok. In 1954, Chinese constituted about half the total population of the greater Bangkok area. As William Skinner describes it so nicely, the Chinese community focused inward upon itself, being controlled through dialect associations, secret societies, and such umbrella community associations as the Chinese Chamber of Commerce.[36] It was from the ranks of this new kind of Chinese-Thai that the next, and quite different, wave of successful Chinese entrepreneurs was to emerge.

Relations between the new Chinese immigrants and the Thai community became strained in the first decades of the twentieth century as a result of these new developments, but it was not until 1932 that Thai xenophobia against the Chinese was fully awakened by a nationalist military regime that came to power at that time through a bloodless coup.[37]

The coup was led by a group of Thai military officers who toppled the patrimonial state and established a constitutional monarchy. The king was removed from the exercise of day-to-day power, though the royal household retained much of its wealth and prestige. The military installed a government led by a dominant political party, the People's party, that was administratively centered on key bureaucratic ministries. As in many intensely nationalistic developing countries in the 1930s, the model for the regime was authoritarian fascism. And as in many of the countries that turned authoritarian during this period, political rule was precarious. (Since 1932 there have been twenty-one attempted coups, of which have ten have been successful.)[38]

During the forty-year period from the 1930s to the 1970s, and especially after World War II, when revolving coalitions of military officials and police gained control of the government, political elites attempted to create a national economy by employing import-substitution strategies.[39] They were following the accepted development theories of the day, but the enactment of this strategy in Thailand resulted in competing cliques within the government and gradually turned whole sectors of the economy into political benefices.[40] Government ministries, each staffed by a segment of the elite, took pieces of the economy, allocating different sectors to different bureaucratic units, each of which developed its set of state-owned enterprises.

The Chinese minority, accordingly, developed a fundamentally different, far narrower, and more strained relationship with the Thai elite after the 1932 revolution than it had had before. Chinese intermarriages with Thai elites became rare. Instead, as Skinner has shown, marriage alliances took place primarily within the Chinese community. This practice helped build a degree of ethnic solidarity that had been unknown in the earlier period and is becoming rare again today.[41] Interethnic arm-twisting replaced the patrimonial embrace that had been experienced before the 1932 revolution. The Chinese became a national minority that had to be cut off from external alliances. Chinese resources could be squeezed in service of the state and those who represented the state—the military and civil service elites.

Coupled with the political shift and the change in relations between the Chinese and the Thai elites, there were also significant changes in the economy of Thailand and the rest of Southeast Asia.[42] The decline of international trade and the deliberate promotion of greater self-sufficiency created a propitious environment for local industrial growth.

The key Chinese entrepreneurs to arise during this period differed from those of the earlier era. Most of the economically privileged Chinese of the patrimonial state had been losing their patronage even before 1932, and few were able to make the transition into economic prominence in the second period. "Indeed," notes Suehiro Akira, "it is very rare when one finds the names of the descendants of the prominent tax farmer families in the major industries after the 1932 Revolution."[43] Instead, most of the Chinese who became economically important during the nationalist period achieved success first in small businesses. Their prominence within the Chinese community then made them brokers between the Chinese minority and the Thai elites.[44] Such people became representatives of a new type of Sino-Thai relationship that arose as part of the government's attempt to isolate the "Chinese problem." It was this deliberate government policy and the new isolation of the Chinese that created what was essentially a new kind of pariah entrepreneurial class.

After 1950, the Thai elites began to nationalize the economy. Thai leaders continued to believe that local economies were in fact "national economies" and that to be progressive, they needed to be more or less autonomous and self-sufficient. This belief coincided not only with the previously right-wing developmentalism of prewar fascist regimes but also with the emergent anticolonialist, leftist vision of how formerly colonial economies could best escape backwardness.[45] They further believed that in order to build such an economy, there needed to be state-sponsored and party-sponsored development. Accordingly, through government and party channels, the military elites proceeded to claim those infrastructure and resource-based areas of the economy not already claimed by the Crown Property Bureau and to set up import-substitution industries.[46] The Ministry of Communications developed the airlines, the Ministry of Industry built petroleum refineries and electricity generators, the Ministry of Finance controlled the tobacco monopoly, and the Ministry of Defense and the Ministry of Finance opened banks. So critical were the areas developed by the government during this era that, in 1986, eleven of the nineteen largest companies in Thailand were still owned by government ministries.[47]

What role did Chinese entrepreneurs play in this new economy? The military governments after World War II were short of capital, so to establish their enterprises they turned to the previously stigmatized Chinese, who could provide it. Leading Chinese businessmen were able to mobilize resources within the Chinese community by using their connections, and they began to forge a whole new set of alliances with the military elite. This action not only generated financing for nationalistic projects but also allowed them to make more money for themselves, as well to enrich select Thai officials.

EXAMPLE TWO: PARIAH ENTREPRENEURSHIP AND
THE SOPHONPANICH FAMILY

After the 1932 coup, Thailand's military created a highly factionalized government that helped generate but then preyed on Chinese wealth. The competing elite factions had political positions but only limited access to wealth, and the Chinese had some wealth but only limited access to political protection. These complementary interests created a structural situation in which ethnic oppression and economic privilege worked hand in hand to achieve a more or less stable symbiosis between Thai elites and Chinese businessmen. Those Chinese who wished to enrich themselves during this period had to develop interethnic alliances with a winning faction and lay themselves open to systematic extractions. In exchange, they gained economic privileges. Perhaps the best illustration of this kind of pariah entrepreneurship is the Sophonpanich family.

The family's wealth was first established by Chin Sophonpanich (1910–88). He was born to a Teochiu father, a commercial clerk, and his Thai wife, in Thonburi, near Bangkok. Though he received his primary education in Swatow in China, he returned to Bangkok at seventeen. He worked as a clerk, a laborer, and a noodle seller before establishing his own business selling construction materials. Later, he opened a hardware and canned goods store and began trading with Hong Kong and Singapore.

In 1944, using resources from a number of his own businesses and in cooperation with other close business associates, Chin helped found and became a director of the Bangkok Bank.[48] Immediately after World War II, he established several independent firms in gold trading, currency exchange, and insurance. Together these firms became the base for Chin's Asia Trust group, the assets of which he used to increase his holdings in Bangkok Bank. He became president of the bank in 1952.

Also in 1952, the military government of Thailand issued a directive through the police director-general that required the Chinese to establish three centralized associations: one for organizing gold trading, one for jewelry trading, and one for banking. This was done the better to tap Chinese wealth. Chin became head of the association of commercial bankers. Using connections with some high military figures that he developed through this position, he obtained substantial financial backing for the Bangkok Bank from the Ministry of Economic Affairs. In exchange for its support, several generals were appointed to key positions on the bank's board of directors. The Ministry of Economic Affairs initially owned 60 percent of the total shares of Bangkok Bank.

Chin was then able to play a central role in Bangkok's Chinese community in the early 1950s. Skinner ranked him as the sixth most influential figure in that community in 1952. In large part, this influence was owing to his role as banker and agent for Police General Phao, for whom he often spoke in Chinese councils. Like other Thai Chinese of his era, Chin took a Thai name, Sophonpanich, and declared Thai citizenship. At the same time, he maintained his identity as an overseas Chinese. Indeed, so close was his attachment to his native region that he built a school named after his father in his home village in China. On one occasion, he even disavowed his Thai citizenship during a trip to China in order to avoid the Thai military draft. He also went to the trouble of reinstating it, however. He was a fervent anticommunist and a strong supporter of the Kuomintang regime in Taiwan.[49]

The years between 1957 and 1973 were crucial ones for all Thai banks. In 1957, the military faction that served as Chin's political patron was ousted from power by another military group. As a consequence, Chin had to flee Thailand. He lived in exile in Hong Kong for five years. Leaving his son Chatri in charge of his Thailand-based business, Chin made aggressive investments in the Hong Kong financial markets and established an overseas arm of the Bangkok Bank. He returned to Thailand in 1963 and soon began consolidating his control of the bank.

By 1963, the Thai economy had begun to expand, and the government had relaxed the anti-Chinese laws and changed its naturalization laws to allow Chinese to obtain Thai citizenship more easily. Less subject to threats of arrest and deportation in the new political climate, Chin gradually began to increase his ownership share of the Bangkok Bank. By 1968, the Sophonpanich family's shares exceeded those of the government for the first time. The family holdings were further augmented when Chin was able to take control of the shares of the military leaders who were forced into exile in the coup of 1973. Suehiro's analysis shows that the family controlled 32 percent of the bank in 1982, while the government held only 8.1 percent.[50] The government, however, maintained some control of the bank through a succession of powerful political officials it placed on the board of directors.

In the 1970s and 1980s, the Bangkok Bank group was able to benefit from Thailand's transition to an open global economy, and it became one of Thailand's biggest financial institutions. Although the group now engages in diverse businesses and has continued to expand in recent years to become more international in scope, like other groups formed in the 1930s and 1940s it still bears the imprint of its origins. Its major branches, managed by Chin's sons, remain centered in the financial sector and embedded in the local Thai economy.[51]

INTERNATIONALIZATION OF CAPITALISM IN
THAILAND AND THE OVERSEAS CHINESE
CONNECTION

From the 1932 coup to the Vietnam War era, the Thai economy remained largely a domestic economy, with its international component confined mainly to rice and lumber exports. At first the economy expanded slowly, but in the late 1950s there began a sustained increase in gross national product that continues to this day.[52] During this period the financial sector and large enterprises within the country were largely state owned or state sponsored. On one side, there was the quasi-private, quasi-state-owned Crown Properties Bureau, and on the other, the various government agencies. Both the royal household and the government elites, however, continued to use Chinese capital and expertise to achieve their own interests.

In the late 1960s, the industrial structure of Thailand began to change decisively. A new round of military coups beginning in 1957 kept the elites circulating at the top, making patronage a sometimes risky blessing. Now with sizable capital resources behind them, Chinese entrepreneurs became less willing to court political favors. Moreover, a coup in 1972 resulted in seizure of the financial assets of many major military figures, which in turn began the process of disentangling capital formation from political privilege.

These uncertainties in the political climate were matched by changes in East Asian economies. Rather quickly in the late 1960s and the 1970s, first Japan and then the Asian newly industrializing countries—South Korea, Taiwan, Hong Kong, and Singapore—became aggressively export oriented and created an economic sea change that would soon engulf the entire region. In 1960, only 1.2 percent of Thailand's exports were manufactured goods, but by the early 1970s, investments from Japanese as well as Western multinational corporations began to alter the structure of economic opportunities in the Thai economy.[53] By 1980, with 32.3 percent of its total exports consisting of manufactured goods, Thailand had become a cheap labor platform for firms operating out of Japan, Hong Kong, and Singapore. This trend accelerated in the 1980s, so that by 1988, 67.5 percent of Thailand's total exports were manufactured goods. By the 1990s, Thailand's economy had been totally restructured, moving from a politically bounded domestic economy to an open, export-oriented segment of the global economy.

The internationalization and industrialization of the Thai economy quickly changed the ownership networks linking firms. The largest change was the emergence of export-oriented sectors, particularly in large-scale manufacturing and agriculture. Firms in the manufacturing sector, including companies in automobile assembly (Siam Motors), textiles (Saha Union), and consumer goods (Sahapathanapibul), often grew out of joint ventures with producers in Japan or the United States, or out of contract buying by Western merchandisers. Many of these firms were part of large industrial conglomerates active in a number of areas. Capitalization of these enterprises typically required large amounts of money, as well as technical know-how, and big banks established during the previous economic period, such as Bangkok Bank and Thai Farmers Bank, quickly became leading lenders to the new industrialists. The banks also added industrial firms to their own holdings, but by and large they did not provide the entrepreneurial leadership for the internationalization of the Thai economy. This leadership, instead, was supplied by yet a new group of Chinese entrepreneurs.

Suehiro Akira's excellent study of the enterprise structure of the modern Thai economy provides the context in which to understand the new group of Chinese entrepreneurs. He shows that by the middle of the 1980s, virtually all of the largest firms in the most advanced sectors of the economy were "members of 'groups of companies' rather than large independent firms."[54] These business groups, which dominated all sectors of the economy, were, according to Suehiro, predominantly owned and controlled by the Chinese minority. In his examination of "over seventy leading 'Thai' business groups in the early 1980s," he found that "non–ethnic Chinese groups numbered only three." One of the three was the group of firms owned by the Crown Property Bureau, another was the group owned by the Military Bank, and the third, the Siam Vidhaya group, was owned by a Thai-Indian family. All the other business groups "belonged to naturalized or local-born Chinese, all of whom held Thai citizenship." Chinese-owned big businesses were divided into two main types—finance and banking and the new industrial groups. The bank-centered groups had all originated during the second period, in the 1940s and 1950s, but the industrial groups dated largely from the late 1960s and early 1970s.[55]

The newest Chinese business groups to emerge in Thailand, those of the industrialists, are groups that have taken advantage of Thailand's increasingly large pool of cheap, skilled labor to establish a wide range of export-related industries. As relative newcomers, the industrialists are not part of the traditional leadership of the old Thai-Chinese community. They have maintained closer contacts with the Chinese communities of Hong Kong, Singapore, the People's Republic of China, and Taiwan than have previous generations of Thai-Chinese. If they had any ties at all with the Thai governmental elite and the royalty, the connections tended, initially at least, to be weak. For those able to transform what were originally successful small businesses into large ones, the initial capital appears to have come from joint ventures and bank loans, but their rapid expansion has been funded through the development of a web of alliances among internationally oriented capitalists, usually from overseas Chinese communities. Among the most successful examples are the Charoen Pokphand group and the Sahapathanapibul group. Other examples include the automobile manufacturing enterprises of the Pornprapha family (Siam Motors) and the textile conglomerate Saha Union, as well as Japanese- and Singaporean-financed steel processing concerns. These operations are still dominated by their original rags-to-riches founders.

The new Chinese industrialists became a leading segment of a thoroughly reconstructed Chinese minority in Thailand. As late as the 1960s, Fred Riggs could refer to the Chinese as being "pariah entrepreneurs,"[56] but by the 1990s it was clear to Kevin Hewison that this concept was "increasingly . . . an unrealistic description of actuality."[57] As Kasian Tejapira points out in chapter 3 of this volume, the status of the Chinese has risen greatly in Thailand in recent years. Chinese-Thais are no longer a stigmatized minority, and they are reclaiming their ethnicity and reconstructing it to fit regional and global, instead of merely local, definitions.[58] By the 1990s, the Chinese in Thailand had joined the middle class, had grown powerful again in politics,[59] and had become one of several new forces, including the Thai Buddhist establishment, participating in the bourgeoisification of Thai society.[60]

EXAMPLE THREE: GLOBAL CAPITALISM AND THE
CHAROEN POKPHAND GROUP

In 1994, one of the largest foreign investors in the People's Republic of China was the Charoen Pokphand (CP) group, Thailand's largest transnational business group.[61] Although the younger of the two founding brothers (Chia Ek Chor, the elder, and Chia Seow Nooy) first migrated from Shantou (Swatow) in Guangdong province to Bangkok in 1917, the core firms of the group did not begin to grow rapidly until the early 1970s.[62] During the intervening years, the brothers ran a struggling seed business that in the 1950s began to specialize in supplying animal feed, especially for chickens. In the 1960s, the two developed a formula for combining chicken breeding with feed milling. To put their method into operation, they reached an agreement with Arbor Acres, a firm in the Rockefeller group. The formula proved so successful that by 1969 the company had an annual turnover of U.S. $1 to $2 million.

In about 1970, the entire business began to change rapidly as big banks finally grasped the potential for capitalist agriculture and food processing.[63] One turning point came when an American, fleeing the Vietnam war, started a chicken farm but then left Thailand owing the Bangkok Bank a large amount of money. The bank asked the Charoen Pokphand feed mill to take over the farm. The formula evolved whereby the CP group would loan Thai farmers money, teach them how to raise chickens, and even help them build buildings. They supplied chicks and feed to the farmers, who in turn sold the grown chickens back to the feed mill for marketing. The entire operation depended on the marketing end to sell the processed chickens to high-volume buyers—grocery stores, restaurants, and fast food franchises. In the early days, the CP group allocated each farmer 10,000 chickens, but in recent years the figure has been raised to 50,000.

The company grew quickly during the 1970s because the Central Bank of Thailand had a policy that a certain percentage of its loan portfolio had to go to the agricultural sector. The CP group was one of the safest players. Government banks would channel money into the agricultural sector by loaning money to farmers who agreed to engage in contract farming with the CP group.[64] CP would cosign the loan. What was safe for the banks and good for Thai farmers proved to be greatly advantageous for CP as well.

The CP group then began to grow rapidly by expanding the same business into other countries—first to Indonesia, then to Taiwan, the PRC, Turkey, Portugal, and the Philippines. In each case, the scenario was repeated: inte-grated feed mills, chicken breeding, contract farming, and the processing and marketing of poultry. The marketing end of the commodity chain drove the production end.

By the 1980s, because of its spectacular growth, CP began to receive a lot of attention, and many firms wanted to get into joint ventures with it. The group began to diversify from its original agricultural base. In 1982–83, in central Thailand, it began raising shrimp, using the same formula that had worked with chickens. In 1987, drawing on the founders' close connections in the PRC, the CP group opened manufacturing businesses in Shanghai, making motorcycles with a license from Honda and brewing beer with a license from Heineken. Also in 1987, CP received the 7–11 and Kentucky Fried Chicken franchises for Thailand and started the Makro retail stores (the original Price Club). In 1989, it entered the petrochemical business in a joint venture with Solvay, the giant Belgian firm. And in August 1992, CP signed a contract to build one of the world's largest privately owned public works projects—at the time, second only to the tunnel being built under the English Channel—the telecommunications infrastructure for Thailand, a project worth U.S. $3 billion. Even more recently, in 1994, it signed a joint venture agreement with Walmart to establish super-retail stores throughout East and Southeast Asia.

Despite their great diversity of business, all the firms in the CP group are run similarly. Each relies on networks among independent producers, independent investors, or both. Most of the manufacturing firms are based on joint ventures and subcontracting. Throughout most of the 1980s the CP group was decentralized by country, but in the late 1980s the family members in charge reorganized the group into nine functional units, all run from headquarters in Bangkok. The nine are the Seed, Agro Chemical, and Fertilizer Unit (started in 1921), the Agro Business (integrated feed and animal production, begun in 1951), the International Trading Unit (1980), the Aqua Business (shrimp farming, 1982–83), the Retail and Wholesale Businesses (1987), the Automotive Division (motorcycles, 1987), the Real Estate Unit (1989), Petrochemicals (1989), and Telecommunications (1992).

The group now relies heavily on professional managers. Family members maintain ardently that the group is not run as a family business, although most of the founders' thirteen sons and many other close relatives are or have been among its leading employees. The sons all have seats on the board of directors, and Dhanin and Sument Chiaravanont (sons of the elder brother, Ek Chor) make most of the major decisions. The other sons all own shares in the group, none of which is traded. Family business or not, the CP group is a creation of deal-making, the quintessential characteristic of the overseas Chinese entrepreneur, of which Dhanin Chiaravanont is one of the best-known examples.

CONCLUSION

The Chinese in Thailand have been economically successful for hundreds of years, through many political and economic transformations. Their success, however, cannot be explained strictly in terms of either local conditions or local historical situations. Nor can it be explained through a sociology of minority capitalism. Explanations of this kind must match the generality of the phenomena they attempt to explain.[65] The Chinese are economically successful throughout Southeast Asia, as well as in other locations around the world. Local histories, even a succession of local histories, cannot explain what is, after all, a general occurrence.

Moreover, Chinese business practices in situations where Chinese are in the minority are remarkably similar to those in situations where Chinese are in the majority.[66] A sociology of minority capitalism cannot explain Chinese economic success when their entrepreneurial strategies in locations such as

Hong Kong and Taiwan are similar, if not identical, to those they use in Southeast Asia and other locations where they are in the minority. And if accounts given of the entrepreneurial efforts of Chinese in the People's Republic of China are correct, it appears that the organizational strategies of Chinese entrepreneurs in China are the same as those elsewhere.[67]

Therefore, explanations for Chinese success in Thailand cannot simply be adduced from the details of Thai history, from the biographies of successful Chinese in Thailand, or from a sociology of Chinese minority status. Instead, the explanation requires a careful investigation of the phenomenon generally, and thus even a reasonable hypothesis lies beyond the scope of this chapter.[68]

Analysis of the Chinese in Thailand does, however, offer some theoretical insights into the economic transformations that have occurred in Thailand and into the roles the Chinese played in them. Analytically, and hence somewhat artificially, we can conceptualize the two as, first, an institutionalized context in which economic action occurs, and second, the entrepreneurial strategies themselves. We recognize, of course, that entrepreneurial strategies also influence the institutionalized structure, but it makes sense theoretically to distinguish the two in order to understand better how context and action fit together.

In this chapter we have argued that the structure of political authority interacts with historically developed configurations of economic activities to create an institutional context for economic action and organization. Royal patrimonialism, military factionalism, and regional and international politics have established the structured contexts that shape Chinese entrepreneurship. The Chinese developed entrepreneurial strategies that took advantage of the opportunities they discovered or created in a particular time and place. Tax farming, banking, and global manufacturing—these and other strategies reflect the context of Chinese involvement.

We suggest, however, that successful entrepreneurship in one context does not automatically transfer into another. Entrepreneurship is situational and therefore "path dependent." Successful entrepreneurship is always tied to actual situations of economic involvement. When the Chinese of one era seized upon a course of action, they tried to routinize it to make it more predictable and less risky. By creating a routinized approach to obtaining wealth, Chinese entrepreneurs embedded themselves in a set of political alliances, interdependent economic networks, and habitual economic practices. When the context altered, through either political or economic changes, the previous alliances, embedded networks, and economic practices made it difficult to adapt to new conditions. Old alliances often precluded new ones, established network ties undermined or at least channeled the ability to create new connections, and economic practices successful in one era became woefully out of date in the next. As a consequence, the Chinese who were the leading entrepreneurs at one time did not automatically carry that role forward into the next period.

The story of the Chinese in Thailand, then, is not one of economic or even ethnic continuity. Instead, it is a story of changes, of sudden transformations, of ethnic reconstructions, and of a succession of distinct groups of Chinese entrepreneurs. To tell the story of the Chinese in Thailand accurately is to tell the story of these discontinuities. The only constants have been the disproportionately high level of Chinese success and the extraordinary ability of new groups of immigrant Chinese to adapt to whatever situation they found. What it is about the Chinese that accounts for this success remains poorly explained.

NOTES

We wish to acknowledge the help of Charles Keyes and Tony Reid, who gave us comments on an earlier draft of this chapter, and especially Daniel Chirot, whose advice, encouragement, and careful editorial assistance greatly improved the final version.

1. Georg Simmel, *The Sociology of Georg Simmel,* translated and edited by Kurt H. Wolff (Glencoe, Illinois: Free Press, 1950), pp. 402–8.

2. Paul C. P. Siu, "The Sojourner," *American Journal of Sociology* 58 (July 1952), pp. 34–44.

3. Gary G. Hamilton, "Temporary Migration and the Institutionalization of Strategy," *International Journal of Intercultural Relations* 9 (1985), pp. 405–25; Roger Waldinger, Howard Aldrich, and Robin Ward, *Ethnic Entrepreneurs: Immigrant Business in Industrial Societies* (Newbury Park, California: Sage Publications, 1990).

4. Mark Granovetter, "Economic Action and Social Structure: The Problem of Embeddedness," *American Journal of Sociology* 91 (1985), pp. 481–510; Ivan Light, *Ethnic Enterprise in America* (Berkeley: University of California Press, 1972); Ivan Light and Edna Bonacich, *Immigrant Entrepreneurs: Koreans in Los Angeles, 1965–1982* (Berkeley: University of California Press, 1988); Waldinger, Aldrich, and Ward, *Ethnic Entrepreneurs.*

5. Waldinger, Aldrich, and Ward, *Ethnic Entrepreneurs.*

6. Edna Bonacich, "A Theory of Middleman Minorities," *American Sociological Review* 38 (1973), pp. 583–94.

7. Gary G. Hamilton, "Pariah Capitalism: A Paradox of Power and Depen-

dence," *Ethnic Groups: An International Periodical of Ethnic Studies* 2 (Spring 1978), pp. 1–15.

8. For example, Herman Kahn, *World Economic Development: 1979 and Beyond* (London: Croom Helm, 1979); Tai Hung-chao, *Confucianism and Economic Development: An Oriental Alternative?* (Washington, D.C.: Washington Institute Press, 1989).

9. Maurice Freedman, "The Handling of Money," *Man* 59 (1959), pp. 64–65.

10. Peter L. Berger and Hsin-Huang Michael Hsiao, eds., *In Search of an East Asian Development Model* (New Brunswick, New Jersey: Transaction Books, 1988).

11. The following discussion of the Chinese in Thailand draws freely on our companion paper, "Economic Organization and Chinese Business Networks in Thailand," in Edward K. Y. Chen and Peter Drysdale, eds., *Corporate Links and Direct Foreign Investment in Asia and Pacific* (Pymble, Australia: Harper Education Publishers, 1995), pp. 87–111. In this chapter, we emphasize the structural situation facing the Chinese and their response to it; in the companion paper we emphasize the economic consequences of Chinese entrepreneurship on the trajectory of economic development in Thailand.

12. Kenneth Perry Landon, *The Chinese in Thailand* (New York: Russell and Russell, 1941); Victor Purcell, *The Chinese in Southeast Asia* (London: Oxford University Press, 1965, 2d ed.). For a notable exception, see G. William Skinner, "Creolized Chinese Societies in Southeast Asia," in Anthony Reid, ed., *Strangers, Sojourners, and Settlers: Southeast Asia and the Chinese* (Sydney: Allen & Unwin, 1994).

13. Max Weber's *Economy and Society* (Berkeley: University of California Press, 1978) contains what is still the best general and comparative treatment of patrimonial regimes.

14. Lysa Hong, *Thailand in the Nineteenth Century: Evolution of the Economy and Society* (Singapore: Institute of Southeast Asian Studies, 1984), pp. 9–37; Rabibhadana Akin, "Clientship and Class Structure in the Early Bangkok Period," in G. William Skinner and A. Thomas Kirsch, eds., *Change and Persistence in Thai Society* (Ithaca, New York: Cornell University Press, 1969), pp. 93–124; Kevin Hewison, "Of Regimes, State and Pluralities: Thai Politics Enters the 1990s," in Kevin Hewison, Richard Robison, and Garry Rodan, eds., *Southeast Asia in the 1990s: Authoritarianism, Democracy, and Capitalism* (St. Leonards, Australia: Allen & Unwin, 1993), pp. 161–89.

15. Hong, *Thailand in the Nineteenth Century*, pp. 38–74.

16. Lewis Coser, "The Alien as a Servant of Power: Court Jews and Christian Renegades," *American Journal of Sociology* 37 (1972), pp. 574–80; Shmuel N. Eisenstadt, *The Political Systems of Empires* (New York: Free Press, 1963). More generally, Max Weber's *Economy and Society* (Berkeley: University of California Press, 1968) treats patrimonial regimes throughout history.

17. G. William Skinner, *Chinese Society in Thailand* (Ithaca, New York: Cornell

University Press, 1957); Viraphol Sarasin, *Tribute and Profit: Sino-Siamese Trade 1652–1853* (Cambridge, Massachusetts: Council on East Asian Studies, Harvard University, 1977); Hong, *Thailand in the Nineteenth Century.*

18. Skinner, *Chinese Society in Thailand*, pp. 24, 26.

19. Sarasin, *Tribute and Profit.*

20. Skinner, *Chinese Society in Thailand*, pp. 80–90.

21. David Wyatt, *The Politics of Reform in Thailand: Education in the Reign of King Chulalongkorn* (New Haven, Connecticut: Yale University Press, 1969).

22. Skinner, *Chinese Society in Thailand.*

23. Hong, *Thailand in the Nineteenth Century*, pp. 111–33.

24. Suehiro Akira, *Capital Accumulation in Thailand, 1855–1985* (Tokyo: Centre for East Asian Cultural Studies, 1989).

25. Suehiro, *Capital Accumulation*, p. 93.

26. Cited in Landon, *The Chinese in Thailand*, pp. 34–43.

27. Jennifer Cushman, "The Khaw Group: Chinese Business in Early Twentieth-Century Penang," *Journal of Southeast Asian Studies* 17:1 (March 1986), pp. 58–79. The quote is on page 58. More generally, see Jennifer Cushman, *Family and State: The Formation of a Sino-Thai Tin-Mining Dynasty, 1797–1932* (Oxford: Oxford University Press, 1991).

28. Cushman, "The Khaw Group," p. 64.

29. Suehiro, *Capital Accumulation*, pp. 64–65.

30. Cushman, *Family and State.*

31. Cushman, *Family and State* and "The Khaw Group."

32. Suehiro, *Capital Accumulation*, pp. 89–90.

33. Skinner, *Chinese Society in Thailand*, pp. 102–109.

34. Lawrence Crissman, "The Segmentary Structure of Urban Overseas Chinese Communities," *Man* 2:2 (1967), pp. 185–204; Edgar Wickberg, "Overseas Chinese Adaptive Organizations, Past and Present," in Ronald Skelton, ed., *Reluctant Exiles* (Armonk, New York: M. E. Sharpe, 1994).

35. Skinner, *Chinese Society in Thailand*, pp. 203–207.

36. G. William Skinner, *Leadership and Community in the Chinese Community in Thailand* (Ithaca, New York: Cornell University Press, 1958).

37. Landon, *The Chinese in Thailand.*

38. Gerald Fry, "Thailand's Political Economy: Change and Persistence," in Cal Clark and Steve Chan, eds., *The Evolving Pacific Basin in the Global Political Economy: Domestic and International Linkages* (Boulder, Colorado: Lynne Rienner, 1992), pp. 83–105.

39. Kevin Hewison, *Bankers and Bureaucrats: Capital and the Role of the State in Thailand* (New Haven, Connecticut: Monograph Series 34, Center for International and Area Studies, Yale University, 1989), pp. 76–91.

40. Fred Riggs, *Thailand: The Modernization of a Bureaucratic Polity* (Honolulu: East-West Center, 1967), pp. 242–310.

41. Skinner, *Leadership and Community.*

42. Christopher Baker, "Economic Reorganization and the Slump in South and Southeast Asia," *Comparative Studies in Society and History* 23 (1981), pp. 325–49.

43. Suehiro, *Capital Accumulation,* p. 110.

44. Skinner, *Chinese Society in Thailand;* Skinner, *Leadership and Community;* G. William Skinner, "Overseas Chinese Leadership: Paradigm for a Paradox," in Gehan Wijeyewardene, ed., *Leadership and Authority: A Symposium* (Singapore: University of Malaysia Press, 1968), pp. 191–207.

45. Gary Gereffi and Donald Wyman, eds., *Manufacturing Miracles: Paths of Industrialization in Latin America and East Asia* (Princeton, New Jersey: Princeton University Press, 1990); Hewison, *Bankers and Bureaucrats.*

46. Riggs, *Thailand;* Suehiro, *Capital Accumulation,* pp. 122–34.

47. *Million Baht Business Information* (Bangkok, 1989).

48. Hewison, *Bankers and Bureaucrats,* pp. 192–205.

49. Skinner, *Leadership and Community,* pp. 99–100.

50. Suehiro, *Capital Accumulation,* p. 247.

51. Chin carefully groomed his sons to take over the family businesses. The second son, Chatri (b. 1934), inherited his father's position at the Bangkok Bank and is one of the most prominent businessmen in Thailand today. Unlike other major Thai business figures, he was educated in Swatow and Hong Kong. His younger brothers and sister were educated in a combination of elite Thai schools, Australian elementary schools, and British and American universities, where they studied economics, engineering, and science. In 1986, three of Chatri's sons had positions on the Bangkok Bank board of directors, a fourth (Chai) was director of Bangkok First Investment and Trust, and a fifth (Cherdchu) was a major figure in Bangkok First Investment and Trust, as well as a director for Asia Insurance (Hong Kong).

52. Malcolm Falkus, "The Economic History of Thailand," *Australian Economic History Review* 21 (March 1991), pp. 53–71.

53. Tambunlertchai Somsak and Suthiphand Chirathivat, "Management of Thailand's International Economic and Trade Relations," in Suchart Prasithrathsint, ed., *Thailand on the Move: Stumbling Blocks and Breakthroughs* (Bangkok: Thai University Research Association, 1990), pp. 189–232. See also Akrasanee Narongchai, Karel Jansen, and Jeerasak Pongpisanupichit, *International Capital Flows and Economic Adjustment in Thailand* (Bangkok: Thailand Development Research Institute, Research Monograph 10, 1993).

54. Suehiro, *Capital Accumulation,* pp. 218–19.

55. Suehiro, *Capital Accumulation,* p. 9.

56. Riggs, *Thailand.*

57. Hewison, "Of Regimes, State and Pluralities," p. 177.

58. Chee Kiong Tong, "Centripetal Authority, Differentiated Networks: The Social Organization of Chinese Firms in Singapore," in Gary Hamilton, ed., *Business Networks and Economic Development in East and Southeast Asia* (Hong Kong: Centre of Asian Studies, University of Hong Kong, 1991).

59. Hewison, "Of Regimes, State and Pluralities."

60. Charles F. Keyes, "Buddhist Economics and Buddhist Fundamentalism in Burma and Thailand," in Martin E. Marty and R. Scott Appleby, eds., *Fundamentalism and the State: Remaking Polities, Economies, and Militance* (Chicago: University of Chicago Press, 1993), pp. 367–409.

61. This history of the Charoen Pokphand group is based on interviews with several sons of Chia Seow Nooy.

62. Around 1965 the family took Thai names, because there was some prejudice among Thai officials at the time and family members judged that it was safer to do so. Chiaravanont is a Thai version of the Chinese family name.

63. Manarungsan Sompop and Suwanjindar Suebskun, "Contract Farming and Outgrower Schemes in Thailand," in David Glover and Lim Teck Ghee, eds., *Contract Farming in Southeast Asia* (Kuala Lumpur: Institute for Advanced Studies, University of Malaysia, 1992), pp. 10–70.

64. Glover and Ghee, *Contract Farming in Southeast Asia.*

65. William H. Sewell, "Marc Bloch and the Logic of Comparative History," *History and Theory* 6 (1967), pp. 208–18.

66. S. C. Redding, *The Spirit of Chinese Capitalism* (Berlin: Walter de Gruyter, 1990); Gary G. Hamilton, ed., *Asian Business Networks* (Berlin: Walter de Gruyter, 1994).

67. There is now a growing literature on Chinese entrepreneurship in a wide variety of social and political settings that proves this. See, for example, Siu-lun Wong, "The Chinese Family Firm: A Model," *British Journal of Sociology* 36 (1985), pp. 58–72; Siu-lun Wong, "The Applicability of Asian Family Values to Other Sociocultural Settings," in Peter Berger and Michael Hsiao, eds., *In Search of an East Asian Development Model* (New Brunswick, New Jersey: Transaction Books, 1988); and Siu-lun Wong, *Emigrant Entrepreneurs: Shanghai Industrialists in Hong Kong* (Hong Kong: Oxford University Press, 1988). On Taiwan, see Susan Greenhalgh, "Families and Networks in Taiwan's Economic Development," in Edwin A. Winckler and Susan Greenhalgh, eds., *Contending Approaches to the Political Economy of Taiwan* (Armonk, New York: M. E. Sharpe, 1988), pp. 224–48; Gary G. Hamilton and Nicole Woolsey Biggart, "Market, Culture, and Authority: A Comparative Analysis of Management and Organization in the Far East," *American Journal of Sociology* 94 (Supplement, 1988), pp. S52–S94; and Gary G. Hamilton and Cheng-shu Kao, "The Institutional Foundations of Chinese Business: The Family Firm in Taiwan," *Comparative Social*

Research 12 (1990), pp. 95–112. On Southeast Asia, see Redding, *The Spirit of Chinese Capitalism;* Eddie C. Y. Kuo, "Ethnicity, Polity, and Economy: A Case Study of the Mandarin Trade and the Chinese Connection," in Hamilton, *Business Networks,* pp. 155–75; and Tong, "Centripetal Authority." On the People's Republic of China, see Ezra F. Vogel, *One Step Ahead in China: Guangdong under Reform* (Cambridge, Massachusetts: Harvard University Press, 1989); Victor Nee, "Organizational Dynamics of Market Transition: Hybrid Forms, Property Rights, and Mixed Economy in China," *Administrative Science Quarterly* 37 (1992), pp. 1–27; and Victor Nee and Frank W. Young, "Peasant Entrepreneurs in China's 'Second Economy': An Institutional Analysis," *Economic Development and Cultural Change* 39 (1991), pp. 293–310.

68. For an attempt at a more general answer, see Gary G. Hamilton, "Overseas Chinese Capitalism," in Tu Wei-ming, ed., *Confucian Traditions in East Asian Modernity* (Cambridge, Massachusetts: Harvard University Press, 1996), pp. 328–42.

11 / Strengths and Weaknesses of Minority Status for Southeast Asian Chinese at a Time of Economic Growth and Liberalization

LINDA Y. C. LIM AND L. A. PETER GOSLING

Southeast Asia is distinguished from other ethnically diverse, economically developing regions by the coincidence of extreme ethnic and religious diversity with relative interethnic peace and rapid economic growth over three decades.[1] Stability and prosperity have been achieved, even though small minorities of ethnic Chinese dominate the region's private-sector economies while once-colonized indigenous majorities control the modern nation-state.[2]

In this essay we seek to analyze, in a comparative regional context, the complex interplay between economic growth, ethnicity, and national policy in determining the state of interethnic relations between the entrepreneurial minority and the majority populations. The central question we address is the extent to which the particular character of Southeast Asia's contemporary economic growth is likely to assuage or aggravate ethnic tensions.

In theory, economic growth improves ethnic relations because it removes the tensions caused by potential interethnic competition over scarce resources, jobs, and business opportunities. The growth in absolute shares of an expanding economic pie reduces concern over relative shares. This is, arguably, what has happened in Southeast Asia, where sustained economic prosperity has minimized the economic basis for interethnic rivalry. Ethnic conflict has been most entrenched in Myanmar, with its poor record of economic growth, whereas Malaysia—with potentially the most volatile ethnic mix, resulting from a colonial-era ethnic division of labor—has not exploded in ethnic violence because economic growth, aided by state policy, has delivered material benefits to all groups.[3] In southern Thailand, a Malay-based ethnic separatist movement disintegrated as Thailand's economic growth accelerated in the 1980s, whereas the similar Moro nationalist movement in the southern Philippines has persisted in part because of a weaker national economy.

285

But economic growth also has the potential to undermine ethnic harmony: first, if the growth is unevenly distributed across ethnic groups, or if it is predicated on or generates occupational or class distinctions that correlate with particular ethnic groups; second, if economic success leads to the enhancement of ethnic identity and a resurgence of ethnic pride among ascendant groups, which others resent; and third, if economic growth increases interethnic contact between previously segregated ethnic groups, giving rise to more opportunity for ethnic friction. All of these developments have also occurred in Southeast Asia as part of its recent rapid economic growth, which has enhanced the historically dominant role of ethnic Chinese in the business sector.[4]

To the local Chinese business families domiciled in the region for generations have been added, since the late 1980s, foreign Chinese investors from Hong Kong, Taiwan, and Singapore. Growing intraregional flows of goods, capital, and labor increasingly involve interethnic exchanges, occurring as they do within the larger geographical context of Asia-wide rapid economic growth, including the spectacular rise of the People's Republic of China (PRC).[5] And it is not only overseas Chinese capital and capitalists who have been flooding into Southeast Asia, but also overseas and PRC Chinese tourists and PRC Chinese labor. Even PRC businesses are starting to trickle in.

The increasingly visible Chinese dominance of Southeast Asia's modern economic life, interwoven as it is with cultural and political divisions, could indeed exacerbate underlying ethnic tensions, despite the counteracting effects of economic growth.

THE EVOLVING CHINESE ECONOMIC ROLE IN SOUTHEAST ASIA

Chinese immigrants and their descendants have played a disproportionate role in the commercial life of Southeast Asia since (and even before) the European colonial era.[6] In the postcolonial era, nationalistic indigenous governments acted to curtail the economic role of Chinese and foreign enterprises and to promote indigenous commercial activity.[7] Restrictive licenses, protective tariffs, ownership limitations, preferential credit allocations, and outright bans on Chinese commercial activity in particular sectors were typical policies. This discriminatory infrastructure elicited a range of adaptive responses from the Chinese, including so-called Ali-Baba ventures with indigenous "sleeping partners" in whose names enterprises were registered, direct and indirect payments to local and national government officials to circumvent restrictions or secure protection, and cultivation of powerful indigenous political patrons and sponsors, particularly where there were ruling military regimes.[8]

Through these and other means, Southeast Asian Chinese businesses succeeded in maintaining the bulk of their operations intact, thereby retaining their dominance of the local private sector. In many cases, they even emerged as the main beneficiaries of nationalist restrictions on foreign-owned enterprises, since these restrictions limited the competition they faced in domestic markets. When foreign enterprises were "localized" in response to national ownership requirements, Chinese were often the only established private-sector parties with the capital and expertise to acquire and operate them. When import-substituting industrialization programs were launched, local ownership requirements helped Chinese acquire foreign technology, because foreign investors often turned to them as the only local partners with the requisite capital and connections. Further "local content" requirements in industries such as automobiles also created new business opportunities for local Chinese enterprises.

Because the ASEAN (Association of South East Asian Nations) governments were anticommunist and ideologically committed to private enterprise and capitalism (albeit often with an equally strong commitment to state enterprise in key sectors), they were limited in their ability and willingness to completely disenfranchise the Chinese, who constituted the main private-enterprise actors in the local modern sector.[9] Chinese control of distribution networks ensured that disenfranchisement would severely disrupt the economic growth to which postcolonial nationalist governments were committed, partly as a component of their strategy for fighting communism. The authoritarian, even military, nature of most of these governments protected Chinese business interests by keeping in check any potential grassroots disaffection. The governments themselves were easily paid off for their tacit support of Chinese economic interests. Continued local Chinese investment and reinvestment in their Southeast Asian home economies also propelled economic growth.

In the 1980s, the ASEAN economies embarked on structural adjustment and liberal market-oriented economic reform programs involving trade and investment liberalization, financial reforms, deregulation, and privatization of state-owned enterprises. Such policies—including fiscal and monetary restraint and reduced protection from foreign competition—hurt the local private sector by increasing its costs, reducing subsidies, and increasing competition. These policies, arguably, were more readily effected in Southeast Asia than in other developing countries because the politically weak (or at least politically dependent) Chinese-dominated local private sector could not and did not resist them. Ethnic distinctions rendered the Southeast Asian state sufficiently "autonomous" from local capital that it could effect necessary policies which hurt business without encountering serious resistance. The persistence of an ethnic division of labor may thus be considered to have been conducive to the enactment of macroeconomic policies required for sustained economic growth.

These policies may indeed have inflicted temporary pain on the Chinese-dominated private sector. But it is equally arguable that in the longer run the Chinese have benefited disproportionately, since they are the best endowed and most competitive members of the private sector and thus are best placed to take advantage of new market opportunities created by economic liberalization, including opportunities for the establishment of joint ventures with new foreign investors. Chinese enterprises, especially the larger ones, are also better insulated than indigenous enterprises against the tight money policies, credit rationing, and high interest rates characteristic of macroeconomic stabilization policies. This is because they have disproportionate access to alternative sources of (often, ethnic Chinese) capital abroad, to informal ethnic-based credit networks at home, to internal financing in Chinese conglomerates (many of which own their own banks), and to preferred customer status among other local banks (most of which are Chinese owned).

Investment liberalization permitted a huge influx of overseas Chinese capital and enterprise into Southeast Asia in the late 1980s, responding to currency realignment, labor shortages, and capital surpluses in the source economies of Taiwan, Hong Kong, and Singapore. This capital influx accelerated economic growth, particularly in labor-intensive, export-oriented manufacturing industries. It also increased the ethnic Chinese share of the booming private sector and linked the Southeast Asian economies closer to those of the ethnic Chinese homelands of their new foreign investors.[10]

At the same time, China's spectacular market-based economic growth has attracted profit-seeking and sentimentally motivated investments from overseas Chinese businesses in Southeast Asia. For example, the Charoen Pokphand (CP) group of Thailand is reported to be the largest single foreign investor in China, and many Indonesian and Filipino Chinese conglomerates are investing heavily in their founders' home provinces in China, most notably Fujian.[11] The prime ministers of Singapore, Malaysia, and Thailand and the president of the Philippines all led large delegations of mostly ethnic Chinese businesspeople to China in 1993. China itself is becoming a major growth market for Southeast Asian commodity and manufactured exports, while competing with the region both for international (including overseas

Chinese) investments and in world export markets. Some Chinese enterprises are starting to invest in Southeast Asia, and all countries in the region are increasingly concerned about burgeoning flows of illegal Chinese foreign labor.

In short, rapid regionwide economic growth has turned Southeast Asia into a "South China Sea" of ethnic Chinese capital and labor movements, greatly increasing the visibility and the actual presence of both foreign and local Chinese in regional economies. As the ASEAN countries move toward closer regional economic integration through the newly established ASEAN Free Trade Area (AFTA), and as they accord a greater role to the private sector both domestically and in the process of regional integration, cross-national links between ethnic Chinese businesses in the region are likely to increase further.[12] It remains for us to consider what impact this Chinese economic role has had and is likely to have on ethnic relations in Southeast Asia.

THE IMPACT ON ETHNIC RELATIONS

In traditional Southeast Asian culture and society, profit-seeking trade (as opposed to barter or exchange for use) was regarded as an activity involving tension between buyer and seller and therefore connoting high social cost. It was thus best undertaken by "outsiders," persons not intimately involved in the social fabric of a particular village society.[13] Throughout the region, trade beyond the simplest level of local exchange (conducted primarily by peasant women and often "disguised" as a social activity) tended to be the terrain of alien groups, including migrants from elsewhere in Southeast Asia. The Chinese are only the most recent, most widespread, and most successful of these ubiquitous "middleman minorities"—originally tolerated as simply one more variant of an established and socially accepted pattern. Social tension generated by trade, which could be internally disruptive in cohesive village societies and cultures that traditionally avoided confrontation, could be dissipated by being turned into ethnic tension directed against "outsiders."

But this ethnic tension, in turn, was held in check by factors including cultural predispositions against violence, the recognized, if also resented, social service provided by the trader, and, later, the power and protection of European colonial authorities. The Europeans not only sanctioned but also encouraged the spreading commercial activities of Chinese middlemen, because they fulfilled a necessary role as intermediaries in the colonial export economy and, being a numerically small group of aliens, did not pose a potential political threat to European colonial rule. In the immediate postcolonial era, resentments against Chinese traders did occasionally erupt into violence, particularly in Indonesia, but it was rarely long-lasting or generalized throughout individual countries or the region as a whole. Military protection and patronage became a factor in the survival and prosperity of Chinese business.

At the same time, the Chinese themselves adopted a partly coerced, partly voluntary strategy of overt assimilation, which earned them a degree of tolerance in host societies historically used to the accommodation of diverse ethnic groups. This assimilation involved the diminution of ethnic Chinese characteristics and expressions such as language, names, the public practice of Chinese religion and culture, and even personal behavior. Southeast Asian Chinese in Thailand, Indonesia, and the Philippines took pains to assimilate local cultural characteristics and norms of behavior, publicly displaying their commitment to their countries of domicile by becoming outwardly more "Thai" or "Indonesian" than "Chinese."[14]

Part of this process occurred naturally through long residence, which included birth, upbringing, and education in the local host society and, especially after the communist takeover of China in 1949, distance and prolonged separation from the "mother country." Intermarriage played a role wherever religion was no barrier, as was the case in Thailand and the Philippines but not in Muslim Malaysia and Indonesia. Many Southeast Asian governments also forbade the learning or use of the Chinese language and of Chinese names, which forcibly accelerated the pace of cultural assimilation. Other than in Chinese-dominated Singapore, the least assimilation occurred in Malaysia, because of its proportionately large Chinese population, the presence of another significant though smaller alien minority, the Indians, and a national philosophy of multiracialism in a largely immigrant population.

Thus, traditional practice, government policy, and voluntary assimilation as a strategy of ethnic accommodation all combined with continuous economic growth to ensure relative interethnic peace and stable ethnic relations in postcolonial Southeast Asia.

But this situation has changed to some degree with the heightened economic presence and cultural profile of both foreign and local Chinese in the region since the late 1980s. Further, state policies throughout the region have encouraged these changes. Governments eager to attract foreign investment not only liberalized investment rules, bringing an influx of foreign Chinese investors, but also relaxed domestic restrictions on expressions of Chinese culture. In Indonesia, a twenty-five-year-old ban on the importation and use of written Chinese characters has been lifted, and Chinese language schools are now allowed to operate. In Malaysia, Chinese cultural activities such as lion dance performances, once a red flag signaling ethnic chauvinism and a refusal to assimilate, have blossomed, and Chinese schools and community groups have been the beneficiaries of donations from Taiwan investors. The Malaysian government has relaxed permanent residence requirements for ethnic Chinese, extending eligibility to Taiwan investors and their families. In Thailand, the willingness of Sino-Thais and Chinese to acknowledge their ethnic identity has increased, as have the use of Chinese languages, the number of Chinese language schools, and public celebrations of Chinese festivals such as the Chinese New Year. Even in Indonesia, the most restrictive country, public celebrations of Chinese New Year were permitted for the first time in 1993.

In short, after decades of adapting their ethnicity to local political requirements and cultural norms—practicing "situational ethnicity"—the hitherto bicultural Chinese of Southeast Asia are suddenly reverting to open expressions of their original Sinic culture and flaunting rather than hiding their commercial success. It is now not only socially acceptable but even socially and certainly economically desirable to be Chinese.[15] The ascent to power of democratically elected ethnic Chinese political leaders such as President Aquino of the Philippines, who, while president, made a highly publicized visit to her family's ancestral village in China's Fujian province, and Prime Minister Chuan Leekpai of Thailand appears to set the official seal of approval on overt Chinese ethnic identity.

At the same time, the establishment of official relations with China—once isolated from its Southeast Asian neighbors—has led to vastly expanded trade and investment links, mainly mediated by locally domiciled Chinese firms, and to greatly increased travel by Southeast Asian Chinese to China. Increasingly affluent Chinese from Taiwan, Hong Kong, Singapore, Malaysia, and China have become the largest group of tourists in Southeast Asia. Even Vietnam and Myanmar receive a few hundred thousand tourists from neighboring southern Chinese provinces every year. Approximately the same number of illegal Chinese migrant workers are believed to be in Thailand, with smaller but increasing numbers in Malaysia and the Philippines.[16] Thus, Chinese visibility, customer and employer contact, and even labor-market competition with indigenous ethnic groups have increased.

The continued rise of China as a world political and economic power increases both the prestige and the value of being Chinese.[17] Historically, in the precolonial era, China was acknowledged as an "overlord" by many of the smaller states of Southeast Asia; in the postcolonial era it provided material and moral support to pro-China and often ethnic-Chinese–dominated communist insurgency movements in the region. This support was dropped in the 1980s, effectively killing these movements, as China sought to become economically involved with the successful capitalist countries of Southeast Asia, transforming itself from a security threat into an economic partner.

So far, the increased economic presence and cultural profile of both foreign and local ethnic Chinese in Southeast Asia does not appear to pose a threat to continued harmonious ethnic relations with the indigenous populations. In a region accustomed and committed to economic growth, the Chinese are seen as bringers of prosperity rather than as competitors for scarce resources. But this does not mean that there are no underlying or potential sources of ethnic tension. There is, first, understandable jealousy and resentment of an alien ethnic minority seen to benefit disproportionately from economic growth. There is a perception that an increasingly unequal class structure correlates with ethnicity. This resentment is exacerbated when increased Chinese wealth is accompanied by conspicuous consumption and the "flaunting" of Chinese ethnic pride, and when there is the perception that the Chinese have not always "played fair" in their economic ascendancy, particularly when they have resorted to corrupt practices and political influence to advance their business interests. As political liberalization and pressures for greater democracy increase in Southeast Asia, the willingness of Chinese businesses to ally with and support corrupt authoritarian regimes becomes both better known and less tolerable to the general population.

A second source of potential ethnic tension generated by Chinese-led economic growth in Southeast Asia is the perception of diminished "loyalty" on the part of local Chinese to their countries of domicile and their correspondingly greater attachment to pan-Asian Chinese economic interests and ethnic identity. In the Philippines, many Chinese-Filipino big business families have been criticized for establishing dual residency in Taiwan and the Philippines. In Indonesia, there are grumblings about the large outward investments that Chinese-Indonesian business groups are making in China, out of the proceeds of their often privileged Indonesian ventures, and at a time when Indonesia itself expects to face a shortage of capital. The resentment is greater when these outward investments are seen to fuel China's competitiveness with Southeast Asia, especially in labor-intensive manufactured exports to the world market, a sector in which the two already compete for capital and technology, including that from overseas Chinese sources. Southeast Asian investments in China are a consequence partly of domestic financial liberalization, partly of the business diversification strategies of Southeast Asian Chinese enterprises, partly of China's attraction as a competitive and profitable investment location, and partly of sentiment for the motherland, especially the home provinces of the investors.

But Southeast Asian Chinese enterprises also invest in neighboring countries, including both the ASEAN and the socialist countries, especially Vietnam.[18] The push of the ASEAN private sector for a regional free trade area and for regional investment projects can be seen as an initiative of ethnic Chinese business leaders, who are the most able to compete outside of their home countries without government protection but with the assistance of their considerable ethnic business networks.[19] Both these outward investments by Southeast Asian Chinese businesses and the increased dependence of Southeast Asian economies on inward investments from foreign-domiciled overseas Chinese businesses reduce the capacity of Southeast Asian governments to control Chinese economic activity in their own territories.

Besides complaints about the outflow of Chinese capital, there have been complaints about an influx of Chinese labor, particularly in Thailand and the Philippines, where there are tens if not hundreds of thousands of illegal migrant workers from the PRC, most of whom are likely to be employed in small, Chinese-owned enterprises. Local workers resent the competition and the resulting downward pressure on their wages. A small but growing cadre of PRC skilled and professional workers is also emerging in the region, but generally not to an enthusiastic welcome by local fellow-workers, even in Singapore.[20]

A third and related factor that could lead to heightened ethnic tension in Southeast Asia's increasingly Chinese-led growth economy relates to the uncertain role of China in the region. In the post–cold war world, China is emerging as an increasingly assertive and potentially belligerent regional power, staking territorial claims to islands in the South China Sea, far from its shores, and rapidly building up its military capabilities in ways that potentially threaten its Southeast Asian neighbors. China already competes with Southeast Asia for international, and especially overseas Chinese, capital and technology and in world export markets. It clearly sees the extensive networks of capital-rich overseas Chinese businesses as part of its strategy for achieving not only domestic development but also international economic power.[21]

China's own economic participation in Southeast Asia is increasing through expanding two-way trade, direct investments, and multicountry joint regional development projects, such as the "Golden Quadrangle" and Mekong River projects, with mainland Southeast Asian states. Such economic relations are likely to presage greater political and cultural influence, especially when military links are also involved, as in the case of Myanmar, which is reportedly being "taken over by China" to the discomfiture of its neighbors and its own leaders.[22] Insofar as Southeast Asian countries feel threatened by China, they will feel threatened by its increasing links with and potential patronage of locally domiciled Chinese. Competition between the PRC and Taiwan for the allegiance of Southeast Asian Chinese can also, on occasion, affect domestic politics and policies in the region.[23]

Linked to all these factors is the changing cultural behavior of Southeast Asian Chinese themselves. To the extent that adaptiveness and assimilation to indigenous Southeast Asian cultures contributed to the social acceptability of the Chinese minority and tolerance of its dominant business activities in the past, any reversion to explicitly Sinic cultural patterns as a result of recent Chinese-led economic growth could pose a threat to the continuation of this ethnic tolerance. Increased ethnic pride and expression based on economic supremacy could lead to chauvinism on the part of the Chinese themselves, while highlighting their separateness from local communities. This could induce anti-Chinese resentment on the part of the indigenous populations. As one observer put it:

> The transformation of China, the achievements of the newly industrializing economies of East Asia and the growth of intra-Pacific trade and investment, in which the overseas Chinese are key players, are all working together to reduce incentives for the Chinese to assimilate in Southeast Asian societies.
>
> They are also encouraging the Chinese minorities to identify more closely with China. Although profitable in the short run, this is a very dangerous trend for the Chinese in Southeast Asia, where an obsession with profit is matched only by insensitivity towards the feelings of their host nations.
>
> The economic success of China and the overseas Chinese in exploiting regional and international links that are beyond the reach of many indigenous businessmen is breeding an arrogance—and a countervailing force of ethnic nationalism—that the Chinese may live to regret.[24]

Even Lee Kuan Yew, Singapore's former prime minister and a vocal advocate for China and expanded overseas Chinese links with China, has warned that such links could adversely affect race relations in the ASEAN countries, and he has cautioned ethnic Chinese businessmen from the region to "be sensitive" to indigenous feelings on this issue. Speaking in Hong Kong to a gathering of Chinese entrepreneurs from around the world in 1993, he said:

> We are all ethnic Chinese. We share certain characteristics through a common ancestry and culture. We can build up trust and rapport more easily between

ourselves. But we must be honest and recognize the fact that at the end of the day, our fundamental loyalties are to our home country, not to our ancestral country.[25]

How does this interplay of domestic and regional, economic, political, and cultural factors affect ethnic relations between the Chinese minority and indigenous majorities in particular ASEAN nations? We turn now to the contemporary peculiarities of the individual national situations, focusing especially on the likely impact on interethnic relations of ongoing political and economic liberalization.

THAILAND

Economic liberalization naturally favors private business while reducing the role and influence of bureaucrats and the state. In Thailand, the rapid, export-oriented growth of the economy since the 1980s, led by the private sector, has greatly increased the wealth and relative power of the urban-based, Sino-Thai–dominated business community while limiting that of the rural-based, Thai-dominated military and provincial bureaucracy. Local and sector-specific business associations—mostly dominated by ethnic Chinese but motivated by business rather than ethnic concerns—have played an important role in influencing government economic policy during this period.[26]

Political democratization has accentuated the trend. The Chatichai Choonhavan government elected in 1988 gave top priority to business-led economic growth, and the antimilitary "pro-democracy movement" of 1992 was essentially based in Bangkok (a disproportionately Sino-Thai city) and led by educated middle-class youths, including many from the business community. Both groups are also disproportionately Sino-Thai.

Electoral politics, too, have led, arguably, to the growth of "money politics," because funds are important for the establishment and maintenance of political parties and the mounting of political campaigns. Most Thai parties must therefore have backers from the business community. Even in provincial cities, political influence is increasingly wielded not by government officials but by local businesspeople, who tend to be of ethnic Chinese origin.[27] Economic influence at the top of the political pyramid thus compensates for the limited influence that Sino-Thais can exert on national polls, given their small proportion (10 percent) of the electorate.[28]

The coincidence of increased political and economic influence for a small ethnic minority might be expected to generate some ethnic tension. Furthermore, this shift in the domestic balance of power is occurring within a larger regional context in which nearby China is flexing its enhanced economic and military muscles, in which Sino-Thai business families are making huge, high-profile investments in developing China's economy, which competes with Thailand's, in which large inflows of overseas Chinese (especially Taiwan) capital have now slowed because of this competition, and in which inflows into Thailand of illegal PRC migrant labor have increased. These developments might be expected to cause at least some indigenous Thais to resent the disproportionate benefit the Sino-Thai business community has derived from economic growth, to doubt the "loyalty" to Thailand of some in this community, to chafe at the potential costs to Thai workers of China's competitive economic growth and illegal migrant streams, and, especially in the case of the conservative, anticommunist Thai military, to fear China as a potential security threat.

That ethnic tension based on such sentiments does not appear to have developed yet in Thailand reflects the influence of several factors. First, despite unequal distribution, the sustained, very rapid rate of growth of the Thai economy has led to some "trickle-down" diffusion of prosperity, even to rural areas, which might tend to diffuse ethnic-based tensions. Second, the relatively high rate of cultural and biological "assimilation" of ethnic Chinese to the Thai population obscures the distinction between Thai and Sino-Thai, dampens awareness of the latter's disproportionate economic power, and wins Thai acceptance of Sino-Thais as fellow nationals whose economic power is not resented the way that of "aliens" might be.

Third, there is no organized opposition to the business ascendancy of Sino-Thais on either ethnic or class grounds. On the political "left," this is because of the demise of communist-led or communist-leaning grassroots protest movements such as the worker-farmer-student coalitions of the 1970s. On the political "right," the Thai military has been weakened by both economic and political reform and by its cooptation by segments of the Chinese business community. Indeed, the military itself might become increasingly dependent on Chinese business for financial support, because of declines in government budget allocations and in U.S. military aid following the end of the cold war and the establishment of peace in Indochina.

Heightened ethnic tension and anti-Chinese sentiment are likely to result only if these three conditions change—if economic growth and its trickle-down slow dramatically, if there is a reversal in the process of Chinese cultural assimilation toward "re-Sinification," and if organized opposition to ethnic Chinese economic dominance develops. But the Thai economy has not experienced a single year of negative GDP growth for forty years, through times of internal and external economic and political turmoil alike, and it is difficult to envisage the specific circumstances that would reverse this trend. Growth, in turn, keeps potential organized opposition in check.

The question of a possible evolution in Sino-Thai ethnic identity is a more difficult one. The long historical experience of the Chinese in Thailand and their high degree of prior assimilation to Thai culture and society make it unlikely that they will suddenly embrace a heightened Chinese ethnic identity. Hewison and Thongyou's study of Sino-Thai provincial business elites suggests that the new generation is much more "Thai" than its parents and likely to remain so.[29] But various forms of Chinese ethnic identification, including education in the Chinese language, remain deep-rooted in Sino-Thai society and have already been given a boost by increasing Sino-Thai domestic political and economic power and by increased linkages with China through expanded two-way travel and growing use of the Chinese language in business communications.[30]

At the same time, the greater freedom of expression resulting from political democratization, along with the disproportionate representation of Sino-Thais in urban consuming populations and in intellectual and artistic communities, has resulted in a shift toward "re-Sinification" in the blossoming Sino-Thai urban popular culture and in consumption patterns that are being diffused throughout the country by the media and market forces. Possible resentment among indigenous Thais may be muted to the extent that they accept this new culture as "Thai" rather than as "Chinese"—that is, to the extent that Sino-Thai culture, as propagated by Sino-Thai–controlled media and consumer outlets, succeeds in "taking over" or "absorbing" indigenous Thai culture.

INDONESIA

In Indonesia, a nation of great indigenous ethnic diversity, the Chinese constitute a small minority, less than 4 percent of the population. They have not intermarried with indigenous Indonesians to a significant degree, largely because of their reluctance to convert to Islam. They are characterized by more diverse patterns of cultural assimilation, and they are scattered throughout Indonesia's vast archipelago rather than concentrated in a single primate city like Bangkok, as the Sino-Thais are.[31]

Partly as a consequence of these special characteristics, the ethnic Chinese business community in Indonesia has had to develop closer ties with the military regime that has ruled the country since 1966. These personalistic ties have served to protect the Chinese from potential harassment as a distinctive, nonindigenous ethnic minority identified with commercial monopoly power at many levels of the economy. They have also provided the Indonesian ruling regime with a degree of control over the private sector, which, because it is Chinese dominated, does not pose a political threat to the military's rule in the way an independent indigenous, or *pribumi,* business class might. The Indonesian state has thus been able to use the Chinese business community to effect certain state developmental goals and has benefited from patronage opportunities created by the dependence of Chinese business on its protection.

An oft-cited example is the case of the Salim group, whose rise to business prominence began with the ascent to power of General Suharto in 1966. Salim's founder, Liem Sioe Long, an immigrant from China's Fujian province, established a relationship with Suharto when he was still a provincial general that paid off handsomely when Suharto became president. Capitalizing on this relationship and the related ability to secure licenses and subsidies and generally "get things through" the labyrinthine Indonesian bureaucracy responsible for overseeing the highly regulated economy, Salim grew by forming alliances with foreign industrial and commercial enterprises. From them it obtained the technology and market expertise, connections, and information that it has used to become, reportedly, the world's largest Chinese-owned conglomerate, accounting for an estimated 8 percent of the Indonesian GDP.

In return, Salim has entered into various strategic sectors of the economy, such as steel, that the Indonesian government wished to see developed, and it has assisted or participated in the business ventures of various of President Suharto's children.[32] It is not the only Chinese-Indonesian conglomerate that has established such a pattern of mutual reciprocity in relations with both the ruling regime and the first family of Indonesia. The government's *pribumi* policy, which is supposed to favor indigenous Indonesian businesses over "alien" Chinese and foreign enterprises, often reduces to Chinese businesses taking *pribumi* partners from ruling elite circles, in part to ensure the political and bureaucratic influence often necessary to operate successfully in Indonesia's complex business environment.

Chinese business in Indonesia has done extremely well for itself under the Suharto regime, owing both to its privileged access to sectoral business opportunities and to the growth generated by the regime's economic policies. Economic reforms in the 1980s gave Chinese business growth a further disproportionate boost, resulting in murmurings of dissatisfaction among indigenous opposition groups and intellectuals. Continued perceptions of unequal benefit from the fruits of economic growth and liberalization could pose a threat to further economic reforms. To forestall this, Suharto held a much-publicized "summit" meeting with the nation's biggest Chinese ty-coons in May 1991, at which he exhorted them to distribute equity in their enterprises to indigenous cooperatives—to date, apparently with little effect.

Since then, new controversies have added to growing indigenous and foreign criticisms of Chinese-Indonesian business practices.[33] Expanding economic linkages with China are the major precipitating force in this regard. Chinese-Indonesian conglomerates have been criticized for "capital flight" because of their reportedly massive investments in China, especially in infrastructure, which Indonesia also desperately needs. In 1993, one company was criticized for importing PRC construction workers for a power plant, when creating employment was a major public policy concern and many Indonesians needed wage jobs.[34] So far, the Indonesian government has defended the right of its Chinese citizens to invest abroad freely, insisting that the benefits from such investments will come back to Indonesia because "we can make them come back"—an allusion, no doubt, to the control it still wields over the politically dependent and vulnerable Chinese business community.

It has not helped that the most prominent Indonesian businessmen investing in China are *totok* Chinese, the less-assimilated recent immigrants whose command of the Indonesian language is imperfect and who are suspected of having stronger sentimental ties to their home provinces in China than to Indonesia. It is precisely in these parts of China that their foreign investments are concentrated. Observed increases in the expression of Chinese culture, use of the Chinese language, lavish celebrations of Chinese New Year, and so on by some in this group have also heightened doubts about their "loyalty." The behavior of the *totok* big business conglomerates even causes apprehension among the more assimilated *peranakan* Chinese, including those in business, who fear that, being smaller-scale, less politically protected, and more confined to the Indonesian home economy, they are the ones who will bear the brunt of any violent anti-Chinese backlash.

At the same time—in contrast to Thailand, where Sino-Thais are officially accepted as being fully Thai nationals—the Indonesian government itself does not always accept even *peranakan* Chinese, whose ancestors have lived in Indonesia for generations, as full Indonesians. Separate treatment of them continues in many spheres, including insistence on the preservation of Chinese names for official recording purposes. This adds to the insecurity the Chinese feel, driving them to seek protection from influential indigenous political leaders and to diversify their economic assets abroad.

Eventual political democratization in Indonesia—which has yet to proceed very far—poses a potential threat to the Chinese business community there. Because their very small numbers are widely dispersed throughout

Indonesia, the Chinese would have no electoral voice in a democratic political system, in contrast to the disproportionate influence they have in the
current regime. Democracy would also be likely to reduce public tolerance
for "corruption" or for the patronage networks that have been developed
between the Chinese and members of the current indigenous ruling regime.[35] By reducing the power of the military, democracy would also undermine the political protection it has long afforded to the Chinese community.
The close alliance of some of the largest Chinese business conglomerates
with the authoritarian, military-backed regime—specifically with the Suharto family's politically favored and increasingly extensive and monopolistic business interests—makes the situation of both parties potentially highly
insecure when Suharto's tenure as president ends and there is an eventual
transition to democracy.[36]

For the moment, two factors are likely to hold back any major outbreak of
anti-Chinese sentiment or policy in Indonesia. The first is the continued
trickle-down effect from Indonesia's rapid economic growth, to which the
Chinese business community and the Suharto regime have positively contributed. The second is the probability that Indonesia's movement toward democracy will be slow. The government crackdown against an increasingly
contentious press in 1994 is evidence of this.[37] Other factors that could
contribute to the staving off of ethnic tension include de-monopolization of
the Indonesian private sector through further economic reforms and greater
sensitivity on the part of the Chinese business community to indigenous
concerns about its activities at home and abroad. It is likely that what the
Chinese do as businessmen—that is, whether they adhere to corrupt business practices or exploit their workers—is much more important than what
they do as Chinese. Ariel Heryanto has argued that the violent labor unrest
in Medan in April 1994, which led to the destruction of Chinese commercial
property and the death of a Chinese businessman (and which, significantly,
drew an official protest from China), reflected anti-employer class conflict
rather than anti-Chinese ethnic conflict.[38] Ethnic Chinese leaders themselves
reportedly met after this incident:

> They agreed that there was a need to ensure greater adherence to labour require-
> ments, including prompt payment of wages, overtime and other work benefits . . .
> giving greater attention to workers' welfare. Greater attention would also be paid
> to their obligations to society through community development projects and the
> like.[39]

A week later, anti-Chinese pamphlets circulated in several major Indonesian
cities.

PHILIPPINES

"Pure" ethnic Chinese account for less than 2 percent of the Philippine population, but Chinese have long intermarried with the country's "indigenous" Spanish mestizo elite, and it is estimated that about 10 percent of the population has some Chinese ancestry. As in Indonesia and Thailand, Chinese in the Philippines range in cultural identity from highly assimilated, long-domiciled Chinese mestizos to relatively recent immigrants who retain most of their original ethnic characteristics and culture. Both groups, particularly the latter, are disproportionately represented in the private business community. But unlike in the other ASEAN countries, in the Philippines they have to contend with competition from a dominant, entrenched, indigenous mestizo business class with agrarian and urban-industrial business interests. This class has traditionally relied on the Philippine state to protect it from foreign competition and occasionally to restrict domestic Chinese competition as well.

During the Marcos military government of the 1970s and early 1980s, Chinese business flourished, owing in part to the many patronage opportunities provided by the regime. Also, as Marcos sought to dismantle the rival business empires of members of the old "landed oligarchy," who posed an economic barrier and potential political threat to his ambitions and those of his "crony capitalists," the established indigenous businesses lost ground. The "apolitical" Chinese, on the other hand, were willing to work with the military regime so long as they could continue their businesses largely undisturbed. The Chinese community in general also benefited from Marcos's liberalization of immigration laws.

With the fall of Marcos, the Chinese transferred their support to his elected successor, Corazon Aquino, who freely acknowledged her ethnic Chinese heritage. During her administration (though more because of the opportunity for sustained growth rather than for ethnic reasons), the Philippines received a wave of domestic and foreign Chinese investment from nearby Hong Kong and Taiwan. Unlike other investors, the Chinese were not discouraged by repeated attempted military coups during the Aquino administration, seeing them merely as opportunities to acquire assets at bargain prices. Often with the assistance of external sources of capital, Chinese businesses also took advantage of new market opportunities provided by the government's economic reform policies, thereby expanding their control over the Philippine economy.[40]

The increasingly visible business dominance of the Chinese has resulted in some ethnic tensions. Filipinos were outraged at an immigration corruption scandal involving large numbers of illegal Chinese immigrants, and criticism has been voiced of Chinese-Filipino tycoons who move their capital freely between multiple domiciles in the Philippines, Taiwan, Hong Kong, and China. The anticorruption public fervor that developed after the collapse of the Marcos regime also bred resentment against the corrupt practices that had long been virtually routine in Chinese-Filipino business as a means of getting around often discriminatory government regulations. But only since the election of General Fidel Ramos as Aquino's successor in 1992 has the Chinese business community in the Philippines faced more serious problems.

Ramos's election coincided with a downturn in the Philippine economy and signaled the continued progress of democratic politics and institutions, including moves to "clean up" government. Yet there followed a spurt of violent kidnappings and murders of members of Chinese business families, which the government seemed powerless to stop. The kidnappings have been variously attributed to, among other things, local military and police groups' attempting to acquire alternate sources of income as their national political and economic power waned with democratization, and international Chinese criminal gangs' targeting the Philippines because of its laxer and more corrupt public security environment. Even if the kidnappings were not ethnically motivated, the ensuing protests from the governments of China and Taiwan threatened to increase ethnic tension by seeming to put the Chinese in the Philippines under the protection of foreign powers whose interests they might even be serving.

In late 1993, a further chill descended on the ethnic Chinese business community in the Philippines when the Ramos administration targeted its six richest tycoons for investigation for massive tax evasion.[41] This move came just six months after the six had accompanied Ramos on a state visit to China, and shortly after they had agreed to his request to form consortia to invest in infrastructural development in the Philippines. The government said its motive was merely to "promote fair competition," including the dismantling of monopolies obtained through political connections. According to this interpretation, the six tycoons were being investigated not because of their ethnicity but simply because of the sheer size of their business operations. Government investigators looking for large potential revenue gains for the overstretched government budget, according to this explanation, felt that this is where there was the greatest opportunity for a windfall.

Whatever the case, it is likely that the Chinese business community was targeted not only because of its ability to pay but also because, as part of a tiny ethnic minority under a democratic political regime, it lacked both the electoral clout and the state protection to fight back. This made the Chinese more popular, lucrative, and vulnerable targets than their rivals from the indigenous mestizo business community, who were strongly represented in Congress. It remains to be seen whether the Philippine Congress's periodic consideration of legislation to end monopoly licenses, quotas, and other such arrangements is even indirectly aimed at undermining the business empires of Chinese-Filipino tycoons, to the advantage of their now politically more powerful indigenous mestizo rivals, as some suspect it is. These rivals may seek to use the instruments of the democratic state to recover market positions lost to the Chinese over the past two decades.[42]

The kidnappings and the tax investigations contributed to a steep drop in 1993 of both domestic and foreign Chinese investment, which was already being reduced by competition for capital from China and Vietnam. But the kidnappings ended, the economy recovered and for the first time in two decades seemed poised for sustained growth, and investment from Taiwan began pouring back in, especially for the industrial conversion of the former U.S. naval base at Subic.[43] It now seems likely that the trickle-down from increased growth to which the Chinese contribute will serve to stifle any elite- or mass-based anti-Chinese actions in the near future.

MALAYSIA

Although ethnic Chinese also dominate private business in Malaysia, the situation there is strikingly different in several respects. First, the Chinese make up a third of the Malaysian population, and the degree of assimilation of most of them to indigenous culture and society is significantly less than it is in Thailand, Indonesia, or the Philippines. A second minority, descendants of immigrants from India, accounts for more than 10 percent of the population, leaving the indigenous Malays, many of them also of immigrant origin, with only a slight majority. Second, Malaysia has been an electoral democracy since independence in 1957, with dominant, ethnic-based political parties and without a politically powerful military. Third, the Malay-dominated government has undertaken affirmative action policies to increase the representation of ethnic Malays in the modern sector of the economy. A twenty-year New Economic Policy (NEP) established in 1971 imposed ethnic quotas for corporate equity ownership, public and private sector employment, and university admission. State enterprises were set up to develop sectors of the economy by and for Malays, and policies were enacted to create both a Malay bourgeoisie and a Malay industrial proletariat.[44]

Conventional wisdom in economic thinking posits a trade-off between growth and distribution. In the Malaysian case, this suggests that ethnic redistribution should result in some reduction of economic growth, since ethnic discrimination might be expected to reduce investment, especially by the Chinese who dominate the private sector. Also, according to economic theory, this trade-off should reduce productivity because of interferences with market mechanisms—for example, preferential access to jobs and business opportunities is given to less-competitive groups, or the less-efficient public sector is favored over the private. Yet the record indicates that economic growth in Malaysia actually accelerated during the 1970s and 1980s, when the NEP was in force. Ethnic redistribution and poverty reduction goals were also largely met by 1990, even though some criticism of the NEP's achievements has continued because of claims that it distributed its benefits unevenly and led to a distortion of the class structure.

This apparently anomalous result may be explained in several ways. First, the NEP sought to achieve "distribution through growth" by changing the distribution of an expanding economic pie to increase the relative Malay share without diminishing the absolute shares of other ethnic groups. Second, a successful overall economic growth strategy emphasizing industrialization and export diversification more than outweighed any diminution of growth resulting from ethnic redistribution policies.

Third, specific components of the redistributional policy itself had growth-enhancing effects. Extensive public investment in infrastructure and education for the Malay community contributed to the development of physical and human capital. The policy of attracting foreign multinationals to create mass industrial employment opportunities for Malays contributed to capital inflows, technology transfers, productivity growth, and export market demand far greater than could have been generated by the mostly small-scale Chinese domestic private sector alone.

Fourth, market forces and private enterprise were allowed to provide alternative educational, employment, and entrepreneurial opportunities for the non-Malay population. Chinese unable to secure public- or private-sector wage and salary employment because of ethnic quotas could still become self-employed in entrepreneurial ventures, and small businesses were exempt from following NEP ownership and employment rules. Private schools and colleges opened up to provide higher education at affordable rates for those unable to secure desired public university places owing to ethnic quotas.

Fifth, even NEP requirements were flexibly and pragmatically enforced in order not to conflict with the prior objective of economic growth. In response to recession in the mid-1980s, for example, the government relaxed

NEP ownership requirements to attract more foreign investment. The resultant influx of capital, including much from non-Malay Chinese, pushed economic growth to record levels, with the subsequent achievement of full employment. Upon termination of the NEP in 1990, the government substituted a New Development Policy (NDP), which pursues NEP goals in a more "flexible" manner, without explicit numerical quotas.

Thus, Malaysia's policy of ethnic redistribution has not adversely affected, and may even have promoted, economic growth. There has been no return to the ethnic violence of 1969, and the economic position of Malays has improved greatly both in absolute terms and in relation to that of the Chinese. Malay dissatisfaction with Chinese economic success has thus diminished considerably. The Chinese, too, have benefited from economic growth: their share of the modern sector of the economy has actually doubled since 1970 (from 23 percent to 46 percent of the total), because Chinese capitalists and rentiers were in the best position to take advantage of the declining share of foreign corporate stockholders and, to some extent, of the gradual privatization of state enterprises. The Malay ownership share of the corporate sector increased from 2 percent to nearly 20 percent over the same period.

Besides economic advancement, Chinese Malaysians can take satisfaction in the growing liberalization afforded to Chinese cultural expressions of ethnic identity, now that ethnic relations are more "relaxed." This is the result of three separate developments. The first is the government's move toward greater economic liberalization and its emphasis on the private sector. This move includes continuing deregulation and the promotion of a more supportive attitude toward local Chinese business, as well as official attempts to attract foreign Chinese investment. The government has even emphasized the presence of a sizable local Chinese population as an attraction for new Chinese capital. The second development is the political split in the ruling Malay party, UMNO, that occurred in the late 1980s and made it necessary for both factions to court non-Malay votes at the ballot box. The Chinese threw their electoral support largely behind the government faction, and this has been appreciated. A third development is the Malay-dominated government's enthusiasm for expanded business relations with China, which has resulted in many Malay-led official business missions to China, unprecedented government financial support for Chinese schools, and the encouragement of Chinese language learning among all ethnicities.[45] Deputy Prime Minister Anwar Ibrahim, a Malay nationalist, has successfully cultivated the Chinese community, and in a highly symbolic gesture at a recent public event, he personally wrote in Chinese characters, "We are all one family."[46]

Overall, Malaysia appears to have achieved both rapid economic growth and ethnic harmony. Progressive liberalization of the private enterprise market economy, along with an electoral system in which the Chinese community's one-third share of the electorate gives it some influence over voting outcomes, has provided sufficient opportunities for Chinese economic prosperity despite distributive policies favoring Malays in education and business. The NEP's twin goals of "eliminating the identification of race with economic function" and "eradicating poverty" are close to being achieved, and strong economic growth is expected to continue.

But, as in other diverse societies (such as the United States), ethnic tensions are unlikely to disappear completely. The entrenchment of ethnicity as a dominant variable in public policy has resulted in an ethnic polarization of Malaysian society, with the various ethnic groups tending to lead ethnically separate and distinct rather than racially integrated social lives. In the process, particularistic ethnic social and cultural characteristics and behavior have been enhanced.

For the Chinese, ethnic identification has increased, and cultural assimilation may have declined—for example, with the spread of Chinese education and use of Mandarin, a development encouraged by greater economic opportunities and interaction with an external Chinese trading world. The sheer size of the ethnic Chinese community also reduces both the need and the incentive for interaction and hence integration with the majority Malay population. The increasing economic prosperity and self-sufficiency of the Malays may also feed a heightened sense of ethnic identification on their part. For some, this identification has taken a religious, Islamic form. It is conceivable, therefore, that ethnic integration could be gradually rejected by both groups as the economic necessity for it declines. The end result would be a society divided ethnically, not on horizontal (class) lines but on a vertical (purely ethnic) basis.

Yet there are forces working to counter such a division. A major one is the homogenizing influence of the "international" secularistic and materialistic culture that comes with modern industrial growth. It has an impact on lifestyles, consumption patterns, and values. Already studies have shown that the values of Malays and Chinese are converging along occupational lines.[47] There is also evidence of increased cross-ethnic cultural sharing motivated by commercial purposes.[48] In other words, neither increasing ethnic cleavage nor a move toward greater integration is precluded, because there are countervailing forces working simultaneously in both directions.

Singapore, the only Southeast Asian country with a Chinese majority, is 75 percent Chinese. This has, on occasion, been a sensitive issue in relations with its neighbors. The Singapore economy itself still functions very much as a "middleman" in intraregional flows of commercial, industrial, and financial services as well as merchandise trade. Statistics on Singapore's trade with Indonesia remain an undisclosed "state secret," presumably because they might reveal the extent of giant Indonesia's trade dependence on its tiny neighbor. Being much richer than its neighbors, just as the Chinese community as a whole is vis-à-vis indigenous majorities in the other ASEAN countries, Singapore may be similarly vulnerable to their envy, resentment, and charges of exploitation.

This structural vulnerability is increased by Singapore's own past admiration for, and emulation of, the Israeli model of an armed-to-the-teeth small state set amid larger, potentially hostile Muslim neighbors (the "Jews in a sea of Arabs" analogy). Singapore still maintains close military and diplomatic links with Israel, despite the hostility of Malaysia and Indonesia toward that nation, a hostility echoed in the sentiments of many among Singapore's own sizable (15 percent) Malay Muslim minority. The country's relationship with Israel has occasionally even led to diplomatic friction between Singapore and its neighbors, as was the case when an Israeli prime minister paid a controversial visit to Singapore in the 1980s.

Despite, or perhaps because of, Singapore's Chinese majority, Chinese ethnic identity has been a public policy issue subject to periodic manipulation by the state to suit its changing purposes. After independence, the 1960s and 1970s saw the decline of Chinese media and educational institutions, which had been identified with left-wing politics and opposition to the mostly English-educated leadership of the ruling People's Action party (PAP).[49] This period also coincided with Western hegemony in the world economy and the dominant role of Western multinationals in Singapore itself, particularly in the manufacturing sector.

Later in the 1970s and into the 1980s, the PAP began reconstituting a state-sanctioned version of Chinese ethnicity. It centered on stamping out use of the southern Chinese dialects that were the mother tongues of most Chinese Singaporeans and the foundations for dialect-based Chinese social organizations that could be politicized. The use of Mandarin was promoted instead, for purposes that were social (to "unify the Chinese community"), cultural (to transmit "traditional values"), and economic (to facilitate trade with China). This period coincided with the rediscovery and propagation, in

Western, particularly American, academic and intellectual circles, of "Confucian values" (favoring education, savings, and hard work, not to mention obedience to central state authority) as an explanation for East Asia's spectacular economic success. It also coincided with China's embrace of outward-oriented market economic reforms.

By the 1990s, official policy had reaccorded legitimacy to the use of Chinese dialects, to dialect-based names, and to "home province" affiliation. This was the product of three concurrent developments. First, the growing regional and global economic presence of Taiwan (whose native dialect is a version of Fujianese, the dominant Chinese dialect in Singapore and the rest of Southeast Asia) led to the expressed recognition that "same dialect helps business." Second, the policy was reinforced by the spectacular economic growth of southeastern coastal China and recognition of the importance of provincial links to Southeast Asian Chinese investments there—Singapore aspires to compete with Hong Kong as the middleman for these capital flows. Third, within Singapore itself, electoral opposition to the PAP apparently shifted from the English-educated middle class to the dialect-speaking working class, which had a hard time learning two foreign languages (English and Mandarin) simultaneously, as required by the state school system. Ostensibly because speaking in dialect had helped an opposition candidate win election to parliament, Prime Minister Goh Chok Tong himself spoke in Hokkien during a 1992 by-election.

In the mid-1990s, although dialect use has declined in Singapore, it is accepted and even celebrated as one of the few things that "touches the heart" in a supermodern urban situation where most traces of the Chinese population's migrant history have been obliterated, reconfigured, or sanitized by progress. But Mandarin remains supreme in its role as transmitter of cultural values conducive to the Confucian ideal of the patriarchal family and authoritarian state. The government considers the transmission of this ideal important to counter any tendencies toward political liberalization and weakened family cohesion that Singaporeans might develop as a consequence of their current affluence, Westernized education, modern life-style, and extensive contact with the rest of the world (including newly democratic Taiwan and South Korea).

Mandarin is also an invaluable aid to Singapore's ambition to play an important role in China's economic development by extending state as well as private enterprise links with the PRC and acting as a middleman and bilingual-bicultural intermediary between China and the rest of the world, including other Southeast Asian and Western countries. China's apparently inexorable economic ascendancy and the relative economic decline of the

West have even caused Lee Kuan Yew to speculate on the need for Singaporeans to adapt their established business practices (which, for example, eschew corruption) to what is acceptable and necessary in China today.

The foregoing analysis supports our a priori contention that economic growth has indeed contributed to more harmonious ethnic relations between the Chinese minority and indigenous majority populations in Southeast Asia. Without growth benefiting indigenous Southeast Asians, it is unlikely that the disproportionate economic benefit to local and foreign Chinese would be so readily accepted. The national benefits to be gained from more economic engagement with "greater China" (the PRC, Taiwan, and Hong Kong) have also enhanced the value of local Chinese business communities to their Southeast Asian home nations.

For the Chinese in Southeast Asia, even those in Chinese-dominated Singapore, ethnicity has always been historically constituted in response to social, political, and economic circumstances. But recent developments are themselves predicated on a historical base, and it appears that the commitment of most Chinese to their Southeast Asian home countries is stronger today than it has ever been. It is grounded not only in economic but also in affective, social, and cultural roots. As Lee Kuan Yew has put it (on several occasions):

> After two or three generations away from China, we have become rooted in the country of our birth.... The Chinese-Thai is a Thai, and in the end he wants Thailand to prosper so that his assets in Thailand can grow and his children's future in Thailand can be secure. So, too, Chinese-Singaporeans, Chinese-Indonesians, Chinese-Malaysians and Chinese-Filipinos. They may invest and visit China frequently, but few want to make China their homes.[50]

Yet Lee goes on to argue that ethnic Chinese should nonetheless build and maintain worldwide networks, or *guanxi,* among themselves as a valuable tool for business advancement.[51] Certainly, ethnic links can enhance intraethnic economic relations, but, as Philip Bowring has noted, they are a "two-edged sword" that, if not handled with care, could undermine interethnic relations.[52] No doubt aware of this, Chinese-Indonesian tycoons, significantly, did not attend the international gathering of Chinese entrepreneurs at which Lee spoke.

So, despite the greater commitment to their home countries noted by Lee, increased domestic tolerance and expanded external economic linkages are contributing to the re-Sinification of the Southeast Asian Chinese as they discover that enhancing their Chinese characteristics and behavior is now both possible at home and desirable, even profitable, abroad.

From the perspective of indigenous Southeast Asians, national economic growth is more than ever intertwined with, and even dependent on, the business activity of local and foreign Chinese. It is against their national economic self-interest to act in any way that might jeopardize this growth. But because the growth process itself is unequal, it could nevertheless generate frictions that, although not ethnic in origin, might be ethnic in manifestation, as suggested by the Medan incident of anti-employer labor unrest.[53] In places where most of the employers who offer unsatisfactory working conditions happen to be Chinese, it might even be in the economic self-interest of particular indigenous worker groups, as a bargaining tactic, to contest with them on an ethnic as well as on a class basis. Similarly, where illegal Chinese migrant workers exert downward pressure on the wages and working conditions of low-skilled indigenous workers, the latter's economic self-interest might add an ethnic element to class-based conflict with the foreign workers and their mostly Chinese employers.

Whether the enhanced ethnic pride, cultural assertiveness, and pan-Chinese ethnic identification of Chinese minorities in Southeast Asia will generate or exacerbate ethnic, class, or other tension depends on the local political economy. Malaysia, for example, has the most "unassimilated" Chinese population in the region, yet an outbreak of ethnic violence is probably least likely there. Successful economic development has drawn most Malays out of poverty, Malays control the state and have made major inroads into the private sector as capitalists in their own right, the employer class includes many other foreign nationalities in addition to Chinese and Malays, wages and working conditions are rather good and improving, and there are few illegal Chinese migrant workers.

In Indonesia, the Chinese are more culturally assimilated, but their perceived economic monopoly and close association with the authoritarian regime, which is seen as favoring and protecting them while restricting the freedoms of the indigenous workers they are accused of exploiting, have already led to anti-Chinese reactions. In Thailand, acceptance of an evolving Sino-Thai cultural identity as legitimately Thai and even as representative of Thai urban cultural identity, which it dominates, may make anti-Chinese reactions unlikely, but the long-term impact of Sino-Thai capital outflows to China and illegal migrant worker inflows from China is uncertain. In the Philippines, the long-standing acceptance of culturally assimilated Chinese-Filipinos may be challenged by re-Sinification and the growing foreign, as well as local, Chinese economic presence—but this too may be counterbalanced by accelerating economic growth.

Ultimately, three major developments hold the key to the future evolution of ethnic relations involving the Chinese in Southeast Asia: the progress of market capitalism, the progress of political democracy, and the role of China in the region. If continued economic liberalization entrenches market capitalism, sustaining economic growth, reducing Chinese monopoly power, raising indigenous incomes, and improving wealth and income distribution, it will help ensure interethnic peace. But market capitalism also brings attendant inequalities that could be correlated with ethnicity and thus become a threat to interethnic peace. Political democratization could reduce the political influence of the Chinese business elite and increase awareness and resentment of their corrupt business practices. Or it could, equally, increase Chinese political influence because of the importance of money and fundraising to party politics in contemporary democracies (the United States and Japan, for example), and this in turn could limit indigenous enthusiasm for democracy. Finally, whether China emerges as a belligerent or a benign power in the political-security sphere, and whether it emerges primarily as a competitor or as a partner in the economic sphere, could influence indigenous attitudes toward the local and foreign Chinese in their midst.

In short, the current situation of the Chinese in Southeast Asia suggests that economic growth eases but does not eliminate ethnic tensions. Improvement of interethnic relations has not eliminated forces that might reverse the trend. The ultimate outcome depends on much more than economics, even though we have argued that economic influences have predominated until now. The complex and dynamic interplay of domestic and international cultural and political variables with economic ones will ultimately determine the state of interethnic relations in any particular historical situation. These will almost certainly vary both between countries in Southeast Asia and over time in the entire region in a manner that is responsive to individual, group, and state actions. This is why it is so important to keep track of the situation in each country as it develops, and to be aware that both desirable and undesirable outcomes remain possible.

NOTES

1. Regarding ethnic and religious diversity, Indonesia alone, for example, contains between 80 and 250 ethnolinguistic groups (depending on how they are defined), who practice variants of Islam (90 percent of the population), Christianity,

Hinduism, and indigenous animistic religions. Muslims are the largest religious minority in the predominantly Catholic Philippines and in Buddhist Thailand. The European colonial era saw the immigration of Indians and especially Chinese into the region and the superimposition of European languages and cultures (Spanish, Dutch, British, French). Regarding interethnic peace, there have been occasional outbreaks of ethnic violence during this period, particularly anti-Chinese riots in Indonesia, but these have not been frequent, prolonged, sustained, or disruptive of the general polity and social order, nor have they involved large numbers of deaths. Ethnic tensions and frictions and ethnic separatist movements do exist, but for the most part they have not resulted in widespread or persistent interethnic violence. And regarding rapid economic growth, among the capitalist ASEAN countries, Indonesia, Malaysia, Singapore, and Thailand—but not the Philippines—have enjoyed real GDP growth rates averaging 6 to 7 percent annually for the past twenty-five years.

2. For example, ethnic Chinese in 1991 accounted for 3.5 percent of the Indonesian population but had a 73 percent share of listed equity. Equivalent figures for Malaysia were 29 percent and 61 percent, respectively; for the Philippines, 2 percent and 50 percent; and for Thailand, 10 percent and 81 percent. See Sakura Bank–Nomura Research Institute, cited in *Asiaweek*, "A Taxing Dilemma," October 20, 1993, p. 58. Listed equity refers to only a small proportion of the total private-sector wealth in these countries, where most Chinese companies are family owned and not publicly listed. But respected estimates for the private sector as a whole tend to parallel these figures.

3. Malaysia did experience one post-independence incidence of interethnic violence, the May 1969 riots, but they occurred before Malaysia's take-off into rapid industrial growth and have not been repeated in the quarter-century since.

4. Linda Y. C. Lim, "The New Ascendancy of Chinese Business in Southeast Asia: Political, Cultural, Economic, and Business Implications" (paper presented at the annual meeting of the Association for Asian Studies, New Orleans, Louisiana, April 1991); Louis T. Wells, Jr., "Mobile Exporters: New Foreign Investors in East Asia," in Kenneth Froot, ed., *Foreign Direct Investment* (Chicago: University of Chicago Press, 1993), pp. 173–96; Clyde D. Stoltenberg and Linda Y. C. Lim, "Investment in Southeast Asia," in Mitchell Silk, ed., *Taiwan Trade and Investment Law* (Hong Kong: Oxford University Press, 1994), pp. 247–68.

5. See Linda Y. C. Lim, "The Emergence of a Chinese Economic Zone in Asia?" *Journal of Southeast Asia Business* 8:1 (Winter 1992), pp. 41–46; Linda Y. C. Lim, "The Role of the Private Sector in ASEAN Economic Cooperation," in Lynn Mytelka, ed., *South-South Co-operation in a Global Perspective* (Paris: OECD Development Centre, 1994), pp. 125–68.

6. There is a voluminous literature on this subject. For recent overviews, see

Wang Gungwu, *China and the Chinese Overseas* (Singapore: Times Academic Press, 1991), and Yeu-Farn Wang, "Chinese Entrepreneurs in Southeast Asia: Historical Roots and Modern Significance" (Stockholm University, Center for Pacific Asia Studies, Working Paper no. 34, May 1994). For various attempts to explain Chinese economic competitiveness in the region, see Yuan-li Wu and Chun-Hsi Wu, *Chinese Development in Southeast Asia: The Chinese Dimension* (Stanford, California: Hoover Institution Press, 1980); Linda Y. C. Lim and L. A. Peter Gosling, eds., *The Chinese in Southeast Asia*, vol. 1, *Ethnicity and Economic Activity*, and vol. 2, *Identity, Culture and Politics* (Singapore: Maruzen International, 1983); Victor Simpao Limlingan, *The Overseas Chinese in ASEAN: Business Strategies and Management Practices* (Manila: Vita Development Corp, 1986); James Mackie, "Chinese Businessmen and the Rise of Southeast Asian Capitalism," *Solidarity* 123 (July–September 1989), pp. 96–107; James Mackie, "Changing Patterns of Chinese Big Business in Southeast Asia," in Ruth McVey, ed., *Southeast Asian Capitalists* (Ithaca, New York: Southeast Asia Program, Cornell University, 1992), pp. 161–90; S. Gordon Redding, *The Spirit of Chinese Capitalism* (Berlin: Walter de Gruyter, 1990); L. A. Peter Gosling, "Analysing the Chinese 'Edge' in Business in Southeast Asia" (paper presented at the annual meeting of the Association for Asian Studies, New Orleans, Louisiana, April 1991); and Louis Kraar, "Overseas Chinese: Lessons from the World's Most Dynamic Capitalists," *Fortune*, October 31, 1994, pp. 91–114.

7. Frank Golay, Ralph Anspach, Ruth Pfanner, and Eliezer Ayall, *Underdevelopment and Economic Nationalism in Southeast Asia* (Ithaca, New York: Cornell University Press, 1969).

8. Many of these adaptive business practices would likely have characterized Chinese business operations in the immigrant traders' home provinces of coastal southern China as well, given the often parasitic control that Chinese officialdom was wont to exert over private enterprise, and still does in China today.

9. In the PRC, the Chinese motherland, Chinese private enterprise was more seriously disenfranchised by communism than it was by ethnic discrimination in Southeast Asia.

10. New foreign investments into Southeast Asia from Taiwan and Hong Kong declined in the early 1990s as investors diversified and responded to the competing attractions of China, but they are now recovering.

11. On the Charoen Pokphand group, see Carl Goldstein, "Full Speed Ahead," *Far Eastern Economic Review*, October 21, 1993, pp. 66–70, and chapter 10 in this volume, by Gary G. Hamilton and Tony Waters.

12. Lim, "The Role of the Private Sector in ASEAN Economic Cooperation."

13. Brian L. Foster, "Ethnicity and Commerce," *American Ethnologist* 1:3 (1974), pp. 437–48.

14. The "dual ethnicity" of Southeast Asian Chinese has long fascinated scholars.

Some recent studies are those of Lim and Gosling, *The Chinese in Southeast Asia;* Jennifer Cushman and Wang Gungwu, eds., *Changing Identities of the Southeast Asian Chinese since World War II* (Hong Kong: Hong Kong University Press, 1988); Edgar Wickberg, "Some Comparative Perspectives on Chinese Ethnicity in the Philippines," *Asian Culture* 14 (April 1990), pp. 23–37; and Teresita Ang See, "Integration and Identity: Social Changes in the Post–World War II Philippine Chinese Community," *Asian Culture* 14 (April 1990), pp. 38–46.

15. See chapter 3 in this volume, by Kasian Tejapira.

16. Eng Fong Pang and Linda Y. C. Lim, "Economic Growth, Structural Change, Regional Integration and International Labor Migration in Asia" (paper presented at a seminar on "Migration and the Labour Market in Asia in the Year 2000," organized by the OECD, the Japanese government, and the Japan Institute of Labour, Tokyo, January 19–20, 1995).

17. Currently the world's third largest national economy after the United States and Japan, China is projected to be the largest within twenty years—about 40 percent bigger than the second largest, the United States, by the year 2020.

18. Lim, "The Role of the Private Sector in ASEAN Economic Cooperation"; Linda Y. C. Lim, "Models and Partners: Singapore and Malaysia in Vietnam's Economic Reforms," in Richard Donner, ed., *Marketization in Southeast Asia* (Ithaca, New York: Cornell University Southeast Asia Program, forthcoming).

19. Gary G. Hamilton, ed., *Business Networks and Economic Development in East and Southeast Asia* (Hong Kong: Centre of Asian Studies, University of Hong Kong, 1991); Kraar, "Overseas Chinese"; Andrew Tanzer, "The Bamboo Network," *Forbes,* July 18, 1994, pp. 138–44.

20. The influx of mostly illegal migrant labor from the PRC is a cause of concern in Japan, Korea, and Taiwan as well, but ethnic tensions are most likely to result in Southeast Asia. Note that intraregional labor flows also include indigenous Southeast Asians. See Pang and Lim, "Economic Growth, Structural Change."

21. For analyses of China's changing relations with the overseas Chinese, see M. R. Godley, "Reflections on China's Changing Overseas Chinese Policy," *Solidarity* 123 (July–September 1989), pp. 108–12; Chee-Beng Tan, "People of Chinese Descent and China," *Solidarity* 123 (July–September 1989), pp. 113–20; and Wang, *China and the Chinese Overseas.*

22. *The Economist,* "China takes over Myanmar," October 8, 1994.

23. Natalia Soebagjo, "Chinese Power Play in Indonesia and the Role of the Ethnic Chinese" (paper presented at the annual meeting of the Association for Asian Studies, New Orleans, Louisiana, April 1991).

24. George Hicks, "Developments that Reduce Incentive for Overseas Chinese to Assimilate," *International Herald Tribune* (reprinted in the *Straits Times,* Singapore, January 30, 1993).

25. *Straits Times Weekly,* November 27, 1993, p. 1.

26. Anek Laothamatas, *Business Associations and the New Political Economy of Thailand* (Boulder, Colorado: Westview Press for the Institute of Southeast Asian Studies, Singapore, 1992).

27. Kevin Hewison and Maniemai Thongyou, "The New Generation of Provincial Business People in Northeastern Thailand" (Murdoch University, Asia Research Centre, Working Paper no. 16, 1993).

28. Note, however, that the electoral weight of Sino-Thai voters is disproportionately concentrated in urban constituencies, particularly Bangkok, that carry disproportionate weight in national politics.

29. Hewison and Thongyou, "The New Generation."

30. Kwok Bun Chan and Chee Kiong Tong, "Rethinking Assimilation and Ethnicity: The Chinese in Thailand," *International Migration Review* 27:1 (Spring 1993), pp. 140–68.

31. Leo Suryadinata, *Pribumi Indonesians, the Chinese Minority and China* (Singapore: Heinemann Asia, 1992, 3d ed.), provides an excellent overview of the situation of ethnic Chinese in Indonesia.

32. For an account of the Salim family enterprises, see Adam Schwartz, "Empire of the Son" and related articles, *Far Eastern Economic Review,* March 14, 1991, pp. 46–50, 52–53. For more general analyses of Chinese business and politics in Indonesia, see Andrew McIntyre, *Business and Politics in Indonesia* (Sydney: Allen & Unwin for the Asian Studies Association of Australia, 1990); and Richard Robison, "Industrialization and the Economic and Political Development of Capital: The Case of Indonesia," in McVey, ed., *Southeast Asian Capitalists,* pp. 65–88.

33. Foreign criticisms of Chinese-Indonesian business practices come from two main sources: (1) non-Chinese, particularly Western, multinationals, which, like indigenous Indonesian entrepreneurs, find it difficult to compete with Chinese enterprises in the supposedly "newly open" Indonesian market because they lack their established personal connections; and (2) international donor agencies, particularly the World Bank, which are concerned that the market-oriented reforms they propose and help to engineer are being subverted by monopolistic private-sector practices that reduce competition, discourage foreign investment, and undermine political support for continued reforms. International donors, however, were not in favor of Suharto's May 1991 equity-distribution proposal because they felt it interfered with the market mechanism and went against the grain of the economic reforms up to that time.

34. The company, which was eventually forced to repatriate the Chinese workers, claimed in mitigation that they possessed skills that were absent in the native Indonesian work force. This in turn led to the charge that the company should provide training to Indonesians rather than rely on a foreign work force.

35. A case in point is the public uproar over unsecured bad loans made by a state bank to Chinese businessman Eddie Tansil, who was subsequently sentenced to seventeen years in jail as a result of the 1994 Bapindo scandal.

36. Paul Jacob, "Anti-Chinese Moves Targeted at Indonesian Leadership" and "Chinese Indonesians Reaffirm National Identity," *The Sunday Times* (Singapore), June 26, 1994.

37. A potentially significant development here is the establishment by Bob Hasan, a Chinese timber tycoon with close links to the Suharto regime, of a new magazine following the closure of several pro-democracy journals. It may signal an attempt to control the media through private ownership rather than through public censorship.

38. Ariel Heryanto, "A Class Act," *Far Eastern Economic Review*, June 16, 1994, p. 30.

39. Jacob, "Chinese Indonesians Reaffirm National Identity."

40. Roberto Tiglao, "Gung-ho in Manila," *Far Eastern Economic Review*, February 15, 1990, pp. 68–71.

41. *Asiaweek*, "A Taxing Dilemma," October 20, 1993, pp. 57–62.

42. For example, the first target of the tax commissioners was Lucio Tan, head of the Asia Brewery company, which had aggressively and successfully challenged—including in bitter lawsuits—the long-held near-monopoly of the mestizo-controlled San Miguel company in the domestic beer market. The tax commissioner was a former employee of a company also headed by San Miguel's chairman, and Tan was a major funder of one of Ramos's opponents in the 1992 presidential campaign. See *Asiaweek*, "A Taxing Dilemma," p. 62.

43. Linda Y. C. Lim, "Economic Outlook ASEAN 1995–1996," in *Regional Outlook: Southeast Asia 1995–1996* (Singapore: Institute of Southeast Asian Studies, 1995), pp. 34–50.

44. The NEP has been extensively studied. For a selection of references, see Donald R. Snodgrass, *Inequality and Economic Development in Malaysia* (Kuala Lumpur: Oxford University Press, 1980); Tat-Wai Tan, *Income Distribution and Determination in West Malaysia* (Kuala Lumpur: Oxford University Press, 1982); Ozay Mehmet, *Development in Malaysia* (London: Croom Helm, 1986); James Jesudason, *Ethnicity and the Economy: The State, Chinese Business and Multinationals in Malaysia* (Singapore: Oxford University Press, 1989); K. S. Jomo, *Growth and Structural Change in the Malaysian Economy* (New York: St. Martin's Press, 1990); K. S. Jomo, "Whither Malaysia's New Economic Policy?" *Pacific Affairs* 64:4 (Winter 1990–91), pp. 469–99.

45. Even before the economic, political, and cultural liberalizations of the late 1980s, the Chinese had signaled some satisfaction with their position in Malaysia by the lack of large-scale capital flight or sustained emigration. The earlier 1980s outflow of Chinese professionals from Malaysia, mostly to Australia and chiefly in response

to declining higher education opportunities for their children in Malaysia, has since stopped. With the excellent performance of the Malaysian economy and liberalization of the education system, many Chinese migrants to recession-ridden Canada and Australia are reportedly interested in returning to Malaysia.

46. Cited in *Asiaweek*, "Wealth and Worries," August 24, 1994, pp. 38–42; see also *Asiaweek*, September 7, 1994.

47. Frederic Deyo, "Chinese Management Practices and Work Commitment in Comparative Perspective," in Lim and Gosling, *The Chinese in Southeast Asia*, vol. 1, pp. 215–65; Nik A. Rashid Ismail, "Value Systems of Malay and Chinese Managers," in Manning Nash, ed., *Economic Performance in Malaysia* (New York: Professors World Peace Academy, 1988), pp. 95–110.

48. Examples are the sponsoring of Malay dance and cultural troupes by Chinese businesses catering to Malay customers and the proliferation of Chinese lion dance troupes whose members are non-Malays performing for remuneration at Chinese business events. See Mohd Nor Mohd Anis, "Dances for Hire: Performances for the Inauguration of Chinese Business Premises in Malaysia" (paper presented at the annual meeting of the Association for Asian Studies, New Orleans, Louisiana, April 1991); also, personal communications from Anis.

49. For example, the government closed down Southeast Asia's only Chinese-language university, the privately funded Nanyang University, and clamped down on Chinese newspapers. But the closure of Chinese and other vernacular (Malay, Tamil) schools had as much to do with economics (in an English-language-dominated modern economy) as with politics (fears that these schools would be breeding grounds for ethnically based political discontent).

50. Quoted in George Hicks and J. A. C. Mackie, "A Question of Identity," *Far Eastern Economic Review*, July 14, 1994, pp. 46–51.

51. In China, the term *guanxi* connotes a network of clientelistic relationships based on mutually beneficial exchanges, and more than a hint of what Westerners might consider corruption.

52. Philip Bowring, "Chinese Minorities in South-East Asia Have Reason to Be Careful," *International Herald Tribune* (reprinted in the *Straits Times*, Singapore, January 30, 1993).

53. Heryanto, "A Class Act," p. 30.

Contributors

STEVEN BELLER is the author of *Vienna and the Jews 1867–1938: A Cultural History* (1989), *Herzl* (1991), and *Francis Joseph* (1996). He is now writing a history of modern Austria.

DANIEL CHIROT is a professor of international studies and of sociology at the University of Washington in Seattle. He is the author of *Modern Tyrants: The Power and Prevalence of Evil in Our Age* (1994), *How Societies Change* (1994), *Social Change in the Modern Era* (1986), *Social Change in the Twentieth Century* (1977), and *Social Change in a Peripheral Society: The Creation of a Balkan Colony* (1976).

L. A. PETER GOSLING is professor emeritus of geography, anthropology, and Southeast Asian studies at the University of Michigan. He is the author of *Population Redistribution: Patterns, Policies and Prospects* (1979) and *Population Resettlement in the Mekong River Basin* (1979). He is the editor (with Linda Lim) of the two-volume *The Chinese in Southeast Asia* (1983), and is now working with Lim on a book on Chinese business in Southeast Asia.

GARY G. HAMILTON is a professor of sociology at the University of Washington in Seattle. He is the author of *Governor Reagan, Governor Brown* (1984) and (with Marco Orr and Nicole Biggart) of *The Economic Organization of East Asian Capitalism* (1997). A volume of his collected articles has been published recently with the title *Chinese Capitalism? The Organization of Chinese Economies* (1997). He is also the editor of *Asian Business Networks* (1996).

K. S. JOMO is a professor of economics and administration at the University of Malaysia in Kuala Lumpur. He is the author of many books, including

318

Growth and Structural Change in the Malaysian Economy (1990), *A Question of Class* (1986), *Beyond 1990* (1989), *Trade Unions and the State in Peninsular Malaysia*, with Patricia Todd (1994), and *U-Turn?* (1994). He has also edited many books on Malaysia and economic change.

VICTOR KARADY is a senior research director at the French National Center for Scientific Research and at the Centre de Sociologie of the Maison des Sciences de l'Homme in Paris, and a professor of history at the Central European University of Budapest. He is the editor of the definitive collection of Emile Durkheim's works, *Emile Durkheim, 1858–1917* (three volumes, 1975, in French), and also the editor of the collected works of Marcel Mauss and Maurice Halbwachs. He is the editor of *Zsidosag az 1945 utani Magyarorszagon*, a collection of articles on Hungarian Jews (1984, in Magyar). More recently he has been the editor (with Yehuda Don) of *A Social and Economic History of Central European Jewry* (1989) and (with W. Mitter) of *Education and Social Structure in Central Europe* (1990).

KASIAN TEJAPIRA is a lecturer in political science at Thammasat University in Bangkok. He is the author of *Looking Through the Dragon Design: Selected Writings on Chineseness in Siam* (1994, in Thai) and *Pigtail: A Pre-history of Chineseness in Siam* (1992). He is also a noted journalist and was formerly a radical activist and guerrilla fighter in the jungle of northeastern Thailand.

HILLEL J. KIEVAL is a professor of history and international studies at the University of Washington in Seattle. He is the author of *The Making of Czech Jewry: National Conflict and Jewish Society in Bohemia, 1870–1918* (1988) and of two forthcoming books on the history of ritual murder accusations against Jews in Central Europe in the late nineteenth and early twentieth centuries and the history of Czech Jews from 1780 to 1918.

LINDA Y. C. LIM is associate professor of business at the University of Michigan's School of Business Administration. She is the author (with Pang E. Fon) of *Trade, Employment and Industrialisation in Singapore* (1986), and (with Thomas Brewer and Kenneth David) of *Investing in Developing Countries: A Guide for Executives* (1986). She is also the coauthor of *Foreign Direct Investment and Industrialization in Malaysia, Singapore, Taiwan and Thailand* (1991). She writes frequently about Southeast Asian and East Asian business and foreign trade, and is working on a book with Peter Gosling on Chinese business in Southeast Asia. She edited, with Gosling, the two-volume *The Chinese in Southeast Asia* (1983).

ANTHONY REID is professor of Southeast Asian history at the Research School of Pacific and Asian Studies at the Australian National University. He is the author of *The Contest for North Sumatra: Atjeh, the Netherlands and Britain, 1858–1898* (1969), *The Indonesian National Revolution, 1945–1950* (1974), *The Blood of the People: Revolution and the End of Traditional Rule in Northern Sumatra* (1979), and the two-volume work *Southeast Asia in the Age of Commerce, 1450–1680* (1988, 1993). He is also the editor of twelve books of collected articles on Southeast Asia.

TAKASHI SHIRAISHI is a professor of history at Cornell University and at the University of Kyoto. He is the author of *An Age in Motion: Popular Radicalism in Java, 1912–1926* (1990); *Indonesia, Kokka to Seiji* (1992); and *Sukarno to Suharto* (1996). He is also the editor of several works on Southeast Asia and Japanese-Southeast Asian relations.

TONY WATERS recently served as deputy project coordinator in Ngara, Tanzania, for the Lutheran World Federation's project to assist Rwandan refugees. He is now a lecturer in sociology at Chico State University in California. He is the author of numerous articles about ethnicity and refugee problems.

EDGAR WICKBERG is a professor emeritus of history at the University of British Columbia in Vancouver. He is the author of *Chinese in Philippine Life, 1850–1898* (1965) and (with Harry Con) the editor of *From China to Canada: A History of the Chinese Communities in Canada* (1982)

Index

Civil rights, 129
Civil service, 136, 150n27, 242
Clan names: Chinese, 85
Cochin China, 55
Cohen, Abner, 36
Cohen, Gary, 103
Cohen, Hermann, 108
Collective organizations, 53
Colonialism, 54, 55, 56; Chinese and,
46–47; in Dutch East Indies, 187–88;
in Java, 194–202, 203–5; in Malaya,
238–41, 246; in Philippines, 154–59,
161–63; in Southeast Asia, 10–11, 14,
50, 289; tutorial, 174–75
Comintern, 54
Commerce, 30n3, 214–15, 238, 297–98
Commercialism, 43
Commercialization, 64–65
Communalism, 23–25, 28–29
Communism, 11, 240, 291–92; in China,
60, 313n9; Chinese and, 14, 53–54; in
Hungary, 125, 133–37, 139, 140, 141–
46; Jews and, 13, 128; in Thailand, 79,
83–86
Communist party, 12, 53–54, 145
Communist Party of Malaya, 240
Community, 51; moral, 214–15; Philip-
pine Chinese, 157–58, 162–63
Competition, competitiveness, 36
Compradores, 264
Concessions, 195
Confucianism, 237, 308
Conversion, 158–59; of Chinese, 14, 156;
in Hungary, 134, 135; of Jews, 13,
104–5, 134, 227–28n13; in Philippines,
155, 157
Cossacks, 42
Council of Trust for Indigenous Peo-
ples, 242
Couperous, Louis: The Hidden Force, 204
CP. See Charoen Pokphand
Cracow, 128
Credit Anstalt, 113
Croatia, Croats, 15, 19, 22
Crown Property Bureau, 264, 270, 273,
274
Crusades, 41

Cultivation system, 194–95, 197
Cultural classification, 160
Cultural mandates 78
Culture(s), 50, 112, 113
Curtin, Philip, 36
Cushman, Jennifer, 265
Czechoslovakia, 15, 44, 126, 132–34, 144
Czech Republic, 22
Czernovitz, 128

Daim, 252
Damrong, Prince, 79, 267
Darma Hatmoko, 193
Darwinism, 10, 11, 38, 51, 110
Datong University, 83
Debrecen, 134
Demak, 42
Democracy, 23, 25, 292, 300
"Democracy in Siam" (Prajadhipok),
79–80
Diaspora, 36, 39, 60, 66n8
Dipanegara, 47
Disease, 10; as metaphor, 100–101
Division of labor, 93n24; ethnic, 219–20,
288
Djawi Hiswara (newspaper), 191, 203
Djawi Kanda (newspaper), 191, 203
Drumont, Edouard: Jewish France, 9
Dual ethic, 214
Dühring, Eugen, 109
Dutch, 32n20, 41, 43; in Java, 46, 194–
202, 203–5, 207n19
Dutch Colonial Service, 195
Dutch East India Company, 44–46, 195
Dutch East Indies, 14, 32n20, 44–45,
239, 240; colonial rule in, 187–89,
194–202, 203–5; native national move-
ments in, 191–94; political system in,
189–90, 200

Eastern Shipping Lines, 267
East Indies, 11
East Timor, 40
Economic growth, 311–12n1; and ethnic-
ity, 285–86
The Economic History of the Overseas
Chinese (Suguru), 80